PRIVACY & CONFIDENTIALITY PERSPECTIVES

PRIVACY & CONFIDENTIALITY PERSPECTIVES

ARCHIVISTS & ARCHIVAL RECORDS

EDITED WITH AN INTRODUCTION BY
Menzi L. Behrnd-Klodt & Peter J. Wosh

THE SOCIETY OF AMERICAN ARCHIVISTS
ESTABLISHED 1936

Chicago

The Society of American Archivists
527 S. Wells Street, 5th Floor
Chicago, IL 60607 USA
312/922-0140 Fax 312/347-1452
www.archivists.org

© 2005 by the Society of American Archivists.
All Rights Reserved.

Printed in the United States of America

Library of Congress Cataloging-in-Publication Data
Privacy and confidentiality perspectives : archivists and archival records /
edited, with an introduction, by Menzi L. Behrnd-Klodt & Peter J. Wosh.
    p. cm.
  Includes bibliographical references and index.
  ISBN 1-931666-10-5 (alk. paper)
  1. Archives—Access control. 2. Archives—Law and legislation.
3. Privacy, Right of. I. Behrnd-Klodt, Menzi L. II. Wosh, Peter J. III. Title.

  CD986.5.P75 2005
  323.44'83—dc22

                                                                2005045128

TABLE OF CONTENTS

ACKNOWLEDGMENTS VII

INTRODUCTION 1

LEGAL PERSPECTIVES 9

   1. The Right to Privacy
      Samuel D. Warren and Louis D. Brandeis   15
   2. Privacy
      William L. Prosser   31
   3. The Tort Right of Privacy: What It Means
     for Archivists . . . and for Third Parties
      Menzi L. Behrnd-Klodt   53

ETHICAL PERSPECTIVES............................. 61

   4. Information Privacy, Liberty, and Democracy
      Heather MacNeil   67
   5. The Archivist's Balancing Act: Helping Researchers
     While Protecting Individual Privacy
      Judith Schwarz   82
   6. Privacy Rights and the Rights of Political Victims:
     Implications of the German Experience
      Elena S. Danielson   93
   7. Ethical Issues in Constructing a Eugenics Web Site
      Martin L. Levitt   112

ADMINISTRATIVE PERSPECTIVES 127

   8. In Secret Kept, In Silence Sealed: Privacy in
     the Papers of Authors and Celebrities
      Sara S. Hodson   131
   9. Southern Family Honor Tarnished? Issues of Privacy
     in the Walker Percy and Shelby Foote Papers
      Timothy D. Pyatt   149
  10. Balancing Privacy and Access: Opening the Mississippi
     State Sovereignty Commission Records
      Sarah Rowe-Sims, Sandra Boyd, and H. T. Holmes   159

11. Archival Access to Lawyers' Papers: The Effect
   of Legal Privileges
   Menzi L. Behrnd-Klodt — 175
12. The Buckley Stops Where? The Ambiguity and Archival
   Implications of the Family Educational Rights
   and Privacy Act
   Mark A. Greene and Christine Weideman — 181

INSTITUTIONAL PERSPECTIVES ... 199

13. Trust and Professional Agency in the Archives
   of Religious Organizations: An Archival Perspective
   on Confidence Keeping
   Mark J. Duffy and Christine M. Taylor — 205
14. Delta Blues: Changing Conceptions of Privacy and
   Property, and Their Implications for Corporate Archives
   Paul C. Lasewicz — 226
15. Confidences in Medical and Health Care Records
   from an Archive Perspective
   Barbara L. Craig — 246
16. The United Methodists and Their Open Records Policy
   L. Dale Patterson — 257

APPENDICES ... 269

1: Selected U.S. Constitutional Amendments — 269
2: Selected U.S. Federal Statutes Concerning Privacy — 271
3: The Family Educational Rights and Privacy Act: Legislative
   Amendments and Judicial Interpretations
   Menzi L. Behrnd-Klodt — 280
4: The Brave New World of 21st-Century Medical Records
   Privacy in the U.S. and Canada, Contrasted with the
   European Data Privacy Model
   Menzi L. Behrnd-Klodt — 285

NOTES ... 295

EDITORS AND CONTRIBUTORS ... 371

INDEX ... 377

ACKNOWLEDGMENTS

This book grew out of our mutual conviction that archivists need a reader concerning privacy and confidentiality issues, as well as from our experience in presenting privacy and confidentiality sessions to standing-room–only crowds at professional conferences. Interest remains high, and we hope that this book provides new insights and contributes to the lively and ongoing conversation.

It has been a challenging and intellectually rewarding experience to work on this book. We appreciate the fact that so many archival colleagues willingly dedicated their time and talents to create the articles contained herein, and we thank them for their fine contributions. We also wish to acknowledge the support of the Society of American Archivists, and we especially owe many thanks to Teresa Brinati for her assistance and patience, as well as to Richard Cox for his thoughtful suggestions. Our own editorial partnership survived several NFL seasons, happily because our respective teams rarely play each other. Their traditional annual early exits from playoff contention left plenty of cold winter months free for writing and editing. Menzi wishes to thank her husband, Gerald J. Klodt, for his steadfast support throughout the project and always. Peter wishes to thank his wife, Patricia L. Schall, for putting up with the project, the attendant clutter, and him.

MENZI L. BEHRND-KLODT AND PETER J. WOSH

June 2005

INTRODUCTION

Privacy concerns invariably generate deeply felt and emotional public responses. Modern democratic cultures struggle with conflicting demands for open access to information and the need to protect individual privacy. By the beginning of the twenty-first century, many observers seemed convinced that the balance had tilted decidedly away from individual rights. National polls reflected this perception, revealing that nearly nine of ten Americans believed that their privacy was under siege.[1] Legal and ethical observers also painted an ominous and depressing portrait. Rodney A. Smolla, a privacy expert and law professor at the University of Richmond, represented this viewpoint well, reciting a litany of disquieting trends and familiar villains that appeared to threaten privacy at the dawn of the new millennium. He pointed especially to the tabloid culture and rise of the paparazzi, the evaporation of boundaries between public and private life, a focus on the lives of ordinary people for entertainment and news in mass culture, technologies that penetrate privacy in unprecedented ways, increased surveillance by governmental authorities, the cozy partnership between law enforcement officials and media outlets, an increased use of shaming as a form of social control and criminal punishment, the inherently public nature of on-line communication and the failure of Internet service providers to guarantee confidentiality, and the ambivalent legal protection afforded to individuals on such matters as reproduction, sexual conduct, or assisted suicide.[2] Regardless of whether one accepts or rejects Smolla's specific historical arguments, he accurately captured popular perceptions and cogently summarized the generally perceived wisdom concerning contemporary threats to privacy. If anything, concerns have heightened following the terrorist attacks on New York and Washington in 2001. A federal climate decidedly favoring both secrecy and surveillance prevailed within the United States during the first few years of the twenty-first century. President George W. Bush's executive order that sought to overturn access provisions of the Presidential Records Act, Attorney General John Ashcroft's memo to federal agencies that encouraged more restrictive approaches to Freedom of Information Act requests, and the passage of the USA PATRIOT Act in 2001 all point toward policies that limit access to public records while simultaneously restricting ordinary citizens' privacy rights.[3]

Still, privacy itself remains a somewhat confusing notion. Despite the ambiguity inherent in the term, an effort to define privacy more precisely, and to distinguish it from related concepts, seems worthwhile at the outset of this book. No single intellectual foundation for privacy exists, though most academics agree that it refers to people and to the purposes for which personal information is gathered, used, and/or disclosed. *Privacy* protection generally implies that personal information will not be revealed to others and that individuals will have the right to make private decisions and choices without governmental interference. Privacy also describes the exclusiveness of personal physical and psychological "space." *Confidentiality*, in contrast, refers to the sensitive nature of certain information and to the circumstances surrounding its disclosure or protection. *Security* indicates the attributes of a protective record-keeping system, such as the effort to prevent unauthorized disclosures and alterations or loss of data, as well as the effort to maintain the integrity of data. *Access* means the ability to see, inspect, use, or disclose information. It may or may not include the right to further transmit the information.

None of these concepts exists in a social or historical vacuum. The confluence of history, law, ethics, social science, public opinion, and technology all shape the changing definitions concerning privacy. Material and social environments, as well as shifting intellectual perspectives, significantly influence the development of privacy concepts. Other important external variables condition public opinion as well. Families, corporations, educational and religious institutions, organizations, communities, political parties, and pressure and interest groups affect popular perceptions. Powerful traditions, habits, ideas, and ideals further help to shape the social climate. And human inertia, greed, altruism, prejudice, ignorance, and sheer accident also play their particular roles. Obviously, the ground continues to shift and the issue remains in a permanent state of flux. This book reflects privacy perspectives at one specific moment in American cultural history, and it focuses on issues involving one particular professional community: archivists.

In fact, archivists did not begin to grapple intensely with privacy issues until relatively recent times, though the concept enjoys a long and interesting history. Samuel D. Warren and Louis D. Brandeis generally receive credit for articulating the "right to privacy" and bringing it to the attention of the American legal profession in 1890, but only federal legislation in the late 1960s and early 1970s stimulated archivists to seriously consider privacy matters. The Freedom of Information Act of 1966 (FOIA) (5 U.S.C. § 552) and the Privacy Act of 1974 (5 U.S.C. § 552a) radically revamped the public informational landscape. Federal agencies developed internal mechanisms for implementing the FOIA. Journalists, historians, advocacy organizations, and private citizens flooded government offices with requests for documentation. Most states and many municipalities drafted freedom of information laws based at least in part on the federal statutes. Many religious, corporate, and cultural institutions revised their own privacy policies in the late 1960s and 1970s as a result of the broader sociopolitical climate that led to the drafting of these laws. The Family Educational Rights and Privacy Act of 1974 (FERPA) (20 U.S.C. § 1232g) further raised questions concerning the confidentiality and administration of student records for all academic archivists. And, in the aftermath of the Watergate crisis, the U.S. Congress finally defined presidential records as public documents and clearly stipulated access provisions.

Still, the archival literature remained remarkably thin through the mid-1970s. Frank B. Evans's comprehensive *Modern Archives and Manuscripts: A Select Bibliography*, which was published by the Society of American Archivists (SAA) in 1975, found virtually no discussion concerning the FOIA in archival or library periodicals.[4] Rather, almost all of the relevant discourse seemed to occur in law journals, government documents, and social science quarterlies. A few scattered articles concerning federal legislation, manuscript access restrictions, and FERPA appeared within archival journals, but the recordkeeping community directed little sustained attention toward the topic.[5] This situation began to change in the late 1970s, in part because archivists began to understand the far-reaching privacy implications of new federal legislation. Research trends also played a role, as historians and social scientists began making greater use of such documentation as social work case files, church sacramental registers, public welfare records, and patient medical histories in their efforts to penetrate the lives of people who left behind few written records. Archivists recognized the research value of such materials, but also understood the confidentiality issues and practical problems that often prevented them from acquiring and accessioning such files.[6] Finally, technological considerations caused archivists to pay greater attention to privacy. The enormous proliferation of data banks, the accumulation of vast amounts of information on individuals by public and private institutions, and the possibility of linking and manipulating data through sophisticated computer programs made archivists more aware of the need to carefully develop access policies for potentially sensitive materials in their organizations.

Sue E. Holbert's *Archives & Manuscripts: Reference & Access*, the basic manual that was published by the Society of American Archivists in 1977, reflects the way in which privacy issues had begun to assume greater prominence within archival circles.[7] Holbert reviewed the federal legislation concerning freedom of information and privacy; raised issues concerning the historic legal privileges of patient-physician, confessor-priest, and client-lawyer; and alerted archivists to the sensitive nature of data that might reside in diverse venues ranging from corporate offices to labor unions to private welfare organizations. Her popular manual reflects the characteristic archival emphasis on opening more records for research and limiting restrictions wherever possible. Holbert warns readers against "shackling many types of research" relating to ordinary people by excessively restricting access to personal information. She worries that an excessive concern with privacy might "lead institutions to avoid the acquisitions of papers and records known to be potential sources of trouble, thus further limiting the availability of resources in critical subject areas." Still, Holbert acknowledges that "archivists must be careful to protect privacy" even as they need to find ways to serve scholars and social historians more effectively. This basic manual constitutes one of the earliest efforts in the archival literature to explore the complex relationship between privacy and access, and it played a role in stimulating greater professional discussion.[8]

Between the late 1970s and the mid-1990s, archivists participated in a lively and constructive debate over basic privacy issues on several fronts. Three book-length archival monographs devoted significant attention to the topic, openly reflecting professional disagreements rather than consensus. Gary M. Peterson and Trudy Huskamp Peterson prepared the basic SAA manual *Archives & Manuscripts: Law* in 1985, which extensively reviewed the FOIA and its various exemptions, as well as other federal and state privacy legislation. The Petersons' manual also contains the somewhat surprising statement that "privacy is by far the most pervasive consideration in restricting material in archives," reflecting a decided shift away from the embrace of open access that characterized much writing in the 1970s.[9] In 1988, the Mid-Atlantic Regional Archives Conference (MARAC) published a symposia volume around the theme *Constitutional Issues and Archives*, which highlights disagreements and eschews easy solutions. The MARAC contribution presents opposing viewpoints on the right to privacy and the right to know, and it discusses such controversial topics as privacy act expungements, emphasizing debate and controversy throughout.[10] Heather MacNeil's influential *Without Consent: The Ethics of Disclosing Personal Information in Public Archives,* which appeared in 1992, further reflects the lack of consensus. MacNeil defines the archivist's role as ensuring "a just and equitable balance" between the competing forces of open access and privacy interests. She clearly tilted the balance toward personal rights, however, arguing that "consideration for the welfare and integrity of individuals generally, and their right to privacy specifically, must prevail over the advancement of knowledge." All of these contributions reflect a thoughtful, cautious, and reasonably balanced approach toward privacy and confidentiality questions, even if concrete answers and certitude appear more difficult to achieve.[11]

Privacy issues emerged more regularly within the professional periodical literature during the 1980s and early 1990s as well. Legislative issues proved a popular topic as archivists discussed federal policies,[12] state statutes,[13] and FERPA.[14] Other authors turned their attention to topics that had a greater impact on private institutions, such as ethical considerations,[15] case studies involving particularly troublesome administrative issues,[16] and detailed examinations of particular kinds of records.[17] Privacy-related sessions drew overflow crowds at archival conferences. SAA established a Privacy and Confidentiality Roundtable, which began monitoring relevant legislation, reviewing new books in the field, and encouraging the production of scholarly and bibliographic work concerning the topic. Archivists may have failed to achieve a complete consensus concerning any one universal professional approach toward privacy, but the recent literature and conference discussions reflect the intensity, quality, and necessity of ongoing debate.[18]

This book seeks to advance these debates and to engage the profession in a more complex analytical consideration of privacy-related questions. The editors have attempted both to locate and to commission articles that offer some historical context for current concerns, that reflect innovative new approaches to resolving privacy dilemmas, and that develop sophisticated theoretical frameworks upon which to consider issues in broad and overarching ways. No effort has been made to bring together all of the existing literature, to cover every aspect of the field, or to create a reference work that serves as a basic manual. Comprehensiveness has been sacrificed in the interest of stimulating deeper reflection, provoking discussion, and offering archivists a variety of ways in which to consider their current practices and methodologies. No single ideological stance dominates the book. The editors instead welcomed contributions that promised to illustrate the ways in which archivists have applied their various philosophical principles to resolve specific privacy problems. The authors differ considerably in style and approach, but they reflect the multiplicity of perspectives that archivists need to consider when confronted with difficult issues.

Accordingly, the book has been divided into four general sections, each of which considers archival privacy and confidentiality from a particular vantage point: legal, ethical, administrative, and institutional. Individual sections include more detailed editorial introductions, but it seems useful to briefly review the topics here. The first section, Legal Perspectives, focuses on the key concepts that define American privacy law. It reprints two classic law review articles that most influenced the course of twentieth-century jurisprudence concerning privacy, and it also includes a reflection on tort law by one of the editors of this volume. Legal Perspectives reminds archivists of the broader frameworks that both limit and constrain their actions, as well as the historical factors and assumptions that have shaped privacy law. The second section, Ethical Perspectives, presents primarily new work by archivists who approach the issues from a more philosophical perspective. The authors illustrate the ambiguities inherent in professional codes of ethics, the difficulties of applying consistent principles to practical situations, and the diverse viewpoints that exist within the archival community. The third section, Administrative Perspectives, contains contributions by archival administrators who have attempted to resolve especially troublesome real-world situations in their own repositories. Conflicts between donor desires and researcher requests, difficulties in protecting third-party privacy rights in governmental records, problems in carrying out judicially imposed records restrictions, and efforts to simply figure out how to follow confusing laws all receive attention. Finally, the Institutional Perspectives section addresses the fact that specific institutional contexts often play the most critical role in resolving privacy questions. The authors focus on the unique problems that face archivists in the corporate, religious, and health care sectors. Organizational and professional cultures, no less than legal and ethical considerations, influence attitudes concerning privacy and confidentiality for most archivists.

Legal, ethical, administrative, and institutional perspectives overlap considerably, as the contributions in this book make abundantly clear. Several themes in particular cut across these boundaries and reappear consistently throughout the volume. Perhaps least surprisingly, most authors pay close attention to recent technological developments. The relationship between technological change and privacy is not new, as the legal history makes clear. The formulation of the "right to privacy" that

Samuel D. Warren and Louis D. Brandeis articulated in 1890 owed much to concerns over the development of cheap handheld cameras and the proliferation of the penny press. By the mid-twentieth century, privacy advocates typically cited "the computer age" as an important factor that allowed governmental and corporate entities to intrude into previously confidential realms of individual existence. Computerized records linkage soon emerged as a major issue, as individuals worried about vast data banks of information that documented their health histories, financial status, and personal habits. Clearly, such concerns have been exacerbated in recent years as daily newspapers bombard consumers with articles involving identity theft, cyberspace cookies, corporate records linkage, the exploitation of individual images, and government surveillance. Electronic records issues dominate much contemporary thought about privacy, and they predictably concern many of the contributors to this volume as well.

The intersection of the public and private sectors in American life constitutes another recurring theme. Most public legislation, such as the FOIA, the Privacy Act, the USA PATRIOT Act, and open records laws, primarily affect access to government records that are held in agencies and repositories. Few federal and state privacy statutes directly govern private entities. Notable exceptions do exist, such as FERPA and the Health Insurance Portability and Accountability Act of 1996 (HIPAA), as well as other regulatory legislation that applies to specific industries. Public policy, however, exerts an influence over developments in the corporate and nonprofit worlds that transcends the narrowly legislative. Federal and state governments collect and trade in private information. They require businesses and organizations to provide data, thereby eroding privacy. Governmental entities also constitute an enormous presence in everyday American life, often fueling mistrust and suspicion, even as many citizens welcome the benefits and opportunities that they provide. Regardless of individual viewpoints concerning the proper role of government in society, many contemporary notions concerning privacy and confidentiality are driven by the actions of government and the reactions of citizens, as well as by the need to provide information in order to receive public benefits. Though most of the articles in this volume directly address privacy issues in the nonpublic sector, governmental policies and practices clearly cast an enormous shadow.

Finally, this book testifies to the fact that the concept of privacy continues to change based on a complex variety of historical, cultural, social, institutional, and personal factors. Archivists typically react to broader sociopolitical changes, and the profession continues to deliberate its appropriate role in public debate. Many contributors to this volume argue for a more aggressively activist stance. Some place a burden on archivists to keep privacy protection high among their core professional values and to build privacy protection into their administrative policies. Others document the specific ways in which archivists have played an important role in increasing access to particular materials while satisfying donor privacy concerns. A few go even further, arguing that archivists should restructure their roles within their institutions to capitalize on their positions as guardians of trust and confidence. But cautionary notes also appear. Archivists occasionally have been overly vigilant in restricting access to materials concerning human sexuality, for example, thereby damaging and distorting the historical record. Aggressive efforts to protect third-party rights may border on censorship and even place institutions at greater legal risk. Responsible professionals appear divided about whether their proper role involves uniformly administering preexisting access policies, or actively shaping those policies. This book cannot resolve these issues, but it can stimulate further conversation. James O'Toole once insightfully observed that "archivists think like archivists; they analyze and understand archival and records problems in their own special way." No particular perspective concerning privacy dominates archival thought, but archivists do think about privacy in their own special way. Perhaps this collection of essays will bring us closer to defining and articulating precisely what that special way of thinking encompasses. If so, the profession may have a unique and significant role to play in the never-ending social discussion concerning privacy, confidentiality, security, access, and records.[19]

LEGAL PERSPECTIVES

Definitions

The right of privacy is considered a purely personal right[1] of living individuals,[2] designed to protect peace of mind. Privacy protects persons from unwarranted publicity, public scrutiny of personal affairs, or making private matters public without consent. Privacy rights primarily protect feelings and sensibilities to prevent emotional harm. Related property rights protect the privacy of personal names and images and the commercial value of celebrities' names and images. An individual's right of privacy thus generally does not extend to protect family members, unless their individual privacy rights also are violated, in which case they receive separate legal protection.[3]

The right of privacy is not absolute, but rather relates to the customs of specific times and places. Only ordinary, as opposed to hypersensitive, sensibilities are protected. An invasion of privacy occurs as the result of an act that a reasonable person could anticipate might, and probably would, cause mental or emotional distress to one of ordinary feelings and intelligence in similar circumstances. Thus, a claim for invasion of privacy may be won only if the claimant has suffered unreasonable and serious interference with protected personal interests.

Individual privacy rights do not necessarily supersede the public's right to know, but require the balancing of competing interests. Individual privacy rights generally do not forbid publication of matters of legitimate public interest about a public person[4] or events of general concern, nor does the right of privacy provide protection for those who are in a public or semipublic place when caught by news cameras.

Constitutional Origins

American privacy rights arise from, but are not explicitly mentioned in, the U.S. Constitution.[5] The Bill of Rights, protector of the rights of the minority against majority rule, broadly affirms privacy concepts by limiting the *government's* power to interfere with individual liberty. The First Amendment[6] guarantees free speech and free exercise of religion, assuring privacy of personal beliefs and associations. The Fourth Amendment protects "persons, houses, papers, and effects" from unreasonable governmental search and seizure. The Fifth Amendment protects individuals from being forced to testify against their interests, thus guaranteeing privacy. The Ninth Amendment reserves otherwise unenumerated rights to the people. The Fourteenth Amendment limits government's power to deprive persons of life, liberty, or property without due process of law and to deny equal protection under the laws. From these roots, notions of privacy have become integral in American life, though the law of privacy is a fairly recent development.

From Warren and Brandeis to Prosser and Beyond

This section of the privacy reader reproduces two classic articles that greatly influenced twentieth-century privacy discussions in the United States, and it concludes with an article on the related tort right of privacy by Menzi L. Behrnd-Klodt. Legal scholars agree that serious discussions of privacy in twentieth-century law and culture began with the 1890 *Harvard Law Review* article by Samuel D. Warren (1852–1910) and Louis D. Brandeis (1856–1941).[7] "The Right to Privacy," as William L. Prosser (1898–1972) notes in his article reprinted here, owed something to Warren's growing outrage over Boston's sensationalist press. Newspaper coverage of both his 1883 marriage to Mabel Bayard, the daughter of a wealthy Delaware senator, and her subsequent social soirees, convinced Warren that citizens possessed a fundamental "right to be let alone." In their important article, Warren and Brandeis defined this legal right of individuals for the first time, drawing upon precedents from the law of defamation, literary property, and eavesdropping to protect each person's "inviolate personality," even though disclosures were not particularly intimate or offensive. They argued that private information "belonged" to the individual to whom it related and could be used by others only with the consent of its "owner." Their articulation of the right to privacy proved extraordinarily influential over the course of the twentieth century, serving as the basis for Supreme Court decisions and legal analysis on topics ranging from wiretapping to abortion to the right to die.

Archivists can find much to ponder in Warren and Brandeis's seminal article. Clearly social, technological, and legal factors contributed to their formulation. Do the authors' conclusions remain socially relevant in the twenty-first century, especially in light of new frontiers in intellectual property considerations and copyright law? When does public interest supersede the "right to be let alone"? Where do unpublished manuscripts, personal diaries, and private correspondence fit into their arguments? The archival profession may play a constructive role in negotiating the complex mixture of legal and ethical considerations that seems so central to Warren and Brandeis.

The Right to Privacy: First and Fourteenth Amendments

American privacy law has developed incrementally since 1890. A recurrent thread is based on both the First Amendment's protections of freedom of the press, association, and liberty, and the Fourteenth Amendment's guarantees of due process and equal protection.

In 1902, New York's highest court held that a woman whose picture was misappropriated and printed on flour packages had no right of privacy.[8] The New York State Legislature immediately passed limited privacy legislation. Three years later, the Georgia Supreme Court explicitly recognized a legal right of privacy when it ruled that publishing a man's picture as an advertisement without his consent was an invasion of his right of privacy.[9]

In the early twentieth century, the Fourteenth Amendment's Due Process clause was interpreted to guarantee the individual's freedom to make personal decisions that were not adverse to legitimate state interests. Only "compelling" state interests could justify any governmental restriction on the exercise of constitutional rights. Laws that prohibited the teaching of children in languages other than English and that required attendance at public rather than private schools were held to be examples of restrictions on personal freedom that lacked a compelling public interest.[10] In 1931, the U.S. Supreme Court, with Brandeis sitting as one of the justices, provided a succinct and surprisingly modern summary of the right of privacy:

> (1) The right of privacy was unknown to the ancient common law. (2) It is an incident of the person and not of property—a tort for which a right of recovery is given in some jurisdictions. (3) It is a purely personal action, and does not survive, but dies with the person. (4) It does not exist where the person has published the matter complained of, or consented thereto. (5) It does not exist where a person has become so prominent that by his

very prominence he has dedicated his life to the public, and thereby waived his right to privacy. There can be no privacy in that which is already public. (6) It does not exist in the dissemination of news and news events, nor in the discussion of events of the life of a person in whom the public has a rightful interest, nor where the information would be of public benefit, as in the case of a candidate for public office. (7) The right of privacy can only be violated by printings, writings, pictures, or other permanent publications or reproductions, and not by word of mouth. (8) The right of action accrues when the publication is made for gain or profit.[11]

The *Restatement of Torts*, completed in 1939 as a compilation of the state of the law, articulated the right of privacy. William Prosser's seminal analysis in his *Handbook of the Law of Torts*[12] was later incorporated into the *Restatement (Second) of Torts*. Together, the analysis in these two works greatly influenced the development of late twentieth-century American law. Many state privacy statutes incorporate almost verbatim Prosser's description of the four aspects of privacy rights.[13] Excerpts from Prosser's 1960 "Privacy" article, which is reprinted in chapter 2, appear in numerous American legal opinions on privacy.

During the late twentieth century, a constitutional right of privacy developed based upon notions of individual freedom of choice and the right to private decision making in personal and family matters, as inherent in the concept of liberty. The Supreme Court recognized privacy rights in sexual matters, marriage, and procreation, all fundamental to the very existence and survival of the human race. Laws that interfered with the exercise of these basic rights received strict judicial scrutiny.[14] In *Poe v. Ullman*, the majority of the court did not decide whether Connecticut laws could prohibit dispensing of contraceptives, but dissenting Justice Harlan argued that the laws violated the due process rights of married persons, invaded upon marital privacy, and intruded upon the most intimate details of marriage.[15] By 1965, mirroring both Justice Harlan's dissent and the state of society, the U.S. Supreme Court invalidated such laws and recognized for the first time a constitutional right to privacy apart from the Fourth Amendment protection against unlawful search and seizure.[16]

The state's role in regulating marriage and other intimate personal decisions also implicates privacy rights and, by the late twentieth century, demanded strict court scrutiny of restrictive statutes. Thus, in the 1960s and 1970s, the U.S. Supreme Court struck down laws prohibiting interracial marriage, requiring prepayment to access divorce courts, requiring court permission to marry if there were minor children to support, and unduly restricting abortion, child rearing, and education.[17] The right of privacy now includes both an individual interest in avoiding disclosure of personal matters and an interest in independence in making certain important decisions.[18] Cases about the right to die, same-sex marriage, and personal decisions made by pregnant women appear likely to be decided under similar standards.

The Right to Privacy: Fourth and Fifth Amendments

The second major twentieth-century theme in privacy law emanated from the Fourth Amendment's protections against unreasonable governmental search and seizure and the Fifth Amendment's protection against self-incrimination. As early as 1886, the U.S. Supreme Court interpreted the Fourth Amendment to protect private papers from seizure.[19] In 1928, the court declined to extend this constitutional protection to telephone conversations, ruling that overhearing did not involve illegal entry, search, or seizure. Justice Brandeis's dissent, however, recognized that changes in technology require an extension of Fourth Amendment concepts, and his prescient commentary has since received widespread acceptance.[20] In 1967, in *Katz v. United States,* the U.S. Supreme Court created a "reasonable expectation of privacy" standard applicable to persons:

> What a person knowingly exposes to the public, even in his own home or office, is not a subject of Fourth Amendment protection. . . . But what he seeks to preserve as private, even in an area accessible to the public, may be constitutionally protected. . . . [O]nce it is recognized that the Fourth Amendment protects people—and not simply "areas"—against unreasonable searches and seizures it becomes clear that the reach of the Amendment cannot turn upon the presence or absence of a physical intrusion into any given enclosure.[21]

A private area is one where an individual has a reasonable expectation of privacy that outweighs the government's interest in conducting a search, factoring in the degree of intrusion involved. Such constitutional protections now protect personal communications, personality, politics, and thoughts.

Today, however, the government may collect and widely distribute personal data with few privacy limitations, particularly during criminal investigations. Individuals have no legitimate expectation of privacy in their bank records, becoming virtual third parties to their own transactions by surrendering their privacy rights when a bank begins to keep their records.[22] Telephone companies provide customer information to police investigations without notifying customers.[23] Homeowners have no legitimate expectation of information privacy in yards that are readily observable to the public, nor in trash placed at the curb for collection.[24] Employees have limited privacy rights in the workplace, where personal items may be seized and secret filming may occur without violating privacy rights.[25] The "war on terrorism" has led to even greater government collection and dissemination of personal information, as many existing federal privacy protections were abolished or restricted by the USA PATRIOT Act in 2001 (see appendix 2).

Conclusion

American privacy rights are at a critical legal juncture. Privacy concerns remain high, but national security interests and fears of terrorism threaten to radically curtail American privacy rights and citizens' abilities to control their personal information. Whether these currently predominant tensions will overwhelm the privacy landscape and cause permanent, constitutionally based changes remains to be determined. This section of the reader, however, sets the stage for later discussions by outlining the development of privacy principles and the legal structure of privacy. It offers insight into the ways in which the peculiar historical development of American privacy law can inform contemporary debate and discussion.

1 The Right to Privacy

Samuel D. Warren and Louis D. Brandeis

> It could be done only on principles of private justice, moral fitness, and public convenience, which, when applied to a new subject, make common law without a precedent; much more when received and approved by usage.
>
> (WILLES, J., in Millar v. Taylor, 4 Burr. 2303, 2312.)

That the individual shall have full protection in person and in property is a principle as old as the common law; but it has been found necessary from time to time to define anew the exact nature and extent of such protection. Political, social, and economic changes entail the recognition of new rights, and the common law, in its eternal youth, grows to meet the demands of society. Thus, in very early times, the law gave a remedy only for physical interference with life and property, for trespasses *vi et armis*. Then the "right to life" served only to protect the subject from battery in its various forms; liberty meant freedom from actual restraint; and the right to property secured to the individual his lands and his cattle. Later, there came a recognition of man's spiritual nature, of his feelings and his intellect. Gradually the scope of these legal rights broadened; and now the right to life has come to mean the right to enjoy life—the right to be let alone; the right to liberty secures the exercise of extensive civil privileges; and the term "property" has grown to comprise every form of possession—intangible, as well as tangible.

Thus, with the recognition of the legal value of sensations, the protection against actual bodily injury was extended to prohibit mere attempts to do such injury; that is, the putting another in fear of such injury. From

---

This article originally published in *Harvard Law Review* 4 (1890):193.

the action of battery grew that of assault.[1] Much later there came a qualified protection of the individual against offensive noises and odors, against dust and smoke, and excessive vibration. The law of nuisance was developed.[2] So regard for human emotions soon extended the scope of personal immunity beyond the body of the individual. His reputation, the standing among his fellow-men, was considered, and the law of slander and libel arose.[3] Man's family relations became a part of the legal conception of his life, and the alienation of a wife's affections was held remediable.[4] Occasionally the law halted—as in its refusal to recognize the intrusion by seduction upon the honor of the family. But even here the demands of society were met. A mean fiction, the action *per quod servitium amisit*, was resorted to, and by allowing damages for injury to the parents' feelings, an adequate remedy was ordinarily afforded.[5] Similar to the expansion of the right to life was the growth of the legal conception of property. From corporeal property arose the incorporeal rights issuing out of it; and then there opened the wide realm of intangible property, in the products and processes of the mind,[6] as works of literature and art,[7] goodwill,[8] trade secrets, and trademarks.[9]

This development of the law was inevitable. The intense intellectual and emotional life, and the heightening of sensations which came with the advance of civilization, made it clear to men that only a part of the pain, pleasure, and profit of life lay in physical things. Thoughts, emotions, and sensations demanded legal recognition, and the beautiful capacity for growth which characterizes the common law enabled the judges to afford the requisite protection, without the interposition of the legislature.

Recent inventions and business methods call attention to the next step which must be taken for the protection of the person, and for securing to the individual what Judge Cooley calls the right "to be let alone."[10] Instantaneous photographs and newspaper enterprise have invaded the sacred precincts of private and domestic life; and numerous mechanical devices threaten to make good the prediction that "what is whispered in the closet shall be proclaimed from the house-tops." For years there has been a feeling that the law must afford some remedy for the unauthorized circulation of portraits of private persons;[11] and the evil of the invasion of privacy by the newspapers, long keenly felt, has been but recently discussed by an able writer.[12] The alleged facts of a somewhat notorious case brought before an inferior tribunal in New York a few months ago,[13] directly involved the consideration of the right of circulating portraits; and the question whether our law will recognize and protect the right to privacy in this and in other respects must soon come before our courts for consideration.

Of the desirability—indeed of the necessity—of some such protection, there can, it is believed, be no doubt. The press is overstepping in every direction the obvious bounds of propriety and of decency. Gossip is no longer the resource of the idle and of the vicious, but has become a trade, which is pursued with industry as well as effrontery. To satisfy a prurient taste, the details of sexual relations are spread broadcast in the columns of the daily papers. To occupy the indolent, column upon column is filled with idle gossip, which can only be procured by intrusion upon the domestic circle. The intensity and complexity of life, attendant upon advancing civilization, have rendered necessary some retreat from the world, and man, under the refining influence of culture, has become more sensitive to publicity, so that solitude and privacy have become more essential to the individual; but modern enterprise and invention have, through invasions upon his privacy, subjected him to mental pain and distress, far greater than could be inflicted by mere bodily injury. Nor is the harm wrought by such invasions confined to the suffering of those who may be made the subjects of journalistic or other enterprise. In this, as in other branches of commerce, the supply creates the demand. Each crop of unseemly gossip, thus harvested, becomes the seed of more, and, in direct proportion to its circulation, results in a lowering of social standards and of morality. Even gossip apparently harmless, when widely and persistently circulated, is potent for evil. It both belittles and perverts. It belittles by inverting the relative importance of things, thus dwarfing the thoughts and aspirations of a people. When personal gossip attains the dignity of print, and crowds the space available for matters of real interest to the community, what wonder that the ignorant and thoughtless mistake its relative importance. Easy of comprehension, appealing to that weak side of human nature which is never wholly cast down by the misfortunes and frailties of our neighbors, no one can be surprised that it usurps the place of interest in brains capable of other things. Triviality destroys at once robustness of thought and delicacy of feeling. No enthusiasm can flourish, no generous impulse can survive under its blighting influence.

It is our purpose to consider whether the existing law affords a principle which can properly be invoked to protect the privacy of the individual; and, if it does, what the nature and extent of such protection is.

Owing to the nature of the instruments by which privacy is invaded, the injury inflicted bears a superficial resemblance to the wrongs dealt with by the law of slander and of libel, while a legal remedy for such injury seems to involve the treatment of mere wounded feelings, as a substantive cause of action. The principle on which the law of defamation rests, covers, however, a radically different class of effects from those for which attention is now asked. It deals only with damage to reputation, with the injury done to the individual in his external relations to the community, by lowering him in the estimation of his fellows. The matter published of him, however widely circulated, and however unsuited to publicity, must, in order to be actionable, have a direct tendency to injure him in his intercourse with others, and even if in writing or in print, must subject him to the hatred, ridicule, or contempt of his fellow-men,—the effect of the publication upon his estimate of himself and upon his own feelings not forming an essential element in the cause of action. In short, the wrongs and correlative rights recognized by the law of slander and libel are in their nature material rather than spiritual. That branch of the law simply extends the protection surrounding physical property to certain of the conditions necessary or helpful to worldly prosperity. On the other hand, our law recognizes no principle upon which compensation can be granted for mere injury to the feelings. However painful the mental effects upon another of an act, though purely wanton or even malicious, yet if the act itself is otherwise lawful, the suffering inflicted is *damnum absque injuria*. Injury of feelings may indeed be taken account of in ascertaining the amount of damages when attending what is recognized as a legal injury;[14] but our system, unlike the Roman law, does not afford a remedy even for mental suffering which results from mere contumely and insult, from an intentional and unwarranted violation of the "honor" of another.[15]

It is not however necessary, in order to sustain the view that the common law recognizes and upholds a principle applicable to cases of invasion of privacy, to invoke the analogy, which is but superficial, to injuries sustained, either by an attack upon reputation or by what the civilians called a violation of honor; for the legal doctrines relating to infractions of what is ordinarily termed the common-law right to intellectual and artistic property are, it is believed, but instances and applications of a general right to privacy, which properly understood afford a remedy for the evils under consideration.

The common law secures to each individual the right of determining, ordinarily, to what extent his thoughts, sentiments, and emotions shall be communicated to others.[16] Under our system of government, he can never be compelled to express them (except when upon the witness stand); and even if he has chosen to give them expression, he generally retains the power to fix the limits of the publicity which shall be given them. The existence of this right does not depend upon the particular method of expression adopted. It is immaterial whether it be by word[17] or by signs,[18] in painting,[19] by sculpture, or in music.[20] Neither does the existence of the right depend upon the nature or value of the thought or emotion, nor upon the excellence of the means of expression.[21] The same protection is accorded to a casual letter or an entry in a diary and to the most valuable poem or essay, to a botch or daub and to a masterpiece. In every such case the individual is entitled to decide whether that which is his shall be given to the public.[22] No other has the right to publish his productions in any form, without his consent. This right is wholly independent of the material on which, or the means by which, the thought, sentiment, or emotion is expressed. It may exist independently of any corporeal being, as in words spoken, a song sung, a drama acted. Or if expressed on any material, as a poem in writing, the author may have parted with the paper, without forfeiting any proprietary right in the composition itself. The right is lost only when the author himself communicates his production to the public,—in other words, publishes it.[23] It is entirely independent of the copyright laws, and their extension into the domain of art. The aim of those statutes is to secure to the author, composer, or artist the entire profits arising from publication; but the common-law protection enables him to control absolutely the act of publication, and in the exercise of his own discretion, to decide whether there shall be any publication at all.[24] The statutory right is of no value, *unless* there is a publication; the common-law right is lost *as soon as* there is a publication.

What is the nature, the basis, of this right to prevent the publication of manuscripts or works of art? It is stated to be the enforcement of a right of property;[25] and no difficulty arises in accepting this view, so long as we have only to deal with the reproduction of literary and artistic compositions. They certainly possess many of the attributes of ordinary property: they are transferable; they have a value; and publication or reproduction is a use by which that value is realized. But where the value of the production is found not in the right to take the profits arising from publication, but in the peace of mind or the relief afforded by the ability to prevent any publication at all, it is difficult to regard the right as one of property, in the common acceptation of that term. A man records in a letter to his son, or in his diary, that he did not dine with his wife on a certain day. No one into whose hands those papers fall could publish them to the world, even if possession of the documents had been obtained rightfully; and the prohibition would not be confined to the publication of a copy of the letter itself, or of the diary entry; the restraint extends also to a publication of the contents. What is the thing which is protected? Surely, not the intellectual act of recording the fact that the husband did not dine with his wife, but that fact itself. It is not the intellectual product, but the domestic occurrence. A man writes a dozen letters to different people. No person would be permitted to publish a list of the letters written. If the letters or the contents of the diary were protected as literary compositions, the scope of the protection afforded should be the same secured to a published writing under the copyright law. But the copyright law would not prevent an enumeration of the letters, or the publication of some of the facts contained therein. The copyright of a series of paintings or etchings would prevent a reproduction of the paintings as pictures; but it would not prevent a publication of a list or even a description of them.[26] Yet in the famous case of Prince Albert v. Strange, the court held that the common-law rule prohibited not merely the reproduction of the etchings which the plaintiff and Queen Victoria had made for their own pleasure, but also "the publishing (at least by printing or writing), though not by copy or resemblance, a description of them, whether more or less limited or summary, whether in the form of a catalogue or otherwise."[27] Likewise, an unpublished collection of news possessing no element of a literary nature is protected from piracy.[28]

That this protection cannot rest upon the right to literary or artistic property in any exact sense, appears the more clearly when the subject-matter for which protection is invoked is not even in the form of intellectual property, but has the attributes of ordinary tangible property. Suppose a man has a collection of gems or curiosities which he keeps private: it would hardly be contended that any person could publish a catalogue of them, and yet the articles enumerated are certainly not intellectual property in the legal sense, any more than a collection of stoves or of chairs.[29]

The belief that the idea of property in its narrow sense was the basis of the protection of unpublished manuscripts led an able court to refuse, in several cases, injunctions against the publication of private letters, on the ground that "letters not possessing the attributes of literary compositions are not property entitled to protection;" and that it was "evident the plaintiff could not have considered the letters as of any value whatever as literary productions, for a letter cannot be considered of value to the author which he never would consent to have published."[30] But these decisions have not been followed,[31] and it may now be considered settled that the protection afforded by the common law to the author of any writing is entirely independent of its pecuniary value, its intrinsic merits, or of any intention to publish the same, and, of course, also, wholly independent of the material, if any, upon which, or the mode in which, the thought or sentiment was expressed.

Although the courts have asserted that they rested their decisions on the narrow grounds of protection to property, yet there are recognitions of a more liberal doctrine. Thus in the case of Prince Albert v. Strange, already referred to, the opinions both of the Vice-Chancellor and of the

Lord Chancellor, on appeal, show a more or less clearly defined perception of a principle broader than those which were mainly discussed, and on which they both placed their chief reliance. Vice-Chancellor Knight Bruce referred to publishing of a man that he had "written to particular persons or on particular subjects" as an instance of possibly injurious disclosures as to private matters, that the courts would in a proper case prevent; yet it is difficult to perceive how, in such a case, any right of property, in the narrow sense, would be drawn in question, or why, if such a publication would be restrained when it threatened to expose the victim not merely to sarcasm, but to ruin, it should not equally be enjoined, if it threatened to embitter his life. To deprive a man of the potential profits to be realized by publishing a catalogue of his gems cannot *per se* be a wrong to him. The possibility of future profits is not a right of property which the law ordinarily recognizes; it must, therefore, be an infraction of other rights which constitutes the wrongful act, and that infraction is equally wrongful, whether its results are to forestall the profits that the individual himself might secure by giving the matter a publicity obnoxious to him, or to gain an advantage at the expense of his mental pain and suffering. If the fiction of property in a narrow sense must be preserved, it is still true that the end accomplished by the gossip-monger is attained by the use of that which is another's, the facts relating to his private life, which he has seen fit to keep private. Lord Cottenham stated that a man "is entitled to be protected in the exclusive use and enjoyment of that which is exclusively his," and cited with approval the opinion of Lord Eldon, as reported in a manuscript note of the case of Wyatt *v.* Wilson, in 1820, respecting an engraving of George the Third during his illness, to the effect that "if one of the late king's physicians had kept a diary of what he heard and saw, the court would not, in the king's lifetime, have permitted him to print and publish it;" and Lord Cottenham declared, in respect to the acts of the defendants in the case before him, that "privacy is the right invaded." But if privacy is once recognized as a right entitled to legal protection, the interposition of the courts cannot depend on the particular nature of the injuries resulting.

These considerations lead to the conclusion that the protection afforded to thoughts, sentiments, and emotions, expressed through the medium of writing or of the arts, so far as it consists in preventing publication, is merely an instance of the enforcement of the more general right of the individual to be let alone. It is like the right not to be assaulted or beaten, the right not to be imprisoned, the right not to be maliciously prosecuted, the right not to be defamed. In each of these rights, as indeed in all other rights recognized by the law, there inheres the quality of being owned or possessed—and (as that is the distinguishing attribute of property) there may be some propriety in speaking of those rights as property. But, obviously, they bear little resemblance to what is ordinarily comprehended under that term. The principle which protects personal writings and all other personal productions, not against theft and physical appropriation, but against publication in any form, is in reality not the principle of private property, but that of an inviolate personality.[32]

If we are correct in this conclusion, the existing law affords a principle which may be invoked to protect the privacy of the individual from invasion either by the too enterprising press, the photographer, or the possessor of any other modern device for recording or reproducing scenes or sounds. For the protection afforded is not confined by the authorities to those cases where any particular medium or form of expression has been adopted, nor to products of the intellect. The same protection is afforded to emotions and sensations expressed in a musical composition or other work of art as to a literary composition; and words spoken, a pantomime acted, a sonata performed, is no less entitled to protection than if each had been reduced to writing. The circumstance that a thought or emotion has been recorded in a permanent form renders its identification easier, and hence may be important from the point of view of evidence, but it has no significance as a matter of substantive right. If, then, the decisions indicate a general right to privacy for thoughts, emotions, and sensations, these should receive the same protection, whether expressed in writing, or in conduct, in conversation, in attitudes, or in facial expression.

It may be urged that a distinction should be taken between the deliberate expression of thoughts and emotions in literary or artistic compositions and the casual and often involuntary expression given to them in the ordinary conduct of life. In other words, it may be contended that the protection afforded is granted to the conscious products of labor, perhaps as an encouragement to effort.[33] This contention, however plausible, has, in fact, little to recommend it. If the amount of labor involved be adopted as the test, we might well find that the effort to conduct one's self properly in business and in domestic relations had been far greater than that involved in painting a picture or writing a book; one would find that it was far easier to express lofty sentiments in a diary than in the conduct of a noble life. If the test of deliberateness of the act be adopted, much casual correspondence which is now accorded full protection would be excluded from the beneficent operation of existing rules. After the decisions denying the distinction attempted to be made between those literary productions which it was intended to publish and those which it was not, all considerations of the amount of labor involved, the degree of deliberation, the value of the product, and the intention of publishing must be abandoned, and no basis is discerned upon which the right to restrain publication and reproduction of such so-called literary and artistic works can be rested, except the right to privacy, as a part of the more general right to the immunity of the person—the right to one's personality.

It should be stated that, in some instances where protection has been afforded against wrongful publication, the jurisdiction has been asserted, not on the ground of property, or at least not wholly on that ground, but upon the ground of an alleged breach of an implied contract or of a trust or confidence.

Thus, in Abernathy v. Hutchinson, 3 L. J. Ch. 209 (1825), where the plaintiff, a distinguished surgeon, sought to restrain the publication in the "Lancet" of unpublished lectures which he had delivered at St. Bartholomew's Hospital in London, Lord Eldon doubted whether there could be property in lectures which had not been reduced to writing, but granted the injunction on the ground of breach of confidence, holding "that when persons were admitted as pupils or otherwise, to hear these lectures, although they were orally delivered, and although the parties might go to the extent, if they were able to do so, of putting down the whole by means of short-hand, yet they could do that only for the purposes of their own information, and could not publish, for profit, that which they had not obtained the right of selling."

In Prince Albert v. Strange, 1 McN. & G. 25 (1849), Lord Cottenham, on appeal, while recognizing a right of property in the etchings which of itself would justify the issuance of the injunction, stated, after discussing the evidence, that he was bound to assume that the possession of the etchings by the defendant had "its foundation in a breach of trust, confidence, or contract," and that upon such ground also the plaintiff's title to the injunction was fully sustained.

In Tuck v. Priester, 19 Q. B. D. 639 (1887), the plaintiffs were owners of a picture, and employed the defendant to make a certain number of copies. He did so, and made also a number of other copies for himself, and offered them for sale in England at a lower price. Subsequently, the plaintiffs registered their copyright in the picture, and then brought suit for an injunction and damages. The Lords Justices differed as to the application of the copyright acts to the case, but held unanimously that independently of those acts, the plaintiffs were entitled to an injunction and damages for breach of contract.

In Pollard v. Photographic Co., 40 Ch. Div. 345 (1888), a photographer who had taken a lady's photograph under the ordinary circumstances was restrained from exhibiting it, and also from selling copies of it, on the ground that it was a breach of an implied term in the contract, and also that it was a breach of confidence. Mr. Justice North interjected in the argument of the plaintiff's counsel the inquiry: "Do you dispute that if the negative likeness were taken on the sly, the person who took it might exhibit copies?" and counsel for the plaintiff answered: "In that case there would be no trust or consideration to support a contract." Later, the defendant's counsel argued that "a person has no property in his own features; short of doing what is libellous or otherwise illegal, there is no restriction on the photographer's using his negative." But the court, while expressly finding a breach of contract and of trust sufficient to justify its interposition, still seems to have felt the necessity of resting the decision also upon a right of property,[34] in order to bring it within the line of those cases which were relied upon as precedents.[35]

The process of implying a term in a contract, or of implying a trust (particularly where the contract is written, and where there is no established usage or custom), is nothing more nor less than a judicial declaration that public morality, private justice, and general convenience demand the recognition of such a rule, and that the publication under similar circumstances would be considered an intolerable abuse. So long as these circumstances happen to present a contract upon which such a term can be engrafted by the judicial mind, or to supply relations upon which a trust or confidence can be erected, there may be no objection to working out the desired protection through the doctrines of contract or of trust. But the court can hardly stop there. The narrower doctrine may have satisfied the demands of society at a time when the abuse to be guarded against could rarely have arisen without violating a contract or a special confidence; but now that modern devices afford abundant opportunities for the perpetration of such wrongs without any participation by the injured party, the protection granted by the law must be placed upon a broader foundation. While, for instance, the state of the photographic art was such that one's picture could seldom be taken without his consciously "sitting" for the purpose, the law of contract or of trust might afford the prudent man sufficient safeguards against the improper circulation of his portrait; but since the latest advances in photographic art have rendered it possible to take pictures surreptitiously, the doctrines of contract and of trust are inadequate to support the required protection, and the law of tort must be resorted to. The right of property in its widest sense, including all possession, including all rights and privileges, and hence embracing the right to an inviolate personality, affords alone that broad basis upon which the protection which the individual demands can be rested.

Thus, the courts, in searching for some principle upon which the publication of private letters could be enjoined, naturally came upon the ideas of a breach of confidence, and of an implied contract; but it required little consideration to discern that this doctrine could not afford all the protection required, since it would not support the court in granting a remedy against a stranger; and so the theory of property in the contents of letters was adopted.[36] Indeed, it is difficult to conceive on what theory of the law the casual recipient of a letter, who proceeds to publish it, is guilty of a breach of contract, express or implied, or of any breach of trust, in the ordinary acceptation of that term. Suppose a letter has been addressed to him without his solicitation. He opens it, and reads. Surely, he has not made any contract; he has not accepted any trust. He cannot, by opening and reading the letter, have come under any obligation save what the law declares; and, however expressed, that obligation is simply to observe the legal right of the sender, whatever it may be, and whether it be called his right of property in the contents of the letter, or his right to privacy.[37]

A similar groping for the principle upon which a wrongful publication can be enjoined is found in the law of trade secrets. There, injunctions have generally been granted on the theory of a breach of contract, or of an abuse of confidence.[38] It would, of course, rarely happen that any one would be in the possession of a secret unless confidence had been reposed in him. But can it be supposed that the court would hesitate to grant relief against one who had obtained his knowledge by an ordinary trespass—for instance, by wrongfully looking into a book in which the secret was recorded, or by eavesdropping? Indeed, in Yovatt v. Winyard, 1 J. & W. 394 (1820), where an injunction was granted against making any use of or communicating certain recipes for veterinary medicine, it appeared that the defendant, while in the plaintiff's employ, had surreptitiously got access to his book of recipes, and copied them. Lord Eldon "granted the injunction, upon the ground of there having been a breach of trust and confidence;" but it would seem to be difficult to draw any sound legal distinction between such a case and one where a mere stranger wrongfully obtained access to the book.[39]

We must therefore conclude that the rights, so protected, whatever their exact nature, are not rights arising from contract or from special trust, but are rights as against the world; and, as above stated, the principle which has been applied to protect these rights is in reality not the principle of private property, unless that word be used in an extended and unusual sense. The principle which protects personal writings and any other productions of the intellect or of the emotions, is the right to privacy, and the law has no new principle to formulate when it extends this protection to the personal appearance, sayings, acts, and to personal relation, domestic or otherwise.[40]

If the invasion of privacy constitutes a legal *injuria,* the elements for demanding redress exist, since already the value of mental suffering, caused by an act wrongful in itself, is recognized as a basis for compensation.

The right of one who has remained a private individual, to prevent his public portraiture, presents the simplest case for such extension; the right to protect one's self from pen portraiture, from a discussion by the press of one's private affairs, would be a more important and far-reaching one. If casual and unimportant statements in a letter, if handiwork, however inartistic and valueless, if possessions of all sorts are protected not only against reproduction, but against description and enumeration, how much more should the acts and sayings of a man in his social and domestic relations be guarded from ruthless publicity. If you may not reproduce a woman's face photographically without her consent, how much less should be tolerated the reproduction of her face, her form, and her actions, by graphic descriptions colored to suit a gross and depraved imagination.

The right to privacy, limited as such right must necessarily be, has already found expression in the law of France.[41]

It remains to consider what are the limitations of this right to privacy, and what remedies may be granted for the enforcement of the right. To determine in advance of experience the exact line at which the dignity and convenience of the individual must yield to the demands of the public welfare or of private justice would be a difficult task; but the more general rules are furnished by the legal analogies already developed in the law of slander and libel, and in the law of literary and artistic property.

1. The right to privacy does not prohibit any publication of matter which is of public or general interest.

    In determining the scope of this rule, aid would be afforded by the analogy, in the law of libel and slander, of cases which deal with the qualified privilege of comment and criticism on matters of public and general interest.[42] There are of course difficulties in applying such a rule; but they are inherent in the subject matter, and are certainly no greater than those which exist in many other branches of the law—for instance, in that large class of cases in which the reasonableness or unreasonableness of an act is made the test of liability. The design of the law must be to protect those persons with whose affairs the community has no legitimate concern, from being dragged into an undesirable and undesired publicity and to protect all persons, whatsoever their position or station, from having matters which they may properly prefer to keep private, made public against their will. It is the unwarranted invasion of individual privacy which is reprehended, and to be, so far as possible, prevented. The distinction, however, noted in the above statement is obvious and fundamental. There are persons who may reasonably claim as a right, protection from the notoriety entailed by being made the victims of journalistic enterprise. There are others who, in varying degrees, have renounced the right to live their lives screened from public observation. Matters which men of the first class may justly contend, concern themselves alone, may in those of the second be the subject of legitimate interest to their fellow citizens. Peculiarities of manner and person, which in the ordinary individual should be free from comment, may acquire a public importance, if found in a candidate for political office. Some further discrimination is necessary, therefore, than to class facts or deeds as public or private according to a standard to be applied to the fact or deed *per se*. To publish of a modest and retiring individual that he suffers from an impediment in his speech or that he cannot spell correctly, is an unwarranted, if not an unexampled, infringement of his rights, while to state and comment on the same characteristics found in a would-be congressman could not be regarded as beyond the pale of propriety.

The general object in view is to protect the privacy of private life, and to whatever degree and in whatever connection a man's life has ceased to be private, before the publication under consideration has been made, to that extent the protection is to be withdrawn.[43] Since, then, the propriety of publishing the very same facts may depend wholly upon the person concerning whom they are published, no fixed formula can be used to prohibit obnoxious publications. Any rule of liability adopted must have in it an elasticity which shall take account of the varying circumstances of each case—a necessity which unfortunately renders such a doctrine not only more difficult of application, but also to a certain extent uncertain in its operation and easily rendered abortive. Besides, it is only the more flagrant branches of decency and propriety that could in practice be reached, and it is not perhaps desirable even to attempt to repress everything which the nicest taste and keenest sense of the respect due to private life would condemn.

In general, then, the matters of which the publication should be repressed may be described as those which concern the private life, habits, acts, and relations of an individual, and have no legitimate connection with his fitness for a public office which he seeks or for which he is suggested, or for any public or quasi public position which he seeks or for which he is suggested, and have no legitimate relation to or bearing upon any act done by him in a public or quasi public capacity. The foregoing is not designed as a wholly accurate or exhaustive definition, since that which must ultimately in a vast number of cases become a question of individual judgment and opinion is incapable of such definition; but it is an attempt to indicate broadly the class of matters referred to. Some things all men alike are entitled to keep from popular curiosity, whether in public life or not, while others are only private because the persons concerned have not assumed a position which makes their doings legitimate matters of public investigation.[44]

2. The right to privacy does not prohibit the communication of any matter, though in its nature private, when the publication is made under circumstances which would render it a privileged communication according to the law of slander and libel.

Under this rule, the right to privacy is not invaded by any publication made in a court of justice, in legislative bodies, or the committees of those bodies; in municipal assemblies, or the committees of such assemblies, or practically by any communication made in any other public body, municipal or parochial, or in any body quasi public, like the large voluntary associations formed for almost every purpose of benevolence, business, or other general interest; and (at least in many jurisdictions) reports of any such proceedings would in some measure be accorded a like privilege.[45] Nor would the rule prohibit any publication made by one in the discharge of some public or private duty, whether legal or moral, or in conduct of one's own affairs, in matters where his own interest is concerned.[46]

3. The law would probably not grant any redress for the invasion of privacy by oral publication in the absence of special damage.

The same reasons exist for distinguishing between oral and written publications of private matters, as is afforded in the law of defamation by the restricted liability for slander as compared with the liability for libel.[47] The injury resulting from such oral communications would ordinarily be so trifling that the law might well, in the interest of free speech, disregard it altogether.[48]

4. The right to privacy ceases upon the publication of the facts by the individual, or with his consent.

    This is but another application of the rule which has become familiar in the law of literary and artistic property. The cases there decided establish also what should be deemed a publication—the important principle in this connection being that a private communication of circulation for a restricted purpose is not a publication within the meaning of the law.[49]

5. The truth of the matter published does not afford a defence. Obviously this branch of the law should have no concern with the truth or falsehood of the matters published. It is not for injury to the individual's character that redress or prevention is sought, but for injury to the right of privacy. For the former, the law of slander and libel provides perhaps a sufficient safeguard. The latter implies the right not merely to prevent inaccurate portrayal of private life, but to prevent its being depicted at all.

6. The absence of "malice" in the publisher does not afford a defence.

    Personal ill-will is not an ingredient of the offence, any more than in an ordinary case of trespass to person or to property. Such malice is never necessary to be shown in an action for libel or slander at common law, except in rebuttal of some defence, *e.g.*, that the occasion rendered the communication privileged, or, under the statutes in this State and elsewhere, that the statement complained of was true. The invasion of the privacy that is to be protected is equally complete and equally injurious, whether the motives by which the speaker or writer was actuated are, taken by themselves, culpable or not; just as the damage to character, and to some extent the tendency to provoke a breach of the peace, is equally the result of defamation without regard to the motives leading to its publication. Viewed as a wrong to the individual, this rule is the same pervading the whole law of torts, by which one is held responsible for his intentional acts, even though they are committed with no sinister intent; and viewed as a wrong to society, it is the same principle adopted in a large category of statutory offences.

The remedies for an invasion of the right of privacy are also suggested by those administered in the law of defamation, and in the law of literary and artistic property, namely:

1. An action of tort for damages in all cases.[50] Even in the absence of special damages, substantial compensation could be allowed for injury to feelings as in the action of slander and libel.
2. An injunction, in perhaps a very limited class of cases.[51]

It would doubtless be desirable that the privacy of the individual should receive the added protection of the criminal law, but for this, legislation would be required.[52] Perhaps it would be deemed proper to bring the criminal liability for such publication within narrower limits; but that the community has an interest in preventing such invasions of privacy, sufficiently strong to justify the introduction of such a remedy, cannot be doubted. Still, the protection of society must come mainly through a recognition of the rights of the individual. Each man is responsible for his own acts and omissions only. If he condones what he reprobates, with a weapon at hand equal to his defence, he is responsible for the results. If he resists, public opinion will rally to his support. Has he then such a weapon? It is believed that the common law provides him with one, forged in the slow fire of the centuries, and today fitly tempered to his hand. The common law has always recognized a man's house as his castle, impregnable, often, even to its own officers engaged in the execution of its commands. Shall the courts thus close the front entrance to constituted authority, and open wide the back door to idle or prurient curiosity?

2 Privacy

William L. Prosser

In the year 1890 Mrs. Samuel D. Warren, a young matron of Boston, which is a large city in Massachusetts, held at her home a series of social entertainments on an elaborate scale. She was the daughter of Senator Bayard of Delaware, and her husband was a wealthy young paper manufacturer, who only the year before had given up the practice of law to devote himself to an inherited business. Socially Mrs. Warren was among the èlite [*sic*]; and the newspapers of Boston, and in particularly the *Saturday Evening Gazette,* which specialized in "blue blood" items, covered her parties in highly personal and embarrassing detail. It was the era of "yellow journalism," when the press had begun to resort to excesses in the way of prying that have become more or less commonplace today;[1] and Boston was perhaps, of all of the cities in the country, the one in which a lady and a gentleman kept their names and their personal affairs out of the papers. The matter came to a head when the newspapers had a field day on the occasion of the wedding of a daughter, and Mr. Warren became annoyed.[2] It was an annoyance for which the press, the advertisers and the entertainment industry of America were to pay dearly over the next seventy years.

Mr. Warren turned to his recent law partner, Louis D. Brandeis, who was destined not to be unknown to history. The result was a noted article, *The Right to Privacy,*[3] in the *Harvard Law Review,* upon which the two men collaborated. It has come to be regarded as the outstanding example of the influence of legal periodicals upon the American law. In the Harvard

---

This article originally published in the *California Law Review* 48 (1960): 383–423. Reprinted with permission.

Law School class of 1877 the two authors had stood respectively second and first, and both of them were gifted with scholarship, imagination, and ability. Internal evidences of style, and the probabilities of the situation, suggest that the writing, and perhaps most of the research, was done by Brandeis; but it was undoubtedly a joint effort, to which both men contributed their ideas.

Piecing together old decisions in which relief had been afforded on the basis of defamation, or the invasion of some property right,[4] or a breach of confidence or an implied contract,[5] the article concluded that such cases were in reality based upon a broader principle which was entitled to separate recognition. This principle they called the right to privacy; and they contended that the growing abuses of the press made a remedy upon such a distinct ground essential to the protection of private individuals against the outrageous and unjustifiable infliction of mental distress. This was the first of a long line of law review discussions of the right of privacy,[6] of which this is to be yet one more. With very few exceptions,[7] the writers have agreed, expressly or tacitly, with Warren and Brandeis.

The article had little immediate effect upon the law. The first case to allow recovery upon the independent basis of the right of privacy was an unreported decision[8] of a New York trial judge, when an actress very scandalously, for those days, appeared upon the stage in tights, and the defendant snapped her picture from a box, and was enjoined from publishing it. This was followed by three reported cases in New York,[9] and one in a federal court in Massachusetts,[10] in which the courts appeared to be quite ready to accept the principle. Progress was brought to an abrupt halt, however, when the Michigan court flatly rejected the whole idea, in a case[11] where a brand of cigars was named after a deceased public figure. In 1902 the question reached the Court of Appeals of New York, in the case of *Roberson v. Rochester Folding Box Co.*[12] in which the defendant made use of the picture of a pulchritudinous young lady without her consent to advertise flour, along with the legend, "The Flour of the Family." One might think that the feebleness of the pun might have been enough in itself to predispose the court in favor of recovery; but in a four-to-three decision, over a most vigorous dissent, it rejected Warren and Brandeis and declared that the right of privacy did not exist, and that the plaintiff was entitled to no protection whatever against such conduct. The reasons offered were the lack of precedent, the purely mental character of the injury, the "vast amount of litigation" that might be expected to ensue, the difficulty of drawing any line between public and private figures, and the fear of undue restriction of the freedom of the press.

The immediate result of the *Roberson* case was a storm of public disapproval, which led one of the concurring judges to take the unprecedented step of publishing a law review article in defense of the decision.[13] In consequence the next New York Legislature enacted a statute[14] making it both a misdemeanor and a tort to make use of the name, portrait or picture of any person for "advertising purposes or for the purposes of trade" without his written consent. This act remains the law of New York, where there have been upwards of a hundred decisions dealing with it. Except as the statute itself limits the extent of the right, the New York decisions are quite consistent with the common law as it has been worked out in other states, and they are customarily cited in privacy cases throughout the country.

Three years later the supreme court of Georgia had much the same question presented in *Pavesich v. New England Life Insurance Co.*,[15] when the defendant's insurance advertising made use of the plaintiff's name and picture, as well as a spurious testimonial from him. With the example of New York before it, the Georgia court in turn rejected the *Roberson* case, accepted the views of Warren and Brandeis, and recognized the existence of a distinct right of privacy. This became the leading case.

For the next thirty years there was a continued dispute as to whether the right of privacy existed at all, as the courts elected to follow the *Roberson* or the *Pavesich* case. Along in the thirties, with the benediction of the *Restatement of Torts*,[16] the tide set in strongly in favor of recognition, and the rejecting decisions began to be overruled. At the present time the right of privacy, in one form or another, is declared to exist by the overwhelming majority of the American courts. It is recognized in Alabama,[17] Alaska,[18] Arizona,[19] California,[20] Connecticut,[21] the District of Columbia,[22] Florida,[23] Georgia,[24] Illinois,[25] Indiana,[26] Iowa,[27] Kansas,[28] Kentucky,[29] Louisiana,[30] Michigan,[31] Mississippi,[32] Missouri,[33] Montana,[34] Nevada,[35] New Jersey,[36] North Carolina,[37] Ohio,[38] Oregon,[39] Pennsylvania,[40] South Carolina,[41] Tennessee,[42] and West Virginia.[43] It will in all probability be recognized in Delaware[44] and Maryland,[45] where a federal and a lower court have accepted it; and also in Arkansas,[46] Colorado,[47] Massachusetts,[48] Minnesota,[49] and Washington,[50] where the courts at least have refrained from holding that it does not exist, but the decisions have gone off on other grounds. It is recognized in a limited form by the New York statute,[51] and by similar acts adopted in Oklahoma,[52] Utah,[53] and Virginia.[54]

At the time of writing the right of privacy stands rejected only by a 1909 decision in Rhode Island,[55] and by more recent ones in Nebraska,[56] Texas,[57] and Wisconsin,[58] which have said that any change in the old common law must be for the legislature, and which have not gone without criticism.

In nearly every jurisdiction the first decisions were understandably preoccupied with the question whether the right of privacy existed at all, and gave little or no consideration to what it would amount to if it did. It is only in recent years, and largely through the legal writers, that there has been any attempt to inquire what interests are we protecting, and against what conduct. Today, with something over three hundred cases in the books, the holes in the jigsaw puzzle have been largely filled in, and some rather definite conclusions are possible.

What has emerged from the decisions is no simple matter. It is not one tort, but a complex of four. The law of privacy comprises four distinct kinds of invasion of four different interests of the plaintiff, which are tied together by the common name, but otherwise have almost nothing in common except that each represents an interference with the right of the plaintiff, in the phrase coined by Judge Cooley,[59] "to be let alone." Without any attempt to exact definition, these four torts may be described as follows:

1. Intrusion upon the plaintiff's seclusion or solitude, or into his private affairs.
2. Public disclosure of embarrassing private facts about the plaintiff.
3. Publicity which places the plaintiff in a false light in the public eye.
4. Appropriation, for the defendant's advantage, of the plaintiff's name or likeness.

It should be obvious at once that these four types of invasion may be subject, in some respects at least, to different rules; and that when what is said as to any one of them is carried over to another, it may not be at all applicable, and confusion may follow.

The four may be considered in detail, in order.

I.
Intrusion

Warren and Brandeis, who were concerned with the evils of publication, do not appear to have had in mind any such thing as intrusion upon the plaintiff's seclusion or solitude. Nine years before their article was published there had been a Michigan case[60] in which a young man had intruded upon a woman in childbirth, and the court, invalidating her consent because of fraud, had allowed recovery without specifying the ground, which may have been trespass or battery. In retrospect, at least, this was a privacy case. Others have followed, in which the defendant has been held liable for intruding into the plaintiff's home,[61] his hotel room,[62] and a woman's stateroom on a steamboat,[63] and for an illegal search of her shopping bag in a store.[64] The privacy action which has been allowed in such cases will evidently overlap, to a considerable extent at least, the action for trespass to land or chattels.

The principle was, however, soon carried beyond such physical intrusion. It was extended to eavesdropping upon private conversations by means of wire tapping[65] and microphones;[66] and there are three decisions,[67] the last of them aided by a Louisiana criminal statute, which have applied the same principle to peering into the windows of a home. The supreme court of Ohio, which seems to be virtually alone among our courts in refusing to recognize the independent tort of the intentional infliction of mental distress by outrageous conduct,[68] has accomplished the same result[69] under the name of privacy, in a case where a creditor hounded the debtor for a considerable length of time with telephone calls at his home and his place of employment.[70] The tort has been found in the case of unauthorized prying into the plaintiff's bank account,[71] and the same principle has been used to invalidate a blanket *subpoena duces tecum* requiring the production of all of his books and documents,[72] and an illegal compulsory blood test.[73]

It is clear, however, that there must be something in the nature of prying or intrusion, and mere noises which disturb a church congregation,[74] or bad manners, harsh names and insulting gestures in public,[75] have been held not to be enough. It is also clear that the intrusion must be something which would be offensive or objectionable to a reasonable man, and that there is no tort when the landlord stops by on Sunday morning to ask for the rent.[76]

It is clear also that the thing into which there is prying or intrusion must be, and be entitled to be, private. The plaintiff has no right to complain when his pre-trial testimony is recorded,[77] or when the police, acting within their powers, take his photograph, fingerprints or measurements,[78] or when there is inspection and public disclosure of corporate records which he is required by law to keep and make available.[79] On the public street, or in any other public place, the plaintiff has no right to be alone, and it is no invasion of his privacy to do no more than follow him about.[80] Neither is it such an invasion to take his photograph in such a place,[81] since this amounts to nothing more than making a record, not differing essentially from a full written description, of a public sight which any one present would be free to see. On the other hand, when he is confined to a hospital bed,[82] and in all probability when he is merely in the seclusion of his home, the making of a photograph without his consent is an invasion of a private right, of which he is entitled to complain.

It appears obvious that the interest protected by this branch of the tort is primarily a mental one. It has been useful chiefly to fill in the gaps left by trespass, nuisance, the intentional infliction of mental distress, and whatever remedies there may be for the invasion of constitutional rights.

II.
Public Disclosure of Private Facts

Because of its background of personal annoyance from the press, the article of Warren and Brandeis was primarily concerned with the second form of the tort, which consists of public disclosure of embarrassing private facts about the plaintiff. Actually this was rather slow to appear in the decisions. Although there were earlier instances,[83] in which other elements were involved, its first real separate application was in a Kentucky case[84] in 1927, in which the defendant put up a notice in the window of his garage announcing to the world that the defendant owed him money and would not pay it. But the decision which has become the leading case, largely because of its spectacular facts, is *Melvin v. Reid,*[85] in California in 1931. The plaintiff, whose original name was Gabrielle Darley, had been a prostitute, and the defendant in a sensational murder trial. After her acquittal she had abandoned her life of shame, become rehabilitated, married a man named Melvin, and in a manner reminiscent of the plays of Arthur Wing Pinero, had led a life of rectitude in respectable society, among friends and associates who were unaware of her earlier career. Seven years afterward the defendant made and exhibited a motion picture, called "The Red Kimono," which enacted the true story, used the name of Gabrielle Darley, and ruined her new life by revealing her past to the world and her friends. Relying in part upon a vague constitutional provision that all men have the inalienable right of "pursuing and obtaining happiness," which has since disappeared from the California cases, the court held that this was an actionable invasion of her right to privacy.

Other decisions have followed, involving the use of the plaintiff's name in a radio dramatization of a robbery of which he was the victim,[86] and publicity given to his debts,[87] to medical pictures of his anatomy,[88] and to embarrassing details of a woman's masculine characteristics, her domineering tendencies, her habits of profanity, and incidents of her personal conduct toward her friends and neighbors.[89] Some limits, at least, of this branch of the right of privacy appear to be fairly well marked out, as follows:

First, the disclosure of the private facts must be a public disclosure, and not a private one. There must be, in other words, publicity. It is an invasion of the right to publish in a newspaper that the plaintiff does not pay his debts,[90] or to post a notice to that effect in a window on the public street[91] or cry it aloud in the highway;[92] but, except for one decision of a lower Georgia court which was reversed on other grounds,[93] it has been agreed that it is no invasion to communicate that fact to the plaintiff's employer,[94] or to any other individual, or even to a small group,[95] unless there is some breach of contract, trust or confidential relation which will afford an independent basis for relief.[96] Warren and Brandeis[97] thought that the publication would have to be written or printed unless special damage could be shown; and there have been decisions[98] that the action will not lie for oral publicity; but the growth of radio alone has been enough to make this obsolete,[99] and there now can be little doubt that writing is not required.[100]

Second, the facts disclosed to the public must be private facts, and not public ones. Certainly no one can complain when publicity is given to information about him which he himself leaves open to the public eye, such as the appearance of the house in which he lives, or to the business in which he is engaged. Thus it has been held that a public school teacher has no action for a compulsory disclosure of her war work and other outside activities.[101]

Here two troublesome questions arise. One is whether any individual, by appearing upon the public highway, or in any other public place, makes his appearance public, so that any one may take and publish a picture of him as he is at the time. What if an utterly obscure citizen, reeling along drunk on the main street, is snapped by an enterprising reporter, and the picture given to the world? Is his privacy invaded? The cases have been much involved with the privilege of reporting news and other matters of public interest,[102] and for that reason cannot be regarded as very conclusive; but the answer appears to be that it is not. The decisions indicate that anything visible in a public place may be recorded and given circulation by means of a photograph, to the same extent as by a written description,[103] since this amounts to nothing more than giving publicity to what is already public and what any one present would be free to see.[104] Outstanding is the California case,[105] in which the plaintiff, photographed while embracing his wife in the market place, was held to have no action when the picture was published. It has been contended[106] that when an individual is thus singled out from the public scene, and undue attention is focused upon him, there is an invasion of his private rights; and there is one New York decision to that effect.[107] It was, however, later explained upon the basis of the introduction of an element of fiction into the accompanying narrative.[108]

On the other hand, it seems clear that when a picture is taken surreptitiously, or over the plaintiff's objection, in a private place,[109] or one already made is stolen,[110] or obtained by bribery or other inducement of breach of trust,[111] the plaintiff's appearance which is thus made public is at the time still a private thing, and there is an invasion of a private right, for which an action will lie.

The other question is as to the effect of the fact that the matter made public is already one of public record. If the record is a confidential one, not open to public inspection, as in the case of income tax returns,[112] it is not public, and there can be no doubt that there is an invasion of privacy. But it has been held that no one is entitled to complain when there is publication of his recorded date of birth or his marriage,[113] or his military service record;[114] and the same must certainly be true of his admission to the bar or to the practice of medicine, or the fact that he is driving a taxicab. The difficult question is as to the effect of lapse of time, and the extent to which forgotten records, as for example of a criminal conviction, may be dredged up in after years and given more general publicity. As in the case of news,[115] with which the problem may be inextricably interwoven, it has been held that the memory of the events covered by the record, such as a criminal trial,[116] can be revived as still a matter of legitimate public interest. But there is the leading case of *Melvin v. Reid*,[117] which held that the unnecessary use of the plaintiff's name, and the revelation of her history to new friends and associates, introduced an element which was in itself a transgression of her right of privacy. The answer may be that the existence of a public record is a factor of a good deal of importance, which will normally prevent the matter from being private, but that under some special circumstances it is not necessarily conclusive.

Third, the matter made public must be one which would be offensive and objectionable to a reasonable man of ordinary sensibilities.[118] All of us, to some extent, lead lives exposed to the public gaze or to public inquiry, and complete privacy does not exist in this world except for the eremite in the desert. Any one who is not a hermit must expect the more or less casual observation of his neighbors and the passing public as to what he is and does, and some reporting of his daily activities. The ordinary reasonable man does not take offense at mention in a newspaper of the fact that he has returned from a visit, or gone camping in the woods, or that he has given a party at his house for his friends; and very probably Mr. Warren would never have had any action for the reports of his daughter's wedding. The law of privacy is not intended for the protection of any shrinking soul who is abnormally sensitive about such publicity.[119] It is quite a different matter when the details of sexual relations are spread before the public gaze,[120] or there is highly personal portrayal of his intimate private characteristics or conduct.[121]

Here the outstanding case is *Sidis v. F-R Publishing Corporation*.[122] The plaintiff, William James Sidis, had been an infant prodigy, who had graduated from Harvard at sixteen, and at the age of eleven had lectured to eminent mathematicians on the fourth dimension. When he arrived at adolescence he underwent some unusual psychological change, which brought about a complete revulsion toward mathematics, and toward the publicity he had received. He disappeared, led an obscure life as a bookkeeper, and occupied himself in collecting street car transfers, and studying the lore of the Okamakammessett Indians. The *New Yorker* magazine sought him out, and published a not unsympathetic account of his career, revealing his present whereabouts and activities. The effect upon Sidis was devastating, and the article unquestionably contributed to his early death. The case involved the privilege of reporting on matters of public interest;[123] but the decision that there was no cause of action rested upon the ground that there was nothing in the article which would be objectionable to any normal person. When this case is compared with *Melvin v. Reid*,[124] with its revelation of the past of a prostitute and a murder defendant, what emerges is something in the nature of a "mores" test,[125] by which there will be liability only for publicity given to those things which the customs and ordinary views of the community will not tolerate.

This branch of the tort is evidently something quite distinct from intrusion. The interest protected is that of reputation, with the same overtones of mental distress that are present in libel and slander. It is in reality an extension of defamation, into the field of publications that do not fall within the narrow limits of the old torts, with the elimination of the defense of truth.[126] As such, it has no doubt gone far to remedy the deficiencies of the defamation actions, hampered as they are by technical rules inherited from ancient and long forgotten jurisdictional conflicts, and to provide a remedy for a few real and serious wrongs that were not previously actionable.

III.

False Light in the Public Eye

The third form of invasion of privacy, which Warren and Brandeis again do not appear to have had in mind at all, consists of publicity that places the plaintiff in a false light in the public eye. It seems to have made its first appearance in 1816, when Lord Byron succeeded in enjoining the circulation of a spurious and inferior poem attributed to his pen.[127] The principle frequently, over a good many years, has made a rather nebulous appearance in a line of decisions[128] in which falsity or fiction has been held to defeat the privilege of reporting news and other matters of public interest, or of giving further publicity to already public figures. It is only in late years that it has begun to receive any independent recognition of its own.

One form in which it occasionally appears, as in Byron's case, is that of publicity falsely attributing to the plaintiff some opinion or utterance.[129] A good illustration of this might be the fictitious testimonial used in advertising,[130] or the Oregon case[131] in which the name of the plaintiff was signed to a telegram to the governor urging political action which it would have been illegal for him, as a state employee, to advocate. More typical are spurious books and articles, or ideas expressed in them, which purport to emanate from the plaintiff.[132] In the same category are the unauthorized use of his name as a candidate for office,[133] or to advertise for witnesses of an accident,[134] or the entry of an actor, without his consent, in a popularity contest of an embarrassing kind.[135]

Another form in which this branch of the tort frequently has made its appearance is the use of the plaintiff's picture to illustrate a book or an article with which he has no reasonable connection. As remains to be seen,[136] public interest may justify a use for appropriate and pertinent illustration. But when the face of some quite innocent and unrelated citizen is employed to ornament an article on the cheating propensities of taxi drivers,[137] the negligence of children,[138] profane love,[139] "man hungry" women,[140] juvenile delinquents,[141] or the peddling of narcotics,[142] there is an obvious innuendo that the article applies to him, which places him in a false light before the public, and is actionable.

Still another form in which the tort occurs is the inclusion of the plaintiff's name, photograph and fingerprints in a public "rogues' gallery" of convicted criminals, when he has not in fact been convicted of any crime.[143] Although the police are clearly privileged to make such a record in the first instance, and to use it for any legitimate purpose pending trial,[144] or even after conviction,[145] the element of false publicity in the inclusion among the convicted goes beyond the privilege.

The false light need not necessarily be a defamatory one, although it very often is,[146] and a defamation action will also lie. It seems clear, however, that it must be something that would be objectionable to the ordinary reasonable man under the circumstances, and that, as in the case of disclosure,[147] the hypersensitive individual will not be protected.[148] Thus minor and unimportant errors in an otherwise accurate biography, as to dates and place, and incidents of no significance, do not entitle the subject of the book to recover,[149] nor does the erroneous description of the plaintiff as a cigarette girl when an inquiring photographer interviews her on the street.[150] Again, in all probability, something of a "mores" test must be applied.

The false light cases obviously differ from those of intrusion, or disclosure of private facts. The interest protected is clearly that of reputation, with the same overtones of mental distress as in defamation. There is a resemblance to disclosure; but the two differ in that one involves truth and the other lies, one private or secret facts and the other invention. Both require publicity. There has been a good deal of overlapping of defamation in the false light cases, and apparently either action, or both, will very often lie. The privacy cases do go considerably beyond the narrow limits of defamation, and no doubt have succeeded in affording a needed remedy in a good many instances not covered by the other tort.

It is here, however, that one disposed to alarm might express the greatest concern over where privacy may be going. The question may well be raised, and apparently still is unanswered, whether this branch of the tort is not capable of swallowing up and engulfing the whole law of public defamation; and whether there is any false libel printed, for example, in a newspaper, which cannot be redressed upon the alternative ground. If that turns out to be the case, it may well be asked, what of the numerous restrictions and limitations which have hedged defamation about for many years, in the interest of freedom of the press and the discouragement of trivial and extortionate claims? Are they of so little consequence that they may be circumvented in so casual and cavalier a fashion?

IV.

Appropriation

There is little indication that Warren and Brandeis intended to direct their article at the fourth branch of the tort, the exploitation of attributes of the plaintiff's identity. The first decision[151] had relied upon breach of an implied contract, where a photographer who had taken the plaintiff's picture proceeded to put it on sale; and this is still one basis upon which liability continues to be found.[152] By reason of its early appearance in the *Roberson* case,[153] and the resulting New York statute,[154] this form of invasion has bulked rather large in the law of privacy. It consists of the appropriation, for the defendant's benefit or advantage, of the plaintiff's name or likeness.[155] Thus in New York, as well as in many other states, there are a great many decisions in which the plaintiff has recovered when his name[156] or picture,[157] or other likeness,[158] has been used without his consent to advertise the defendant's product, or to accompany an article sold,[159] to add luster to the name of a corporation,[160] or for other business purposes.[161] The statute in New York,[162] and the others patterned after it[163] are limited by their terms to use for advertising or for "purposes of trade," and for that reason must be somewhat more narrow in their scope than the common law of the other states;[164] but in general, there has been no significant difference in their application in the field that they cover.

It is the plaintiff's name as a symbol of his identity that is involved here, and not his name as a mere name. There is, as a good many thousand John Smiths can bear witness, no such thing as an exclusive right to the use of any name. Unless there is some tortious use made of it, any one can be given or assume any name he likes.[165] The Kabotznicks may call themselves Cabots, and the Lovelskis become Lowells, and the ancient proper Bostonian houses can do nothing about it but grieve. Any one may call himself Dwight D. Eisenhower, Henry Ford, Nelson Rockefeller, Eleanor Roosevelt, or Willie Mays, without any liability whatever. It is when he makes use of the name to pirate the plaintiff's identity for some advantage of his own, as by impersonation to obtain credit or secret information,[166] or by posing as the plaintiff's wife,[167] or providing a father for a child on a birth certificate,[168] that he becomes liable. It is in this sense that "appropriation" must be understood.

On this basis, the question before the courts has been first of all whether there has been appropriation of an aspect of the plaintiff's identity. It is not enough that a name which is the same as his is used in a novel,[169] a comic strip,[170] or the title of a corporation,[171] unless the context or the circumstances,[172] or the addition of some other element,[173] indicate that the name is that of the plaintiff. It seems clear that a stage or other fictitious name can be so identified with the plaintiff that he is entitled to protection against its use.[174] On the other hand, there is no liability for the publication of a picture of his hand, leg and foot,[175] his dwelling house,[176] his automobile,[177] or his dog,[178] with nothing to indicate whose they are. Nor is there any liability when the plaintiff's character, occupation, and the general outline of his career, with many real incidents in his life, are used as the basis for a figure in a novel who is still clearly a fictional one.[179]

Once the plaintiff is identified, there is the further question whether the defendant has appropriated the name or likeness for his own advantage. Under the statutes this must be a pecuniary advantage; but the common law is very probably not so limited.[180] The New York courts were faced very early with the obvious fact that newspapers and magazines, to say nothing of radio, television and motion pictures, are by no means philanthropic institutions, but are operated for profit. As against the contention that everything published by these agencies must necessarily be "for purposes of trade," they were compelled to hold that there must be some closer and more direct connection, beyond the mere fact that the newspaper is sold; and that the presence of advertising matter in adjacent columns does not make any difference.[181] Any other conclusion would undoubtedly have been an unconstitutional interference with the freedom of the press.[182] Accordingly, it has been held that the mere incidental mention of the plaintiff's name in a book[183] or a motion picture[184] or even in a commentary upon news which is part of an advertisement,[185] is not an invasion of his privacy; nor is the publication of a photograph[186] or a newsreel[187] in which he incidentally appears.

This liberality toward the publishers was brought to an abrupt termination, however, when cases began to appear in which false statements were made. It was held quite early in New York[188] that the publication of fiction concerning a man is a use of his name for purposes of trade, and that in such a case the mere sale of the article is enough in itself to provide the commercial element. It follows that when the name or the likeness is accompanied by false statements about the plaintiff,[189] or he is placed in a false light before the public,[190] there is such a use. The result of this rule for the encouragement of accuracy in the press is that the New York court has in fact recognized and applied the third form of invasion of privacy[191] under a statute which was directed only at the fourth.

It seems sufficiently evident that appropriation is quite a different matter from intrusion, disclosure of private facts, or a false light in the public eye. The interest protected is not so much a mental as a proprietary one, in the exclusive use of the plaintiff's name and likeness as an aspect of his identity. It seems quite pointless to dispute over whether such a right is to be classified as "property."[192] If it is not, it is at least, once it is protected by the law, a right of value upon which the plaintiff can capitalize by selling licenses. Its proprietary nature is clearly indicated by a decision of the Second Circuit[193] that an exclusive license has what has been called a "right of publicity,"[194] which entitles him to enjoin the use of the name or likeness by a third person. Although this decision has not yet been followed,[195] it would seem clearly to be justified.

V.
Common Features

Judge Biggs has described the present state of the law of privacy as "still that of a haystack in a hurricane."[196] Disarray there certainly is; but almost all of the confusion is due to a failure to separate and distinguish these four forms of invasion, and to realize that they call for different things.

Typical is the bewilderment which a good many members of the bar have expressed over the holdings in the two *Gill* cases in California. Both of them involved publicity given to the same photograph, taken while the plaintiff was embracing his wife in the Farmers' Market in Los Angeles. In one of them,[197] which involved only the question of disclosure by publishing the picture, it was held that there was nothing private about it, since it was a part of the public scene in a public place. In the other,[198] which involved the use of the picture to illustrate an article on the right and wrong kind of love, with the innuendo that this was the wrong kind, liability was found for placing the plaintiff in a false light in the public eye. The two conclusions were based entirely upon the difference between the two branches of the tort.

Taking them in order—intrusion, disclosure, false light, and appropriation—the first and second require the invasion of something secret, secluded or private pertaining to the plaintiff; the third and fourth do not. The second and third depend upon publicity, while the first does not, nor does the fourth, although it usually involves it. The third requires falsity or fiction; the other three do not. The fourth involves a use for the defendant's advantage, which is not true of the rest. Obviously this is an area in which one must tread warily and be on the lookout for bogs. Nor is the difficulty decreased by the fact that quite often two or more of these forms of invasion may be found in the same case, and quite conceivably all four.[199]

There has nevertheless been a good deal of consistency in the rules that have been applied to the four disparate torts under the common name. As to any one of the four, it is agreed that the plaintiff's right is a personal one, which does not extend to the members of his family,[200] unless, as is obviously possible,[201] their own privacy is invaded along with his. The right is not assignable;[202] and while the cause of action may[203] or may not[204] survive after his death, according to the survival rules of the particular state, there is no common law right of action for a publication concerning one who is already dead.[205] The statutes of Oklahoma, Utah and Virginia,[206] however, expressly provide for such an action. It seems to be generally agreed that the right of privacy is one pertaining only to individuals, and that a corporation[207] or a partnership[208] cannot claim it as such, although either may have an exclusive right to the use of its name, which may be protected upon some other basis such as that of unfair competition.[209]

So far as damages are concerned, there is general agreement that the plaintiff need not plead or prove special damages,[210] and that in this respect the action resembles one for libel or slander per se. The difficulty of measuring the damages is no more reason for denying relief here than in a defamation action.[211] Substantial damages may be awarded for the presumed mental distress inflicted, and other probable harm, without proof.[212] If there is evidence of special damage, such as resulting illness, or unjust enrichment of the defendant,[213] or harm to the plaintiff's own commercial interests,[214] it can be recovered. Punitive damages can be awarded upon the same basis as in other torts, where a wrongful motive or state of mind appears,[215] but not in cases where the defendant has acted innocently, as for example in the belief that the plaintiff has given his consent.[216]

At an early stage of its existence, the right of privacy came into head-on collision with the constitutional guaranty of freedom of the press. The result was the slow evolution of a compromise between the two. Much of the litigation over privacy has been concerned with this compromise, which has involved two closely related, special and limited privileges arising out of the rights of the press.[217] One of these is the privilege of giving further publicity to already public figures. The other is that of giving publicity to news, and other matters of public interest. The one primarily concerns the person to whom publicity is given; the other the event, fact or other subject-matter. They are, however, obviously only different phases of the same thing.

VI.
Public Figures and Public Interest

A public figure has been defined as a person who, by his accomplishments, fame, or mode of living, or by adopting a profession or calling which gives the public a legitimate interest in his doings, his affairs, and his character, has become a "public personage."[218] He is, in other words, a celebrity—one who by his own voluntary efforts has succeeded in placing himself in the public eye. Obviously to be included in this category are those who have achieved at least some degree of reputation[219] by appearing before the public, as in the case of an actor,[220] a professional baseball player,[221] a pugilist,[222] or any other entertainer.[223] The list is, however, broader than this. It includes public officers,[224] famous inventors[225] and explorers,[226] war heroes[227] and even ordinary soldiers,[228] an infant prodigy,[229] and no less a personage than the Grand Exalted Ruler of a lodge.[230] It includes, in short, any one who has arrived at a position where public attention is focused upon him as a person. It seems clear, however, that such public stature must already exist before there can be any privilege arising out of it, and that the defendant, by directing attention to one who is obscure and unknown, cannot himself create a public figure.[231]

Such public figures are held to have lost, to some extent at least, their right of privacy. Three reasons are given, more or less indiscriminately, in the decisions: that they have sought publicity and consented to it, and so cannot complain of it; that their personalities and their affairs already have become public, and can no longer be regarded as their own private business; and that the press has a privilege, guaranteed by the Constitution, to inform the public about those who have become legitimate matters of public interest. On one or another of these grounds, and sometimes all, it is held that there is no liability when they are given additional publicity, as to matters reasonably within the scope of the public interest which they have aroused.[232]

The privilege of giving publicity to news, and other matters of public interest, arises out of the desire and the right of the public to know what is going on in the world, and the freedom of the press and other agencies of information to tell them. "News" includes all events and items of information which are out of the ordinary humdrum routine, and which have "that indefinable quality of information which arouses public attention."[233] To a very great extent the press, with its experience or instinct as to what its readers will want, has succeeded in making its own definition of news. A glance at any morning newspaper will sufficiently indicate the content of the term. It includes homicide[234] and other crimes,[235] arrests[236] and police raids,[237] suicides,[238] marriages[239] and divorces,[240] accidents,[241] a death from the use of narcotics,[242] a woman with a rare disease,[243] the birth of a child to a twelve year old girl,[244] the filing of a libel suit,[245] a report to the police concerning the escape of a black panther,[246] the reappearance of one supposed to have been murdered years ago,[247] and undoubtedly many other similar matters of genuine, if more or less deplorable, popular appeal.[248]

The privilege of enlightening the public is not, however, limited to the dissemination of news in the sense of current events. It extends also to information or education, or even entertainment and amusement,[249] by books, articles, pictures, films and broadcasts concerning interesting phases of human activity in general,[250] and the reproduction of the public scene as in newsreels and travelogues.[251] In determining where to draw the line the courts have been invited to exercise nothing less than a power of censorship over what the public may be permitted to read; and they have been understandably liberal in allowing the benefit of the doubt.

Caught up and entangled in this web of news and public interest are a great many people who have not sought publicity, but indeed, as in the case of the accused criminal, have tried assiduously to avoid it. They have nevertheless lost some part of their right of privacy. The misfortunes of the frantic woman whose husband is murdered before her eyes,[252] or the innocent bystander who is caught in a raid on a cigar store and mistaken by the police for the proprietor,[253] can be broadcast to the world, and they have no remedy. Such individuals become public figures[254] for a season; and "until they have reverted to the lawful and unexciting life led by the great bulk of the community, they are subject to the privileges which publishers have to satisfy the curiosity of the public as to their leaders, heroes, villains and victims."[255] The privilege extends even to identification and some reasonable depiction of the individual's family,[256] although there must certainly be limits as to their own private lives into which the publisher cannot go.[257]

What is called for, in short, is some logical connection between the plaintiff and the matter of public interest. The most extreme cases of the privilege are those in which the likeness of an individual is used to illustrate a book or an article on some general topic, rather than any specific event. Where this is appropriate and pertinent, as where the picture of a strikebreaker is used to illustrate a book on strike-breaking,[258] or that of a Hindu illusionist is employed to illustrate an article on the Indian rope trick,[259] it has been held that there is no liability, since the public interest justifies any invasion of privacy. On the other hand, where the illustration is not pertinent, and a connection is suggested which does not exist, as where the face of an honest taxi driver appears in connection with an article on the cheating practices of the trade,[260] or the picture of a decent model illustrates one on "man hungry" women,[261] the plaintiff is placed in a false light, and may recover on that basis. The difference is well brought out by two cases in California and New York. In one of them[262] a photograph of the plaintiff arguing with a would-be suicide on a bridge was held properly used to illustrate an article on suicide. In the other[263] the picture of a boy in the slums, taken while he was innocently talking baseball on the street, was used with an article about juvenile delinquency, entitled "Gang Boy," and he was allowed to recover.

VII.
Limitations

It is clear, however, that the public figure loses his right of privacy only to a limited extent,[264] and that the privilege of reporting news and matters of public interest is likewise limited. The decisions indicate very definitely that both privileges apply only to one branch of the tort, that of disclosure of private facts about the individual. The famous motion picture actress who "vants to be alone"[265] unquestionably has as much right as any one else to be free from intrusion into her home or her bank account; and so has the individual whose divorce is the sensation of the day.[266] The celebrity can undoubtedly complain of the appropriation of his name or likeness for purposes of advertising, or the sale of a product,[267] and so can the victim of an accident.[268] It was once held that even the Emperor of Austria had a right to object when his name was bestowed on an insurance company.[269] And while it seems to be agreed that the courts are not arbiters of taste, and the fact that a publication is morbid, gruesome, lurid, sensational, immoral, and altogether cheap and despicable will not forfeit the privilege,[270] it is also clear that either the public figure[271] or the man in the news[272] can maintain an action when false or fictitious statements are published about him, or when his picture is used with an innuendo which places him in a false light before the public.[273]

But even as to the disclosure of private facts, it appears that there must be some rather undefined limits upon these privileges. Warren and Brandeis[274] thought that even a celebrity was entitled to his private life, and that he would become a public figure only as to matters already public and those which directly bore upon them. The development of the law has not been so narrow. It has recognized a legitimate public curiosity about the personalities of celebrities, and about a great deal of otherwise private and personal information concerning them. Their biographies can be written,[275] and their life histories and their characters set forth before the world in unflattering detail. Discreditable facts about them can be exposed.[276] And as our newspapers demonstrate daily, the public can be treated to an enormous amount of petty gossip as to what they eat for breakfast, wear, read, do with their spare time, or say to their friends.

Some boundaries, however, still remain; and one may venture the guess that the private sex relations of actresses and baseball players, to say nothing of inventors and the victims of automobile accidents, are still not in the public domain.[277] As some evidence of popular feeling in such matters, one might look to the statutes in several states[278] prohibiting the public disclosure of the names of victims of sex crimes. The private letters, even of celebrities, cannot be published without their consent;[279] and the good Prince Albert was once held to have an action when his private etchings were exhibited to all comers.[280] An excellent illustration of the privacy of a public figure is a case[281] in a trial court in Los Angeles, not officially reported, in which the actor Kirk Douglas, after engaging in some undignified antics before a home motion picture camera for his friends, was held to have a cause of action when the film was put upon public exhibition.

Very probably there is some rough proportion to be looked for, between the importance of the public figure or the man in the news, and of the occasion for the public interest in him, and the nature of the private facts revealed. Perhaps there is very little in the way of information about the President of the United States, or any candidate for that high office,[282] that is not a matter of legitimate public concern; but when a mere member of the armed forces is in question, the line is drawn at his military service, and those things that more or less directly bear upon it.[283] And no doubt the defendant in a spectacular murder trial which draws national attention can expect a good deal less in the way of privacy than an ordinary citizen who is arrested for ignoring a parking ticket. But thus far there is very little in the cases to indicate just where such lines are to be drawn.

One troublesome question, which cannot be said to have been fully resolved, is that of the effect of lapse of time, during which the plaintiff has returned to obscurity. There can be no doubt that one quite legitimate function of the press is that of educating or reminding the public as to past history, and that the recall of former public figures, the revival of past events that once were news, can properly be a matter of present public interest. If it is only the event itself which is recalled, without the use of the plaintiff's name, there seems to be no doubt that even a great lapse of time does not destroy the privilege.[284] Most of the cases have held that even the use of his name[285] or likeness[286] is not enough in itself to lead to liability. Thus a luckless prosecuting attorney who once made the mistake of allowing himself to be photographed with his arm around a noted criminal was held to have no remedy when the picture was republished fifteen years later in connection with a story of the criminal's career.[287] Such decisions indicate that once a man has become a public figure, or news, he remains a matter of legitimate recall to the public mind to the end of his days.

There is, however, *Melvin v. Reid*,[288] in which it was held that the use of the name of a former prostitute and murder defendant made the publisher liable when a motion picture narrated her story; and there are a few other cases[289] that look in the same direction. One may speculate that the real reason for the decision in the *Melvin* case was not the use of the name in connection with past history, but the disclosure of the plaintiff's whereabouts and identity, which were no part of the revived "news," or perhaps that the explanation lay in the shocking enormity of the revelation of a woman's past when she was trying to lead a decent life, and that again something in the nature of a "mores" test is to be applied. There is, however, almost nothing in the cases to throw any satisfactory light upon such speculations. All that can be said is that there appear to be situations in which ancient history cannot safely be revived.

VIII.
Defenses

Next in order are the various defenses to the claim of invasion of privacy. It is clear first of all that the truth of the matter published does not arise in the cases of intrusion, and can be no defense to the appropriation of name or likeness, nor to the public disclosure of private facts.[290] It may, however, be in issue where the third form of the tort is involved, that of putting the plaintiff in a false light in the public eye,[291] and to that extent it has some limited importance, and cannot be entirely ruled out.

Chief among the available defenses is that of the plaintiff's consent to the invasion, which will bar his recovery as in the case of any other tort.[292] It may be given expressly, or by conduct, such as posing for a picture with knowledge of the purposes for which it is to be used,[293] or industriously seeking publicity of the same kind.[294] A gratuitous consent can be revoked at any time before the invasion;[295] but if the agreement is a matter of contract it is normally irrevocable, and there is no liability for any publicity or appropriation within its terms.[296] But if the actual invasion goes beyond the contract, fairly construed, as by alteration of the plaintiff's picture,[297] or publicity materially differing in kind or in extent from that contemplated,[298] the consent is not effective to avoid liability. The statutes[299] all require that the consent be given in writing. As against the contention that this can still be "waived" by consent given orally, the rule which has emerged in New York is that the oral consent will not bar the cause of action, but is to be taken into account in mitigation of damages.[300]

Other defenses have appeared only infrequently. Warren and Brandeis[301] thought that the action for invasion of privacy must be subject to any privilege which would justify the publication of libel or slander, reasoning that that which is true should be no less privileged than that which is false. There is still no reason to doubt this conclusion, since the absolute privilege of a witness,[302] and the qualified one to report the filing of a nominating petition for office[303] or the pleadings in a civil suit[304] have both been recognized. The privilege of the defendant to protect or further his own legitimate interests has appeared in a case or two, where a telephone company has been permitted to monitor calls,[305] and the defendant was allowed to make use of the plaintiff's name in insuring his wife without his consent.[306] It has been held that where uncopyrighted literature is in the public domain, and the defendant is free to publish it, the name of the plaintiff may be used to indicate its authorship,[307] and that when the plaintiff has designed dresses for the defendant it is no invasion of his privacy to disclose his connection with the product in advertising.[308]

The conflict of laws, so far as the right of privacy is concerned, is in the same state of bewildered confusion as that which surrounds the law of defamation. The writer has attempted to deal with it elsewhere,[309] and will not repeat it here.

Conclusion

It is evident from the foregoing that, by the use of a single word supplied by Warren and Brandeis, the courts have created an independent basis of liability, which is a complex of four distinct and only loosely related torts; and that this has been expanded by slow degrees to invade, overlap, and encroach upon a number of other fields. So far as appears from the decisions, the process has gone on without any plan, without much realization of what is happening or its significance, and without any consideration of its dangers. They are nonetheless sufficiently obvious, and not to be overlooked.

One cannot fail to be aware, in reading privacy cases, of the extent to which defenses, limitations and safeguards established for the protection of the defendant in other tort fields have been jettisoned, disregarded, or ignored. Taking intrusion first, the gist of the wrong is clearly the intentional infliction of mental distress, which is now in itself a recognized basis of tort liability.[310] Where such mental disturbance stands on its own feet, the courts have insisted upon extreme outrage, rejecting all liability for trivialities, and upon genuine and serious mental harm, attested by physical illness, or by the circumstances of the case. But once "privacy" gets into the picture, and the fact of intrusion is added, such guarantees apparently are no longer required. No doubt the cases thus far have been sufficiently extreme; but the question may well be raised whether there are not some limits, and whether, for example, a lady who insists upon sun-bathing in the nude in her own back yard should really have a cause of action for her humiliation when the neighbors examine her with appreciation and binoculars.

The public disclosure of private facts, and putting the plaintiff in a false light in the public eye, both concern the interest in reputation, and move into the field occupied by defamation. Here, as a result of some centuries of conflict, there have been jealous safeguards thrown about the freedom of speech and of the press, which are now turned on the left flank. Gone is the defense of truth, and the defendant is held liable for the publication of entirely accurate statements of fact, without any wrongful motive. Gone also is the requirement of special damage where what is said is not libel or slander "per se"—which, however antiquated and unreasonable the rigid categories may be, has at least served some useful purpose in the discouragement of trivial and extortionate claims. Gone even is the need for any defamatory innuendo at all, since the publication of non-defamatory facts, or of even laudatory fiction concerning the plaintiff, may be enough. The retraction statutes, with their provision for demand upon the defendant, and the limitation to prove special damage if a demand is not made, or is complied with, are circumvented; and so are the statutes requiring the filing of a bond for costs before a defamation action can be begun. These are major inroads upon a right to which there has always been much sentimental devotion in our land; and they have gone almost entirely unremarked. Perhaps more important still is the extent to which, under any test of "ordinary sensibilities," or the "mores" of the community as to what is acceptable and proper, the courts, although cautiously and reluctantly, have accepted a power of censorship over what the public may be permitted to read, extending very much beyond that which they have always had under the law of defamation.

As for the appropriation cases, they create in effect, for every individual, a common law trade name, his own, and a common law trade mark in his likeness. They confer upon him rights much more extensive than those which any corporation engaged in business can expect under the law of unfair competition. These rights are subject to the verdict of a jury. And there has been no hint that they are in any way affected by any of the limitations which have been considered necessary and desirable in the ordinary law of trade marks and trade names.

This is not to say that the developments in the law of privacy are wrong. Undoubtedly they have been supported by genuine public demand and lively public feeling, and made necessary by real abuses on the part of defendants who have brought it all upon themselves. It is to say rather that it is high time that we realize what we are doing, and give some consideration to the question of where, if anywhere, we are to call a halt.

All this is a most marvelous tree to grow from the wedding of the daughter of Mr. Samuel D. Warren. One is tempted to surmise that she must have been a very beautiful girl. Resembling, perhaps, that fabulous creature, the daughter of a Mr. Very, a confectioner in Regent Street, who was so wondrous fair that her presence in the shop caused three or four hundred people to assemble every day in the street before the window to look at her, so that her father was forced to send her out of town, and counsel was led to inquire whether she might not be indicted as a public nuisance.[311] This was the face that launched a thousand lawsuits.

3 The Tort Right of Privacy: What It Means for Archivists . . . and for Third Parties

Menzi L. Behrnd-Klodt

Prosser's Analysis and *The Restatement (Second) of Torts*

William L. Prosser's analysis has been especially influential in defining the privacy tort[1] and shaping American privacy law and philosophy. The tort right to privacy is distinct from the constitutional right to privacy, which is based in the Bill of Rights and protects fundamental personal rights from governmental action. Prosser's contribution consists of outlining four aspects of the tort right of privacy that subsequently were refined and adopted in 1977 in the *Restatement (Second) of Torts, Privacy,* Chapter 28A, Invasion of Privacy, Sections 652B–E.[2] The following four aspects have been enacted into law in whole or in part by many state legislatures.

Section 652B. Intrusion Upon Seclusion or Solitude

> One who intentionally intrudes, physically or otherwise, upon the solitude or seclusion of another or his private affairs or concerns, is subject to liability to the other for invasion of his privacy, if the intrusion would be highly offensive to a reasonable person.

This privacy right protects against (a) intentional interference or intrusion (b) in a manner that is highly offensive to a reasonable person (c) on a protected interest in seclusion or solitude or a matter that a person has a right to keep private, or intrusion for which there is no otherwise valid reason. Such a physical intrusion must involve an area that is truly private in order to be protected. Examples might include breaking into a home or examining a wallet or purse. Acquiring information or taking photographs in a private space also may violate this right of privacy, but not if they occur in public or at a public event or in a public place, including the workplace.[3] Other unlawful nonphysical intrusions include electronic surveillance or wiretapping. Such intrusions cause psychological distress, and it is the act of the intrusion that causes the legal harm. It is irrelevant whether the intruder learned any private or embarrassing data, or whether any publicity of private facts occurred. This type of invasion of privacy rarely will concern archivists.

Section 652C. Appropriation of Name or Likeness

> One who appropriates to his own use or benefit the name or likeness of another is subject to liability to the other for invasion of his privacy.

This aspect of privacy resembles a property right in protecting an ordinary individual's interest in the exclusive use and benefit of his or her own identity. One who misappropriates or misuses another's name, image, activities, or personal characteristics causes mental or physical injury or harm.

A related, and confusingly similar, concept is "the right of publicity,"[4] which protects the property interest of celebrities in the publicity value of their names, personalities, likenesses, and public images. Some state laws also protect live performances, entertainment styles, voices, hairstyles, caricatures, distinctive facial features[5] and other personal elements,[6] and distinctive nicknames[7] closely identified with personalities, as well as their slogans or verbal "signatures."[8] Misappropriation requires misuse by another for profit or commercial advantage without consent, thereby depriving a celebrity of possible earnings. It also mistakenly may imply celebrity endorsement of a product or service. Misappropriation of a name or identity for no commercial gain injures the psyche of ordinary individuals, although noncelebrities may recover damages for noncommercial appropriation of their names or pictures.[9]

The courts may distinguish between unlawful commercial invasions of privacy and legitimate editorial references to celebrities, public figures, and individuals, depending on whether the use involves advertising or commerce.[10] To recover damages, a celebrity must have established some intrinsic value in a name or likeness. Mere publication of a name or likeness is not misuse. Some courts confuse "appropriation" and "right of publicity" concepts in considering the privacy rights of ordinary individuals by requiring that a name or likeness have actual or potential commercial value in order for damages to be awarded.

Descendability/Immortality. Under established legal principles, the personal right to privacy expires upon death. The right of publicity, however, may survive death, and like trademark and character rights, may be commercially exploited, used, licensed, assigned, or transferred during the celebrity's lifetime and after death. California,[11] Florida,[12] Kentucky,[13] New York,[14] Oklahoma,[15] Tennessee,[16] Texas,[17] Utah,[18] and Virginia[19] permit rights of publicity to be inherited. Heirs may assert ownership of the deceased person's name, likeness, or traits. The Supreme Court of Georgia has held that Martin Luther King, Jr. had a common-law right of publicity that is inheritable regardless of whether it was exploited during his lifetime, a concept that presumably applies to other celebrities as well.[20] In other states, however, descendability/immortality rights hinge on whether the celebrity exploited his or her commercial value while alive.

Opponents of the concept of descendability/immortality argue that the right of publicity, as a component of the right to privacy, is inherently individual and personal, and that the rationale and need for this protection expires with the individual. Should heirs be able to "control history" by controlling all profit-making portrayals of the deceased? Why should celebrities be accorded such rights, but not ordinary citizens who also may exploit their names or likenesses for some commercial value? These and other questions remain to be answered by the courts and legislatures.

Section 652D. Publicity Given to Private Life or Disclosure of Private Facts

One who gives publicity to a matter concerning the private life of another is subject to liability to the other for invasion of his privacy, if the matter publicized is of a kind that
(a) would be highly offensive to a reasonable person, and
(b) is not of legitimate concern to the public.

This invasion of privacy requires an intentional or, in some states, unreasonable or reckless public disclosure of private facts. Such facts must have no legitimate concern to the public, must identify the individual, and must be highly offensive to a reasonable person. To be protectable, the information must be truly private. It is irrelevant legally whether the disclosed facts are true or false, because the act of disclosure itself causes the harm. The disclosure or publicity need not involve publication, but must be so intimate and unwarranted as to outrage the community's notion of decency, or cause emotional distress, embarrassment, shame, and humiliation.

Third-party considerations. Of the four aspects of privacy law described in this article, archivists likely must worry only about this aspect. Even if all of the elements of an unlawful disclosure of private facts exist, however, liability, lawsuits, and damages do not necessarily follow, nor are archives and archivists always at risk.[21] The principle that the truth is a defense to certain statements and disclosures protects the publication of true facts, probably even in privacy actions.[22] The circumstances under which this tort should concern archivists are limited, but it is worthwhile to examine these elements and influences in greater detail.

1. Public disclosure. For privacy to be invaded, private facts must be publicized, but what suffices as "public disclosure" or "publicity" must be determined in each instance. "Publication" includes any communication to a third person, while "publicity" means communicating private facts to the public at large. The difference is not the means of communication, which may be oral, written, or by any other means, but whether the communication is private or whether it reaches, or is sure to reach, the public.[23]

2. Identification of the individual. The public disclosure must identify an individual by name, or other unique facts that would make it sufficient for a reasonable person to understand who is described or depicted.

3. Private facts or information. The issue is whether the disclosure involves private facts or information that are secret, confidential, not already public, or observable in a public place. There is no invasion of privacy in disclosing, redisclosing, or publishing public information.[24] If one voluntarily discloses personal information, the courts are divided about whether the facts are public or private. The outcome may depend on the circumstances in each case, or the size of the group to which the individual communicates the information.

4. Highly offensive to a reasonable person and of no legitimate concern to the public. The disclosure of true, but embarrassing, private facts may be an unconscionable invasion of privacy. A determination of unconscionability requires consideration of whether the disclosed facts are highly offensive to a reasonable person and of no legitimate concern to the public. Community standards, as well as the nature of the action and its connection with the harm caused, also come into play.[25] There may be no liability unless the discloser actually knew or should have *reasonably foreseen* that the person would be offended. In considering whether a disclosure is "highly offensive to a person of ordinary sensibilities," courts often rely on the following threshold:

> The law is not for the protection of the hypersensitive, and all of us must, to some reasonable extent, lead lives exposed to the public gaze. Anyone who is not a hermit must expect the more or less casual observation of his neighbors and the passing public as to what he is and does, and some

reporting of his daily activities. The ordinary reasonable person does not take offense at mention in a newspaper of the fact he has returned home from a visit, or gone camping in the woods, or given a party at his house for his friends. It is quite a different matter when the details of sexual relations are spread before the public eye, or there is a highly personal portrayal of his intimate private characteristics or conduct.[26]

First Amendment values underlie determinations of whether disclosed private facts are matters of legitimate public concern. Public figures have fewer privacy rights than do ordinary citizens in most instances, not only because their activities are of public interest and concern, but also theoretically owing to their implied consent to the disclosures. Courts disagree on whether a public figure, or anyone in the public eye, can be a completely private individual again. In some cases, a person becomes newsworthy for a short period of time and later disappears from public view.[27] In other cases, it may be impossible to separate an individual from a particular event, or from all events. The question, however, needs to be determined in each instance.

5. Community standards. Society's views inevitably intrude when analyzing whether an invasion of privacy has occurred and whether it is "shocking to community standards of decency," a standard that has changed enormously in the last fifty years:[28]

> In determining what is a matter of legitimate public interest account must be taken of the customs and conventions of the community; and in the last analysis what is proper becomes a matter of community mores. The line is to be drawn when the publicity ceases to be the giving of information to which the public is entitled, and becomes a morbid and sensational prying into private lives for its own sake, with which a reasonable member of the public, with decent standards, would say that he had no concern.[29]

Section 652E. Publicity Placing a Person in a False Light

> One who gives publicity to a matter concerning another that places the other before the public in a false light is subject to liability to the other for invasion of his privacy, if
>   (a) the false light in which the other was placed would be highly offensive to a reasonable person, and
>   (b) the actor had knowledge or acted in reckless disregard as to the falsity of the publicized matter and the false light in which the other would be placed.

False light claims involve defamation and damage to reputation. The essence of false light publicity is the intentional distribution of false facts or images, or the deliberate presentation of true facts or images that create a false impression or implication to the public. The facts need not be private, but their misrepresentation must be major and highly offensive to a reasonable person, with widespread publicity. The harm flows from the combination of unreasonable conduct and false, or falsely presented, content. Publication of reasonable, accurate, newsworthy facts that simply embarrass and offend, or that merely criticize another, do not violate privacy. A public official or public figure likely also must establish actual malice and harm to his or her reputation.

A Note on Defamation

The legal distinctions between defamation and invasion of privacy are not sharply drawn. Lawsuits often include both claims, and courts may mix the two legal theories in order to achieve a desired outcome. Defamation involves false statements that injure character or reputation and may occur by publication to only one person. The truth of the matter at issue is a defense to a defamation claim. The right of privacy concerns injury to peace of mind, causing mental or emotional distress and often requiring wide public disclosure of the offending facts. Truth may be, but generally is not, a defense to invasion of privacy.

Invasion of Privacy—Risks and Defenses: Whither Archivists?

Many archivists fear that a professional misstep may result in an invasion of privacy lawsuit. In fact, few, if any, such suits have been successfully litigated against archives. Privacy cases, like other lawsuits, are determined based on the facts and circumstances in each instance. Although privacy litigation may grow out of the use of archival records, lawsuits most likely will involve authors, publishers, and photographers who misuse information, rather than the archivists or their employers who provide access to records. Nonetheless, this section provides some general, and hopefully reassuring, comments that summarize the risks associated with providing access to records containing facts and information about third parties.

Various standard legal procedural defenses may be available in an invasion of privacy lawsuit. The expiration of the statute of limitations[30] may bar any action. Consent to a disclosure may foreclose a lawsuit, although the nature and extent of the consent and disclosure may be the core of the issue. An immunity to a lawsuit may be invoked if the disclosures had been required by law or a court order, constituted part of a court proceeding or official duties, were legally privileged, or otherwise had been authorized by law.

Only the subject of a disclosure of private facts may bring a claim. The disclosure of private facts cause of action does not survive death, nor may it be inherited by family members.[31] Only a reasonable expectation of privacy is protected by law. Consequently, the facts and circumstances of the claimed invasion, as well as consideration of whether the interests that have been asserted are reasonable or are merely those of a hypersensitive individual, must be evaluated. No liability exists for publicizing matters that are already a matter of public record. It may be possible to assert that information placed in an archives is made public or voluntarily disclosed to others by the donor, thereby insulating the archives and archivists from liability for invasion of a donor's privacy.

The First Amendment defense of newsworthiness has a role in privacy law, particularly in misappropriation cases.[32] No misappropriation occurs when notes or a photograph is taken but not used, and there may be no misappropriation if a fact or photograph is used to illustrate a noncommercial and newsworthy story, even if without consent. Truthful uses of names, likenesses, or facts, including biographies, histories, documentaries, and other media portrayals, also may be newsworthy and protected by the First Amendment. Any liability for misrepresentation of disclosed facts under the false light tort would rest on the offending author or publisher.

Public figures and celebrities, as well as ordinary persons who are present at public events or sites, likewise have fewer privacy rights and less recourse against use or disclosure of information or photographs:

> People who do not desire the limelight and do not deliberately choose a way of life or course of conduct calculated to thrust them into it nevertheless have no legal right to extinguish it if the experiences that have befallen them are newsworthy, even if they would prefer that those experiences be kept private.[33]

It seems highly unlikely that archivists directly will invade the privacy of others. Concerns about liability for negligent conduct, however, should be considered. Liability for negligent conduct may occur only when one person violates a legal duty of care to another, thereby causing harm. In general, such a legal duty or obligation is created by contract, law, regulation, court order, affirmative assumption, or human interdependence, such as the responsibility of parents for children. A breach of a legal duty that results in harm, with an adequate causal connection, may create liability. Where no such legal duty exists, however, there is no negligence or legal responsibility.

Archivists should be cautious about *affirmatively* assuming additional legal obligations that may be difficult to complete, and which may be problematic if the obligations are ignored or negligently fulfilled. If an archives agrees to a donor's request to protect the privacy of third parties whose identities appear in the donor's files, for example, the archives undertakes special, and perhaps onerous, duties. Any individual failure to protect privacy according to the higher standards could lead to legal action against the archives and perhaps even individual archivists. A further difficulty may arise if archivists *voluntarily* seek to protect the feelings, sensibilities, and personal information about third parties who may not know that their data is present in archival records. While perhaps admirable, such a goal may be troublesome to achieve, particularly when trying to determine what information is private or embarrassing to whom, and from whom it must be withheld. Archivists who undertake any such affirmative restriction voluntarily set a high standard of conduct that may be difficult to execute. By maintaining exceptional, and perhaps unnecessarily high, standards, archivists must make consistently perfect judgments about privacy concerns and future research needs. This increases the possibility of poor decisions, takes time, and has the potential to create public relations problems. Any error may lead to liability for failure to follow newly created policies or customs. Consequently, archivists should be very wary of undertaking unusual legal obligations or duties to donors or to third parties. Only carefully should archivists undertake proactive attempts to locate, identify, and prevent access to private information, and they need not, and should not, impose higher standards than are necessary.

Conclusion

The social scientist Alida Brill aptly writes that "perhaps the case-by-case approach to privacy that we have developed confounds rather than clarifies privacy. We need instead to develop a broad-based and normative understanding of privacy rather than a restricted and political policy of privacy. . . . Currently we are entrapped in a kind of 'regulated' privacy, encoded by law and upheld or dismissed by the courts."[34] American privacy law is far from uniform. Still, it has evolved rapidly over the past century, settling on a consensus that a right to privacy is important to maintain for society and individuals. The fact that wide variation exists, with no clear rules to guide and instruct archivists, perhaps testifies to privacy's flexibility and signals future changes.

ETHICAL PERSPECTIVES

Ethical considerations often govern day-to-day decision making concerning privacy and confidentiality questions. A fundamental tension between guaranteeing open access to records and protecting the personal privacy of individuals remains at the heart of much of the professional debate. The Society of American Archivists began confronting the issue directly in the early 1970s through a series of statements and guidelines. Initially, most archivists during the Watergate era rallied to the cause of open access. The SAA's Committee on Reference, Access, and Photoduplication, for example, prepared a statement on research materials in 1973 that heavily favored liberal access policies. The committee declared that repositories should commit themselves to "preserving manuscript and archival materials and to making them available for research as soon as possible." Though acknowledging that public institutions had a legal mandate to protect privacy, and conceding that donors had a right to impose "reasonable" conditions on use, the statement urged all archivists to minimize access restrictions. The SAA suggested that repositories should discourage donors from controlling use, place time limits on restrictions, periodically reevaluate closed records, "and work toward providing access to material no longer harmful to individuals or to national interest."[1]

The SAA statement attempted to codify a perceived professional consensus in the mid-1970s, but other dissenting voices entered the conversation during the 1980s and 1990s. Individually and collectively, archivists found it difficult to develop a rigorously consistent position on access issues, and many embraced ambiguity instead. The Society of

American Archivists' Code of Ethics, originally drafted in 1980 and revised with commentary in 1992, reflected the change and revealed some confusion concerning appropriate archival roles.[2] Three sections of the code specifically addressed privacy and confidentiality issues: IV—Relations with Donors and Restrictions, VII—Privacy and Restricted Information, and VIII—Use and Restrictions. Section IV echoed the 1973 committee statement by instructing archivists to "discourage unreasonable restrictions on access and use," but it also observed that professionals "may occasionally suggest . . . restrictions to protect privacy." The code commentary concerning section IV explained that donors often did not understand the sensitivity of their materials. It characterized archivists as knowledgeable and neutral professionals who might "when necessary, recommend that donors make provision for protecting the privacy and other rights of the donors themselves, their families, their correspondents, and associates." Section IV thus charged archivists with the task of actually intervening in the negotiation process in order to increase restrictions in some instances. Section VII further underscored the code's concern with privacy, affirming that archivists should "respect the privacy of individuals who created, or are the subjects of, documentary materials of long-term value, especially those who had no voice in the disposition of the materials." Once again, the code apparently encouraged archivists to expand their role by remaining vigilant about third-party rights and occasionally overruling donors to increase restrictions on materials. Section VIII, however, seemed to argue for a very different notion of professional responsibility. It plainly and forthrightly instructed archivists to "discourage the imposition of restrictions by donors." Faced with conflicting advice about their professional responsibilities, archivists often found themselves in the uncomfortable position of applying ambiguous professional guidelines on a case-by-case basis.

The articles in this section of the reader reflect contemporary archivists' efforts to come to terms with these kinds of problems. They also illustrate the increasingly complex and nuanced views concerning privacy that began to permeate the profession by the early 1990s. Heather MacNeil's influential 1992 book, *Without Consent: The Ethics of Disclosing Personal Information in Public Archives*, constitutes one of the earliest and most important attempts to broaden the archival dialogue.[3] MacNeil effectively argues throughout her monograph that archivists need to consider more carefully their moral and ethical obligations when allowing access to highly sensitive and deeply personal documents. *Without Consent* focuses primarily on public records and the proliferation of government-held personal information, but it frames the entire discussion within a larger historical and sociocultural context. It quickly became required reading in graduate education programs and stimulated many working archivists to reconsider the ways in which they handled sensitive records. MacNeil's contribution to this volume extends and advances her earlier work, exploring the ways in which liberal democratic cultures have defined and debated privacy-related questions.

Other North American archivists had also begun to reflect on the complex ethical issues surrounding privacy by the early 1990s. Judith Schwarz's especially influential article concerning privacy, reprinted below, first appeared in the *Journal of American History* in 1992. As a charter member of the pioneer group of scholars who virtually invented the field of gay and lesbian history in the 1970s, Schwarz remained committed to opening sensitive materials to responsible scholarly inquiry. Yet, as a founder of the Lesbian Herstory Archives in New York City, and as a professional archivist who previously had worked in a variety of repositories, she also remained cognizant of the institutional considerations and personal factors that necessitated access restrictions. Schwarz structured her approach to access around the notion of "balance," a term that also appears frequently in MacNeil's scholarship. The balance concept continued to dominate most archival discussions of confidentiality questions throughout the 1990s. Archivists increasingly viewed themselves as neutral brokers who balanced the competing demands and interests of donors and users. By embracing the notion of balance, however, archivists sometimes found it difficult to present a coherent professional perspective on privacy and access questions. They also distanced themselves somewhat from the unqualified support for open access that united their research clientele. This occasionally strained cross-disciplinary relationships and hindered cooperative advocacy efforts with historians and other academics.

Indeed, the archival balancing act appeared to be tilting toward providing greater privacy safeguards during the 1990s. Specifically, an increased sensitivity to the rights of third parties pervaded much of the archival literature. MacNeil worried about the fact that the individuals whose names appeared in religious records, social welfare case files, corporate archives, congressional papers, and social history databases typically presumed that their institutional dealings would remain confidential. Schwarz addressed the issue of human sexuality, as well as the sensitivity and prudery that motivated many archivists and donors to restrict access to information concerning family members and loved ones. Third-party considerations loom especially large in another article contained in this section of the reader. Elena Danielson discusses records relating to the East German State Security Service (Stasi) following the collapse of the Berlin Wall in 1989–1990, offering an instructive comparison with similar situations in other Eastern European countries. Former Communist functionaries attempted to destroy and suppress information concerning political repression, while dissidents and other citizens demanded access to their files. Democratic politicians feared that opening intelligence records would lead to a period of revenge, murder, manslaughter, and politically motivated retribution. Former Communist collaborators, many of whom sought to retain political and social influence following unification, argued for lengthy temporal restrictions on access to the records. Victims wished to view their own files and to learn the identities of spies and informants partly to reconcile themselves with the past. Danielson documents the complex ethical challenges, wrenching philosophical debates, practical political compromises, and unique archival challenges faced by post-Communist regimes. Her analysis carefully considers the unique factors that produced varied situations in each European nation, but she also illustrates the possibility of crafting a global ethical approach to the records of repressive regimes. She provides a useful international perspective concerning privacy, reminding North American archivists that debates concerning openness, third-party rights, and confidentiality transcend state boundaries and require creative solutions.

Martin Levitt's article, which concludes this consideration of ethical perspectives, also deals with an innovative solution to a very specific problem. During the 1990s, he became involved in an effort to create an educational Web site that documented the history of the eugenics movement through the reproduction of primary sources and explanatory text. The project staff struggled with the issue of relating the history of the movement without giving credence to its scientifically discredited and distasteful conclusions. Archivists, historians of science, scientists, educators, legal scholars, representatives of advocacy groups for the physically challenged, and ethicists collaborated on the endeavor. They carefully weighed the privacy rights of individuals depicted in photographs and documents against the social benefits of providing an open and intelligent discussion concerning eugenics. Ultimately, the project relied on a broad-based editorial advisory panel to consider the ethical implications and craft an appropriate solution. Levitt's case study thus offers a practical example of an approach favored by Heather MacNeil, who has suggested that archives establish ethical review boards to help them address complex access questions. The story of the eugenics Web site also illustrates the way in which technological changes have altered the archival landscape, creating both greater opportunities to violate individual privacy and possible remedies for tricky ethical dilemmas.

Considered together, these four studies probably raise more questions than answers. They suggest that no easy ethical consensus appears on the horizon within the archival community. Political factors, technological developments, and changing academic research trends have placed new demands and pressures on archivists to satisfy a broad constituency of donors, users, and third parties. Codes of ethics provide some guidance, but the ambiguity inherent in many privacy-related situations usually frustrates any effort to apply consistent policies or to construct formulaic responses. Above all, these articles suggest that ethical issues involving privacy continue to proliferate and that abstract principles cannot be applied easily or uniformly to unique historical and sociocultural situations. Archivists need to continue participating in the rich discussions and debates that have characterized the past twenty years.

4 Information Privacy, Liberty, and Democracy

Heather MacNeil

In principle, archivists recognize an individual's moral right to privacy. The Society of American Archivists' Code of Ethics, for example, contains a provision stating that "[a]rchivists respect the privacy of individuals who created, or are the subjects of, documentary materials of long-term value, especially those who had no voice in the disposition of the materials."[1] In the world of public records, this ethical principle echoes the legal principles underpinning data protection laws.[2] The main premise of such laws is that the personal information that individuals must disclose to the government in connection with any of their transactions should be held to a trust relationship and should create a duty of nondisclosure, subject to specific and limited exceptions. When government records containing personal information are transferred to archival custody, the responsibility for preserving that trust relationship passes to the archivist.

The trust relationship is a specific manifestation of a general principle concerning the ownership of public records in a democracy, a principle long familiar to government archivists. In 1943, Margaret Cross Norton, an early proponent of the public service role of government archivists, wrote: "the first of the basic principles involved in the care of public records is that under a democratic form of government the people are sovereign. That is, the records of the government belong to the people and the official who creates, files, and services the records is merely acting as custodian for the people."[3] As trusted custodians, government archivists are charged with the responsibility to safeguard the integrity of the records in their care.[4] This responsibility carries with it an implicit obligation to protect the integrity of particular relationships between citizens and their government to which the records bear witness, as well as to intercede on behalf of record subjects to protect their privacy interests.

At the same time, the role that government archivists play as trusted custodians must be balanced with the role that they play as communicators of society's documentary memory. The latter role carries with it an obligation to encourage and to promote the greatest possible access to archival holdings. In the public sphere, such obligation is supported and reinforced by freedom of information laws. The principle underlying such laws is that, generally speaking, every citizen should have the right to obtain access to government records to heighten the accountability of government, enable citizens to contribute to debates on public policy, and encourage fairness in administrative decision-making processes affecting individuals.[5]

Given these dual roles of trusted custodian and access guarantor, archivists are uniquely qualified to contribute to societal debates concerning the appropriate balance in a democratic society between the individual's right to be private and society's need for knowledge. Judging from the dearth of substantial discussion in the archival literature, however, it is fair to conclude that archivists are generally disinclined to participate in such debates. To the limited extent that they do participate, it appears that, while they do not dispute the significance of individual rights to privacy, they are more inclined to publicly promote the importance and value of increased accessibility to archival holdings. The purpose of this article is to explore the reasons why the right to information privacy constitutes a democratic interest that is as compelling and indisputable as the democratic interest in promoting accessibility. This article will examine defenses of the right to information privacy that are grounded in the interconnectedness of privacy, liberty, and democracy. It will also suggest some of the ways in which an understanding of that connectedness might inform archival policies and practices relating to the administration of access to government records containing personal information.

Our moral interest in privacy and the grounds on which we claim a legal right to it derive from a respect for individual autonomy, expressed as the individual's freedom from the scrutiny and judgment of others in certain areas of their lives. The legal scholar Ruth Gavison has defined privacy as "the extent to which we are known to others [our secrecy]; the extent to which we are the subject of others' attention [our anonymity]; and the extent to which others have physical access to us [our solitude]."[6] From this definition it follows that the individual's right to privacy assumes the right to a reasonable degree of secrecy, anonymity, and solitude. Of course, the concept of "reasonable degree" constitutes a continually negotiated criterion.

The association of privacy with individual moral autonomy is a distinctively Western cultural notion that has developed only gradually over the centuries. In ancient times, the word *private* meant literally a state of deprivation and carried the negative connotation of withdrawal from public life; Aristotle insisted that an individual who lived only a private life could not be fully human. But according to Raymond Williams, who has traced the etymology of the word, around the fifteenth century, *private* acquired a slightly different meaning that manifested itself in "a conventional opposition to *public*, as in private house, private education . . . private club, private property. In virtually all of these uses, the primary sense was one of *privilege*; the limited access or participation was seen not as deprivation but as advantage."[7] Privacy thus came to be associated with a sense of individual, personal privilege similar in kind to the privileges associated with class position. As the communications theorist Oscar Gandy observes, "[t]he importance of this privilege in relation to the demands or requirements of the state on an emerging bourgeoisie is a distinction that ought not be lost."[8] Equally important was the gradual evolution of the senses of withdrawal and seclusion associated with privacy into those of independence and intimacy. Beginning around the sixteenth century and continuing into the seventeenth and eighteenth centuries, Williams suggests, "seclusion in the sense of a quiet life was valued as privacy, and this developed beyond the sense of solitude to the senses of decent and dignified withdrawal . . . and beyond these to the generalized values of private life."[9]

This development was closely connected to the emergence, in the eighteenth century, of individual "natural" rights, which were considered essential to the individual's growth and fulfillment in society. Rousseau valorized privacy as the ground of philosophical truth, for "a man cannot speak the truth about the world unless he cuts himself off from it."[10] In the nineteenth century, the philosopher and social reformer John Stuart Mill placed the individual's right to privacy at the heart of his defense of liberty, maintaining that a close connection existed between the availability of a protected zone of privacy and an individual's ability to develop her individuality and creativity. He drew a clear distinction between what he termed "self-regarding" (i.e., private) conduct and "other-regarding" (i.e., public) conduct and argued, in the interests of liberty, against any regulation of the former: "[T]he only purpose for which power can be rightfully exercised over any member of a civilised community, against his will, is to prevent harm to others. . . . In the part which merely concerns himself, his independence is, of right, absolute. Over himself, over his own body and mind, the individual is sovereign."[11] Although today it is generally recognized that the borderline between self- and other-regarding conduct is considerably more fluid and contentious than Mill's treatise admits, the moral principle of respect for persons underlying his defense of privacy remains a distinguishing characteristic of the classical liberal ethic, which is a conviction "centering on the basic thesis that individuals are not to be treated as mere property of the state but instead are to be respected as autonomous, independent beings with unique aims to fulfill."[12]

Contemporary concerns for privacy within the liberal tradition relate primarily to the amount of information known about an individual and have emerged in response to situations created by information-gathering practices ignored in traditional interpretations of invasion of privacy. The threat to the modern individual's privacy is embodied most strikingly in the surveillance power of large information-gathering organizations in society. Advances in communication and information technologies have resulted in an enormous expansion in the amount of personal information held in computer databases. Today, digitized data concerning all major personal characteristics—vital statistics, social and geographic mobility, wealth, income, education, political affiliations—can be easily collected, stored, linked with other data, and disseminated widely within and between organizations. Civil libertarians believe that, even if nothing intrinsically private or improperly derogatory is stored in a database, dangerous possibilities exist. The vast quantities of ostensibly innocuous information on citizens, combined with the technological capacity to link information from a variety of sources, will result in a less spontaneous and, ultimately, less free society. Moreover, there is widespread concern that organizations will use the information in ways that were not intended, or consented to, at the time of collection. A major target of citizen concern has been the government because it constitutes the largest information-gathering organization in society.

Throughout history, individuals have been willing to surrender a certain degree of privacy in return for physical, social, and legal protection under the terms of the social contract underlying relations between citizens and their government. Based on the fact that "every civilized community, perhaps any real community requires, in order that it may exist at all, a mutual recognition of rights on the part of its members, which is a tacit contract,"[13] social contract theory specifies the privileges and responsibilities foregone by citizens and placed in trust with the governing agency. Social contract theorists also extol the benefits that citizens receive in return, such as good government, protection from external threat, and a guarantee of selected individual rights. These rights, they theorize, can only be relinquished with the consent of the individual.

Within the social contract framework, privacy rights and consent are inextricably linked. This is especially true in pluralist societies where, in the absence of a single canonical vision of what constitutes the good, the only feasible option is to ground the moral authority of the state on the permission of the governed.[14] As the ethical philosopher Tristram Engelhardt, Jr. explains:

> In such circumstances, rights to privacy announce the plausible limits of the authority of others and of the state over the individual by disclosing the boundaries of consent. Or to put matters more positively, rights to privacy mark where individuals continue to maintain authority over themselves.[15]

In the interest of the social contract, citizens are obligated to surrender a certain amount of their privacy. The government's right to collect and store information about citizens is not, however, an unlimited one, nor does it imply the right to disseminate personal information to third parties for unspecified purposes. The disclosure of personal information to third parties is contrary to the basic principle that individuals should be able to determine for themselves when, how, and to what extent information about them is communicated to others. Individuals have little control over whether or not their privacy is invaded by the government since they are often denied benefits and services if personal information is not provided. For the government then to disseminate or permit others access to that information for use in unspecified ways is viewed as a serious threat to an individual's information privacy.

The collection, processing, and sharing of personal information by such large bureaucratic organizations as governments are sources of unease because they render citizens vulnerable to an insidious system of impersonal observation and control against which they are largely defenseless. The poststructuralist philosopher Michel Foucault finds in the Panopticon a powerful symbolic expression of that system. Conceived by Jeremy Bentham in 1791, the original Panopticon was a model of a scientific prison. Foucault describes the principle on which its architectural design is based:

> [A]t the periphery, an annular building; at the centre, a tower; this tower is pierced with wide windows that open onto the inner side of the ring; the peripheric building is divided into cells, each of which extends the whole width of the building; they have two windows, one on the inside,

corresponding to the windows of the tower; the other, on the outside, allows the light to cross the cell from one end to the other. All that is needed, then, is to place a supervisor in a central tower and to shut up in each cell a madman, a patient, a condemned man, a worker or a schoolboy. By the effect of backlighting, one can observe from the tower, standing out precisely against the light, the small captive shadows in the cells of the periphery. They are like so many small theatres, in which each actor is alone, perfectly individualized and constantly visible.[16]

The major effect of the design, according to Foucault, is

to induce in the inmate a state of conscious and permanent visibility that assures the automatic functioning of power. . . . The Panopticon is a machine for dissociating the see/being seen dyad: in the peripheric ring, one is totally seen, without ever seeing; in the central towers, one sees everything without ever being seen.[17]

This capacity to see without being seen—what Foucault calls the Panopticon gaze—is the very essence of power because ultimately the power to dominate rests on the differential possession of knowledge.[18]

In the wake of Foucault, several critical commentators have adopted the Panopticon metaphor to draw specific attention to the surveillance potential of new and emerging communication and information technologies. Communications scholars Kevin Robins and Frank Webster suggest that such technologies are an extension and transformation of the Panoptic machine: "What these technologies support, in fact, is the same dissemination of power and control, but freed from the architectural constraints of Bentham's stone and brick prototype. On the basis of the 'information revolution,' not just the prison or factory, but the social totality, comes to function as the hierarchical and disciplinary Panoptic machine."[19] In "Driving to the Panopticon," the philosopher Jeffrey Reiman also draws on the Panopticon metaphor to elucidate the risks to individual privacy posed by the information-gathering practices of large organizations:

Information-gathering in any particular realm may not seem to pose a very grave threat precisely because it is generally possible to preserve one's privacy by escaping into other realms. Consequently, as we look at each kind of information-gathering in isolation from the others, each may seem relatively benign. However, as each is put into practice its effect is to close off yet another escape route from public access, so that when the whole complex is in place, its overall effect on privacy will be greater than the sum of the effects of the parts. . . . I call this whole complex . . . the *informational panopticon*.[20]

As Reiman's comments make clear, the overall effect of the informational panopticon is to reduce the amount of private space available to individual members of society, thereby weakening the physical and psychological boundaries that society tries to sustain between the private and public domains and reinforcing people's sense that personal information, sooner or later, will become publicly known.

Given that our moral interest in privacy is rooted in a respect for individual moral autonomy and that the capacity for autonomy depends on an individual's freedom to withdraw from the scrutiny of others, it is clear that the fear raised by the spectre of the informational panopticon is the fear of loss of autonomy. Oscar Gandy describes the specific threat that the informational panopticon poses to individual autonomy in the following way:

> The panoptic sort [by which he means the practice of disciplinary classification and surveillance] threatens the autonomy of the individual by increasing the range of activities that may be brought under the watchful eye of significant others. If every action generates a record and if this record is available to a wider and wider sphere of interested, or potentially interested others with the power to make decisions about a person's options, the freedom of action becomes self-limiting. The limitation on autonomy that derives from the belief that one is being watched is not restricted to formally illegal behaviors. Depending on the individual, the constraint spreads to include behaviors that may be merely questionable or are out of fashion. The limitations on autonomy that characterize the panoptic sort are evermore broad because it is unclear just who is watching and what their interests and standards might be.[21]

A generalized system of surveillance threatens individual autonomy because it bypasses an individual's normal decision-making capacity and interferes with the voluntary nature of her actions. As more and more aspects of people's lives become the subject of impersonal observation and recording, individuals risk losing their sense of self-ownership; they are unable to withdraw themselves from public scrutiny and are constantly reminded that they are someone else's data.[22] Such a society provides limited scope for the expression of individuality and personal identity, encouraging instead social conformity and conventionality.

The impoverishment of personal identity and individuality represents perhaps the most troubling threat posed by the informational panopticon. This is because it implies the diminution of an individual's inner life. A hallmark of the liberal vision is the belief that an individual's inner life is essential to a free society. And it is here that we find the profound connection among liberalism, privacy, and democracy. Reiman describes that connection in the following way:

> The liberal vision is guided by the ideal of the autonomous individual, the one who acts on principles which she has accepted after critical review rather than simply absorbing them unquestioned from outside. Moreover, the liberal stresses the importance of people making sense of their own lives, and of having authority over the sense of those lives. All this requires a kind of space in which to reflect on the entertain beliefs, and to experiment with them—a private space. . . . Deeper still, however, the liberal vision has an implicit trust in the transformational and ameliorative possibilities of private inner life. Without this, neither democracy nor individual freedom have worth. Unless people can form their own views, democratic voting becomes mere ratification of conventionality, and individual freedom mere voluntary conformity.[23]

Privacy is necessary to the health of a democratic society, in other words, because it promotes tolerance and pluralism and, in so doing, fosters and encourages independent and critically minded individuals. Ruth Gavison believes that privacy is important for democracy because "it fosters and encourages the moral autonomy of the citizen, a central requirement of a democracy. Part of the justification for majority rule and the right to vote is the assumption that individuals should participate in political decisions by forming judgments and expressing preferences. Thus, to the extent that privacy is important for autonomy, it is important for democracy as well."[24]

It may be argued, of course, that the emphasis that liberal ideology places on the individual's right to privacy is excessive and, far from promoting democracy, constitutes an impediment to the transparency necessary for meaningful democratic participation. The legal scholar Spiros Simitis notes that, when the right to privacy is defined as an individual's right of seclusion or withdrawal from society, "the *citoyen's* access to information ends where the *bourgeois'* claim for privacy begins."[25] Simitis explores the conflict between the individual's "right to be let alone"[26] and the public's need to be informed in his analysis of the principles and purposes underpinning data-protection legislation. He points out that the existence of a democratic society depends on a free flow of information, including personal information; as long as the information that is needed to understand and evaluate political and economic processes is withheld or suppressed, democratic participation remains an empty phrase. Simitis equates the free flow of information with transparency and argues that the search for greater transparency is justified by the goal of allowing the individual to understand social reality better and thus to form a personal opinion on its decisive factors as well as on possible changes. The citizen's right to participate in the government of affairs "presupposes individuals who not only disperse the necessary information but also have the capacity to transform the accessible data into policy expectations. Transparency is, in other words, a basic element of competent communicative action and consequently remains indispensable as long as social discourse is to be promoted, not inhibited."[27]

As the collection and analysis of personal information becomes a standard instrument of government administration, however, it tends to constrain the very social discourse it is supposed to promote. Simitis believes this is because

> Habits, activities, and preferences are compiled, registered, and retrieved to facilitate better adjustment, *not* to improve the individual's capacity to act and to decide. . . . [The processing of personal information] increasingly appears as the ideal means to adapt an individual to a predetermined, standardized behavior that aims at the highest possible degree of compliance with the model patient, consumer, taxpayer, employee, or citizen. In short, the transparency achieved through automated processing creates possibly the best conditions for colonization of the individual's lifeworld. Accurate, constantly updated knowledge of her personal history is systematically incorporated into policies that deliberately structure her behavior. The more routinized automated processing augments the transparency, however, the more privacy proves to be a pre-requisite to participate in social discourse.[28]

In other words, the so-called transparency achieved through the collection and processing of personal information is hardly distinguishable from the "permanent visibility" envisaged in Bentham's Panopticon. Rather than promote meaningful democratic participation, such transparency threatens instead to erode individual autonomy and, consequently, democratic decision making.

If data-protection laws are to achieve the desired end of promoting democratic participation, Simitis argues, they must be structured around a model based on the human capacity for such participation, in which the right to privacy is equated with the right to informational self-determination, rather than around an informational seclusion model, in which privacy is defined as the individual's right to be let alone. The problem with the informational seclusion model of privacy is that it tends to situate the essence of privacy in the ability to choose it and in the ability to see that the choice is respected. The power of choice is emphasized rather than the way in which such power should be exercised. The privacy-as-participation model, on the other hand, is more concerned with sorting out the conditions under which personal information may be shared or withheld, based on an assessment of the consequences of that sharing or withholding for both the individual and society.

The limits of the seclusion model have been noted by other legal scholars. Paul Schwartz, for example, in his examination of the strengths and weaknesses of current data-protection laws, points out that

> [I]n the computer age, the critical issue is no longer limited to *whether* personal information should be collected and processed, but *how* these data should be used. Significantly more personal data are collected and used as a result of the increasing use of computer technology. Indeed, by reducing personal information to a fluid digital form, the computer encourages the sharing of data within organizations. Data protection law should respond by countering the computer's omniscience with a compromise between the concealment and exposure of personal information. A right to be let alone does not help address the question of how this compromise should be struck.[29]

Data-protection legislation, Schwartz maintains, should protect and promote the values of what he terms *deliberative autonomy* and *deliberative democracy*. To do so, it must provide safeguards to preserve individuals' capacity for decision making, and it must structure the use of personal information to shield individuals from state or community intimidation that would undermine their capacity for democratic participation.[30]

Over the past decade or so, the privacy-as-participation model has been adopted by a number of European legislators and courts. A salient characteristic of this model is the explicit connection it makes between the protection of privacy and a wide range of constitutional rights. The West German Federal Constitutional Court, for example, has argued that "[n]either freedom of speech, nor freedom of association nor freedom of assembly can be fully exercised as long as it remains uncertain whether, under what circumstances, and for what purposes personal information is collected and processed. [On this view], the right to privacy involves more than any one particular right: it determines the choice between a democratic and an authoritarian society."[31]

As both Simitis and Schwartz make clear, current debates over information privacy are, fundamentally, debates over the limits of personal freedom—that is, the extent to which people are, or should be, entitled to be free from scrutiny and judgment in certain areas of their lives, when there are others who claim to be entitled to prevent them from exercising that freedom. Part of the price we pay for community membership is the sacrifice of some degree of privacy when this is required either to fulfill ourselves as social beings or to further other compelling societal interests. The problem then becomes one of balancing the individual's claim to privacy against the state's claim to regulate conduct for the collective welfare, against the claim of other individuals to exercise their legitimate rights, and against the individual's own need for participation in wider communities.[32]

The mutual dependence of the public and private realms, the legal scholar Lloyd Weinreb suggests, follows logically from the premise that it is the nature of human beings to live in community:

> Hobbes, for example, . . . famously observed that outside a community bound together by normative conventions, the life of man would be "solitary, poor, nasty, brutish, and short"—that is to say, not (fully) human. Without a community, he argued, there is lacking the predicate for responsible action, which distinguishes a human being from all other kinds of being and makes him a person. . . . A community, on the other hand, is made up of individual human beings and, without contribution from them, has no existence as more than an aggregate of individuals. . . . Both fundamentally and at a more practical level, the individual and the community are interdependent.[33]

Given this interdependence, individual rights to privacy should be interpreted, not as a means of drawing isolationist boundaries but, rather, as a means of protecting relational ties.[34] In the end, providing citizens with the capacity to participate in the life of a community and to contribute to the formation of a free and just society is the most compelling defense of privacy within a democracy. "Whatever its many dangers and shortcomings," Mark Kingwell observes, "a well-ordered private realm makes a just public realm possible. Among other things, it makes the public/private distinction itself a matter for specifically public discourse, a contested border war. For only there can we offer arguments that will be assessed by our fellow citizens."[35]

The understanding that freedom of information and privacy together provide the necessary conditions for democratic participation and deserve equal protection constitutes the essential starting point for public debates concerning the nature and limits of privacy rights. It also constitutes the essential starting point for the formulation of archival policies and procedures for administering access to government records containing personal information. This follows from the fact that government archivists are both public custodians of the records, with a duty to safeguard the privacy interests contained in them, and communicators of society's documentary memory, with a responsibility to facilitate access to the records that embody it.[36]

"Integral to the notion of proper archival management of records, especially those which require decision-making," the archivist Ruth Simmons argues, "is the necessity to demonstrate a pattern of practice which shows care and concern."[37] Proper archival management in the context of protecting privacy rights implies a number of obligations on the part of archivists. At the institutional level, it means establishing defensible procedures for administering access to records containing personal information. At the professional level, it means advocating the development of privacy-related laws and guidelines that strike a just and equitable balance between the individual's need for both community membership and moral autonomy. At the societal level, it means participating in the public debate concerning ways and means to protect information privacy in an increasingly public society.[38]

The archival management of access to records containing personal information should properly begin before records come into archival custody. As records are scheduled for transfer, the conditions under which they are to be held by the archives need to be clarified and documented: What details are available about the kinds of personal information contained in the records? Do statutory or other explicit provisions exist for protecting the confidentiality of such information? Are there any provisions requiring disclosure? If confidentiality provisions apply, are there any exceptions to the general rule of nondisclosure? What are the exceptions? Who has the authority to decide whether conditional access is permissible for research or statistical purposes and how are decisions to be documented, made known, and accounted for? At what point in time can the records safely be made generally available for research purposes?

In many jurisdictions, restrictions on access to records containing personal information will be determined by existing legislation and regulations. However, the defined restrictions may leave important questions unanswered, such as the duration of the restrictions. Moreover, data protection laws typically permit archival institutions to make records containing personal information available for research purposes on the condition that the archives establish formal guidelines for administering access to such records. Institutional guidelines for administering access to records containing personal information are essential because they provide a defensible procedural substitute for obtaining the informed consent of record subjects. If they are to serve as an acceptable substitute for consent—meaning that they are capable of satisfying the moral requirement of respect for persons underlying the principle of consent—such guidelines should, at a minimum, identify the categories of information restricted for reasons of personal privacy[39] as well as the duration of restrictions on general access. They should also specify a procedure for reviewing requests for access to restricted records, establish a harms test to guide access decisions, and establish an appeal process for researchers who are denied access.

The process of establishing access guidelines requires a sensitivity on archivists' part, first, to the common law principle that rights to privacy do not diminish significantly over the lifetime of the individual to whom the information relates and second, to the common sense principle that, in some cases, these rights are not extinguished even with the death of that individual. Detailed analyses of the nature of the privacy interests inherent in different types of records are urgently required to enable archivists to make more thoughtful and informed judgments about the varying degrees of sensitivity associated with specific records and the types of harm implicated in their disclosure. Whatever decisions are taken, it is generally accepted that restrictions of indeterminate duration are unacceptable. Archivists should be prepared to defend any limitations on access and publicize them for the benefit of users through formal statements of access policy and in relevant finding aids. To ensure consistency in administering access to restricted records, standard operating procedures covering such areas as screening, withdrawal, cross-referencing, and periodic re-review of restricted records also should be instituted.[40]

For most archivists, the dilemmas that arise from legitimate but conflicting interests—the individual's right to privacy and society's need for knowledge—present themselves in the workplace and require solutions within that institutional context through formal policies and procedures such as those just described. At the same time, privacy issues affect the archival profession as a whole and, therefore, need to be discussed and debated by the profession as a whole. According to the traditional taxonomic model of professionalism, one of the attributes of a profession is *institutionalized altruism,* which Richard Cox describes as "a structural system that promotes behavior of its practitioners beneficial to others. This type of service orientation includes concerns for staying abreast of developments in a field so that clients are not harmed and standards are maintained to protect clients."[41] The archival profession's commitment to institutionalized altruism is enshrined in its various codes of ethics.[42]

One means by which the archival profession might demonstrate that altruism in the specific area of privacy is to formally articulate, for the benefit of both archivists and users, the basic ethical standards that should inform the archival administration of access to records containing personal information. Alice Robbin has proposed a set of ethical standards for the protection of personal information held in data archives that can be usefully adapted for the purposes of more traditional archives. The standards identify the archivists' obligation to protect the public trust with which personal information has been given; to maintain a high standard of professional competence with respect to the nondisclosure of confidential information; to demonstrate a sensitivity to the social codes and moral expectations of the public community that they serve; to safeguard the confidentiality of personally identifiable information; to establish and publicize conditions for protecting confidential records; and to establish appropriate security measures to prevent unauthorized access to data processing and storage devices that maintain personal information.[43] Ethical standards serve a number of useful purposes. They are a valuable educational and training device for promoting discussion of privacy issues affecting archivists. In the event of violations of privacy in an archival context, ethical standards provide criteria or points of reference by which to assess situations. They further provide a solid foundation on which to build more specific policies and procedures for the protection of records containing personal information.

The archivist's obligation to protect and promote the value of information privacy is not confined to the domain of historical records; it extends to current records as well. Most privacy acts are built around a set of internationally accepted fair information practices that are designed to "minimize intrusiveness in the collection of personal information; maximize fairness in its use; and provide reasonable and enforceable expectations of confidentiality."[44] Fair information practices should be seen as an essential component of any recordkeeping standard either developed or recommended for use by the archival profession. Of course, in promoting fair information practices, archivists need to strike a balance between the individual's right to be forgotten, which is implicit in certain of those practices, and society's need for memory. In other words, archivists should advocate a humane standard for the collection, use, and retention of records containing personal information but, at the same time, they must remain vigilant against overly rigid interpretations of fair information practices that could threaten the legitimate preservation of records possessing long-term value.

By contributing to the societal debate concerning the protection of personal privacy in an increasingly public society, archivists might demonstrate their professional altruism. As a consequence of their involvement in the management of both current and historical records, archivists are intimately acquainted with the moral, legal, and practical dilemmas associated with collecting, preserving, and disseminating enormous quantities of personal information. A detailed account of the nature and extent of these problems from an archival perspective should be communicated to legislative bodies and other policy makers to ensure that the concerns of the profession are heard and to provide relevant audiences with information that will assist them in developing and modifying access- and privacy-related statutes, regulations, and policies.[45] In the same spirit of altruism, archivists could build alliances with other interested groups—related professional associations, public officials, government agencies, users, civil libertarians, lawyers, and politicians—and work with them to draft model data-protection laws and guidelines structured around the protection and promotion of privacy as a condition of democratic participation.

In "Archival Principles and Records of the New Technology," Trudy Peterson observes that

> When we begin to hold quite current information in machine-readable form in an archives—information that is easy to link with other information in our possession and to send by telephone lines anywhere in the world in a matter of minutes—we are creating a frightening concentration of information. We must be exceptionally sensitive to our responsibilities to the public as users and to the public as subjects of our records. Modern records force the issue; and while it is possible—although expensive—to produce "public use versions" or "disclosure-free data sets," we still hold unparalleled information on our fellow citizens. We must make sure that our professional ethics are adequate to the challenge.[46]

Intimations of the assurance that Peterson seeks may be found in the opening clause of the International Council on Archives' code of ethics, which states: "The primary duty of archivists is to maintain the integrity of the records in their care and custody. In the accomplishment of this duty they must have regard to the legitimate, but sometimes conflicting, rights and interests of employers, owners, data subjects and users, past, present and future." This statement of principle suggests that interceding on behalf of records subjects to protect their privacy rights is not a disavowal of the archivists' obligation to make records available for use but, rather, a responsible exercising of their overriding duty to respect all the parties whose interests are bound up in the records over time. This article has situated that duty within the specific framework of liberal, democratic ideology and has suggested some of the ways in which an understanding of that framework might inform the archival administration of access to government records containing personal information.

5 The Archivist's Balancing Act: Helping Researchers While Protecting Individual Privacy

Judith Schwarz

Archivists, historians, and other researchers have a strong mutual interest in opening the historical record for the fullest access to information. At the same time, we share concern over how to safeguard individual privacy against the danger that someone's private life can become public without her or his permission, acquiescence, or desire. Weighing issues of privacy while trying to meet the access and informational needs of researchers is one of the most difficult balancing acts that archivists perform in carrying out their professional duties.

My observations on maintaining the confidentiality of records and protecting individual privacy while seeking the most complete openness of the historical record come from three professional experiences. In them I played three different roles and came to see from the inside the contending motives that shape three activities vital to the creation of a historical record. One activity is that of institutions and individuals (or the heirs of individuals) that generate records and decide to open them to researchers. The activity can be called donation; the institutions and individuals, donors. Amid the complex motives of donors, there is often a desire to establish a favorable historical image of the record-creating institution, family, or person. That desire can lead to a destruction of some materials before any are donated and to restrictions on access to what is

---

This article originally published in the *Journal of American History* 29 (June 1992): 179–89. Reprinted with permission.

saved. A second activity is research, and one motive of researchers is the desire to examine all the documents that may bear on their topics. A third activity is collecting materials that document the history of a region, profession, social class, movement, or racial, ethnic, religious, or sexual community. The motives of collectors often include the desire to affirm the documented group's identity and to convince others of its legitimacy by enshrining its particular past. In the nineteenth-century United States, much collecting promoted regional identities, by showing that the Midwest, for example, had an important and dramatic history. Twentieth-century collecting has created archives devoted to the histories of labor, of African Americans, of women, and, lately, of gays and lesbians. Archivists, as custodians of the historical record, must recognize the interests of donors, researchers, and collectors, and they must reconcile their sometimes conflicting demands.

Archivists aware of the need to balance interests when questions of privacy arise can make a special contribution to the study of the history of sexuality. By constructing policies that protect privacy, archivists can encourage donors to save and give revealing materials. By letting researchers know what archives hold, they can help them write about once-taboo sexual topics. By collecting imaginatively, they can make it possible for all of us to ask new questions about the past and to write histories that go deeper and range wider.

Successive experiences taught me the perspectives of an archivist representing a donor institution, a researcher, and a collector. First, during the early 1980s, as records manager for the General Board of Global Ministries (GBOGM) of the United Methodist Church (UMC), I was responsible for the overall administration of the records of seven agencies of the church. I often had to weigh the official confidentiality policies and concerns of the record-creating divisions against researchers' requests for information. Second, since 1976 I have been researching the personal, professional, political, and medical records of 110 women who from 1912 to the 1940s belonged to a unique feminist organization, the Heterodoxy Club, in Greenwich Village, New York City. In using several dozen research facilities, I faced research problems historians often face. When I tried to look beyond the surface level of a woman's life into her more private life, I clearly entered areas that make many people very nervous, including the woman's family, the professional or political institutions with which she was affiliated, and even, at times, the archivists responsible for preserving and granting access to the surviving evidence of the woman's life. Third, since 1978 I have been one of several coordinators guiding the pioneering work of the Lesbian Herstory Archives (LHA) and the Lesbian Herstory

Educational Foundation. We have continually had to wrestle with the issues of confidentiality, censorship, and access for researchers.

Like the archives of other large, ongoing institutions, the records department of the GBOGM existed mainly for the institution, and its staff members were expected to be custodians of the General Board's memory—and sometimes of its good name. Informational items ranged from pristine, elegantly handwritten ledger books from 1840s frontier Methodist Episcopal churches in Ohio to the spreadsheets and databases created on mainframe and personal computers each workday. On any given day, we had to be able quickly to find and retrieve an individual missionary's service papers and letters from the field in India, China, or Africa while also answering requests for next year's budget projections. Requests came from a variety of sources, including General Board staff members, church members, social agencies, historians, researchers, and a family member looking for information on her great-grandmother, who had been stationed in China in 1890, for the upcoming family reunion. Although the Commission on Archives and History, United Methodist Church, at Drew University, Madison, New Jersey, contained most of our oldest paper-based records, many nineteenth-century minute books, periodicals, and missionary documents were still housed in the offices of those who used them on a regular basis. Fundamental problems of confidentiality came up in the daily handling of research requests, such as the request of a highly vocal critic from a United Methodist Church conservative group trying to ferret out "financial waste" in the funding given by divisions of the General Board to programs for incest survivors and birth control information pamphlets.

Classification and written but flexible policies on access give archivists ways to balance conflicting concerns. Among the United States Methodist Church's many records series, a number are classified as "Private" or "Confidential," particularly series from the World Division of the General Board of Global Ministries. They contain information on imprisonment of missionaries in occupied lands during World War II, misconduct of missionaries and bishops, political involvement of missionaries in host countries, and serious differences of opinions between missionaries and the "home office." As is often the case in religious institutions, a strong concern for the good public opinion of the church can often outweigh the case for historical accuracy. Yet we were often proud of helping researchers discover far more than they knew to look for. But what of the family member asking us to waive restrictions on the records of her revered, much-beloved grandfather, who was "kicked upstairs" from his position with an orphanage under the shadow of rumors that he may have forced sexual acts upon children in his care?

The policies on access reflected archivists' efforts to consider not only the interests of the donor institution for which they worked but also the concerns of researchers. In 1982, my predecessor as records manager had written nearly a dozen respected historians, theological professors, archivists, and manuscripts curators, asking for professional and ethical guidance in developing a policy that would protect the missionary and at the same time "make relevant material available to researchers." (A separate issue that could also be addressed would be the vast differences in what she or I would consider "relevant," much less what the researcher might have thought.) The most compelling response came from an eminent church historian, who made a strong case that only "*really* private and/or confidential" matters be so labeled and restricted; even then, he advised, closing records for one hundred years was far too restrictive. He suggested fifty years. The historian suggested that the criterion for closure be used only when the information released "might cause personal harm or deep embarrassment" to a living person.

His advice was taken. The final policy placed a fifty-year restriction from the date of the document's creation on missionary correspondence, program policy, and project documents. For the Confidential and Personal Papers records series, there is now a seventy-five year restriction. Any deviation, including granting family members access, must be approved jointly by the deputy general secretary of the division and the records manager. This policy proved extremely helpful over the years I worked there. I looked forward to discussions of the most problematic requests with the deputy secretary. Her insightful comments were based on a lifetime of dedication and early years as a missionary in the United Methodist Church. In sum, the policy aimed for eventual open access while preserving the privacy of living individuals and protecting the interests of the church.

My experience as a professional interpreter of an inherited organizational confidentiality policy made me slightly more tolerant of the situations I found myself in as a master's degree thesis writer, then in pursuing further research to turn that thesis into a book, *The Radical Feminists of Heterodoxy*.[1]

The motto of Heterodoxy was "The only taboo is on taboo," and the members prided themselves upon a diversity in their political and personal lives that defies belief in these days of single-issue groups and few coalition movements. The women were called "the most unruly group of individualistic women you ever fell among" and included Charlotte Perkins Gilman, labor organizer and American Communist party leader Elizabeth Gurley Flynn, Unitarian minister Marie Jenney Howe, novelists Fanny Hurst and Zona Gale, feminist playwright Susan Glaspell of the Provincetown Players, actress and Theater Guild founder Helen Westley, as well as choreographer Agnes de Mille and her mother Anna George de Mille, several anarchists and labor activists, black civil rights worker Grace Nail Johnson, physicians, and many more who met every other Saturday for forty years to enjoy each other's company, to share information, and sometimes to act upon issues including labor, civil rights, birth control, suffrage, and pacifism. These women were considered so dangerous by the United States government during World War I that they were spied on and harassed by government agents—so much so that they actually changed their meeting place more than once.

In attempting to flesh out and verify the better-known, often erroneous, details of these women's lives, I was never denied access to papers by any of literally dozens of archives and manuscript repositories visited. Archivists and research room librarians were incredibly patient and helpful as I went on fishing expeditions through massive and minimally indexed collections such as the La Follette Family Papers in the Library of Congress, eventually requesting to see over thirty manuscript boxes to turn up only two dozen documents directly related to Heterodoxy (although, of course, much of the rest was very helpful as background material). The only request that was flatly refused was to the Communist party for access to Flynn's papers. After my book was published, her papers were deposited in the Tamiment Library at New York University, leading to the discovery of her important and lengthy live-in relationship with another woman. I am also not sure that the items I was given access to from Federal Bureau of Investigation files on individual members were very helpful, full as they are of entire pages blackened out and unreadable. Mind you, all the club members except Agnes de Mille are dead. Most of the surviving family members have long since come to terms with what they consider their aunt's or grandmother's eccentric beliefs or life choices. The nephew of the novelist and Columbia University professor Helen Hull inherited legal title to her papers deposited at Columbia, and he wanted to be sure that anyone researching his aunt's life was willing to deal with her as a lifelong lesbian. He has the refreshing viewpoint that it is not only relevant information, but absolutely essential in understanding Hull's life. The most difficult part of my life as a researcher has been what many searchers for women's history have faced. Women's papers, particularly those of women not considered notable, were often the last to be processed in an archives and were seldom indexed. More than once in a university archives of a formerly all-male university, I had to plead for access to collections that I knew were there, but that had not been processed thirty years after the papers were deposited. Yes, there are sometimes good reasons to process one collection over another, but thirty years does seem sufficient time, especially for only two manuscript boxes.

Other researchers interested in women's personal and sexual lives have at times been denied access to materials. When they have demanded it, the results have been mixed. At the Mount Holyoke College library in the late 1970s, Anna Mary Wells stumbled upon a large unopened box listed as the papers of former college president Mary Emma Woolley. They had been given to the library at the death of Woolley's lifelong partner, Jeannette Marks. No proviso was attached that restricted their use by researchers. When the box was opened, Wells found several dozen neat brown paper packets containing ardent love letters written by Marks and Woolley to each other over their long life together. "Shocked and embarrassed," Wells said, "my immediate impulse was to abandon my plans for the book" on Woolley.[2] Instead, she read many of them, making verbatim handwritten copies of large sections. When the college administration heard rumors of what Wells (a former student of the two women) had found, the collection was immediately closed to any and all use. President David Truman of Mount Holyoke then told Wells not only that she could not quote from the letters at all but also that he forbade her even to *mention* that they were at Mount Holyoke. In an important and courageous decision, Wells refused to accept Truman's arbitrary and high-handed edict. She sought advice and support from several professional historical and archivist organizations. Fittingly, members of these organizations and many researchers in women's and social history joined together in placing pressure on the college to reopen the collection. Eventually, Wells was allowed to use the many notes she had already taken, but she was not allowed to check her notes against the original letters before publishing *Miss Marks and Miss Woolley*. Truman decided that since one packet (not originally in the large box of letters) read "Not to be opened until 1999," the entire contents of the box should be closed until that date. Now, as a result of continuing pressure from influential historians and others, the letters in the box are once again open to public use, but only by "qualified scholars."

The most notorious example of an archives consigning materials relevant to lesbian history to inaccessibility is known among gay, lesbian, and other sexual history scholars as "the Box Ten Affair." In the late 1970s, Barbara Gittings, then coordinator of the American Library Association's Task Force on Gay Liberation, received an anonymous note in the mail, which she passed on to Jonathan Katz, author of *Gay American History*. The note described a binder of letters at the Minnesota Historical Society (MHS). The letters were exchanged by Rose Elizabeth Cleveland, sister of President Grover Cleveland and his White House hostess during his year as a bachelor president, and Evangeline Marrs Simpson, a widow who later married Henry Whipple, first Episcopal bishop of Minnesota. The unknown writer said that the letters "reveal a lesbian relationship between the two women," and that they were not listed in the card catalog. The gay and lesbian history study group to which Katz, Martin Duberman, Joan Nestle, Deborah Edel, Blanche Wiesen Cook, I, and several others then belonged began calling it "the Box Ten Affair," since MHS officially listed the Whipple-Scandrett Papers as comprising only nine boxes. The love letters were in an unmarked, unlisted *tenth* manuscript box. When Katz questioned the MHS about the letters, he received the reply that the letters "had been closed until 1980," but that "due to current scholarly interest, those materials were reviewed and the decision made to remove the restrictions." It is not clear whether anyone outside the MHS even knew of the existence of the letters, other than Gittings, the members of the study group, and the anonymous note writer. The MHS did not mention the reasoning behind the original decision not to list the material as part of the collection. The suppressed love letters are now open for research use, for which all of us are grateful. But many of us wonder if they would ever have been listed without Katz's inquiry.[3]

His other brush with the suppression of material did not end as well as the Cleveland-Whipple "affair." A feminist historian discovered love letters written to Margaret Sanger in 1916 by Dr. Marie Equi, whom Sanger identified in a note as having been called a lesbian. The historian decided not to pursue the information but made typed copies of the letters, which are in the Margaret Sanger Papers, in the Sophia Smith Collection, Smith College. She then sent copies on to Katz, who was then researching *Gay American History*. He wrote the library for permission to photocopy the letters and inquired about permission to publish them. His request was sent on by the Smith staff to the Sanger family, who retain legal control of the papers. He was refused permission to publish or even to make copies of the letters. After exchanges back and forth with the Sanger family, Katz's inquiries finally provoked one of the two Sanger sons to reply that he could not "understand your interest in this," and that the information was "not important." He added, "There are several aspects of my mother's life which my brother [the executor] and I are unwilling to have explored."[4] I wonder if any other historian has asked about those letters and also been refused permission to quote from them. One can always paraphrase, but it is difficult to paraphrase passionate love letters. Even worse, the woman who wrote the lesbian love letters was not even a member of the family that is withholding them from view.

These examples of institutions' handling of lesbian materials prompt several reflections. The impulse to suppress material or at least to restrict its use for a time seems to spring from desires to protect both the reputations of individuals and families and the welfare of the institutions. A college president such as Truman may feel that the gain from keeping the college free of controversy far outweighs the temporary sacrifice of researchers' access to the private life of a predecessor. Archivists may plausibly believe that by restricting access they encourage donors to entrust sensitive records to their institutions. On the whole, however, archivists figure in these stories as balancers of competing concerns and interests. Thus when researchers have organized and demanded access to materials that archivists controlled, they have often gotten it. The threat to the preservation and the accessibility of materials for the study of lesbian and gay history remains. As long as lesbians and gay men are seen as a threat to the established social order, and lesbianism stays a slanderous accusation long after a woman's death, we will continue to face angry protectors of a deceased relative's or colleague's reputation. That may prove to be a very long time indeed.

As one of the longtime coordinators of the Lesbian Herstory Archives/Lesbian Herstory Educational Foundation (founded in New York City in 1974), I have been intimately involved with the issues of trust, individual privacy, and fear within our own international, national, and local communities of lesbians. The collection has grown to over ten thousand books, over a thousand lesbian and gay periodical series from around the world, nearly two hundred individual manuscript collections, and several thousand biographical and organizational files on women who have identified themselves to us as lesbians or been so identified by the media without their permission. Our newsletter, which is also a running catalog of the parts of the collection that can be publicly identified, is distributed to five thousand individuals and eight hundred libraries, archives, and other organizations throughout the world. All this is done with volunteer labor, mostly by lesbians already carrying full-time paid jobs elsewhere, several of whom have family responsibilities. We answer an average of twenty telephone requests per day and six hundred written requests per year, and we see an equal number of researchers and other visitors.[5]

All of us who care about the preservation and presentation of the fullness of women's and social history should feel enormous pride in the grass-roots work done over nearly two decades by the many gay and lesbian archives, libraries, and special collections in the United States and in other nations. Preservation of the history of thousands upon thousands of women scattered throughout the world in many languages is a monumental task, made all the harder by the understandable focus on self-preservation that forces far too many of us to destroy all written or pictorial evidence of our lives. Not only that, but our very existence in most societies and countries is either totally denied and invisible, or swept under the overall title of homosexuality and considered exactly the same as that of gay men, without recognition of the fundamental differences between male and female experience of life. Even worse, throughout the world lesbians and gay men are declared criminal, perverse, and considered so far beneath contempt that to be caught kissing another person of the same sex can mean imprisonment and even death. Every love letter, every photograph, every taped voice crackling with pain or howling with delight over a favorite "coming out" story, every 1960s lesbian paperback passed down to us tattered and torn from the hands of the average thirty readers per copy before it gets into the LHA collection—these are precious gifts lovingly handled. They are our very reason for existence.

Yet even here archivists must balance conflicting needs, concerns, and interests. We who preserve the remnants of lesbian and gay history face tremendous dilemmas over issues of confidentiality and individual privacy when people's lives may depend upon the security of their deepest held secrets.

LHA gathers and preserves records of lesbian lives and activities so that our own and future generations will have ready access to materials relevant to their lives. LHA is both a life-giving place and a place to commemorate lost lovers and friends. At times it can offer a substitute for something lesbians as a group have been deprived of, the rituals of communal sorrow when death separates us.

When a woman deposits her poems, letters, journals, artwork, leather jacket, T-shirts, or a tape of her music or of a day in her life with us at LHA, we talk with her and ask her to write the accessibility proviso herself. That very act gives her control over how her life will be used by researchers. There are many levels to this. Let us say she is a lesbian mother who has been fortunate enough to keep custody of her children in a divorce case. Will she allow another woman in the same trouble to learn of her story and find useful tactics and information? Can we allow an author of a lesbian reference manual, a college student writing a paper, a journalist researching an article for the *New York Times* or the *Village Voice,* or a filmmaker to quote from her writings or use her photograph? Will that place her in future jeopardy of a new legal attempt to remove her children because she did not keep silent and is now deemed to be flaunting her sexuality, with or without evidence that she ever acted on her self-knowledge? May we list her name when we print an index of the archives' holdings in our newsletter, always knowing that it could be used against her later? Does she prefer us to place her materials under seal and keep them apart from the open access collection for a certain period of time until her family can no longer be threatened? May male researchers see all or part of her collection, and if only part of it, which part?

Joan Nestle, one of the founders of the Lesbian Herstory Archives, said that the most important thing I can tell you is that "to preserve is to give life, but in the very act of preservation, we can destroy a life." Lesbians who declared their sexuality freely and openly in the women's liberation movement heyday of the early 1970s can now lose everything in these terrible conservative times.

I want to close by telling of an instance when we struggled mightily over the issue of individual privacy versus collective memory. The Daughters of Bilitis (DOB) was the first self-declared lesbian group in the United States, and possibly the world. Founded in San Francisco in 1955, it eventually grew by creating local chapters in many American cities. LHA has most of the chapter newsletters, minutes of meetings, and thousands of letters written to the New York City chapter when it had the only published address to which women could write for information on lesbians. In 1984, we were very fortunate to receive the Philadelphia chapter papers from long-time lesbian activist and librarian Gittings. She had kept them in her basement for over twenty years. A woman who had written one or two letters in the early 1960s to DOB found out that the collection had been given to us and wrote a passionately angry letter, demanding that we destroy the entire collection. She argued that by preserving the letters without individual permission from each writer, we would cause great psychic distress and possibly even physical harm to the women involved. Deborah Edel, one of the founding members of LHA, wrote a long letter to open a dialogue with the protester, explaining why we felt the papers should be kept and asking her either to meet or to speak on the telephone with us. After several months of discussion via telephone and letters, she agreed that the collection was in safe hands but still wanted her own letters destroyed. We agreed to send them to her when the collection was processed, but we asked her in the meantime to reflect: If the collection as a whole was safe and should be kept, shouldn't she continue to feel comfortable about her participation in the Daughters of Bilitis, and about being a part of women's, lesbian, and civil rights history?

She later wrote to us, saying, "Yes. I see your point. Keep them all safe from harm, including the harm I might do them." Her sense of stigma and self-hatred was enormous in the beginning, causing us untold hours of anguished labor and concern. Yet an archivist of any minority despised by the society-at-large must be willing to work with people uneasy about the records they have created before their history is destroyed. The donor is not the enemy. She is a victim of the situation that gives us reason to exist—the devaluing of human lives.

Many scholars are now writing the history of lesbian and gay sexuality. They have responded to the increasing self-consciousness of sexual minorities—to the revaluing of lesbian and gay lives—and to changes in the world of scholarship. One such change is in the thinking of historians, many of whom now will entertain the idea that sexuality is socially constructed and thus understandable in historical, rather than purely biological terms. Another change is a greater availability of records. Because researchers have made their interests known, because donors have saved records, because lesbian and gay community archivists have convinced donors that their gifts can be used, in Joan Nestle's words, to give life, new histories can be written.

I plead with all who care for the full rich story of our human history to help us open the archives and research institutions to the full complexity of people's lives, remembering to be inclusive of sexual minorities as well as ethnic, racial, religious, and political minorities. I make a special plea to archivists. When the documents have been collected, process and index them as fully as anything you value. Remember, when appropriate, to use the fearsome words *lesbian* and *gay* and *homosexual*. When the issue is unclear, give us clues such as "female friendships," "Boston marriages," and "cross-dressing images." Name the unnameable as much as is historically accurate from the evidence in front of you. (There have been instances of men and women who lived together but were not heterosexually active with each other. Sometimes they were just good friends or both were gay and sought to head off social and familial criticism. The point is: Never assume anything without solid evidence.)

As for collections that already contain lesbian or gay information, remember—please—that while individual privacy and confidentiality may be of paramount concern while the individual lives, a full disclosure of deceased individuals' history can do little harm and yet add much to the lives of others.

Those of us who care about opening access and those of us who abhor historical censorship in all its forms share a need to inform each other when we hear of instances of censorship, especially of efforts to close archival collections after the death of the collection's creator and against that person's wishes.

6 Privacy Rights and the Rights of Political Victims: Implications of the German Experience

Elena S. Danielson

When repressive regimes collapsed in Eastern Europe, Africa, and Latin America during the 1980s and 1990s, the demand to open police files filled with private information had international support from the human rights movement and carried a certain moral imperative. Coping with the demand has resulted in a number of methods for balancing the need for justice and the right to privacy. Some countries established "truth commissions," while others attempted to establish special courts of inquiry with trusted judges.

The German experience is instructive and has implications for the use of what can be termed the "archives of repression" in a way that successfully validates the rights of victims to know their fate and at the same time makes an effort to preserve their right to privacy. The files were consciously used to create a basis of extrajudicial justice for a society in transition. While the German system was an exception in Eastern Europe, its policy of openness has proven to be an effective method of transitional justice. It almost did not happen. During a confused moment in history, a relatively small number of activists were able to formulate and implement a legal structure to meet the demands from widespread but diffuse citizens' groups.

The Background of the German Policy

As the Berlin Wall fell in 1989–1990, the German Democratic Republic and the Federal Republic of Germany united with great speed and utter confusion. The records of the East German State Security Service

(*Ministerium für Staatssicherheit,* called the MfS or Stasi) were at first neglected by West German authorities preoccupied with the seemingly hopeless task of steering monumental changes that were beyond any governmental control. The Communist security apparatus continued to operate after the fall of the Wall, and party loyalists ran shredding machines around the clock in an effort to destroy incriminating evidence from forty years of intelligence-gathering activity. The shreds, which were saved, actually filled 15,587 mail sacks. In the power vacuum, East German dissidents and some more politically mainstream citizens invaded the Stasi headquarters in Berlin on 15 January 1990 to halt the destruction of records by Stasi functionaries. Certainly the dissidents wanted to preserve the evidence of the fallen regime's oppression for historical reasons. On a more personal level, they also wanted to know exactly who had been reporting the adverse information about them that had affected their jobs, personal freedom, and basic aspects of their lives.[1] The long-term implications of these spontaneous actions only became apparent later.

A remarkable group of people had protested against the repressive German Democratic Republic without any realistic hope of success. In general, German dissidents proved far less aggressive than their counterparts in Poland and the Soviet Union. When the regime fell, ordinary German citizens seemed as surprised as the experts. Quite unexpectedly, a host of fundamental questions had to be resolved. The disposition of the Stasi files was one of many political issues under intense debate. The national archives of West Germany, known as the *Bundesarchiv,* advocated the consistent application of West German archival policy. This plan would have closed the Stasi archives for thirty years, except for privileged government access. Personal files would be closed for longer periods, typically thirty years after the individual's death. This thirty-year rule had been standard practice in West Germany for decades, having been codified in the nation's 1969 archival law. Chancellor Helmut Kohl also adamantly expressed his opposition to opening the files.

Much happened in 1990 during the months between the fall of Communism and unification. Despite the heroic work of the January 15 citizens' groups to save the Stasi archives, the hastily assembled Control Commission for the Dissolution of the Ministry of Security advocated complete destruction of the records, largely out of fear that they would be exploited by the West German intelligence service and its allies, including the CIA. This reasoning was based on the privacy argument, and on the fear that closing the files would not sufficiently protect the information. The concerns were not exaggerated, for in fact the CIA did surreptitiously acquire substantial sets of Stasi records in the course of those confusing days. The privacy argument also masked the fact that the Control Commission promoted the interests of the former Communist regime and was anxious to obliterate the record of its misdeeds. The democratically elected East German prime minister declared that opening the records would usher in an era of politically motivated murder and manslaughter. In effect, he invoked a security argument. His motivation may well have been mixed, as later developments implicated him in unsavory collaboration with the Stasi. In both east and west, persuasive voices advocated actually destroying the files for a third reason. They worried about the debilitating burden of coping with the recent past. In fact these three arguments at first persuaded the interim East German democracy simply to do away with the most troubling records of the Communist era. They began with the electronic security files, which were erased on the orders of the advisory Round Table in February of 1990. Already doubts existed about the wisdom of obliterating history. In something of a panic, a partially successful secret effort was made to duplicate the electronic files on diskettes prior to the official erasure. The doubts increased as disturbing news was reported in the press.

In March of 1990, rumors began circulating about Stasi collaborators. One dissident named Ralf Hirsch was accused of having Stasi connections by a political opponent. With great difficulty, Hirsch succeeded in examining his files even though no clear procedures for allowing access existed. His documents were stamped "very uncooperative," a badge of honor for him that now vindicated his career. "If I hadn't got access to the file, I would have been finished," he observed in a *New York Times* interview on 28 October 1990. "I could have gone out with a noose and hung myself." Evidence of tampering with the historical record added more pressure. Bärbel Bohley, an important dissident, reported that an anonymous caller offered to sell her the Stasi file kept on her activities. Most telling was the case of Wolfgang Schnur, the leading Christian Democratic candidate for the March 18 elections. Stasi records revealed conclusively that he had served for many years as a Stasi collaborator. Schnur's political career was damaged by accurate documentation, not by rumors or by blackmail with secret information as happened in other post-Communist regimes. The need for preserving the files became very clear.

As a result of these developments, the debate in the first freely elected East German parliament, the *Volkskammer* (in power from March to October 1990) soon took a radically different turn. A consensus began to form in favor of using the files to uncover the truth about recent history. Once elected to the *Volkskammer,* an outspoken pastor from Rostock, Joachim Gauck, was unwavering in his advocacy of openness. To the surprise of the establishment, his views prevailed. Against all odds, it became clear within five years of opening the files to victims that Gauck's policy had substantially helped Germany come to terms with the past. In fact, despite great problems, Germany has coped more successfully than the other post-Communist governments that have continued to keep police files tightly restricted under the guise of privacy protection. In the process, a new level of freedom of information was tried, tested, and proved to be an effective tool of democratization.

The results have implications for other countries with agencies that accumulate adverse information on the private lives of their citizens. The historian William G. Rosenberg makes a convincing case that the obvious ethical problems surrounding the release of archives from Communist regimes have a more universal, if less obvious, significance for state archival systems in other countries as well, including democracies. Throughout recent history, the sentiment that people have a right to know the truth about their lives seems to be gaining momentum. It appears in many settings internationally, but most prominently when basic human rights have been violated and when privacy has been invaded by surreptitious surveillance.[2] Simultaneous with this trend, unprecedented acts of terrorism have justified the need for increased monitoring of private communications. The two competing tendencies have yet to achieve a legal balance. The recent German experience with the Stasi Records Act is a positive story with practical implications on finding this balance. Its success can be seen in the details of the legal structure that was established to ensure implementation.

The Stasi Records Act

The Stasi Records Act of 20 December 1991 was greeted initially with great skepticism. It was passed by the united German Parliament with the insistent urging of Joachim Gauck. Bypassing the West German *Bundesarchiv,* the legislation placed the State Security Service records of the former German Democratic Republic in the custody of the Parliament, which was charged with appointing a federal commissioner to administer this particular set of records. Stringent German security and privacy laws would not apply. Most crucially, the law provided for immediate access by victims of political persecution to their own records. As noted above, this unprecedented access reflected the consensus reached in the summer of 1990 by the *Volkskammer.* On 24 August 1990 the *Volkskammer* passed legislation to open the Stasi archives to victims. A major obstacle almost blocked this legislation: the jurisdiction of the *Volkskammer* was unclear, as the body was soon to be superceded by the unified German parliament.

Since so many public figures in both East and West Germany wanted to consign this legislation to the area of benign neglect and to let restrictive West German law apply instead, the initial draft of the unification treaty of 31 August 1990 simply ignored the access demanded by the dissidents. Activists responded quickly. On September 4, they occupied the Stasi archives in building seven of the huge Ministry of Security complex in Berlin and publicized the missing part of the treaty. Some held a hunger strike. There were press releases, folk concerts, and all the classic techniques of grassroots demonstrations. Banners proclaimed slogans such as "To each his file" and "Occupied—The Files Belong to Us." It took hundreds of thousands of demonstrators marching in the streets to bring down the regime in 1989. A much smaller group of activists, probably a few dozen, pressured the government to reaffirm the legislation from 24 August 1990 in a special addition to the unification treaty. The wording specifically addressed the rights of individuals to obtain access to their files. It also advocated the right to privacy for third parties. Significant attention was paid to blocking access to the information for intelligence purposes by other unspecified security services. People whose private lives had been secretly recorded by adversaries were especially sensitive to the potential abuse of the information collected by the Stasi if it fell into the hands of the West German, Soviet, and American security services. Wolfram Kempe, one of the participants, explained: "On September 28, 1990, the Occupation of the Stasi headquarters ended. Without it the unification treaty would be somewhat shorter . . . thousands of people would not have had the opportunity to see their own files and to find out whether their friends or relatives denounced them. And the informants would be vulnerable to blackmail with secrets of the old regime for recruitment by other secret services."[3]

On 3 October 1990, Joachim Gauck was designated as the federal commissioner to oversee the administration of the files. The preservation of the files thus found a strong advocate with a clear concept of how to administer them in order to balance the right to information and the right to privacy. In the confused aftermath of unification, many basic miscarriages of justice occurred simply from a lack of coherent leadership. The Stasi files could easily have been destroyed, as some were, or completely restricted in the name of privacy during the lifetime of those affected by them. Gauck and a relatively small number of activists prevailed against the odds for two reasons: they were able to pull together a feasible plan for implementation, and they represented a groundswell of popular opinion.

Under Part One, Section One of the 20 December 1991 Stasi Records Act that regulated the purposes and scope of the legislation, both the right to know the truth about one's personal history and the right to privacy were addressed. Since these two principles are sometimes seen as contradictory, it is worth considering the exact language as translated by the Gauck Authority:

> This Act regulates the custody, preparation, administration and use of the records of the Ministry for State Security of the former German Democratic Republic and its preceding and succeeding organizations (State Security Service) in order to
>
> 1. facilitate individual access to personal data which the State Security Service has stored regarding him, so that he can clarify what influence the State Security Service has had on his personal destiny;
> 2. protect the individual from impairment of his right to privacy being caused by use of the personal data stored by the State Security Service;
> 3. ensure and promote the historical, political, and juridical reappraisal of the activities of the State Security Service;
> 4. provide public and private bodies with access to the information required to achieve the purposes of this Act.[4]

Of these four provisions, the most urgent at the time that the legislation was drafted involved the immediate need for victims' rights to their personal history. The law also allowed government access to the files so that it might evaluate the suitability of job applicants and screen out former spies and informants from public jobs. A very strongly felt consensus emerged among the former dissidents that those who had benefited from a morally compromised regime should not be placed in positions of trust and should not teach the next generation in the public schools. The right to know and the right to privacy were reconciled by eliminating the basic principle of equal access to files that contain personal data. Victims viewed their own files but could not access those of others. Copying was allowed, and much information eventually entered the public domain. Legal ordinances regulated the fees involved and varied depending on the type of inquiry. Victims paid substantially less than former Stasi employees for photocopies, for example. The letters sent in response to applications for access provided very precise citations to the applicable legal paragraphs.

While protecting the privacy rights of the victims and of third parties, a very specific and well–thought-out exception was made to German privacy law, or *Datenschutz*. Unlike the provisions of the American Privacy Act of 1974, the Stasi Records Act enabled victims of spying to have nearly complete access to the identity of those who informed on them. Not only was information that enabled the victims to identify code names made available to the researchers, but the staff of the archives actively assisted with the decoding of pseudonyms.

It is worth quoting the exact language of the law:

Section 13 (5)

If code names of employees of the State Security Service who gathered or evaluated personal data regarding the data subject, or names of their officers, together with particulars which make it possible to positively identify these employees, can be found in the existing prepared records which the data subject has inspected or for which he has obtained duplicates, the names of such employees shall be provided to the data subject at his request. Sentence 1 shall also apply to other persons who informed on the data subject in writing, if the contents of their reports were written in such a way as to be detrimental to the data subject. The interest of employees and informers in keeping their names secret shall not rule out disclosure of their names.

Many experts warned that the dissidents would not be able to cope with the truth about their personal histories. There were some dire predictions that the fragile social fabric would be torn beyond repair. Now that most citizens have had the opportunity to find out their histories, it can be safely determined that the opening of the files was beneficial to individuals and to German society. If it were not for the quick action of a small group of citizens in September 1990, it is unlikely that the good intentions of the *Volkskammer* would ever have been implemented.

Ten years after the passage of the Stasi Act, the files continue to be a source of controversy. In 2000, Gauck stepped down to make way for a new commissioner, a member of the Green Party named Marianne Birthler. She has also championed the opening of records of historical interest in the face of serious opposition and legal challenges from both of the main political parties. Birthler makes a distinction between the privacy rights of public figures and ordinary citizens. Like her predecessor, she interprets the law as granting ordinary citizens a higher degree of protection than celebrities and political figures who deserve more scrutiny because of their public role. The arguments for and against this interpretation are given full play on a lively Web site.[5]

One aspect of the law has been vindicated during the past decade. The ability of victims to learn the identity of informants has strengthened rather than weakened the democratic process. Even opponents concede that a great service was done by revealing the truth, no matter how inconvenient. This is the conclusion of British journalist and historian Timothy Garton Ash, who published a diary-like narrative tracing the process of reading one's file and reliving events that were being observed and recorded.[6] It is a book that every archivist should read. Garton Ash, unlike most victims, sought out the informants and confronted them to discover their motivations. In this confrontation with a notorious system, he found his informers fundamentally ordinary, venal perhaps, or jealous, but not especially evil. The people who spied on him were polite, punctual, and orderly. They assembled information that was shared through a database with the Soviet KGB and is no doubt available to Russian intelligence. At the end of the narrative, Garton Ash meditates on the British intelligence services MI5 and MI6 and wonders: how similar and how different are the files of repression in a totalitarian state and in a democratic country?

Garton Ash's other books have explained the dynamics of repression and resistance throughout the last twenty years of the Communist era in Eastern Europe. The regimes could not have survived as long as they did without such repressive internal spying and the files that this activity required. Garton Ash interviewed the Gauck Authority archivists about the experience of other readers. There were a few divorces when people learned that spouses had informed on their most private conversations, and sadly some suicides occurred because of the revelations. The main consequences were endless discussions (private and in the press), encounters with history, and a search for a truthful understanding of the past.

What did it take to accomplish this reconciliation with history? In the first ten years since the fall of the Wall, a staff of over two thousand Gauck employees processed approximately 1.5 million applications from citizens to see their files, sometimes called *habeas data*. Clearly some of the requests turned up no files at all, or only small fragments of information. Other requests involved the lengthy searching and the copying of hundreds of documents. Some applicants waited a year or two—sometimes four or five—but the system worked. To expedite processing, archivists identified the people with very small files and simply mailed them copies, rather than trying to provide reading room service for everyone. In most cases, that package in the mail sufficed. Other cases were more complicated and took a great deal of staff time, such as the files on foreign embassies in Berlin. Much time was devoted to helping influential dissidents, who generated stacks of files that documented intercepted mail, telephone taps, reported conversations, plans for dirty tricks, and similar examples of official malfeasance. On the whole, most people felt liberated from doubts and free to act from a more secure base of knowledge. A typical reaction was, "Now that I know my nephew did not spy on me, I can include him in my will."

In addition, the archivists conducted background checks on another 1.5 million cases for civil service applicants. The Gauck authority supported wide-ranging research that resulted in exhibitions, conferences, books, and dissertations. Archivists took on seemingly impossible tasks, such as the re-assembly of shredded documents. Some 400,000 pages have been pieced back together. In all, it is an impressive record in many ways. Certainly a generous budget helped make these achievements possible, with approximately 200,000,000 DM (roughly $1.32 million) spent annually on the project. Two other key factors included the leadership of the Gauck authority and the professionalism of the staff archivists. The motivation of the employees and the support of the government combined to create a remarkable institution in the history of archives management.

The Experience in Other Post-Communist Countries

Other post-Communist states grappled with the same issues.[7] Only Germany, however, implemented a clear process for ensuring victims' rights through opening the records to those affected. Each country took a different trajectory that reflected the unique political forces at work. Several countries tried to address the problem through the judiciary rather than through an archival authority. In the other post-Communist countries more attention was paid to vetting public officials than to providing people with information on their individual lives. "Lustration" became the term used to describe the process of examining people's pasts in order to determine their suitability for public service in a democracy. Two fundamental flaws in this approach quickly became evident. When closed files are used to determine a civil servant's reliability, the charges cannot be verified. Good careers may be ruined. Politicians with a questionable past are vulnerable to blackmail. In addition, closing the files, except for verifying holders of high public office, means that the pervasive spying and culture of denunciation at lower levels of society remains unexamined.

Czechoslovakia passed a lustration law in 1991 for the purpose of using its files to perform background checks on government officials. Collaborators were disqualified from public office for a period of ten years. This use of the files actually functioned rather well, although Vaclav Havel pointed out the problem of publicly verifying allegations with closed files. Czech legislation in July 1993 formally declared the criminality of the previous Communist regime and the legality of the resistance. An office in the justice department was established and staffed with fifty employees in an attempt to come to terms with the crimes of the Communist period. Without substantial funding and adequate staffing, the system could not provide a widespread sense of reconciliation with the past. Repeated scandals rocked the government throughout the 1990s, often based on unsubstantiated charges about past collaboration. The Czechs established a limited system for citizens to see their files in April 1996, but by then much documentation had been destroyed. The legislation covered only 60,000 files. By the end of the decade, many felt that the limitations and delays simply provided a method to prevent information from surfacing until the statute of limitations had run its course. In Slowakia, the feeling is widespread that the number of competent politicians remained so small that reducing the number even further through the process of lustration would decimate the leadership of the entire country. Access to files by ordinary citizens was not even attempted.

In 1992, Boris Yeltsin tried unsuccessfully to outlaw the Russian Communist Party. He assembled documentary evidence of criminality, but the eventual trial led to inconclusive results. The Communist Party continued to function, and many past acts have not been adjudicated. The same leadership was largely retained through the transition to a post-Communist regime. There is however a process for "rehabilitation" of former political prisoners. The identity of the informers was tightly concealed, according to legislation passed in 1992. In theory, victims who have been formally rehabilitated can see their own files, but those who have not been rehabilitated cannot access the information. An attempt at lustration legislation in 1993 failed. Post-Communist Russian archival law of 1993 has adopted the traditional German *Bundesarchiv* guidelines for closing government papers for thirty years and personal papers for seventy-five years, or basically for the lifetime of the people involved. This law in theory places the records of the security service under the national archives of the Russian Federation. In practice, the successor organizations of the KGB and the Russian Ministry of the Interior still control their records from the Communist era and continue to restrict access. Privacy and security arguments have become stronger over time, and some files that had once been opened subsequently were reclassified.

When Communism abruptly fell in Poland in the summer of 1989, the first non-Communist prime minister Tadeusz Mazowiecki advocated making a break with the past, without looking too closely at historical issues. The files of the Polish secret service remained in the hands of the Communist functionaries much longer than in Germany. An estimated 50 percent of the files were destroyed. In addition, forgeries were introduced into the records, corrupting the files as a reliable source. Because the Ministry of the Interior files were both fragmentary and in some cases misleading, politicians used other methods to come to terms with the past. In 1992, the minister of the interior was asked to check on the background of high officials. He issued a list of sixty-four former agents, including the name of the sitting president. The resulting "war of the files" had a destabilizing effect on the government. A long series of lustration laws were proposed and rejected. Finally, in 1997, a court was established to determine questions of guilt and innocence during the Communist period. Political candidates were required to admit any participation in domestic surveillance. The court would vet these statements. In theory, consequences would occur only if officials lied about the past, not if they openly acknowledged collaboration. It was difficult to find judges willing to serve on such a court. Once in operation, the lustration court seemed to unearth unverifiable documents about politicians running for office in a manner that seemed politically motivated. In 1998, Parliament established an Institute for National Memory to clarify questions concerning the recent past. This institution primarily dealt with broad problems and did not open files for large numbers of individual victims. The lives of ordinary citizens have remained clouded by uncertainty about their former friends and suspicions concerning acquaintances who had betrayed them in the past. It is unlikely that any sense of resolution will be achieved in the next generation.

In Hungary, the new custodians of the security files initially advocated openness on the German model. An examination showed evidence of widespread destruction of files, as well as poorly documented transfers of record groups.[8] Soon a new administrator was appointed who implemented more restrictive regulations to limit access and shield the identity of informers. According to Dr. György Markó, director of the Historical Office of the Security Service, victims of surveillance during the Communist era can request to see copies from their files, but cannot access the originals. Historians can apply for permission to conduct research. When asked whether an American historian could conduct such research, the director responded negatively. The reason provided was that the United States does not have privacy legislation comparable to Hungary. A serious German historian, the director explained, could be allowed to gain access, but not a journalist.

In Romania, a committee was established in 2000 to provide access to the files along the lines advocated by Joachim Gauck. This committee was not provided with the basic staff and offices necessary to implement the parliamentary mandate. The committee members were not even told of all of the locations of the files they were to administer.

The result of the struggles over secret police files in Russia and most of Eastern Europe has been a great deal of contention concerning the basic question: who did what to whom? In many cases, citizens of these countries feel that privacy law has been used to obstruct justice.

The comparison of the German experience with the unresolved quandaries of the other post-Communist countries can be seen as a strong argument for opening files to victims of political oppression. Opening the files is increasingly seen as an act of basic human rights. In Germany, the Gauck Authority used archives as a basis for what essentially constitutes a "Truth Commission." This successful model could be useful for other countries, not just in Eastern Europe, but also in Latin America and Africa. While his program originated in a chaotic grassroots movement, Gauck very carefully drafted clear and effective guidelines into the law. Legislation inspired by the human rights movement has generated a momentum that crosses borders. Standards and expectations of openness are often set by practice. For this reason, there may be implications for American practice as well. A fundamental lesson from the experience of the Gauck Authority was the need to understand the moral ambiguity of the freelance informers. The Germans developed a vocabulary to cope with the different categories of people in a repressive regime.

Victims and Perpetrators in Transitional Justice

"Informer," "spy," "tattletale," "snitch," "fink," "canary": the terms for those who supply private information concerning their acquaintances carry a heavily negative connotation with the general public even when the words derive from underworld slang. Unpopular as these informers have been throughout history, official agencies have gone to great lengths to conceal sources of intelligence. In the nongovernmental sphere, journalists feel strongly about their right to protect their sources. In the East German context, particular attention is paid to the "unofficial co-workers" of the state security apparatus. They are known by the initials "IM" or *Inoffizielle Mitarbeiter,* translated as "unofficial informers." It is felt that the official spies, while pernicious, were doing a job for a salary. The freelance, part-time informers were not paid especially well. The implication is that this group informed on friends and family out of a malicious, even criminal, motivation, or from a primitive urge to do harm. Collaborators carry a heavier moral burden in this view. In general, an estimated one hundred thousand freelance informers were not prosecuted in the newly reunified German state. Several reasons account for this seeming apathy. First, the numbers are too large. Second, their work was legal under the laws of a sovereign state. Interestingly, the revelation of names has not resulted in the massive retaliation that was predicted, but it has effectively limited the informants' ability to profit from the new open society. Borrowing an American concept of "sunshine laws," the truth is simply revealed and society responds. In some sense, the failure of the unified state to punish widespread abuses of trust in the former regime is compensated for by opening otherwise privileged information. It is a form of parliamentary rather than judicial justice, an important component of transitional justice in democratizing societies.

Terms identifying the person about whom confidential information is collected have not been standardized. Typical attempts include the following: "the individual to whom the record pertains," "suspect," "data subject," "victim," "the individual affected," "the person in question," and "the subject of investigation." The Stasi files refer simply to "the object." Before the passage of the Stasi Act, the victims of political informants had not traditionally been given the opportunity to learn the identity of their accusers. The reasons ranged from weighty matters of state security and freedom of the press to bureaucratic self-protection. In German, the term is often given as "those affected" (*die Betroffenen*), as in the sense of adversely affected. The official English version, published by the Gauck Authority, translated this term with the more neutral phrase "data subjects." In the literature, the most frequent term used is *Opfer*, or "victim."

Case studies demonstrate a great confusion between the concepts of the victim and the perpetrator. When the privacy of a suspected perpetrator of a crime is violated, he or she becomes a victim of sorts. If pressed to name accomplices, he or she becomes an informer and another type of perpetrator. The privacy of the informant is protected to prevent retaliation and victimization. The informant may be acting out of malicious motives and may supply false information in the role of a perpetrator. The informant may be blackmailed into reporting on friends and simultaneously be victim and perpetrator. Again in the German context, special note is made of those who benefited from the whole apparatus of informing on acquaintances. Those who benefited are *die Begünstigten*, translated into English as the rather confusing "beneficiaries." Instead of distinguishing between victim and perpetrator, the

Germans have made a distinction between those who were harmed from an officially sanctioned but criminal system, and those who benefited. Third parties form the other recognized category whose privacy rights are addressed. The Stasi Act makes generous provisions for the rights of the victims, but sometimes necessarily protects beneficiaries of the old system. Even perpetrators have rights, according to Gauck. The strength of the legislation lies partly in its judiciousness.

Defining the universe of information that governments need to preserve can be awkward. "Records maintained on individuals" is a term defined in the United States Privacy Act of 1974 (5 U.S.C. Section 552a) as follows:

> The term "record" means any item, collection, or grouping of information about an individual that is maintained by an agency, including, but not limited to his education, financial transactions, medical history, and criminal or employment history and that contains his name, or the identifying number, symbol, or other identifying particular assigned to the individual, such as a finger or voice print or a photograph.

The sources of these records are left unexplained. The most important ethical issue is basically ignored. In the East German case, the text makes it explicitly clear that the records include "personal data collected by deliberate, including secret, information-gathering or spying."

A Few Historical Notes

While the Stasi case may be extreme, the situation of spies compiling adverse information on suspects has a long tradition in the history of police files. Maintaining files on such suspects as murderers and thieves with intelligence gathered from informants can easily be justified for the well-being of society. Few would deny the basic justification for a state intelligence and security service. The situation becomes more convoluted when a police apparatus is used to enforce religious or political conformity and when the guardians of the rights of citizens are perceived as violating those rights themselves. Spies were certainly known in antiquity, but not until the development of consistent recordkeeping was it possible to track individuals' casual remarks for reliability.

In many cases, the archives of repression have survived to provide grist for serious research. The Italian historian Carlo Ginzburg made very good use of extensive records to understand the belief structure of literate peasants during the Counter-Reformation. In the sixteenth century, the Roman Inquisition enforced a code of law. Like the Spanish

Inquisition, it used a vast system of records that have largely survived. The court was charged with the enforcement of religious dogma and required an elaborate system of monitoring and recording acts of heresy, and it used forced confessions and denunciations. Verbatim records were kept by a notary, including testimony produced by the defendant undergoing the then-common judicial procedure of torture. Denunciations made by neighbor against neighbor fueled the system, enforcing conformity of belief. Unlike contemporary organized crimes, which the perpetrators take care not to record, political and religious persecutions are characterized by detailed files. [9]

While dogmatic conformity enforced by a culture of denunciation was common in Western Europe by the sixteenth century, it was in Eastern Europe with its fragmented ethnic mosaic that repression became an essential tool of statecraft. In the history of the German, Russian, and Hapsburg empires, religious uniformity was harder to enforce given the welter of languages and nationalities. Stringent methods emerged. Over the course of the nineteenth century, the issues shift almost seamlessly from religious to political dogma. Police were assigned to track subversive conversations by national separatists in the manner that the Inquisition previously rooted out religious heresy. A complex system of internal passports and residency permits was developed to control the population, and this paperwork required an extensive bureaucracy dedicated to maintaining files of private information on individual citizens.

Throughout the nineteenth century, the tsarist regime in Russia was rocked by a series of increasingly violent attacks on government officials. Terrorism created an environment of fear. The assassination of Tsar Alexander II in 1881 by politically motivated radicals made the need for the security services very plain. The *Okhrana* soon began to open mail, eavesdrop on meetings, and gather files on political activists. Polish nationalists were monitored by the *Okhrana,* and Czech nationalists received attention from the Hapsburg authorities. Secret police activity became more effective at the end the nineteenth century as typewriters and modern filing systems made it easier to monitor the activities of subversives. The files burgeoned. The Russian, German, and French police services shared information then, as they sometimes do now.

In the Russian Revolution of 1917, common people rushed to the *Okhrana* offices to burn files that tracked their movements and casual conversations. By 1918, the successful revolutionaries established their own political police, the *Cheka,* roughly modeled on the old tsarist *Okhrana.* The Bolsheviks were even more dedicated to maintaining files on citizens than their predecessors had been. By the 1930s, the Russian

NKVD and German *Gestapo* competed with each other in vigilance. Germans experimented with American-designed punch cards to facilitate the recordkeeping work, which became an obsession.

Once the Red Army defeated Nazi Germany and took over the eastern sector of the country, the two traditions merged in the development of the Communist German state. Feliks Dzerzynskii, founder of the Soviet *Cheka*, was a hero, and his portrait could be found in all of the Stasi offices until 1989. The compounding of German and Soviet file mania can be seen in the sheer mass of files maintained: about 180 kilometers of files, 360,000 photographs, 600,000 negatives, and more than 40,000 file cards. Hundreds of sacks of shredded documents that were found in offices have been labeled, and efforts are being made to piece the shreds back together in legible form. The number of official Stasi employees in 1989 has been calculated as about 91,000 official agents and another 174,000 freelance informers in a population that totaled only 16.4 million. The Russian KGB in 1990 had one employee for every 595 Soviet citizens. The ratio of Stasi employees to citizens has been estimated at 1:180.[10] Files were kept on approximately four million citizens and two million foreigners. Essentially every East German family was affected. Even among Communist countries, the East Germans were credited with developing the most intensive domestic surveillance system in history. When the United States seized the Iraqi security service files, which had been secured by the embattled Kurdish political groups, various East German materials were found mixed in the documentation, probably evidence of an advisory role. Globalization has compounded the complexity of these archival issues.

Globalization of Archival Issues Relating to Files of Repression

From 1993 to 1997, a panel of experts assembled by the International Council of Archives (ICA) analyzed the issues posed by the surviving security services files of the collapsed repressive regimes in Spain, Portugal, Greece, Eastern Europe, Latin America, and Africa. Their report to UNESCO is still one of the best and most succinct outlines of the practical problems involved.[11] They examined the situation in twenty-five countries and were able to gather systematic data on thirteen of these. The range of responses was very broad. Some countries had no written records, but in most cases the records were created out of the necessity to control domestic unrest. In many countries, the records could not be found. Others were openly destroyed. In a few cases, the records were kept for a brief period of judicial review prior to destruction. In most cases, where the files were preserved, they have been maintained as heavily restricted records. Germany appears to have been the most open and most meticulous nation in handling the documentation, but only, as can be seen by the historical sketch, due to the insight and tenacity of a small group of activists.

ICA's UNESCO report makes recommendations for legislation to provide a more consistent legal framework for records access. The main recommendation involves the right to obtain information on the existence of "personal information in whatever form, providing always that the privacy of third parties is guaranteed." As is often the case, this recommendation is self-contradictory. The wording seems to preclude the disclosure of informants' names, along the lines of the American Privacy Act and the Russian rehabilitation rules. The recommendations obliquely make provisions for individuals to obtain special permission to see their own files and provide an opportunity for them to answer allegations that they consider false, along the lines of American credit reports. It does not mandate the massive program initiated by Gauck in Germany. Another area where the report diverges from the Gauck model is its insistence that these records belong to the national archives of the successor state. The report does make allowances for a specialized agency to handle the records on an interim basis if necessary. It also includes a draft Code of Ethics, which describes the process of protecting third-party privacy by copying, redacting, and recopying files as practiced under the U.S. Freedom of Information Act and to a lesser degree by the Gauck Authority. Implementation of this kind of legislation would be very expensive and beyond the means of most underdeveloped countries and emerging democracies.

The UNESCO report represents real progress in comparing the practices in different transitional regimes. Although the report did not aim to provide a single set of regulations that would apply in all cases, its one consistent point is the need to preserve such files after the collapse of a repressive regime, as occurred in Poland, or during the gradual transformation and democratization of the country, as happened in Spain. In most of these situations, there has been a strong desire to destroy the incriminating records of the past and to make a fresh start. It can be assumed that former operatives of the old regime will attempt to destroy evidence. In most of the cases examined, such efforts succeeded to some extent. Historical experience shows that the new, more democratic regimes often prefer not to cope with the burden of the past and that destruction of the historical record is a strong temptation. In Greece, the police files of the previous repressive regime were used to verify restitution claims and then were destroyed to prevent their later misuse. The loss to Greek national history is immeasurable. During times of turmoil, basic guidelines such as the UNESCO proposals can be of great practical utility in tipping the balance in favor of preservation.

The UNESCO report remains tacitly skeptical of the use of the files as a form of an extrajudicial truth commission. It does not advocate allowing hundreds of thousands of victims to see their files and to learn the identity of their accusers. In Europe there is a trend to harmonize privacy laws along the lines of a thirty-year closure for most state records and a seventy-five-to-eighty-year closure for records containing personal information. There is no doubt that this model has been used to obscure the criminal past of many paid and unpaid agents from earlier regimes. Very little operative difference exists between destroying files and closing them for the lifetime of those affected. The countries that invoked privacy to cover up widespread denunciations in fact lost credibility with the public and underwent more turmoil and political instability than Germany did with its policy of openness. As technology and legislation enhance the ability to gather information, citizens will increasingly wish to view such information.

Archives have long been used as evidence in judicial proceedings. In cases where the injustice has been systemic, jailing every perpetrator is simply not feasible. Archivists can use the records in the process of establishing the basic historical truths and accurate personal histories. Special legislation is required in these cases, along with a realistic sense of program costs and an understanding of the care required in administration. Another essential factor in the credibility of the Gauck Authority has been largely missing from the administration of the privacy acts in the United States and other countries. Gauck widely circulated the forms for requesting access to one's files, both in paper and on the Web. Posters announced the availability of the service. Lecture series, open house days, and traveling exhibits familiarized the public with the program. Average German citizens have the impression that the authorities want them to know as much as legally possible about data collected on them as individuals, as well as about the politicians for whom they vote. The concepts of lustration and *habeas data* are linked. The archivists consider this work essential to a democracy and convey this message consistently. Not everyone is happy with the results, but the general legitimacy of the effort has been vindicated. The countries that did not make this effort have yet to recover from the effects of the past.

Conclusion

The German experience makes it very clear that archives play a role in transitional or extrajudicial justice. Preserving and then opening security files of repressive regimes to the subjects builds confidence in the democratic process and creates a sense of justice even in cases beyond the reach of the courts' formal jurisdiction. The other post-Communist regimes that restricted security files by using justifications of privacy or security continue to wrestle with basic issues of legitimacy. In a global situation of shifting borders, changing notions of sovereignty, and unclear jurisdiction, past injustice can sometimes be best addressed by opening records and providing a truth commission or forum for discussion. The individual situation should be looked at carefully. Joachim Gauck was correct on both a theoretical and pragmatic level to honor the rights of victims of anonymous informants. In such cases, it is a great mistake to try to define the role of archives according to narrowly traditional rules. Procedures can be designed that reconcile privacy rights and the right to information about one's life and one's national history.[12]

7 Ethical Issues in Constructing a Eugenics Web Site

Martin L. Levitt

On 11 February 2000, the Dolan DNA Learning Center, an educational division of James D. Watson's[1] Cold Spring Harbor (CSH) Laboratory, made available on the World Wide Web a new site devoted to the history of eugenics (http://www.eugenicsarchive.org/eugenics/). (See figure 1.) The construction of the site was made possible by a grant given by the Ethical, Legal, and Social Issues (ELSI) Program of the National Human Genome Research Institute. The site, intended both as a teaching tool and a catalyst for discussion, raised issues about the ethical use of controversial archival materials in a virtual exhibit. To understand the nature of these issues, it remains important to remember the eugenics movement, and to revisit briefly its history.[2]

Sir Francis Galton (1822–1911) was a British anthropologist and statistician especially interested in human intelligence. Galton coined the word "eugenics" to describe a new "science" dedicated to the prospect of improving the quality of the human species through the manipulation of the gene pool. By encouraging mating among those people with desirable characteristics (such as higher intelligence or physical superiority), eugenicists maintained that gradually these characteristics would permeate the general population. Though he coined the term eugenics in 1883 to describe his ideas, Galton and his colleagues later became aware of apparent connections to the nascent science of genetics, from which they borrowed such ideas as pedigree analysis. These early eugenicists

---

A version of this paper was originally delivered at the Society of American Archivists 65th annual meeting, Washington, D.C., 30 August 2001, in a session titled "Ghosts in the Closet: Controversial Data, Ethical Quandaries."

Image Archive on the American Eugenics Movement

Dolan DNA Learning Center
Cold Spring Harbor Laboratory

SEARCH the Archive
Click here to enter the Archive image database.

Virtual Exhibits
The buttons below link to essays (using the *Flash Player* plugin) that introduce the key events, persons, and social conditions that contributed to the development of eugenics. We suggest you visit these exhibits before searching the images in the Archive. Click here for text-only versions of the virtual exhibits.

- Social Origins
- Scientific Origins
- Research Methods
- Traits Studied
- Research Flaws
- Eugenics Popularization
- Marriage Laws
- Sterilization Laws
- Immigration Restriction

Eugenics Archive grows to 2200+ items

Browse 950 new photos, papers, and data – including extensive collections from noted eugenicists. Discover Francis Galton's work on fingerprint analysis and composite portraiture, and read Charles Davenport's treatise, *Eugenics: The Science of Human Improvement by Better Breeding*, presented in its entirety. Explore Arthur Estabrook's field photos of subjects of his (in)famous studies: *The Jukes in 1915*, *Mongrel Virginians*, and *The Nam Family*. Click the "Search the Archive" button to access the image database.
(New images have ID#s 1255-2320.)

Galton   Davenport   Estabrook

Examine the Chronicle of how society dealt with mental illness and other "dysgenic" traits in the final installment of our website: *DNA Interactive*. Meet four individuals who became objects of the eugenic movement's zeal to cleanse society of "bad" genes during the first half of the 20th century. Then meet a modern-day heroine for an account of mental illness and the lesson it holds for living in the gene age.

The philosopher George Santayana said, "Those who cannot remember the past are condemned to repeat it." This adage is appropriate to our current rush into the "gene age," which has striking parallels to the eugenics movement of the early decades of the 20th century. Eugenics was, quite literally, an effort to breed better human beings – by encouraging the reproduction of people with "good" genes and discouraging those with "bad" genes. Eugenicists effectively lobbied for social legislation to keep racial and ethnic groups separate, to restrict immigration from southern and eastern Europe, and to sterilize people considered "genetically unfit." Elements of the American eugenics movement were models for the Nazis, whose radical adaptation of eugenics culminated in the Holocaust.

Figure 1 The home page of the Eugenics Archive, with explanatory introduction. *Reproduced with permission of the Cold Spring Harbor Laboratory, David Micklos, Executive Director, Dolan DNA Learning Center.*

posited that genetics, and especially its predictive component, seemed to support the scientific plausibility of eugenics. The seminal work of Gregor Mendel established the basis for genetics in a famous paper on pea plant variance. From this work, scientists subsequently codified Mendel's hypotheses as the laws of heredity. Interestingly, Mendel's paper, "Experiments in Plant Hybridization," was published in 1866. The scientific community only rediscovered and began to appreciate the significance of his work thirty-four years later.

Animal husbandry, on the other hand, is the term used to describe the traditional techniques employed to select for certain characteristics in domesticated animal stock, such as horses, dogs, or cattle. Race horse owners, for example, bred the fastest horses to improve the chances of producing more lucrative offspring. While not an exact science, animal husbandry clearly had, over time, successfully changed certain physical characteristics of domesticated animals. Eugenicists asserted that breeding for desirable characteristics could be as effective and useful for humans as it had been for domesticated animals.

Eugenics, therefore, began to coalesce around the first decade of the twentieth century. It arose in part from Mendelian genetics and in part from experimental animal husbandry. Conflated with ideas of social Darwinism and inextricably entwined with racial and ethnic stereotypes, eugenics embraced both scientific pretensions and applied social theory. Eugenicists argued that the application of techniques associated with genetics and breeding to humanity would eliminate or mitigate physical and mental defects. Conversely, the same techniques would naturally allow for the selection of desirable characteristics. The eugenicists proved only too willing to define "desirable characteristics" in scientific-sounding, racist jargon. Eugenicists further asserted that biologically superior humans would have a vast social impact. The eugenics movement, which ultimately lent credibility and a patina of scientific endorsement to notions of racial purity during the Nazi era, manifested itself in different ways throughout the world. In the United States, for example, eugenics tended to be "negative." Eugenicists advocated the use of such techniques as sterilization to prevent the "undesirable" from procreating. In Great Britain, a society of more rigid class structures, eugenicists adopted a more "positive" approach by essentially encouraging the "superior classes" to have more children than the "undesirable classes."

In the United States during the first decade of the twentieth century, Charles Benedict Davenport emerged as a prominent figure in the establishment of the American eugenics movement. Davenport was a Harvard-educated zoologist, whose personal ambition and nearly evangelical enthusiasm for eugenics marked him as a leader in the incipient science.

In 1904, Davenport left a promising career as a professor at the University of Chicago to become director of the Station for Experimental Evolution at Cold Spring Harbor, on the bucolic north shore of Long Island. There, Davenport, funded first by the Carnegie Institution of Washington, and later by wealthy railroad heiress Mrs. E. H. Harriman, recruited like-minded poultry breeder Harry H. Laughlin to establish the Eugenics Records Office (ERO).

The ERO created data collection forms, published material meant to popularize and gain public support for eugenics, and perhaps most importantly for archivists, collected data. Some data arrived unsolicited, but the ERO acquired most through the efforts of student "field work." The ERO's field workers targeted such diverse groups as albinos and the Amish community in Pennsylvania. Armed with "trait books," they went forth to study groups of juvenile delinquents, the feeble-minded, and the criminally insane. The eugenicist's notions of inherent intellectual and moral differences among ethnic and racial groups invariably were "documented" and "corroborated" by data collection techniques both subjective and predisposed to bias. The data collected by the field workers, and later reviewed at Cold Spring Harbor, included family pedigrees, medical histories, and interviews. Much of this material now reposes at the American Philosophical Society in Philadelphia.

The public relations arm of the ERO sponsored "fitter family" contests in which families were judged for their superior characteristics, and it employed traveling exhibits in such venues as state fairs to bring the message of eugenics to a broader popular audience. (See figure 2.) The ERO quickly became the mouthpiece of racist and anti-immigration groups, as eugenicists advanced the notion that such social problems as poverty, crime, alcoholism, prostitution, and insanity resulted from the perpetuation of "bad genes." Eugenics also appealed to many educated Americans as the scientific basis for a program of progressive social engineering and a humane solution to many of the thorniest problems of the human condition. Therefore, for a good part of the first half of the twentieth century, eugenics had a rather broad appeal and a good deal of mainstream support. Eugenics only came to be generally discredited following the revelations of Nazi atrocities justified by eugenical advancement.

Recently, eugenics-related issues have acquired renewed relevance. In the light of the Human Genome Project (HGP), which began in 1990, as well as such technological and scientific achievements as the cloning of mammals, the issues and ethics of manipulating the human gene pool remain unresolved. From a purely mechanical standpoint, much of the technological infrastructure necessary to implement a sophisticated program approximating eugenics is materializing. The HGP seeks to identify

Figure 2 A fitter families exhibit and examination building at the Kansas State Free Fair, 1920. *Reproduced with permission of the American Philosophical Society.*

and map all of the approximately 30,000 genes in human DNA. Undeniably, this project has vastly important implications for medicine, scientific research, and the health industry. ELSI, which funded the eugenics Web site, was conceived as an agency of the HGP designed to address the cultural and ethical issues implicit in this effort. Clearly, the ability to manipulate human genes that will result from the HGP also raises both familiar and new ethical questions. Thus, ELSI conceived the eugenics Web site as a teaching tool and an on-line exhibit that would stimulate classroom discussion about these issues for high school or university students.

Early critical response to the Web site confirmed the predictions of the educators who had participated in its construction. History of science students, ethics classes, high school biology students, and other audiences were often surprised that modern ethical questions related to human gene manipulation had a historical precedent. They began to understand that the capabilities suggested by human gene manipulation in many ways recall the era of eugenics. The archival items selected for on-line exhibition obviously could illustrate how eugenics went astray.

They also served as a means of stimulating classroom conversations about the ethics of today's cutting-edge research in the life sciences. In a high school class, for example, an educator might initiate a discussion of the ethical implications of the HGP by observing that the same technology potentially responsible for providing a means to eliminate genetically linked diseases, such as Tay-Sachs or sickle cell anemia, could also be used to produce "designer babies" for which the parents have preselected desired physical characteristics.

David Micklos, director of the Dolan DNA Learning Center[3] at CSH, originated the idea of collecting archival examples of the eugenics movement as an on-line exhibit and teaching resource. Initially, Micklos and his colleagues thought that a fairly simple exhibit of some 1,200 archival items with appropriate labels might suffice as a teaching tool. Fears arose among grant reviewers, however, concerning the potential misuse of the exhibited material. Scholars understand that eugenics is a discredited field within mainstream scientific and historical thought. Nonetheless, no shortage of racists, bigots, and other fringe groups might appropriate and exploit these archival exhibits if they were offered without some historical context. Concerns over issues of confidentiality and privacy also quickly surfaced, primarily from an ethical, rather than a legal, perspective. Some of the items to be exhibited, though not medical records in a technical sense, had been gathered by lab-coated workers, often students. The research subjects may well have assumed a medical confidentiality. Indeed, the objects of eugenical research often were poorly educated and may not have understood, or been informed, that eugenical records did not constitute medical records. Some of the archival exhibits used relatively recent material from the 1930s, and it seemed possible that some subjects might still be living. Moreover, the defamatory nature of some eugenics records, and the family association with certain eugenical deductions, made it altogether possible that an exhibit could potentially harm descendants. (See figure 3.) Another concern involved the potential for the unscrupulously exploitative and unauthorized use of images that depicted human physical defects.

Micklos and his colleagues responded to these critiques by reformulating the grant to include an Editorial Review Panel, which would serve as an advisory board. Comprised of historians of science, scientists, educators, legal scholars, representatives of the handicapped community, and ethicists, the panel was charged with establishing ethical guidelines for the site and with writing much of the required historical context in the form of essays and image captions.[4] A research team from the Dolan DNA Learning Center visited four repositories, including the American

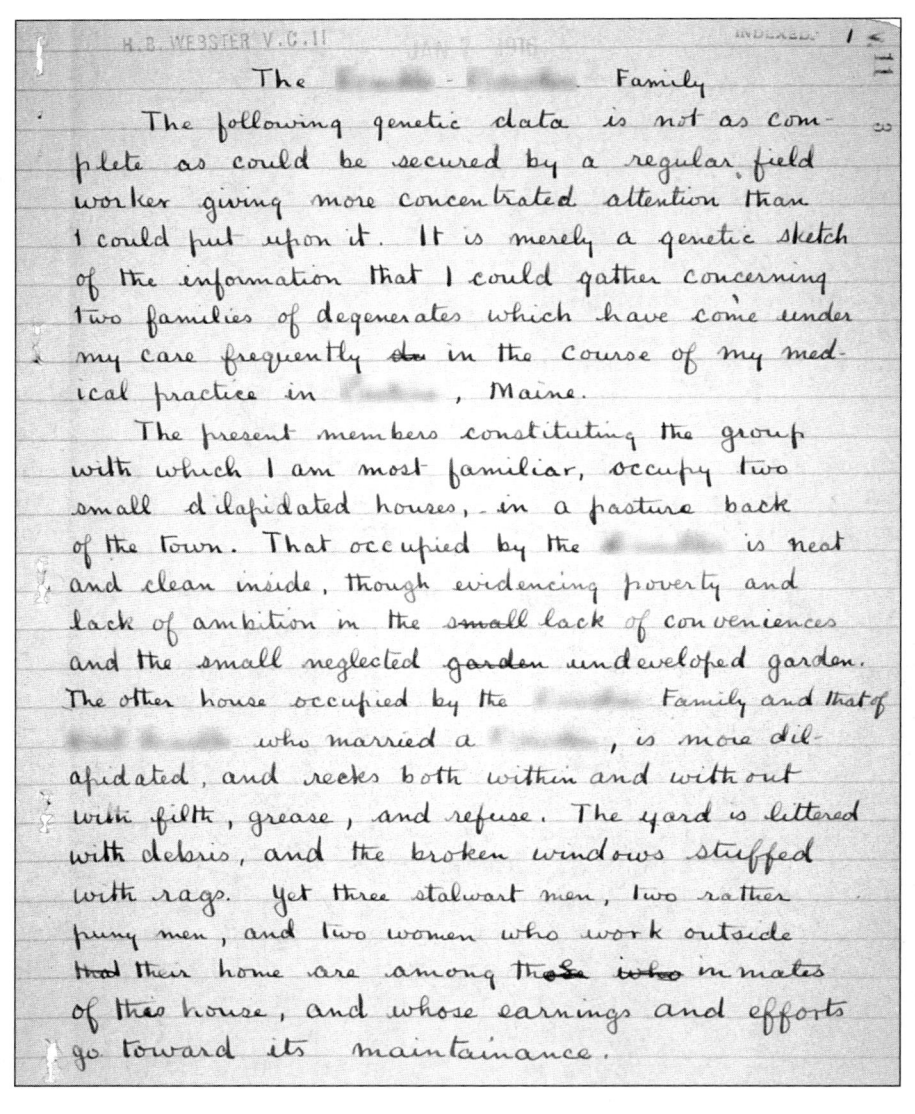

Figure 3 A field report on a certain family from Maine, containing observational data (a "genetic sketch") on a family of "degenerates." Here, to protect the confidentiality of the subjects, we have obscured both the family names and specific geographic locations. *Reproduced with permission of the American Philosophical Society.*

Philosophical Society (APS), Cold Spring Harbor Laboratory Archives, Rockefeller Archives Center,[5] and Truman State University Archives,[6] where they selected and photographed hundreds of items for possible inclusion on the Web site. The team selected items that appeared representative of eugenical thinking, such as pedigrees, evaluations, correspondence of leading eugenicists, photographs of eugenical events, tracts, and propaganda. The APS has perhaps the most extensive collections related to eugenics in the United States. It holds the papers of the Eugenics Record Office, which was started by Davenport at Cold Spring Harbor to develop and collect eugenical data, as well as the papers of the American Eugenics Society, the Charles B. Davenport Papers, and the Frederick Osborn[7] Papers. These four collections alone comprise well over three hundred linear feet of shelf space and are supplemented at the APS by several important but smaller manuscript collections, as well as extensive images and printed materials. The APS, which has a long tradition of acquiring manuscripts relating to the history of science, came to collect eugenics materials by acquiring the papers of Charles Darwin. The Darwin papers created a collection development magnet, attracting new materials related to evolution and Darwin's predecessors, contemporaries, and successors. This emphasis in turn stimulated collecting related to the history of genetics and allied sciences and, as a consequence, eugenics.

Once the document selection team from the Dolan DNA Learning Center had made its research visits, the Editorial Advisory Panel (EAP) convened at Cold Spring Harbor for the first of several meetings to provide context for the images that it had collected. To address the ethical issue of possible misuse of materials mounted on the Web, the EAP solicited nine accompanying essays, essentially geared to an audience of bright high school students, and compiled a suitable bibliography. Experts like Garland Allen of Washington University, Steven Seldon of the University of Maryland, Paul Lombardo of the University of Virginia, and several others crafted thoughtful tracts with such titles as "Social Origins," "Scientific Origins," "Sterilization Laws," "Traits Studied," "Immigration Restrictions," and "Marriage Laws." Each essay opens in its own window and is accompanied by several images with a mixture of photographs and documents. These images carry reference numbers to make them available for searching. Users may also access the archive through twenty-one artificial subject categories including "circus performers," "Mendelian heredity," "poverty and degeneracy," and "sterilization." A shorter essay or theme accompanies each of these categories as well. Pictures in groups appear in frames, with the theme in a left frame and thumbnail prints on the right. Scholars hoped that this variety of accompanying editorial content would stimulate discussion, improve the site as a resource for teaching, and provide the basis for even the most casual visitor to understand some of the issues related to eugenics and the historical significance of the images. The home page carries an introductory statement meant to convey a clear message that the presentation of the images does not constitute an endorsement of eugenics and that eugenics is largely a discredited science. It reads in part:

> We now invite you to experience the unfiltered story of American eugenics—primarily through materials from the Eugenics Record Office at Cold Spring Harbor, which was the center of American eugenics research from 1910–1940. In the Archive you will see numerous reports, articles, charts, and pedigrees that were considered scientific "facts" in their day. It is important to remind yourself that the vast majority of eugenics work has been completely discredited. In the final analysis, the eugenic description of human life reflected political and social prejudices, rather than scientific facts.
>
> You may find some of the language and images in this Archive offensive. Even supposedly "scientific" terms used by eugenicists were often pervaded with prejudice against racial, ethnic, and disabled groups. Some terms have no scientific meaning today. For example, "feeblemindedness" was used as a catch-all for a number of real and supposed mental disabilities, and was a common "diagnosis" used to make members of ethnic and racial minority groups appear inferior. However, we have made no attempt to censor this documentary record—to do so would distort the past and diminish the significance of the lessons to be learned from this material.[8]

The EAP conceded that, even with the accompanying editorial material in place, the possibility remained that fringe groups would misuse the images. At the heart of the decision to go forward was a consensus that the educational benefits of the site outweighed the potential for misuse. By making editorial context part of the site, however, the designers sought to mitigate misuse and make misinterpretation more difficult.

The EAP complemented the extensive use of expert historical context by instructing the site designers to insert a mandatory "use agreement" for researchers, who must click an "I agree" button. Although the essays and a few images are accessible without "signing" the agreement, the search engine and most images cannot be accessed until users agree to the following conditions:

> The images and text in the Digital Archive on the American Eugenics Movement are solely for educational and scholarly uses. The materials may be used in digital or print form in reports, research, and other

projects that are not offered for sale. Materials in this archive may not be used in digital or print form by organizations or commercial concerns, except with express permission.

The potential for misuse still exists, but the EAP concluded that this use agreement might reserve certain legal remedies should misuse occur. More significantly, the panel hoped to alert users that the creators of the site would take the misuse of these images very seriously.

A second ethical concern involved the confidentiality and privacy of the individuals who constituted the subjects of eugenical study, as well as their descendants. The lawyers on the EAP advised their colleagues that, typically, the right to privacy privilege inherent in the doctor-patient relationship ended upon the death of the patient. Due to the age of the documents in question, it seemed likely, though not certain, that the subjects were dead. Even accepting the most conservative assessment of these materials as a kind of medical record, a relaxed position on confidentiality and privacy might be possible. For several reasons, however, the EAP adopted a fairly stringent policy of obscuring subject names in all unpublished documents mounted on the Web site. In certain instances, the editors also suppressed locality information, a rather painstaking process that was accomplished by using Adobe's Photoshop software. The EAP took this step for several reasons.

First, the inclusion of subject names made no substantive contribution to the primary purpose of the site, which involved educating visitors about the history of eugenics and providing an exhibit that would spark classroom discussion about the relationship of science and society. The panel believed, for example, that the presentation of a family pedigree was just as instructive whether or not the subject names were legible. (See figure 4.) Historians naturally worried about the alteration of primary source materials, but were persuaded by the argument that document alterations appear clearly evident and that the source of each document is watermarked on each image page. Any researcher could, if so motivated, find the unadulterated source document in the original archive.

Second, though the material might not meet a strict definition of medical records, much of it had been gathered in such a way that subjects may have *presumed* that the information was confidential. Certainly, case workers often sought the uneducated or the poor as subjects. Thus, it seemed especially likely to the EAP that few subjects would have drawn any distinction between eugenical and medical data. Moreover, although some study subjects could still be alive, it seemed equally troublesome that the nature of the records potentially could embarrass descendants

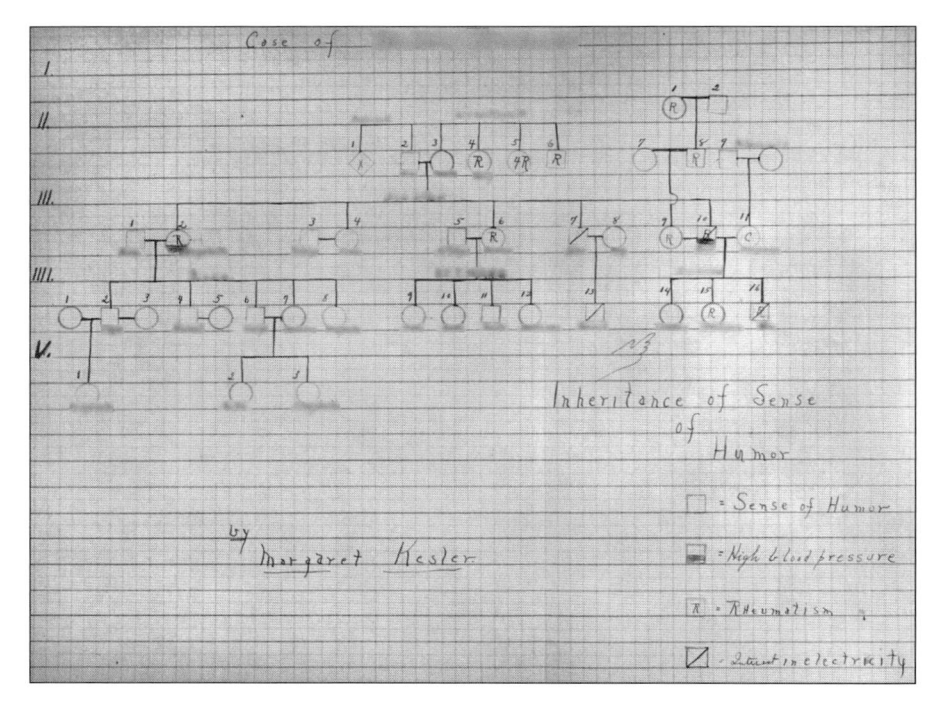

Figure 4 A student pedigree attempting to trace the inheritance of characteristics such as a sense of humor, high blood pressure, and an interest in electricity through five generations. Again, names are obscured. *Reproduced with permission of the American Philosophical Society.*

of subjects. (See figure 5.) A strong sentiment existed that, even if an informant had full knowledge that the collected eugenical data was not confidential, the nature of the data itself could negatively impact relatives who had never been consulted nor given consent.

The original grant specifically prohibited the use of any images of "people under scrutiny" or "individuals who could be construed as human subjects," because of a common-law provision that provides general protection to private individuals from having their images made public without permission. Certain photographs were nevertheless deemed appropriate and legally compliant, and the EAP decided against obscuring faces in unidentified photographic images. One must see, for example, a "fitter family" in order for the images to convey the full impact of the eugenical intent. (See figure 6.) In this case, casual viewers could not identify the people in these images. They did not constitute "human subjects" in the negative context of that concept, and in any

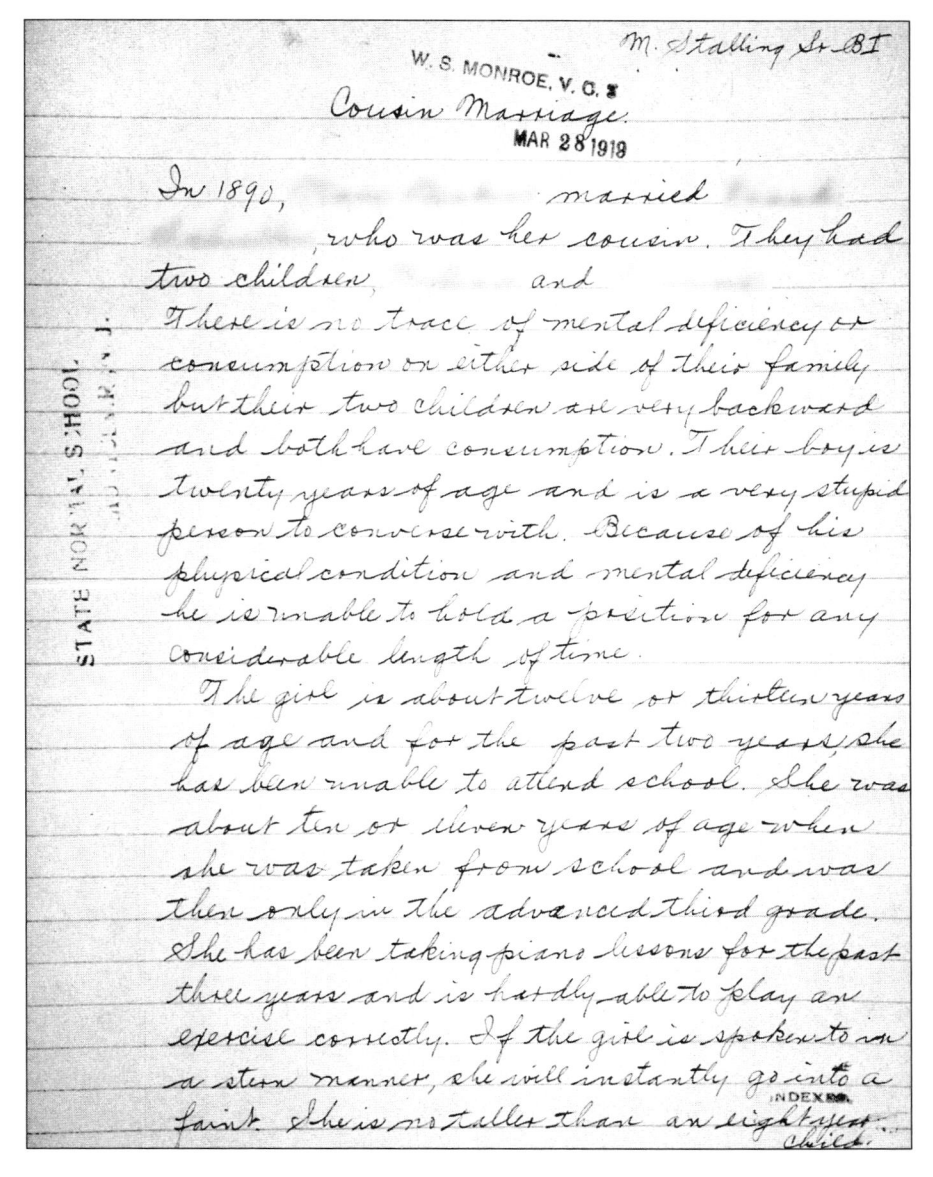

Figure 5 A 1919 student report entitled "Cousin Marriage." The names obscured are both the cousins in question, and also the names of their two children. The children are characterized as "backward"—suffering from "consumption"—and the boy is "a very stupid person to converse with. . . ." *Reproduced with permission of the American Philosophical Society.*

Figure 6 "Large family" winner, Fitter Families Contest, Eastern States Exposition, Springfield, Massachusetts, 1925. *Reproduced with permission of the American Philosophical Society.*

event many of the images had been previously published. The site authors at the DNA Learning Center felt strongly, however, that the original grant restriction, though well intentioned, prevented the inclusion on the Web site of some of the most meaningful and instructive photographs in the collection. They filed a formal request seeking to remove the restriction that prevented the exhibition of such photographs as that of a child pseudonymically called "Buster," who allegedly had been born with "criminal tendencies." The DNA Learning Center staff argued, and the EAP agreed, that such photographs best illustrated "the naïve preconceptions of eugenicists; the dubious measurements made by eugenicists; and the negative light in which some groups were cast by eugenicists."[9] As this article is being written in 2002, ELSI has responded by removing the restriction, and the DNA Learning Center and the EAP will thus shortly add materials previously prohibited from exhibition.

Use of the Web as a means to present controversial material for instructional purposes constitutes a double-edged sword. The Eugenics Archive site has received considerable praise and excellent reviews, and the site clearly has proven useful in a number of classroom settings throughout the nation. E-mail to the site has been overwhelmingly favorable in tone. Nevertheless, the nature of the material, and the potential for its misuse, warrants continuous vigilance and review. To truly appreciate eugenics as an example of science gone awry, and to illustrate eugenical thinking, the site necessarily exhibits what can only be characterized as distasteful materials. The EAP and the DNA Learning Center have made every effort to mitigate the possible misuse of these materials and to place them in their proper historical context. Unfortunately, someone intent on misusing the material probably cannot be prevented from doing so. In this respect, we have gambled that the usefulness of the site, and its potential for teaching, outweighs the possibility of pernicious mischief.

ADMINISTRATIVE PERSPECTIVES

Privacy considerations present formidable administrative challenges for practicing archivists. Every aspect of archival work, from donor negotiations through reference service, requires some sensitivity to questions of confidentiality. Legal restraints and ethical precepts may provide professionals with some basic guidance, but troublesome day-to-day situations typically resist easy resolution. This section draws upon the practical experiences of archivists who have struggled to reconcile the complex and conflicting needs of donors, heirs, families, publishers, attorneys, politicians, researchers, journalists, and repositories. Several themes emerge from the discussion. Some authors emphasize their essential neutrality and highlight their efforts to serve scholarship by negotiating favorable access agreements. They seek to provide donors with an adequate assurance that understandable sensitivities may be addressed through prudent and reasonable restrictions. Ultimately, these archivists seek to permanently preserve a broad and unexpurgated range of research materials that enrich the historical record. Other contributors question the extent to which archivists should assume an activist stance in order to impose restrictions and thereby protect the rights of third parties. Excessive efforts to guarantee privacy occasionally border on censorship, and records professionals may even place their own institutions and themselves at legal risk through arbitrary and overly zealous efforts to serve donor interests. Finally, the discussion underscores the need for the profession to aggressively pursue a more coherent advocacy agenda. Archivists too often have minimal input into records-related legislation and find themselves in a reactionary position, administering confusing and contradictory laws that affect their interests in unanticipated ways. Their flexibility appears limited and legal risks seem unclear as they struggle to satisfy regulatory mandates in a responsible and professional manner. The following articles address these issues from a variety of perspectives.

Sara S. Hodson focuses primarily on privacy and access issues concerning prominent authors and literary manuscripts. She reviews numerous high-profile incidents involving donor restrictions, exclusive access arrangements, and familial threats to destroy records. Modern literary figures and media celebrities appear at the center of many contemporary controversies. Hodson explains several reasons for this phenomenon, which considerably complicates manuscript curatorship. The subjects' very prominence produces a heightened public interest in the most intimate details of their personal lives, especially during the glitzy and tabloid-driven celebrity culture of late twentieth-century America. Archivists who document the lives of the unlettered may face fewer problems on this score. Further, literary collections inevitably contain the subjects' harshly judgmental commentary concerning equally famous colleagues and rivals. The brutal honesty of the documentary record sometimes stimulates heirs and family members to purge and sanitize material to protect reputations and soothe hurt feelings. Copyright also emerges as a major administrative consideration for managing the papers of literary figures, as estates occasionally use intellectual property rights to limit access. In the final analysis, the intense pressure placed upon many manuscript repositories to collect the papers of living authors, and to compete aggressively for contemporary collections, often exacerbates privacy problems and encourages heavy donor-imposed restrictions. Hodson examines these difficult issues and chronicles the administrative implications.

Timothy D. Pyatt explores some of these same problems through the lens of the Southern Historical Collection at the University of North Carolina. He documents the institution's acquisition of the papers of Shelby Foote and Walker Percy, prominent literary figures who shared common literary interests, ties of kinship, Mississippi roots, and a sense of family honor and noblesse oblige that ultimately produced some peculiar curatorial complications. Pyatt provides considerable insight into the tricky process of donor negotiations, illustrating the ways in which family sensitivities at times conflicted with standard institutional policies and generally accepted professional practices. The Foote and Percy Papers forced the repository to confront a wide variety of administrative issues that ranged from aggressive efforts to protect individual reputations to lawsuit threats by an aggrieved third party to an uncomfortable situation that developed when a donor's son was rejected for admission to the university. The Southern Historical Collection managed to resolve these difficulties, and the case study provides archivists with solid practical advice that should help to govern their dealings with donors, estates, and literary agents.

Manuscript repositories seem to generate some of the most interesting administrative controversies involving privacy, but other archival environments also face unique challenges. Sarah Rowe-Sims, Sandra Boyd, and H. T. Holmes review the formidable pressures that faced the Mississippi Department of Archives and History as it began to manage the records of the Mississippi State Sovereignty Commission. The Sovereignty Commission had been established in the 1950s to combat the voting rights movement in Mississippi and to compile investigative and surveillance reports concerning civil rights supporters. Though the commission's records had been ordered sealed for fifty years by the state in the late 1970s, a lawsuit that had been initiated by the American Civil Liberties Union/Mississippi resulted in an agreement to open the records for research in the late 1980s. This presented the archives with conflicting pressures to allow broad public access to journalists and scholars, to satisfy the privacy demands of individuals who had been named in the agency files, and to protect the integrity of the records themselves. The specific challenges presented by the Sovereignty Commission files led the state archives to reappraise its practices concerning privacy-sensitive materials and to establish new procedures that had implications beyond the immediate crisis. Perhaps most significantly, the Sovereignty Commission experience forced the archives to recognize that maintaining a passive approach to recordkeeping does not constitute an administrative option when dealing with modern documentary problems. This lesson, as well as the specific reforms and policies implemented by the Mississippi Department of Archives and History, deserves careful scrutiny by all professional archivists.

Archivists generally celebrate the virtues of access, but Menzi L. Behrnd-Klodt airs a cautionary note by introducing the constraints sometimes imposed by common-law traditions and concepts and occasionally transmitted to the archives at the request of donors who are bound by their own professional obligations. Her specific theme concerns the development of the historic legal privileges within American jurisprudence, with a specific focus on attorney-client privilege. Many archives solicit and maintain lawyers' papers, but not all archivists understand the complications concerning access, ownership, and confidentiality posed by such acquisitions. Behrnd-Klodt discusses the distinctions between privileged and nonprivileged documentation within individual files, reviews debates within the legal profession concerning the duration of the attorney-client relationship, and instructs archivists about the ways in which they can recognize attorney work product materials. She also presents practical advice for archivists, assesses the risks involved in opening lawyers' papers, and explores some solutions that various institutions have developed to satisfy both scholarly and legal demands.

Relatively few laws actually apply to records in nonpublic repositories, but the Family Educational Rights and Privacy Act (FERPA) has plagued academic archivists since its enactment in 1974. Mark A. Greene and Christine Weideman chronicle the confusion and lack of clarity that have clouded this law since its inception.[1] Archivists did not lobby against the legislation, and they proved slow to react. FERPA failed to provide a clear definition of an educational record, and the legislation seemed to imply that student records should be restricted in perpetuity. Some archivists have attempted to clarify legislative intent and receive definitive guidelines from the Family Policy Compliance Office, but the results have proven mixed at best. Greene and Weideman surveyed several colleagues in an effort to gauge current archival practices and understanding of FERPA and found that no professional consensus exists. They also examined some recent judicial decisions, particularly a U.S. Supreme Court case that involved the issue of whether peer grading violated the legislation (*Owasso Independent School Dist. No. 1-011 v. Falvo*, 534 U.S. 426 (2002)). Individual archivists clearly need to remain vigilant and aware of such contemporary court decisions, but the profession also needs to adopt a more aggressive advocacy stance toward legislation involving archival records. For the present, however, as all of the articles in this section demonstrate, archivists must remain comfortable with ambiguity and uncertainty as they craft administrative solutions to the complex array of privacy issues that inevitably intrude into the workplace.

8 In Secret Kept, In Silence Sealed: Privacy in the Papers of Authors and Celebrities

Sara S. Hodson

> The human heart has hidden treasures,
> In secret kept, in silence sealed;–
> The thoughts, the hopes, the dreams, the pleasures,
> Whose charms were broken if revealed.
>
> (*Charlotte Bronte,* "Evening Solace"[1])

Like the human heart with its hidden treasures, collections of modern personal papers often possess personal or sensitive data, kept in secret, sealed in silence. When modern manuscript collections contain personal letters and other writings by those who are still living, such materials can present acutely difficult challenges to the curator or archivist charged with overseeing them. In collecting recently created manuscript material, archival repositories take on the responsibility of properly administering potentially private or confidential material that could, if seen by researchers, violate the privacy rights of a living individual. In the case of both literary archives and the papers of other famous individuals, this potential problem is often exacerbated. This paper will discuss the definitions of privacy, the difficulties of identifying and dealing with private or confidential materials, the competing ethics of providing access while protecting privacy, and the special qualities that make the papers of authors and celebrities a far more difficult administrative challenge for archival professionals than the papers of ordinary people.

The modern concept of privacy, a right to which Americans assume they are entitled, and from which springs the archivist's concern with privacy and confidentiality in collections of modern papers, is a relatively recent addition to the American legal landscape. The first enunciation of privacy rights in the United States came from the 1890 article "The Right to Privacy (the implicit made explicit)" by Samuel Warren and Louis Brandeis.[2] Believing that existing law did not sufficiently cushion individuals against the improper or unwarranted revelation of their private affairs and seeking to combat the propensities of the era's yellow journalists to publish gossip and salacious information, Warren and Brandeis sought explicit protection of individuals' rights to keep private information safe from public exposure. In the more than one hundred years since their article appeared in the *Harvard Law Review*, subsequent definitions and interpretations have elucidated and broadened this right. For example, the legal scholar William Prosser identified four ways in which the invasion of privacy can occur: intrusion upon the individual's seclusion or solitude, or into his or her private affairs; public disclosure of embarrassing or private facts about the individual; publicity that places the individual in a false light in the public eye; and appropriation, for another person's advantage, of the individual's name or likeness.[3]

Any of these invasions of privacy, but especially the first two—intrusion into an individual's private affairs and public disclosure of embarrassing or private facts about an individual—can occur as a result of a manuscript repository acquiring and making available the personal papers of a living or recently deceased person. To what degree should manuscripts curators and archivists be concerned with the possible invasion of privacy by virtue of opening a set of personal papers for research? If such concern is appropriate and justified, what resources exist to provide guidance in identifying sensitive material and deciding whether it safely and wisely may be made available for research?

Conventional wisdom suggests that the right of privacy ends at death, since the dead obviously can no longer be embarrassed by the revelation of personal information. A corollary to this standard tenet acknowledges that modern archives that include the papers of living people do hold the potential for embarrassing those individuals. Even when the creator of a manuscript collection is no longer living, some or even all of his or her correspondents might still be alive and therefore still possess a right of privacy. In fact, the privacy of so-called third parties who may be represented in a collection can be the most worrisome and difficult to address. These third parties had no voice in deciding the fate of the papers and are unlikely to have been consulted about any potential sensitivity in the collection. In addition, archivists must keep in mind that collections of papers contain letters that are, by definition, private communications intended solely for the eyes of their recipient(s), not for viewing and study by researchers or the curious public. Private letters may well reveal sensitive matters or confidential information that is meant solely for a close friend or relative, or for a confidante.

In view of this possibility, how should archivists proceed when dealing with modern papers of persons still living? The Code of Ethics for Archivists, adopted by the Council of the Society of American Archivists in 1992, offers this advice: "Archivists respect the privacy of individuals who created, or are the subjects of, documentary materials of long-term value, especially those who had no voice in the disposition of the materials. They neither reveal nor profit from information gained through work with restricted holdings."[4] The overall ethical tenet is clear: archivists must be aware of, and perhaps take steps to safeguard, the privacy of individuals represented in archival collections. The statement does not provide specific guidance, however, about who will determine what is private, or about what criteria might be appropriate in making such a judgment.

Faced with difficult decisions about identifying sensitive materials, and with only general guidelines to follow, archivists, curators, and their repositories have devised a wide range of policies and practices. At one end of the continuum, many repositories make no effort at all to define privacy. They even-handedly make available all manuscript material, whether by living or dead persons, regardless of the content of the manuscripts. At the other end of the scale, at least one institution has routinely sealed all letters by living individuals, thereby even-handedly guaranteeing protection of the privacy rights of all living persons represented in the collections. This latter institution, the Bodleian Library at Oxford University, England, came under fire for this policy during 1993 and 1994. Eric Jacobs, the authorized biographer of the English author Kingsley Amis, requested copies of Amis's letters that had been housed in the Bodleian. Even after Amis himself requested the copies, the library declined to produce them, citing the policy under which it automatically sealed all letters by living individuals. Ultimately, after considerable unpleasant media attention and lengthy correspondence between Amis and Bodleian officials, the library produced copies for Amis, who promptly turned them over to his biographer.[5]

Few, if any, archivists in the United States would implement such a blanket policy of closure. Unless they and their repositories adhere to a uniform practice of opening everything for research and make no attempt to seal possibly sensitive materials, they will need to devise some policy for governing access to private documents. The most common institutional practice relies on the donor to point out sensitive documents or files. Since the donor typically either created the archive, or is a family member, descendant, or close friend or associate, this approach has the advantage of drawing upon the donor's intimate knowledge of the material at hand and the people, situations, and issues represented in the archive. The donor, armed with this background knowledge, and the curator or archivist, possessing a more detached point of view and awareness of professional ethics and of the law, may discuss or even negotiate what materials in an archive should be sealed, for what reasons, and for how long. Occasionally such negotiations can become intense. Donors often exhibit extraordinary concern about matters of privacy, perhaps in an eagerness to perpetuate or sanitize the good reputation of the creator of the papers. The archivist or curator more typically favors opening the collection and making it freely available to researchers. Once the parties agree on terms of any closure of part or all of a collection, such terms should be written into a deed of gift that is signed by the donor and by a representative of the repository, as a protection for both the donor and the repository.

In agreeing to the terms of restriction that have been requested or recommended by a donor, the curator or archivist must take care that the restriction is fairly and impartially imposed to ensure that the professional ethic of equal access is followed in administering the papers.[6] In earlier days, research libraries routinely implemented inequitable restrictions that had been requested, or insisted upon, by donors. Every institution has its stories of such closures, most or all of which have been quietly corrected in recent decades. According to oft-told tales from the Huntington Library, one manuscript collection had been declared by its donor (a misogynist, we must assume) to be off-limits to women, while another had been sealed to anyone of British descent, and a third could not be seen by Jews, Roman Catholics, or the donor's nephew. Obviously, such restrictions constitute acts of prejudice that lead to inequitable access, in violation of ethical tenets of the library and archival professions.

Similarly, curators and archivists should not acquire, except in extremely unusual circumstances, any papers that carry with them decrees of selective access in which the donor or other designated individual retains the right to decide, on a case-by-case basis, and according to his or her own criteria, who will be able to see the collection. Donors may wish to limit access in order to reserve an archive for the exclusive use of an authorized biographer, or of those who have demonstrated the proper reverence or respect for the papers' creator, or they may simply wish to wield power over the papers and over applicants for the donors' favor. Such selective availability not only contravenes the ethic of free and unfettered access that remains a cornerstone of the archival profession in a democratic society, it can also lead to trouble for both the donor and the curator. Copies of material that have been made available to an authorized researcher, for example, may well fall into the hands of someone who was not allowed to see it. This happened with the famous case of some of the papers of Sigmund Freud, which languished under a double set of restrictions. Anna Freud, the psychoanalyst's daughter, would allow only those whom she trusted to see papers in her possession, while Kurt Eissler, a collector of Freud material, held the reins of access to the Freud Archives that he deposited at the Library of Congress. After Eissler's protégé Jeffrey Masson, who had been given access to the papers, publicly espoused findings to which Eissler objected, he was dismissed from his position as projects director for the Freud Archives. For her part, Anna Freud refused to supply copies of papers to a researcher named Peter Swales, who eventually obtained them anyway, merely by asking a more respected scholar to get them for him. By 1986, Eissler's successor as head of the Freud Archives, Harold Blum, opened all of the papers that had been, or were about to be, published, and he announced that restricted materials would be opened in the near future.[7]

Sometimes, donors must make restriction decisions based upon outside influences, rather than upon their own beliefs or preferences or their own judgment about the sensitivity of the papers. For example, in 1999 the Huntington Library acquired the papers of the Anglo-American author Christopher Isherwood (1904–1986), probably best known for his stories of life in Berlin in the 1930s that were adapted as the musical *Cabaret*. The collection includes the original diaries that Isherwood kept throughout most of his adult life, some of which had been published in expurgated form in 1996.[8] The editor, Katherine Bucknell, in consultation with the collection's donor/seller, Isherwood's heir and long-time partner Don Bachardy, had omitted passages that could be embarrassing to those still living. The publishing firm's attorneys further examined the manuscript of the book for potentially actionable text. Even with this intensive attention to safeguarding privacy, difficulty arose. The attorneys had read and examined the text of the diaries to be published, but they had not checked the footnotes. A revelation of certain information about an individual was discovered in a footnote by a surviving family member who threatened legal action. As a result of this episode, Bachardy, despite his strong belief in free and open access, reluctantly agreed to impose a restriction on the original diaries in the Isherwood archive. Based on the ages and likely life spans of those mentioned in the diaries, a restriction of thirty years was decided upon.

In dramatic contrast, another modern literary collection involved the Huntington in a nascent legal wrangle as a result of the unethical behavior of its creator/seller. The collection consisted of oral history interviews about a twentieth-century author, conducted with some of his remaining friends and family members. The family members who had been interviewed were promised by the collection's creator that only the edited transcripts would be used. The original tapes contained some private information that they wished to seal for a period of time, and I had agreed to take the material under the same condition. Some months after this collection had been purchased by the library, an angry literary agent representing the family members contacted me. The agent claimed that the creator had broken his agreement by publishing a book that contained quotations from, and references to, the expurgated portions of the interviews. The agent threatened legal action by the family if the library did not immediately return to the family the relevant tapes and transcriptions. Returning this material was not acceptable, but I certainly felt that the wronged parties had a valid complaint. More to the point, they could not be dissuaded in seeking redress, so I explained the virtue of sealing the material for a sufficient period of time to ensure that the privacy of the family members would be respected. Following lengthy negotiations that began with the agent insisting on a one-hundred-year closure, we finally reached an agreement for a restriction of fifty years—a far longer period than I would have wished for, but the shortest time span that the irate family members would accept in lieu of taking legal action.

When donors or sellers do not recommend any restrictions for privacy reasons, when they are not aware of potentially sensitive materials in an archive, or when there is simply no one left who can offer any guidance, then the curator or archivist may face a difficult dilemma. In such a situation, if a document or file contains letters or other materials that defame a living individual, or that could cause embarrassment to persons still living if the information were revealed, she or he must decide whether a curator-imposed restriction is necessary and appropriate.

The difficulty, of course, involves establishing criteria and defining what is private in a collection of personal papers. Apart from certain legally protected categories of records, such as patients' and students' records and attorneys' case files, no guidance exists concerning sensitive or embarrassing documentation. Thus the curator or archivist is left to his or her own, or the repository's, discretion to determine which documents in an archive might reveal private information if opened for research. How, then, can the archivist be sure that a restriction is appropriate to the collection and the individuals in it, rather than constituting unconscious or inadvertent censorship? No simple solutions exist. Archivists must take care to seal manuscript material only with the utmost caution, rigorously and objectively analyzing the situation without imposing personal beliefs or values. Of course, this places a nearly impossible demand on an archival professional, and this difficulty leads institutions to apply no restrictions on their own, in the absence of donor requests. If, however, an archivist or curator feels that certain material might contain private information and therefore should be sealed, what criteria can help in reaching a decision when the family or donors either do not know of private material or are not available for advice?

In a previous article on privacy, I recommended that archivists should become as knowledgeable as possible about the moral and social milieu of the individuals represented in the collection and attempt to deal with sensitive materials based on this knowledge.[9] An example of this approach arose in the late 1980s, when I began to process and catalog the papers of Patrick Balfour, 3rd Baron Kinross, a travel writer who died in 1976. Because Kinross was unmarried, with no direct descendants, his papers were consigned to the British dealer Bertram Rota Ltd., which sold the archive to the Huntington Library. Kinross, a gay man, was a confidante to an astonishing number of people, many of them gay and many of them still living. As a result, the correspondence files contain numerous letters pouring out intimate, confessional details. Keeping in mind the injunction in the SAA Code of Ethics to respect the privacy of people in collections, *especially those who had no say in the disposition of the papers* (italics supplied), I felt great concern about the possibility that private matters, in particular the "outing" of closeted gay men who felt their sexuality was their own business and no one else's, could be revealed if the letters were opened for research.

In reviewing the correspondence files, I realized that no archivist could determine whether the private matters in the letters had been confided to Kinross alone or constituted more general knowledge. With no family available for consultation, I had no recourse except either to open all of the letters, despite my concerns, or to try to arrive at some sense of whether opening the confessional letters would reveal intimate, private information about people who would have no idea that their private letters had been housed in a research library in California. Taking into account the tenor both of the correspondence in the archive and of the time in which Kinross and his friends lived, when the outing of gays was controversial and many gays remained firmly behind the closet door, I nearly decided to try implementing restrictions based on a sense of this milieu. Still, this prospect proved very disquieting and I felt no confidence that restrictions could be consistently or sensibly applied. As events transpired, by the time this dilemma had been duly considered and the collection had been processed, sufficient time had passed since Kinross's death that I felt that all the correspondence files could probably be made available safely without much risk to anyone's privacy. Thus, the situation resolved itself more as a sort of decision-by-default, rather than as a result of a considered determination of the proper course of action.

The debate that lay behind this decision-by-avoidance is possibly emblematic of an over-active sense of ethics that may afflict some archivists. The potential for revealing private information more often constitutes an ethical concern than a legal one. In fact, it seems highly unlikely that a manuscript repository would be sued for invasion of privacy or for revealing private information. Even if the risk for institutions appears small or negligible, however, the administrators of many repositories might still feel considerable concern about their legal liabilities and therefore might seal sensitive materials. An alternative view of the legal responsibility for safeguarding privacy holds that a repository could actually be protected legally by never restricting any material at all, thus avoiding any responsibility for identifying and dealing with private or sensitive items. This approach leaves the burden squarely on the researcher, who could be held legally accountable for publishing private information. Indeed, the more likely party to be sued is a researcher who publishes private information, rather than an institution. Whether for legal or ethical reasons, though, it is prudent for archivists and curators to be aware of privacy rights and issues and alert to the presence of potentially sensitive material in collections. If archivists can set aside their ethical worries about betraying the privacy of individuals represented in their collections, then the blanket policy of opening everything in collections can safely protect the repository. The decision about which course to follow will depend on a repository's comfort level. Ethically motivated attempts to respect the privacy of individuals in collections inevitably conflict with the legal gamble that a repository can absolve itself of liability by disassociating itself from privacy decisions.

Whatever policy archivists and their repositories adopt for dealing with sensitive materials, collections of the papers of modern authors and celebrities seem to present a somewhat greater degree of difficulty in the area of privacy than do other kinds of collections. Several reasons account for this. First, authors' and celebrities' papers are high profile, generating much public interest. Second, correspondence and other manuscripts in such collections often deal with personal matters, rather than with historical events or situations. Third, copyright can become intertwined with issues of privacy. Finally, within the past twenty years or so, repositories have increasingly begun to collect the papers of living authors, as the papers are being created. Let us consider each of these reasons in turn.

First, the archives of major authors and other well-known figures document high-profile people and contain high-profile content, leading to a heightened level of interest in those individuals and their activities. In the latter decades of the twentieth century and the opening years of the twenty-first, the growth of tabloid journalism and its offspring, the "tell-all" biography, has spawned a public obsession with knowing scandalous and salacious details about the lives of celebrities. The intrusive interest of the public in the lives of famous people has received comment recently from the relatively anonymous author Charles Webb, whose 1966 novel, *The Graduate,* is famous as the basis for the Dustin Hoffman film. In the news again with the publication of his 2001 novel *New Cardiff,* Webb has suddenly become a focal point for media attention, prompting an interviewer to relate this anecdote of his conversation with Webb: "Asked perhaps one too many personal questions, he responded with a gentlemanly but prickly sense of humor: 'Well, what do you think of this? Next time you're at your dentist, what if you said: By the way, I'd be interested in knowing more about your wife. Can I see a picture of her? Is she your first wife? Have you ever been sued? Are you straight or gay? Do you have affairs? How much money do you make?'"[10] This kind of obsession with the private lives of public or well-known figures has meant that increasing numbers of researchers prowl library stacks, in search of new biographical details that can titillate an often insatiable public.

According to American legal precedent, individuals frequently in the public eye surrender a certain degree of their privacy by virtue of being public figures. Most of us would agree, however, that beyond a certain point, some categories of personal information about famous people are private and should be respected as such. Though we might secretly, and with a certain feeling of shame, savor gossip that reveals a sensitive or scandalous tidbit of information about a celebrity, nonetheless we recognize that a boundary line has been crossed when that information becomes public. The sacrifice of complete privacy on the part of public figures does not usually, and should not, constitute free rein to digest every morsel of that person's private life.

The strong interest that we feel in the lives of famous people is not a new phenomenon, but simply an ever-burgeoning outgrowth of a long and deeply rooted human propensity. Henry James's short story "The Aspern Papers" offers an example from 1887. The real-life seed for the tale came to James's attention earlier that same year, when the young English novelist Vernon Lee recounted to James an anecdote about an elderly lady living in Florence, Mary Jane Clairmont (self-styled as "Claire Clairmont"), formerly the mistress of Byron and the mother of Byron's illegitimate daughter Allegra. A Boston sea captain named Silsbee, who had a passionate interest in Shelley and who knew that Claire Clairmont had in her possession a cache of Shelley and Byron papers, had exhausted every effort to acquire them and finally arranged to rent a room in her villa, where the papers were kept. After Claire died in 1879, her late–middle-aged, spinster niece, who had been casting longing glances in Silsbee's direction, offered him the letters if he would marry her, whereupon he immediately fled the scene.

James recorded this anecdote in his notebook, noting his interest in "the two faded, queer, poor and discredited old English women . . . with these illustrious letters their most precious possession. Then the plot of the Shelley fanatic—his watchings and waitings—the way he *couvers* the treasure. . . . It strikes me much."[11] In James's version of this tale, "The Aspern Papers," his nameless narrator, a would-be scholar-collector, insinuates himself into the household of an elderly woman, just as Silsbee had done, intending to inveigle her into giving him letters that she had received many years before from the now-deceased Jeffrey Aspern, a well-known poet and her secret lover. The star-struck, avaricious narrator voices his plan of attack to his confidante: "The old woman won't have her relics and tokens so much as spoken of; they're personal, delicate, intimate, and she hasn't the feelings of the day. God bless her! If I should sound that note [i.e., an offer of money] first, I should certainly spoil the game. I can arrive at my spoils only by putting her off her guard, and I can put her off her guard only by ingratiating diplomatic arts. Hypocrisy, duplicity are my only chance. I'm sorry for it, but there's no baseness I wouldn't commit for Jeffrey Aspern's sake. First I must take tea with her—then tackle the main job."[12]

The "cult of celebrity" and its effect on personal papers also appears as a theme in other works of fiction. A. S. Byatt's 1990 novel, *Possession,* for example, concerns a struggle between two twentieth-century literary scholars who vie for first access to a cache of love letters that document the hitherto-unknown love affair between two nineteenth-century authors. The issue seems never to have been more strongly in evidence than in recent years. At its most basic, the human fascination with celebrities and public figures is manifestly evident in the tabloid periodicals, which have proliferated in the last few decades and whose screaming headlines seduce the public from every newsstand and supermarket checkout line. Humankind's desire to know everything, even (or especially) intimate details about the lives of celebrities, has also come to pervade the work of both popular and scholarly biographers. As recently as the 1950s and 1960s, when Leon Edel's massive, five-volume biography of Henry James was published, it seemed sufficient to know that James never married, evinced shyness in the company of available women, and might have been sexually conflicted. Fred Kaplan, in his 1992 biography of James, boldly asserted that James was gay. Similarly, in her biography of Anne Sexton, Diane Middlebrook did not merely state that the poet underwent psychological counseling. Rather, she included in her book information from the counseling sessions, causing widespread debate about the ethical proprieties of revealing private medical data, even though the revelation came after the patient's death.[13]

A flurry of news stories from the late 1980s concerning authors' papers and privacy reveals just how large the issue has become. In 1988, Stephen Joyce, James Joyce's grandson, stunned and horrified a conference honoring the Irish novelist when he announced that he had destroyed family letters. Specifically, he burned letters by the playwright and novelist Samuel Beckett and by his aunt, James Joyce's daughter, Lucia, who had died in 1982 after living for thirty years in an English mental institution following the 1951 death of her mother, Nora. He cited his action as a personal one, to protect the family's privacy, and as a justifiable one, since he emphasized that Lucia's life after Nora's death could have no bearing at all for research on James and Nora Joyce. However, his action received widespread condemnation from scholars and from descendants of William Butler Yeats and Ezra Pound, who asserted that the lost letters held great importance for the study of the relationship between Joyce, Beckett, and Lucia. Many felt that such materials about great writers are significant public treasures and must not remain private.[14] In the face of the public outcry against the destruction of the letters, Stephen Joyce passionately defended his action as a necessary one brought about by such revelations of family matters as made in Brenda Maddox's 1988 biography *Nora: The Real Life of Molly Bloom*. Maddox's frank treatment of James and Nora Joyce's erotic relationship, together with her recounting of the last thirty years of Lucia's life, caused considerable consternation in the family. Stephen Joyce aggressively refuted the view that his grandfather's and other family members' letters are public cultural treasures whose private contents can appropriately be revealed, writing: "I have not destroyed any papers or letters in my grandfather's hand, yet. Unlike others close to the Joyce family, I do not sell Joyce papers, letters, memorabilia, etc. I keep those I am fortunate enough to have, buy others and destroy some, such as Lucia's letters to us, which if seen by outsiders and made public would be an intolerable, unbearable invasion of my family's privacy. . . . I firmly believe that there is a part of every man or woman's life, no matter how famous he or she may be, that should remain private. . . . Enough is enough, even too much."[15]

Also in 1988, Janna Malamud Smith, whose father Bernard Malamud had died in 1986, voiced her concerns about the disposition of the author's papers. Citing the Joyce case, Smith deplored the trend toward revelations in biographies of intimate details about their subjects' lives. While acknowledging that authors have surrendered the privacy of themselves and their families, she nonetheless regretted that the families had no power to refute invasive or false accounts of the authors' lives. Struggling in her analysis of the issues to arrive at a reasonable course of action, Smith reached no firm resolution to the dilemma, writing, "Will we burn papers or letters? I do not yet know. . . . Because there are few limits to what biographers these days will write, I imagine many families will become more careful about what they tell. If an audience for his fiction persists, my grandchildren might wish to make public Bernard Malamud's private letters and journals. I doubt I will."[16]

Both Stephen Joyce and Janna Malamud Smith expressed understandably deep and legitimate concern over the revelation of personal details in the increasingly frank biographies that became standard in the latter part of the twentieth century. They both failed to consider the obvious alternative to either destroying sensitive papers or opening them freely to scholars: placing the papers in an archival repository with an agreement that they be sealed for an appropriate period of time. In such instances, the willingness of a library to accept papers that carry a reasonable restriction may ensure that significant but sensitive research materials survive to be used by scholars in future years.

Contrasting dramatically with Stephen Joyce's actions and with Janna Malamud Smith's concerns, the widow and children of John Cheever handled his papers with a remarkable, unqualified openness. The public face of certain aspects of Cheever's private life began with the 1984 publication of his daughter Susan Cheever's memoir, *Home Before Dark,* which disclosed his alcoholism and bisexuality. As she explained her action, "I did it out of anguish and love."[17] Then, in 1988, her brother Ben Cheever edited *The Letters of John Cheever,* in which he notably did not expurgate sexually explicit passages, citing his reason: "I had an implied contract with my readers. You don't leave something out because it is impolite. Had I done so, I would have imposed my priggishness on his life."[18]

The Cheever family's comfort with the revelation of intimate, sensitive details about John Cheever's life is commendable, and it ensures that the letters and other documents that illuminate the private facets of his life will survive and be available for scholarly research. Most authorial families, however, seem unlikely to adopt such an open-minded, apparently selfless stance with regard to sensitive materials. Since these individuals are well-known public figures, the potential revelations of private details about their lives create an enticing prospect to the public and to researchers seeking to publish. Since such a possibility remains so uncomfortable, even repugnant, to the families of these individuals, they are far more likely to react by trying to protect the privacy and memory of the famous individual, as well as their own privacy. The lives of unknown, ordinary people whose papers are in a repository carry far less risk of attracting attention or generating widespread public interest and therefore present a less serious potential problem with regard to privacy issues.

The second, closely related, reason that literary papers carry heightened privacy concerns is that correspondence and other papers in literary archives usually deal with personal matters, while historical collections more often deal with historic events. The correspondence files of a literary manuscript collection tend to be filled with letters in which authors write about themselves—their relationships with others, the events of their own lives, their progress or lack thereof on their current writing projects, and other authors and literary topics in general. This concentration on the personal is in marked contrast to historical collections that often comprise the papers of unknown or ordinary people who have either observed or participated in major historic events, or have been part of issue-related movements or events. Such collections might consist of documents relating to water rights in California in the twentieth century, or to an activist group dedicated to the preservation of natural resources in the United States. In cases like these, often the fact that the people involved are not famous makes their firsthand accounts so important to the historical record. Moreover, even when such collections date from very recent or contemporary times, these collections would not hold the same level of potential for revealing personal information as would the papers of famous authors or other celebrities.

Literary figures, families, or heirs sometimes "sanitize" the archive, or purge personal letters and documents to safeguard privacy before transferring them to a repository. As a result, an archive loses an important personal dimension that in most instances can never be replaced or re-created. One interesting example of a sanitized collection of personal papers dates to 1922, when the Huntington Library acquired the archive of James and Annie Fields from their descendants. Fields (1817–1881) edited and published the *Atlantic Monthly* and was a partner in the Boston firm of Ticknor and Fields, one of the top literary publishing houses of the latter half of the nineteenth century. His wife, Annie, was the socially prominent leader of a literary salon in Boston and, as scholars have begun to recognize in recent years, much more of a participating partner in her husband's literary and business affairs than had previously been known. The collection contains a deep, rich store of literary manuscripts and letters by virtually every major nineteenth-century New England author, including Henry David Thoreau, Ralph Waldo Emerson, Henry Wadsworth Longfellow, Oliver Wendell Holmes, John Greenleaf Whittier, Harriet Beecher Stowe, and Nathaniel Hawthorne. It also contains important documentation concerning American authors active outside the literary center of New England, including Samuel Clemens and Ambrose Bierce, as well as such British figures as Charles Dickens and Edward Lear. This collection illuminates the working lives of these authors, as well as their all-important relationship with their editor and publisher, and it continues to reward researchers with new insights, even after decades of heavy scholarly use. Still, either the sellers or their predecessors in the family removed from the archive nearly all exclusively personal letters to the Fieldses or between them. As a result, the collection is a superb literary and publishing archive, but it presents very little significant insight into the personalities and points of view of James and Annie or into their relationship. One can only assume that the family either doubted the importance of the personal information about the Fieldses, or that it sought to preserve the privacy of the literary couple. This constituted a legitimate concern in 1922, because, although James died in 1881, Annie lived on until 1915. If the family indeed felt concerned about privacy, one can only wish that they had elected to place parts of the collection under closure, rather than to remove permanently its more personal contents. How much richer even this superb collection would be if it had not been sanitized, but had been left intact to afford deep insight into James and Annie themselves. Years after the archive arrived at the Huntington Library, the family donated additional Fields papers. Yet, even this supplementary collection predominantly consists of copy books containing James's and Annie's random notes and their own literary efforts. The collection still lacks much material relating to them personally or to their relationship.

The third factor that sets the papers of authors and celebrities apart from other collections is copyright, which remains much more of an issue in literary or celebrity archives than in historical collections. In the personal papers of ordinary people who are not famous figures, protection or exploitation of copyright of either their image, for example, or of a work of art, literature, or music they have created, is not likely to emerge as an issue in the administration or use of those collections. When considering the papers of well-known figures, in contrast, copyright quite often emerges as a factor. In the case of actors and similar celebrities, the use of their image or likeness might be protected by copyright. The papers of musicians, artists, photographers, and authors typically contain copyrighted creative works. At times, the concepts of copyright and the right of privacy, as they relate to a famous individual's archive, have become intertwined and therefore somewhat confused or muddled. Probably the best-known example of this phenomenon is the case of the unauthorized biography of J. D. Salinger by Ian Hamilton. The fiercely private Salinger refused to cooperate with Hamilton, who was writing a biography of the famously reclusive author. When Hamilton persisted with his plans, Salinger transformed what began as a privacy case into a copyright case by retroactively registering the copyright in his letters held in such libraries as Harvard, Princeton, and the University of Texas, thereby seeking to block Hamilton from quoting the letters. His position was upheld by the courts, which ruled that Hamilton and Random House violated the terms of fair use and must not include in the biography any quotations, or even paraphrases, from Salinger's letters. Finally, Hamilton's rewritten book was issued, less as a biography than as an account of his legal experiences.[19]

The Salinger case illustrates how authors or other celebrities who discover that their letters are preserved and available for research in a library, or who feel threatened by the potential use of those letters, can invoke copyright law as a means of protecting their privacy. A similar situation arises when families, descendants, or other literary heirs of a famous individual seek to oversee the use of a collection by applying their literary rights to control access. This occurred with the Jack London Papers at the Huntington Library. Worrying about both the portrayals of London in published works and about the possible invasion of privacy in a collection whose contents dated up until the mid-1950s, the descendants who held the literary rights stipulated in the 1960s that their approval would be required for anyone to have access to the collection. Even though holders of literary rights more commonly grant permission to scholars to use archival material only *after* the scholars have done their research and written their books or articles, the London estate asserted its right to grant or deny such use *before* scholars could begin to use the collection. Privacy is a strong motivating force in the estate's decision to apply its literary rights in this manner, for, while Jack London died in 1916, his widow, Charmian, lived until 1955. Thus, in the 1960s, at the time the estate established its access arrangements, living people were represented in the correspondence files, and, even more worrisome to the estate, mentioned in Charmian's diaries. Despite the seeming strictness of these arrangements, the estate always responded reasonably, turning away only a small number of would-be researchers and doing so only in the first years of its oversight. Over time, with more and more researchers using the archive and publishing biographical and critical works on London, and with no hint either of invasion of anyone's privacy or of legal action, the estate has significantly relaxed its administration. Indeed, for some time I have administered the estate's granting of permission in nearly all instances, distributing to researchers permission forms already signed by the estate.

The fourth factor that sets authors' archives apart from other collections of personal papers is the increasing trend for repositories to collect authors' papers during the authors' lifetimes, rather than after their deaths. Reflecting authors' awareness of the high market value of their archives, the keen competition among institutions for authors' papers, and the desire by those institutions to nail down a literary archive as soon as possible, this trend increases the likelihood that collections will contain private and sensitive documents. With any recently created collection, privacy can be a concern, because of the so-called third-party privacy rights that inhere to any of the still-living correspondents, as well as to the individuals who are mentioned as subjects in the collection. In such instances, the injunction in the SAA Code of Ethics against violating the privacy of those who had no say in the disposition of the papers must be considered by the archivist or curator in overseeing the collection. When the creator of the papers is still living, the risks and difficulties are multiplied. Moreover as more papers from the author are transferred to the repository, the curator must consult repeatedly with the author about the possible presence of sensitive materials. Each new acquisition must be surveyed with an eye to privacy, both of the author and of other individuals. The longer the time period for an ongoing transfer of papers from an author, the longer the archivist must continue to deal with privacy and with the possibility of sealing certain documents or files as potential issues for that growing collection, even as he or she is addressing similar questions for other collections being acquired.

These situations arose at the Huntington when in 1987 the library began to purchase the papers of British author Kingsley Amis. The initial contact came from a rare book and manuscript dealer, but thereafter each successive transaction took place directly between the library and Amis's literary agent. Throughout this relationship the awareness of privacy issues was present. In one of the transfers of papers, Amis requested that certain material be restricted until his death. One item to be sealed was the autograph manuscript of an unpublished novel he had written called *Difficulties with Girls* (not the same work as a different novel that he did publish under the same title). Amis wanted this manuscript closed because he anticipated that critics and readers would incorrectly interpret it as autobiographical, and he did not want to deal with answering questions about it. The other material that he wished to have closed consisted of a large file of letters to him from the poet Philip Larkin. Larkin had already passed away, so his privacy rights were not an issue. Amis knew, however, that the letters contained frank comments about mutual friends still living, and he did not want those people to know what had been written about them until after his own death. His concern clearly was driven by self-interest, to save himself from the possible anger of the people mentioned. The fact that his papers were now in a library to be opened for research as soon as they were processed, made this an important issue. Had his papers been placed in a repository after his death, this kind of material would not have appeared sensitive. In 1995, when Amis passed away, the sealed items in the collection were opened for research.

More recently, in 1995, the Huntington began acquiring the archive of British novelist Elizabeth Jane Howard, who coincidentally was Kingsley Amis's second wife. According to her request, several groups of correspondence in her papers are closed for various lengths of time, in deference to the privacy of the authors of those letters, who are still living. A slightly different case involves the papers of another British novelist, Hilary Mantel, whose archive began arriving at the Huntington in 2001. According to discussions and correspondence between Ms. Mantel and myself, we have sealed her personal diaries for her lifetime, due to sensitive diary entries. In the Amis, Howard, and Mantel examples, some or all of the restrictions agreed upon by the authors and the library became necessary because the papers had been acquired during, rather than after, the author's lifetime.

The high market value of authors' papers, plus the desire by institutions to acquire literary archives early in order not to miss getting them, leads to another kind of situation that could present archivists with a privacy dilemma. In the early 1970s, the British author Stephen Spender was approached by the Bancroft Library at the University of California, Berkeley, which sought to purchase some of his papers. Spender, pressed for money at the time, sold to the Bancroft his file of the letters written to him by Christopher Isherwood. He subsequently wrote to Isherwood with some degree of slightly blustery embarrassment to confess what he had done, to seek Isherwood's approval of his action, and to urge Isherwood to sell his (Spender's) letters to the Bancroft. That letter now resides in the Huntington Library as part of Isherwood's archive, along with the rest of Spender's letters to him, which Isherwood obviously did not elect to sell. I do not know whether the Bancroft closed Isherwood's letters, but many of the letters certainly had been written very shortly before Spender sold them, so that privacy could well have been an issue. This situation presents a classic case of third-party confidentiality, in which the recipient of letters sells them to a repository without the prior knowledge or approval of the writer of the letters. Whether Isherwood would have approved the Spender sale if he had known in advance remains an interesting question. The combination of the Spender transaction and the subsequent acquisition of the Isherwood archive by the Huntington means that the correspondence between the two men lies at opposite ends of the state of California, split by one of those odd sequences of events that often play such a large part in the placement of collections of personal papers.

Faced with the competing ethics of free and open access to research collections and the safeguarding of people's right to privacy, and in view of the special problems presented in collecting the papers of authors and other high-profile individuals, how can curators and archivists devise appropriate policies for administering modern personal papers? Unfortunately, no good answers exist. There appear few even satisfactory guidelines for handling potentially sensitive letters and manuscripts. Both institutions and archivists must determine acceptable risk levels for the possible legal fallout of violating someone's privacy rights. Based on such practical considerations as the time that can be spent on processing collections and the level of detail that the archivist and other staff members can devote to examining individual items, archivists must arrive at policies and procedures that reflect an awareness of both the legal and ethical aspects of individual privacy, without being held hostage by the difficulties of administering the personal papers of modern figures. Archivists need to acknowledge that there are few if any absolutes in dealing with sensitive manuscript materials. Nearly all modern collections will present difficult gray areas of privacy for archivists to struggle with. Archivists should be fully informed about the issue of privacy and the options available, and they must behave conscientiously in handling sensitive materials. If sensitive professionals make such good faith efforts, there is reason to believe that modern personal papers may be opened responsibly for research while the private, hidden treasures in them are kept in secret and sealed in silence until they can be safely revealed.

9 Southern Family Honor Tarnished? Issues of Privacy in the Walker Percy and Shelby Foote Papers

Timothy D. Pyatt

Introduction

Literary manuscripts did not rank high on Joseph Grégoire de Roulhac Hamilton's agenda when he established the Southern Historical Collection at the University of North Carolina in 1930. His priority was preserving manuscripts that told the story of the plantation and Civil War South, and he excelled at it. For those unfamiliar with the history of the Southern Historical Collection, Hamilton became known as "Ransack" due to his aggressive collecting techniques. He publicized his plans for creating a "national Southern collection" in Chapel Hill in a series of lectures, newspaper articles, and pamphlets. A 1930 pamphlet describes Hamilton's efforts to rediscover the "Old South":

> Among historians and scholars nothing in years has made a stronger appeal than the plan, sponsored by the University of North Carolina, to assemble at Chapel Hill in a fire-proof library, every accessible scrap of paper bearing upon any phase of the history and development of the South. For generations it has been observed by the cautious student of history that the historians have given undue emphasis to the East, and particularly to New England, to the neglect of the South and the West; and that result has been a lopsided, and unintelligent interpretation and appraisement of American history. . . . Here is the plan that will relieve him [the historian] of the impossible task of reaching the material now scattered over a vast territory. It is proposed to assemble it for him. So rich should be the sowing of Chapel Hill that scholars and historians will

make a deep path from the North, the East, and West to the seat of this collection, and the result will be reflected in a juster, saner, less sectional interpretation of our American life.[1]

Hamilton worked tirelessly to fulfill this plan as he scoured the South in the 1930s and 1940s, gathering plantation records and Civil War manuscripts from Mississippi, Louisiana, South Carolina, Georgia, Tennessee, Virginia, and North Carolina. His efforts did not bring "every accessible scrap of paper" documenting the South to Chapel Hill, but Hamilton did collect over two million manuscripts prior to his retirement in 1948. The University of North Carolina thus boasted the largest manuscript collection documenting the American South at that time. The pamphlet's prediction that "historians will make a deep path" to use the Southern Historical Collection proved prescient. Hamilton's efforts to save documentary evidence of the Old South helped to increase awareness of the importance of primary source documentation in the region and to heighten and spur other institutions to gather and build manuscript collections.[2]

Despite Hamilton's focus, he did collect some literary manuscripts from deceased authors. The writings of Caroline Hentz, a nineteenth-century writer from the Northeast who married a University of North Carolina at Chapel Hill faculty member, and scattered works by the slave poet George Moses Horton, rank among his most notable acquisitions. Today the Southern Historical Collection (SHC) forms part of the Manuscripts Department of the University of North Carolina at Chapel Hill (UNC-CH) with holdings of over 19 million manuscripts, 120,000 archival audio and video recordings, and 75,000 photographs. It remains especially rich in the papers of southern planters, families, and politicians. Among the collection's lesser-known strengths are the papers of modern southern writers and publishers. As of the year 2000, the SHC held the papers of over forty writers and the records of twenty publishers.

UNC-CH professor emeritus Louis Rubin, noted author/editor and founder of Algonquin Books, played a key role in initiating the Southern Historical Collection's present program of collecting the papers of southern writers in the early 1970s. Rubin authored or served as editor for almost forty books, including *Southern Writers: A Biographical Dictionary* (1979). He felt that the UNC-CH Library was letting the southern literary renaissance pass by and that, in particular, the papers of notable graduates would be lost to other repositories. Two of the first writers that he encouraged the SHC to pursue were former UNC-CH students Shelby Foote and Walker Percy. Given their close relationship as kinsmen, fellow students, and long-time confidants, it is only fitting to write of Foote and Percy together. Their literary ties, common family tragedies, Mississippi roots, and shared concept of Southern family honor and noblesse oblige link them as personalities.

Acquisition and Access

A brief summary of the lives and careers of Percy and Foote, as well as that of Percy's cousin and Foote's friend William Alexander Percy, helps to place the issues surrounding their papers in context. William Alexander Percy (known as "Will") was born in Greenville, Mississippi, in 1885, the son of U.S. senator Leroy Percy and Camille Percy. He received degrees in literature from the University of the South and in law from Harvard. Percy was raised in the planter family tradition where the planter (as the landed gentry) cared for "his" people, whether they were slaves, sharecroppers, or townsfolk. A World War I hero and civic leader, Percy lived the life of the gentleman lawyer and man of letters. Together with his father, he fought against the Ku Klux Klan in Greenville and headed the local Red Cross efforts in the great Mississippi flood of 1927. He wrote an autobiography evoking the nostalgic Old South, entitled *Lanterns on the Levee*, which helped to solidify the impression of Percy as an unreconstructed southerner. He also raised his three orphaned cousins, one of whom was Walker Percy.

Walker Percy was born in Birmingham, Alabama, in 1916 and received degrees from UNC-CH in chemistry and Columbia in medicine. During his teens he lived with his cousin, William Alexander Percy (whom he called "Uncle Will"), after his father's suicide and his mother's death in an auto accident. As part of his medical training, Percy worked as an intern in Bellevue Hospital in New York where he contracted tuberculosis. After his recovery, he left medicine to focus on writing. He married Mary Townsend in 1946 and moved to Covington, Louisiana. Shortly thereafter he converted to Catholicism. He gained literary prominence with his first published novel, *The Moviegoer*, which won the National Book Award in 1962. He also wrote *The Last Gentleman* (1967), *Love in the Ruins* (1971), *Lancelot* (1977), *The Second Coming* (1980), and *The Thanatos Syndrome* (1987). He published two works of nonfiction, *The Message in the Bottle* (1975) and *Lost in the Cosmos* (1983).

Shelby Foote was born in Greenville, Mississippi, in 1916 and attended UNC-CH. He was a friend and schoolmate of Walker Percy after the latter moved to Greenville, a relationship much encouraged by Will Percy. Foote's various jobs included reporting for the Associated Press and serving in the Marine Corps. After his first novel, *Tournament*, was completed in 1949, he was praised as one of America's finest young post–World War II authors. His other novels are *Follow Me Down* (1950), *Love in a Dry Season* (1951), *Shiloh* (1952), *Jordan Country* (1954), and *September, September* (1978). Foote is probably best known for his three-volume narrative history of the Civil War and for his work on Ken Burns's television documentaries.

UNC-CH acquired the papers of Walker Percy over the course of several years.[3] Negotiations started in 1977 with a discussion of various acquisition options. Percy ruled out making a gift of his papers because he could not take self-created works as a tax deduction at "fair market" value under Internal Revenue Service regulations. In 1980, the UNC-CH Library proposed a loan of the papers. After talking over the proposal with his friend Shelby Foote (who already had placed portions of his papers on loan to the SHC in 1978), Percy agreed and asked UNC-CH lawyers to create a loan agreement. While waiting for the loan to be formalized, Percy in 1981 placed with the SHC the first installment of his papers, which included primarily drafts and typescripts of his books from *The Moviegoer* to *The Second Coming*. Terms of access seemed straightforward. The materials, after processing, would be "made available for scholarly research within the limitations of 'fair use [i.e., as U.S. Copyright Law provides]' in the reading room of the Southern Historical Collection as are other manuscripts. The owner [i.e., Percy] specifically retains copyright and stipulates that there be no photocopying of the manuscripts for readers or correspondents."[4] In addition, Percy required that the library carry separate insurance coverage for his papers.

In 1983, the SHC acquired additional Percy materials, including more drafts of novels already held as well as drafts and materials concerning other publications. Of special note was the typescript for *The Gramercy Winner*, the second of Percy's two early, unpublished novels. The loan agreement finally was formalized (only a brief receipt with copying restrictions noted had been previously completed) with Percy naming his daughter, Mary Pratt Percy Lobdell, as owner of the papers if he should die. The photocopying restriction remained. In 1989, the collection received additional manuscript drafts and, for the first time, letters, including some from authors Allen Tate, Caroline Gordon, and Shelby Foote. The terms of the loan remained the same. After Percy's death in 1990, the collection received a few more items from his widow, Mary "Bunt" Townsend Percy, who had become co-owner of the papers with her daughter.

This arrangement continued until 1994, when the loan was converted to a combination gift/purchase, and some additional materials from Percy's home were added. The photocopying restriction was lifted at the time of the purchase, but the Percys retained copyright and other intellectual property rights. Prior to the sale, the Percy family handled all publication permission requests. Afterward, it employed a literary agent to process such requests.

Like the Walker Percy Papers, the Shelby Foote Papers were acquired over a period of years. In 1978, at the suggestion of Louis Rubin, Shelby Foote placed the manuscript of *The Civil War: A Narrative* on loan to the Southern Historical Collection. Terms of use were the same as for other manuscript collections in the SHC. In 1983, about 265 letters and postcards from Foote to Walker Percy were received on loan along with other letters and drafts and typescripts of Foote's novels, *Tournament, Shiloh, Follow Me Down,* and *Love in a Dry Season,* as well as typescripts for other writings.

The correspondence between Foote and Percy merits some additional explanation. While Percy saved Foote's letters as early as 1948, Foote did not save Percy's letters until around 1960. Neither saved copies of his own letters. In the 1980s, both returned their respective letters to each other. This results in the somewhat confusing arrangement that the papers of the writer, as opposed to the recipient, contain his own letters. Jay Tolson has edited these letters into a highly regarded volume.[5]

Foote and the university have enjoyed a productive relationship, with one possible exception. Foote spoke on the occasion of the Southern Historical Collection's fiftieth anniversary and also served as a writer-in-residence for the English Department. One of the rockier moments occurred in 1980 when his son was placed on stand-by for undergraduate admission. Foote felt disheartened that the university "wanted his papers, but not his son." Fortunately this incident did not prevent the SHC from formally acquiring the papers in 1994 as a gift/purchase with terms similar to the Percy agreement, with the exception that Foote remains the primary contact for publication permission. Both collections have been fully processed with finding aids available on the Web and MARC records loaded onto bibliographic utilities. Their collections have been further promoted through publications and a Web site devoted to North Carolina Writers.

Use and Privacy Issues with Foote and Percy Papers

Research interest in the Percy papers has been keen since their initial acquisition. Jay Tolson[6] and Patrick Samway[7] have written biographies, and Bertram Wyatt-Brown wrote his extensive biography and social history of the Percy family entitled *House of Percy*.[8] Most researcher requests were handled without difficulty, although Percy did occasionally ask for some exceptions to the terms of access that he had negotiated. In the late 1980s, Walker Percy asked Richard Shrader, then acting-curator of the Southern Historical Collection, to reserve the use of a forthcoming addition to his papers to a single researcher designated by Percy. Shrader dissuaded Percy from this course, explaining that once the addition had been given to UNC-CH, professional ethics dictated that the collection provide equal access to all researchers. Percy, after being reminded that he still retained control of publication permission rights, chose to place the addition with the collection without insisting upon exclusive access.

Members of the Percy family remain interested in the papers and their use, as well as the ways in which Walker Percy's life and career are portrayed. Their heightened sense of family honor, a holdover from the Percy planter days, continued even after his death. So it is not surprising that the current generation of Percys, who are very prominent in the political, social, and economic life of the Delta and Southwest, still show concern about how their forebears are described in print. The concept that "the dead have no privacy" does not hold true with the vigilant survivors of the Percy clan. Wyatt-Brown discovered, while writing *House of Percy*, that the family was particularly concerned about any discussion of the sexual orientation of Walker Percy's guardian, Will Percy, and the family's tendency toward depression. In a paper delivered at the 1998 meeting of the Society of American Archivists in Orlando, Florida, Professor Wyatt-Brown explained that, while he was engaged in the research for the *House of Percy*, a prominent member of the family warned him of a possible libel lawsuit. Although other reasons were offered, family members actually worried that Wyatt-Brown might sensationalize other writers' commentary concerning Will Percy's homosexuality. As it turned out, Will Percy's sexuality remained peripheral to the historian's work. Wyatt-Brown realized that to raise the issue was to distort Will Percy's remarkable career as a poet, memoirist, and leader for good government and sound journalism in Mississippi. The result turned out to be more satisfactory to the Percys than the subsequently published bestseller, *Rising Tide*,[9] by John Barry, a fast-paced and thorough history of the Mississippi River and of the great flood of 1927. In dealing with conditions in Greenville, Mississippi, Barry explicitly addressed the sexuality of Will Percy, who headed flood relief work in the Delta district. Barry used sources that Wyatt-Brown chose not to cite because he considered them questionable. The publication of his book did not lead to legal action or public protest, perhaps because such a venture might simply have increased sales without, in the Percys' view, retrieving family privacy and sense of honor. Such are the hazards of writing biographies when vigilant family members shield themselves from negative assessments, whether justified or not.

Ironically, Percy wrote a note of introduction for Wyatt-Brown that would seem to indicate that his research met with Percy's approval. The note, dated 2 July 1988, reads:

> This is to give permission for Bertram Wyatt-Brown to examine my papers in the Southern Historical Collection. I'd appreciate your cooperation, since Mr. Wyatt-Brown is doing some valuable work—with my best wishes, Sincerely, Walker Percy[10]

House of Percy did not appear until several years after Walker Percy's death, and the presence of this note had little effect on the surviving family, if they were even aware of its existence.

In 1996, a Percy devotee created the "Walker Percy Project—an internet literary center"[11] on the World Wide Web. This site, which had been created using materials in the public domain, concerned the Percys. The family initially investigated ways to have it shut down. A pseudo-academic site, it violated no laws or agreements. When the Web site creator requested use of the Percy papers, SHC staff treated him and the site as it did any other researcher. Once the creator learned that the Percy family's literary agent would have to grant permission to mount items from the papers on the Web site, he chose to use other materials.

The family's concern and involvement were also reflected when the library mounted its North Carolina Writers Web site in 1998.[12] The site includes inventories, biographies, and photographs of writers with papers in the Southern Historical Collection. Walker Percy, as a UNC-CH graduate, is represented along with North Carolina natives. Archivists at the collection believe that it possesses access to these materials for such use through the donor agreement. As a goodwill gesture, however, they requested permission from the literary agent to mount a photograph of Percy on the Web site. After a brief review and some explanation, the literary agent allowed the collection to use the photo.

Intimate details concerning personal relationships are also revealed in Jay Tolson's 1997 edition of the correspondence of Shelby Foote and Walker Percy, in which he published letters that exposed the heart and soul of these two authors. The letters often candidly described bouts of writer's block, depression, womanizing, and heavy drinking. They also included Foote's frequently voiced opinion that Percy's conversion to Catholicism would hurt him as a writer. It is fortunate that the letters have survived although, as previously noted, Foote discarded many of the early Percy letters. Of particular relevance is an undated letter by Shelby Foote to Walker Percy from sometime in 1953, when Foote was deeply depressed while suffering through writer's block and the break-up of his marriage. The letter, much of which is written as stream of consciousness in notable contrast to Foote's other well-crafted letters, reads in part:

> I'm not doing so good. Terrible in fact. Much oppressed. Maybe I'll get back on the manic kick again; I dont know. Useless feeling. Lonely. Loneliness is an artist's strength; thats where everything comes from and he knows it even though he hates it; thats why he wont surrender it. But I am finding it intolerable—which indicates how much less an artist I am nowadays. . . . Whats worse, I lost my skill when I lost my concern, my intensity. . . . Whatever I wrote would be very bad and I know it. . . .

Foote ends this moving letter by directing Percy to "Destroy this—not later: now."[13]

Researchers of Foote are fortunate that Percy did not follow his instruction as this letter helps to explain a turning point in his career. The letter was written after a period of great success for Foote; his first five novels had been well received, and he had started work on his sixth, which he felt would be his best yet—an experimental breakthrough novel based on the style of Henry James, James Joyce, and Marcel Proust. Yet Foote hit a block that was unrelieved until 1958 when he was commissioned to write a narrative history of the Civil War. He never completed that novel and did not return to fiction for over twenty-five years until *September, September,* which was published in 1978. This letter helps to explain the transition from fiction to nonfiction.

Documentation such as this letter is priceless to the researcher, but does raise concern about the privacy rights of the donor. The collection received this letter from Foote after Percy returned Foote's letters to him. The existence of these letters allowed Tolson to conduct his research, and he later received permission from both families to publish the letters. The key to success in handling such sensitive material is the archival repository's close working relationship with the author, heirs, and literary agents. In this instance, the Southern Historical Collection worked closely with Percy, Percy's literary agent, and Foote. The archivists made sure that the authors, heirs, and/or literary agents received updated copies of the inventory to the papers as new items were received. The archivists also routinely send current copies of researcher agreements and use policies so that the family can observe how researchers are informed about copyright and publication permission.

Access vs. Donor Rights to Privacy

To create a productive research environment with sensitive modern papers, it is vital to inform potential donors about how their papers might be used. In building UNC-CH's literary collections, other relevant examples of researcher access versus donor rights to privacy have surfaced. One local poet, who has been a leader in creating and encouraging Internet poetry sites, is an enthusiastic donor to the Southern Historical Collection. As is sometimes the case, he excitedly brought the archives everything—from correspondence to baby shoes—to work through. After the papers were processed and the inventory loaded onto the Web site, the poet promptly e-mailed the inventory to all of his literary friends. One of his friends was not amused that the papers were so publicly available and demanded to know whether her correspondence was present in his papers. A quick check revealed that the letters were there. The author informed the poet that she would sue him if they were not removed or restricted. The SHC chose to restrict them for a mutually agreed upon time period.

Similar concerns have surfaced with editorial correspondence present in publishing archives. In the case of the *Southern Economics Journal* and the *Southern Historical Journal* records, UNC-CH has correspondence commenting on rejected articles, as well as candid remarks on poetry submissions in the records of the avant-garde publication, *Oyster Boy Review*. Should a repository delete these materials from the historical record due to third-party privacy concerns? In each case the SHC has had to make compromises. In the case of the two academic journals, the archivists worked with the editorial staff to create the following use conditions:

> These papers may be read for information only. Copying, citation, quotation, or publication of any material written by a living individual is prohibited without the written permission of that individual.

It seemed important to preserve the documentation describing how academic literature is selected and disseminated. In the case of the *Oyster Boy Review* files, after negotiation with the editors, the archivists decided to restrict access entirely to that portion of the records. Even with a lengthy restriction, it still appeared vital to retain the materials. Who would not want a record of the early rejected works of a potential young "Jack Kerouac" or "Allen Ginsburg," even if it would be years before the scholarly community could consult them?

Conclusion

So how do archivists provide quality modern collections without compromising an individual's right to privacy? First, archivists must be honest with potential donors and explain access intentions as well as offer some thoughts on how the papers might be used. The donor should be made aware of the repository's access procedures and be informed about policies concerning copying and publication permission. Archivists should explain to prospective donors how the repository enforces copyright law and makes users aware of any access, copying, and publication restrictions. The repository should share with donors any research and duplication agreements that researchers must complete prior to using collections or requesting copies. Once the papers are placed with the repository, the donor should be consulted about any sensitive materials uncovered during processing and receive a copy of the inventory when completed. Building trust with the donor is vital for a productive long-term working relationship for both the repository and the potential researcher. A good relationship with the donor, or donor's heirs or agent, will also aid the researcher who requests permission to publish. The donor will be familiar with the papers' contents and will have had a chance to discuss access options with the repository before researchers examine the papers. These steps may not always prevent family honor from being tarnished in the eyes of some, but should ensure fair and equal access in the eyes of the researcher and the donor.

10 Balancing Privacy and Access: Opening the Mississippi State Sovereignty Commission Records

Sarah Rowe-Sims, Sandra Boyd, and H. T. Holmes

I.

A popular government, without popular information, or the means of acquiring it, is but a prologue to a farce or tragedy—or perhaps both. Knowledge will forever govern ignorance, and a people who mean to be their own Governors must arm themselves with the power knowledge gives.

James Madison[1]

Government archivists play a crucial role maintaining the health and vitality of the nation. As James Madison identified in the quotation above, the cornerstone of democracy is an informed citizenry with access to records of its government. Archives remain central to the democratic process itself. The archivist of the United States, John Carlin, defines the National Archives as

> a public trust on which our democracy depends. It enables people to inspect for themselves the record of what government has done. It enables officials and agencies to review their actions and helps citizens hold them accountable. It ensures continuing access to essential evidence that documents the rights of American citizens; the actions of federal officials; the national experience.[2]

Such a lofty statement is not mere hyperbole, massaging the limp ego of a low-status profession. Carlin recognizes the archivist as an essential component in government infrastructure and the national consciousness.

This article appears courtesy of the Mississippi Department of Archives and History.

With this duty comes an ominous responsibility, which plunges the archivist into the murky waters of privacy and access rights. This study examines how one state archives rose to the challenge, managing one of the most infamous collections of privacy-sensitive government records of twentieth-century America: The Mississippi State Sovereignty Commission Records.

II.

The History and Legal Mandate of the Mississippi Department of Archives and History (MDAH)

MDAH has a long tradition of protecting Mississippi's finite cultural resources. Founded in 1902 as a state agency, it is the second-oldest state archives in the nation.[3] The creating legislation did not impose official restrictions on access to the records in MDAH's custody. Dunbar Rowland, the agency's first director, was clearly "more interested in providing access than in restricting any materials."[4] In an address to the American Historical Association in 1910, Rowland identified as the "greatest drawback to investigation . . . the inaccessibility of public archives due to unnecessary restrictions."[5] In early MDAH annual reports, Rowland affirmed the agency's "liberal" access policy, stating that "[t]he freest access to documents is allowed to every properly accredited student engaged in serious work."[6]

The Archives and Records Management Act of 1981 and the Mississippi Public Records Act of 1983 defined MDAH's responsibilities more clearly. The 1981 law charged MDAH with the duty to maintain a "program in cooperation with each agency for the selection and preservation of vital records considered essential to the operation of government and to the protection of the rights and privileges of citizens. . . ."[7] Government records were defined as public property and opened to inspection, with the exception of those specifically exempted by state law, court order, contractual agreement or ". . . those records which it is shown the public interest is best served by not disclosing to the public." In addition, the act stated the MDAH would make records available ". . . at a reasonable time and place under rules and regulations adopted by the Board of Trustees."[8]

The 1983 Public Records Act and its subsequent amendments legally reaffirmed access to government records in Mississippi. The statute declared public records to be open and accessible, except for those records exempted by specific legislation. It further stipulated that nonexempt records contained within exempt records be separated and made available by agencies. In 1996, the act was amended to encompass the new demands of electronic media. This amendment required agencies to ensure access to electronic records, exempting software that was proprietary in nature, that was obtained under a licensing agreement, or that was considered "sensitive."[9] It also guarded against proprietary electronic records systems, stressing that agencies must plan for public access in their management of electronic records. The amendment authorized MDAH to assure access, stating that reproduction and storage of records of "enduring value" had to meet archival standards.[10]

III.

The "NKVD among the cotton patches"[11]

In a state whose image has largely been defined by racism, the Mississippi State Sovereignty Commission stands as an especially sinister institution. From 1956 to 1977, this state agency collected information on civil rights activists, acted as a clearinghouse for information on civil rights activities and legislation around the nation, funneled money to prosegregation organizations, and disseminated right-wing propaganda. Ironically, although its loudest proponents championed themselves as part of a Christian crusade against the insidious "red menace" of communism, the commission more closely resembled Big Brother.

The commission was established in the wake of the 1954 United States Supreme Court decision, *Brown v. Board of Education*,[12] which rejected as unconstitutional the notion of segregated "separate but equal" schools. Like other states below the Mason-Dixon Line, Mississippi passed a slew of legislation to shore up the walls of racial separation. Shrouded in the rhetoric of states' rights, the act creating the commission provided the agency with broad powers to spearhead the state's response to *Brown*. The commission's objective was to "do and perform any and all acts and things deemed necessary and proper to protect the sovereignty of the state of Mississippi, and her sister states" from a perceived encroachment by the federal government.[13] The governor served as ex-officio chairman and state legislators composed its membership. The agency staff remained small, consisting of several gubernatorial appointees, a director, a public relations director, and a handful of investigators.

As a result of its broadly defined statutory mandate, the commission performed a myriad of duties. Activities loosely comprised three basic functions: investigative, public relations, and advisory. The focus of each varied according to the whim of the governor and the particular skills of his appointees. Perhaps the most infamous function involved investigation. The commission likened itself to the FBI and the armed services intelligence agencies "during times of war seeking out intelligence information about the enemy and what the enemy proposes to do."[14] Routine work for investigators consisted of traveling around the state compiling reports on civil rights activities in each county. In addition to its investigators, the commission also used paid informants and private detectives.[15]

Actual evidence of "racial agitation" was not necessary to attract the commission's attention. The rumor mill and race baiters fed the commission, and any person or organization that appeared to transgress the racial lines or espouse a vaguely liberal perspective was a likely target. Following the passage of the Civil Rights Act of 1964,[16] the Voting Rights Act of 1965,[17] and other civil rights legislation, the tone of the reports changed. Reports began to use the term "subversive" rather than "agitator." The director asserted that the commission was "not a super snooping agency trying to crack down on any Negro who raises his hand."[18] Investigators were instructed to purge information demonstrating that the commission assisted in preventing voter registration. In reality, the commission continued to fulfill its usual functions, although investigations in the late 1960s began to focus on college campuses and "counter-culture" activities in general.[19]

The commission advised state and local government officials, law enforcement personnel and members of the public. To discourage voter registration, the commission routinely advised local governments to fire any employee who attempted to register. Prior to the 1964 Freedom Summer, it conducted "Clinics" to instruct local law enforcement in how to handle the expected "invasion." With the passage of federal civil rights legislation, the commission focused on ways to circumvent the new regulations.[20]

Officially, Mississippi sought to present the face of racial harmony to the rest of the world. The commission worked in secret to prevent news of racial violence and intimidation from reaching the press. Its public relations director wrote editorials for local newspapers that debunked national media reports. The agency acted as a clearinghouse for civil rights information, and its Speaker's Bureau provided advocates who toured the nation presenting Mississippi's official perspective. The commission facilitated right-wing propaganda activities by funneling state money to such groups as the Citizens' Council and the Washington, D.C.–based Coordinating Committee for Fundamental American Freedoms.[21] The commission also donated small amounts of money to African-American individuals and organizations sympathetic to segregation, hoping to attract those they termed the "thinking Negroes of Mississippi."[22]

By the 1970s in Mississippi, support of an openly racist, state-sanctioned commission no longer appeared politically expedient. In April of 1973, Governor William Waller vetoed the Sovereignty Commission's appropriation and described the agency as "a stigma on the state's government."[23] Even before the ink dried on Waller's veto, public speculation began over the files of the defunct commission. On the first day of the 1977 legislative session, H.B. 276 was introduced to transfer the files and equipment of the commission to the Department of Public Safety.[24] A heated debate ensued in the legislature, as lawmakers introduced other bills designed to dispose of the records in various ways. African-American legislators called for the files to be opened, some legislators argued for a lengthy closure, while others voted for the records literally to be burned.[25]

The vote to destroy the files prompted a firm response from MDAH. The MDAH board of trustees unanimously passed a resolution at its 28 January 1977 meeting "strongly imploring the legislature" not to destroy the records. The board voted to "immediately advise the appropriate members of the Legislature" of its opposition to the "indiscriminate destruction of the records of the State Sovereignty Commission or any state records." MDAH also stated that it would willingly take the records "in accordance with any restrictions the Legislature [chose] to place on them."[26]

Preservation advocates aired their views at the 18 February 1977 House of Representatives Judiciary "B" Committee hearing. The chair of the MDAH board of trustees, former governor William Winter, argued that "there is too much historical value in these records to destroy them without giving historians some way to interpret this era of our history." Winter further asserted that destroying the records seemed "inconsistent with the way we do things and smacks of totalitarianism."[27] MDAH director Elbert Hilliard identified precedents for dealing with records of this nature, citing the National Archives' handling of the records of the United States House Un-American Activities Committee. Hilliard also assured the committee that MDAH had "room to seal and store the records."[28] The result was the enactment on 3 March 1977 of an amended bill to abolish the commission but to seal its records at the archives until 2027.[29] The secretary of state's office immediately transferred nearly 133,000 pages of surviving commission records to MDAH, where they were secured in its vault.[30] Because the records were statutorily sealed when the law was enacted, MDAH archivists did not have the opportunity to assess their physical condition or even confirm the contents of the filing cabinets.[31]

IV.

[W]e feel that it would be the bitterest irony to subject the many people whose files are so gathered to a cavalier and uninhibited media spectacular.[32]

In January 1977, even as the Mississippi House debated the agency's fate, the American Civil Liberties Union/Mississippi (ACLU/M) initiated an intense legal battle in the federal courts to open what it dubbed

Mississippi's "spy files." As the case of *American Civil Liberties Union of Mississippi, Inc., et al. v. Cliff Finch Govenor of State of Mississippi, et al.*[33] wound its tortuous route through the courts, the central element emerged as a debate between access and privacy protection. For seven and a half years after the lawsuit was filed, various court skirmishes occurred. At one point, the suit was dismissed by the federal district court, only to be reinstated by the Fifth Circuit Court of Appeals. During this initial period, the debate centered on the question of whether the records should remain open or closed. Curiously, the arguments and decisions occurred before any commission records were available for discovery. Both sides argued over records that no one had evaluated.

In October 1984, the plaintiffs were finally granted access to the files for discovery.[34] Once the plaintiffs actually read the records, an internal schism developed. As a result, in December 1987, U.S. District Court Judge William H. Barbour, Jr. divided the plaintiff class into two subclasses: access plaintiffs and privacy plaintiffs. Access plaintiffs sought "unlimited public access" to the records, while privacy plaintiffs consisted of those who supported "access to the records for those named in the records, but who further advocate no further access by other parties without the prior consent of each person or persons described in a particular record."[35]

One of the original plaintiffs, freelance journalist Ken Lawrence of Jackson, who favored full disclosure, summarized the access perspective: "[T]here's nothing that anyone would want to keep secret." He continued, "[T]he need we have to understand the outrageous behavior of the state so much overrides the technical claim of privacy that it doesn't make any sense."[36] In contrast, former Tougaloo College professor John Salter, one of the original plaintiffs, who now favored privacy, noted, "[W]e feel that it would be the bitterest irony to subject the many people whose files are so gathered to a cavalier and uninhibited media spectacular."[37]

On 27 July 1989, the court declared the 1977 act sealing the records unconstitutional and ordered the files to be treated like "any other public record according to state and federal law." The judge also stipulated that any class member could "file with the custodian of the Sovereignty Commission files any rebuttal to any allegation, charges or other information about the class member contained in such files."[38] In the ruling, the court strongly defended the importance of disclosure:

> To open the files would further the general principle of informed discussion of the actions of government, while to leave the files closed would perpetuate the attempt of the state to escape accountability.

Opening the files would also end public speculation as to the extent of the acts of the Commission, much of which has far exceeded the record.[39]

The ACLU/M applauded Judge Barbour's ruling, and the state governor and attorney general chose not to challenge the decision.[40]

On the day that the ruling was handed down, MDAH representatives met with the state attorney general to discuss opening the files. After twelve years of litigation, it was evident that the access plaintiffs would allow MDAH little time to prepare. During the discovery process, MDAH archivists assessed both the physical condition of the papers and their processing needs. Faced with an imminent opening, immediate and drastic plans had to be developed for providing access within a matter of a few days. The privacy advocates, however, moved to prevent the opening of the files, and the ruling that opened the files was immediately stayed, pending an appeal to the Fifth Circuit Court of Appeals.[41]

The potential impact of the court's ruling that opened the records moved the MDAH board of trustees into action. Since the passage of the closure act, and during the previous twelve years of litigation, MDAH had been asked neither to comment on the issue and/or process nor to provide testimony regarding any archival issues. The near-reality of having to open the records in a very short time served to focus the vision of the department.

The privacy plaintiffs began talking with MDAH staff about how to provide access to the records with personal identifying information redacted. Armed with this information, the privacy plaintiffs worked with some of the access plaintiffs to develop a compromise settlement, which was given to MDAH for comment.

The proposed settlement would have required the MDAH to

> Open all Commission records to the public after the records had undergone privacy screening; except that records involving certain classes of persons would be opened without screening:
> deceased persons;
> all public officials of local, state and federal government at the time each record was created;
> all paid informers;
> all verified providers of information to the Commission, excepting those persons who provided information on white supremacist groups.
> Notify all class members of their rights, including, but not limited to:
> publication in Mississippi and national newspapers;
> mailing to last known address;
> written notification to all relevant organizations.

The proposed settlement defined "class members" as any individuals who thought their civil rights may have been violated by the commission.[42]

After reviewing the proposed settlement and carefully considering the situation, the MDAH board of trustees strongly endorsed privacy screening and offered a counter proposal that would require the archives to

> Make all Commission records open to the public after the records had undergone privacy screening; except that records involving certain classes of persons would be opened without screening:
> > deceased persons, provided however that the Department would screen for privacy of family members of deceased persons; members of the Commission and public employees of the Commission;
>
> All records would be declared open, public records in 2027
> Notify class through publication in state and national newspapers
> Provide a means for a class member to provide written rebuttal to any records pertaining to him.

To accomplish the privacy screening, the archives proposed converting the records into electronic form and using electronic editing capabilities for rapid privacy screening.[43]

The possibility of such a settlement failed due to the plaintiffs' inability to agree on a final plan. But the MDAH board had identified its responsibility to the matter as it then stood, taken a strong stand on the need for privacy protection, and realized that its opinion needed to be heard by the appeals court. Because the state attorney general had declined to enter an appeal on the district court's ruling, the MDAH board's position would not be heard in court. As required by state law, the board requested the attorney general's permission to hire private counsel to represent the department as a privacy advocate.[44] Three months later, that request was denied.[45]

On 14 September 1990, the Fifth Circuit held that Judge Barbour's ruling "did not adequately take into consideration privacy interest [*sic*] of persons named in agency files" and directed the district court to "devise a plan" to accommodate privacy interests.[46] In September 1993, Judge Barbour held an evidentiary hearing to explore the privacy and access issues. Litigants, including representatives from MDAH, outlined their recommendations for opening the files.[47]

Prior to this point, the archives' role in the case had been solely that of legal custodian of the records. Although MDAH had proven instrumental in saving the records from the funeral pyre, as a state agency it was a defendant in the ACLU litigation. MDAH had never been requested to testify. The hearings now afforded archivists their first opportunity to outline archival concerns to the court. In formulating its plan, MDAH tempered archival requirements with the court's immediate needs and the strictures of time. MDAH adamantly insisted, however, that the physical and intellectual integrity of the files should be preserved. Rejecting microfilming and photocopying options as economically unfeasible for the long term, MDAH advocated imaging in order to leave the originals untouched and provide an exact, authentic electronic copy coupled with an index. This electronic copy could meet both the court's privacy stipulations by allowing archivists to work on a single "copy" of the document and the access needs of researchers by allowing them to see that same "copy." To further ensure authenticity, MDAH rejected optical character recognition (OCR) technology due to the potential for data manipulation. In addition, the poor quality of the originals and inclusion of much handwritten material made the job beyond the capabilities of the OCR technology available at that time. The involvement of archivists in the trial, presenting archival procedures and concerns, was noticed by the court.

On 31 May 1994, Judge Barbour released a memorandum and opinion order, which declared the records open and established a privacy and disclosure procedure. Now sympathetic to archival concerns, Judge Barbour's goal was to maintain "the original integrity of the files, while balancing the competing interests of the various plaintiffs in privacy and disclosure." He also stressed, however, that "no system of disclosure will be perfect."[48] MDAH was given the task of implementing the process within a set time frame. The archival process to be used in complying with the court's order was not mandated, but the following steps in the process were stipulated:

> Compilation by MDAH of an index of all personal names appearing in the records
> Classification by MDAH of each name as either a "victim" of Commission surveillance or a complicit "state actor"
> Notification by MDAH to class members that records were available for review
> Response by class members
> Redaction by MDAH
> Opening of redacted records[49]

Although Judge Barbour set a deadline for the completion of this process, he expected that appeals would delay implementation. MDAH was instructed to proceed with the compilation of the index while awaiting the determination of the final redactions that would be made. The privacy plaintiffs appealed the 1994 order, which was upheld by the Fifth Circuit Court of Appeals. The United States Supreme Court refused to consider the matter. In November 1996, with all avenues of appeal exhausted, the timetable outlined by Judge Barbour's 1994 court order finally went into effect.[50]

Advertisement Period	45 days
Inquiries from interested individuals	90 days
MDAH response to inquiries with copies of records	90 days
Inquirer response to privacy options ("inquiry stage")	30 days
Final preparation prior to public opening	30 days

The appeals afforded MDAH valuable extra time to complete the laborious and tricky task of imaging and indexing the records. At the time that MDAH was ordered to index the records, the agency had no prior experience in dealing with privacy issues of this magnitude. When MDAH became responsible for redacting records to protect personal privacy interests, a total re-engineering of attitude was required.

The resulting changes were most apparent in, and had the most immediate impact on, the indexing and processing of the records. Because an unintentional slip-up on the archivists' part could result in the loss of individual privacy protection, and possibly result in litigation against the agency and its staff, every step of the process was checked, rechecked, and checked again. A team of three archivists was assigned this responsibility, and scanning began. Each scanned image was reviewed by two archivists for accuracy and completeness. Two archivists separately indexed the personal names on each page, and a third archivist checked each page. Ultimately, the index consisted of approximately 300,000 name occurrences comprising approximately 87,000 unique name forms.

The inquiry stage began in January of 1997. MDAH alerted the public by placing advertisements in the local and national press for three successive weeks. These advertisements invited people who believed that their names might appear in the records to write to MDAH. The agency received approximately one thousand initial inquiries within the ninety-day period established by the court, and the MDAH processing team mailed detailed questionnaires to each respondent. This notification procedure also required triple-checking of addresses, mailings, receipts, and requests. Seven hundred completed questionnaires were returned. In the next ninety-day period established by the court, the processing team searched for individuals in the records based on information provided in the questionnaires. Records containing approximately 360 of the individuals' names were located. Again, each search was performed by one archivist and replicated by a second, with the search results approved by a third archivist. To ensure complete privacy, MDAH redacted all other names in these records before providing copies for the respondents.[51] As before, the redactions were done by one archivist, checked by a second, and reviewed by a third. Production of the respondent review copies followed the same process. At the end of the ninety-day period in August of 1997, MDAH mailed the respondents printouts generated from the image database containing every document in which the requested name appeared, along with instructions on how to declare privacy options.[52] Most respondents chose full disclosure, but forty-two people selected a privacy option.[53] The court reviewed the requested privacy redactions and in each case issued a sealed order determining the final redactions. A number of plaintiffs contested the court's redaction and requested the court to review its decision on their records. The decision by the court to rule individually on each redaction request removed a huge burden from MDAH. Initially, discussions had centered on the archivists redacting names and identifying information. MDAH quickly realized that such a task would be nearly impossible. Many whose names were in the records were still living, and the historical period covered by the records had been scrutinized by historians and others. It would have been too easy to positively identify an individual. MDAH feared resulting litigation from such identifications. From the MDAH perspective, the court was truly wise in requiring the individuals to ask for their own redactions, with a final court review of the request.

On 13 January 1998, Judge Barbour ordered all noncontested commission records to be opened in March. Contested records included those of individuals who had made privacy requests and status challenges. In response to the order, MDAH finalized its system to provide public access to the noncontested records.[54]

On 17 March 1998, twenty-one years after the lawsuit was filed, the bulk of the records of the defunct Mississippi State Sovereignty Commission were made available in electronic format on three computer workstations in the MDAH library. Once again, the production of this redacted version required the three-stage procedure of checking each image and index term. Six percent of the records remained in litigation and stayed closed. There was intense national media attention on opening day, and very few researchers appeared. In the following days and weeks, a large number of individuals, many who had never been in an archives before, came to look at the records. Three staff archivists were assigned to handle the large number of requests mailed in by people who could not visit the archives.

Subsequent releases in July 2000 and January 2001 concluded the opening of the files. These newly opened pages incorporated the court-approved redactions requested by a small number of respondents who, in exercising their court-established rights, chose to have certain identifying information permanently expunged from the records. In addition, the releases included over two thousand pages of rebuttal material submitted by individuals named in the files. In 2002, the proprietary in-house electronic version was converted to an open system to make it Web accessible.[55]

V.

No system of disclosure will be perfect.[56]

The fight to open commission records mirrors the issues inherent in the privacy versus access debate. The commission, a state-funded agency, gathered information on thousands of Mississippi citizens and noncitizens. Investigative reports often contained intimate and slanderous details, many of which were the product of hearsay, concerning individual lives.

This type of information was precisely that which the privacy plaintiffs sought to have restricted. Former activists Edwin King and John Salter clearly had an "unwarranted invasion of personal privacy" in mind when, after reviewing documents in the discovery process, they broke from the ACLU/M access camp and doggedly sued to protect privacy rights. In subsequent arguments, Salter and King firmly denounced the commission's illegal activity and demanded government accountability. Still, they always promoted the notion of individual privacy rights. Salter and King also sought to protect the privacy of deceased persons and of those parties who would have no reason to believe that their names might be in the files.

Conversely, the access plaintiffs focused on the public's right to know. The commission's records clearly document a pivotal period in the state and national history. The civil rights movement was in effect a second American revolution, a reaffirmation of the principles that forged a nation from a colony. In recent years, civil rights historiography has evolved from chronicling great men and big events to providing detailed movement studies. The commission records are of immense historical value in establishing a fuller understanding of the role of ordinary men and women in the civil rights movement. County by county and organization by organization, the commission documented civil rights activities. Furthermore, the files reveal in detail the extent of white resistance, illustrating the white establishment's deep-seated commitment to the system of racial apartheid. Although, as with any historical source, the diligent historian will use these records with caution, they undoubtedly provide a treasure trove of hitherto unseen information.

In addition to their historical value, the commission's records can also be used to bring justice in cases of civil rights atrocities. In February 1994, after leaked commission documents prompted a third retrial, Byron De La Beckwith was convicted for the 1963 slaying of Medgar Evers, the Mississippi state field secretary for the National Association for the Advancement of Colored People.[57] On 17 March 1998, MDAH delivered commission documents to the family of Vernon Dahmer, a Hattiesburg businessman and activist who was killed when the Klan firebombed his home in January 1966.[58] These documents were then used in the subsequent trial and conviction of former Ku Klux Klan grand wizard Sam Bowers in August 1998. Newly released commission documents are also being reviewed in connection with the 1964 murders of civil rights workers James Chaney, Andrew Goodman, and Michael Schwerner in Neshoba County and in the February 1967 murder of Wharlest Jackson in Natchez.[59]

The May 1994 ruling, which established the procedure to open the records, attempted to balance the needs of privacy against the demands of access. In his earlier 1989 ruling, Judge Barbour clearly considered public interest to far outweigh privacy concerns. In overturning the 1989 ruling in 1990, however, the Fifth Circuit Court of Appeals stressed that the "disclosure strand of the privacy interest in turn includes the right to be free from the government disclosing private matters in which it does not have a legitimate proper concern."[60] Subsequently, while stating in 1994 "that so long as the Commission files remain sealed, there is a continuing violation of the federal constitutional rights of those named in the files," Judge Barbour acknowledged that the rights of victims "would be violated again if information about these victims is disseminated without their knowledge." In his ruling, Judge Barbour thus recognized the impossibility of finding a perfect solution to this dilemma, stating that "no system of disclosure will be perfect."[61]

VI.

> The ". . . greatest drawback to investigation" was "the inaccessibility of public archives due to unnecessary restrictions."[62]

The Mississippi Sovereignty Commission records left an indelible impression on the archivists charged with their maintenance. Processing such an infamous and historically significant collection constituted a grave responsibility. The case also identified the total absence of an agency policy on handling privacy-sensitive records and led to a reappraisal of current agency practices.

As noted above, MDAH's legal mandate is demanding. For the first several years of litigation, after having successfully saved the records from destruction in 1977, MDAH remained passive. With the first ruling, MDAH found itself merely reacting to events. The Sovereignty Commission saga brought into stark focus that passivity is not an option in a modern information-hungry and litigious society. MDAH needed to establish policies and procedures for dealing with privacy-sensitive materials and to step beyond the traditional role as a mere keeper of records. MDAH acknowledged that responsibility in January 1990 when the board of trustees, contrary to the positions taken by the state governor and attorney general, endorsed privacy screening for the commission records.

Development of a program has not been easy. No state statutory authority provides for privacy in public records unless those records are specifically deemed confidential by a state law. MDAH has had to work without specific statutory authority to provide privacy screening, but has also had to meet the requirements of applicable federal law and court decisions regarding privacy protection. Increasingly, the easy availability of personal information in electronic format requires MDAH to be even more diligent to help prevent the use of archival data for identity theft and similar acts.

Accordingly, MDAH established the position of privacy officer to oversee access issues. Initially, many nineteenth- and early twentieth-century records were closed as statutorily confidential or exempt from public disclosure since the passage of the 1983 Mississippi Public Records Act.[63] Records such as public hospital admission registers had been available for public research for decades, but our initial reading of the current statutes indicated that closure was required. After the records were closed, researchers were required to obtain a court order for access to these previously open records. MDAH later determined that the legal principle of prior publication applied—that is, all of the records that were publicly available prior to the 1983 Public Records Act had in effect been published. Consequently, MDAH reopened the records.

MDAH also became aware of the need for a state archival program to monitor federal court opinions. For example, the Fifth Circuit Court opinion in *Tarlton v. United States*[64] that prisoner records may be confidential resulted in a reassessment of MDAH prisoner records and the closure of a number of records series. Again, after a lengthy review, many of these records were reopened, but one series of probation and parole records containing victim statements remains closed.

Currently, the privacy officer identifies existing collections containing privacy-sensitive records and responds to requests for assistance from processing archivists. The privacy officer consults with MDAH's legal counsel at the Office of the Attorney General to interpret applicable state and federal statutes and case law and to construct access solutions. A general screening policy has been developed that can be modified for specific circumstances. With minimal guidance from the privacy officer, processing archivists are alerted to the type of documents that might require further consideration. Once relevant collections have been earmarked for consideration, the privacy officer either works with the processing archivists or personally conducts a lengthy review of the records. When the privacy officer limits access, finding aids include explanatory statements and the privacy officer remains on-call to assist reference staff. A significant problem remains with the failure of state agencies to design their records to allow the efficient redaction of personal data. Currently, MDAH is prohibited from "determining the nature and form of records" created by other agencies,[65] and until such time as the archival program can influence recordkeeping practices, long-term privacy protection problems will abound.

To date, the privacy officer's primary focus has been to review the validity of existing restrictions. Many closed nineteenth- and early twentieth-century government records have now been reopened. There has also been a concerted effort to generally heighten staff awareness of potential privacy and related legal issues. Staff members have attended workshops on copyright and privacy and confidentiality, and the services of a copyright attorney have been retained. In addition, the records scheduling process has been overhauled. Access issues now receive greater emphasis at the time of records scheduling. Vague determinations rarely slip by.

The tasks are colossal and remain far from completion. Many semi-processed collections lie in limbo awaiting a privacy review. Staffing limitations have required the shelving of a systematic approach to access assessment in favor of ad hoc responses to the most pressing needs. In addition, as MDAH prepared for a new building in 2003, energies shifted to preparations for the move. However, despite all of its current inadequacies, the archives recognizes the importance of protecting privacy and the groundwork is in place.

VII.

Any ethical stance constrains someone's freedom; that does not mean such a stance is unreasonable or unjust. In the end, our acceptance of limitations on the pursuit of knowledge in order to protect a greater common interest is what distinguishes us as moral beings.[66]

Archivists do not exist in a vacuum, but must respond appropriately to the social, cultural, and political environment in which they live and work. Archivists fulfill a dual role. They provide access to the records that they maintain and they protect the subjects of those records. This duality is stressed in the Code of Ethics for Archivists, which states:

> Archivists answer courteously and with a spirit of helpfulness all reasonable inquiries about their holdings, and encourage use of them to the greatest extent compatible with institutional policies, preservation of holdings, legal considerations, individual rights, donor agreements, and judicious use of archival resources. They explain pertinent restrictions to potential users, and apply them equitably.

Use is tempered by privacy considerations. The code directs archivists to ". . . weigh the need for openness and the need to respect privacy rights to determine whether the release of the records or information from records would constitute an invasion of privacy."[67]

Thus, while archivists perform a dual role, they have a single purpose. Access policies should not be viewed as raising the sinister specter of censorship. Access and privacy are not contradictions, but as Heather MacNeil concludes in her study of the ethics of disclosure:

> . . . any ethical stance constrains someone's freedom; that does not mean such a stance is unreasonable or unjust. In the end, our acceptance of limitations on the pursuit of knowledge in order to protect a greater common interest is what distinguishes us as moral beings.[68]

Archivists often are wary of establishing draconian restrictions, yet they must manage their collections in an ethical manner. Access policies should be based on legal obligations and require archivists to keep abreast of evolving state and federal laws. Access policies should encompass responsible collection management and reference policies, but not censorship. They afford archivists the opportunity to truly address and respond to the needs of the public. Access policies require dialogue with the public. By explaining the need for such policies, archivists can articulate their professional responsibilities. Furthermore, by being responsive to and communicating with the public, archivists foster a better understanding of the profession. Thus, access policies enable archivists to show that our profession constitutes a crucial element of the national information infrastructure and remains vital to the democratic process. To reassert John Carlin's statement, the opening of the Sovereignty Commission records affirms the archival role in enabling people to see for themselves just what the state government did and allows Mississippi citizens to hold the government accountable. In the final analysis, fulfilling such a noble function is a rare honor.

11 Archival Access to Lawyers' Papers: The Effect of Legal Privileges

Menzi L. Behrnd-Klodt

Introduction

Archivists encounter legally privileged materials in attorneys' case files, client records of law firms, and corporate legal files. Such materials typically include sensitive personal and confidential information that is unavailable to the public while records are held by their creators. This article considers the nature and effect of the legal privileges in archival records.

American legal privileges derive from centuries-old common law,[1] which protected individual rights and interests valued by society. Versions of the historic privileges are codified in both state and federal law, despite modifications in recent years to prevent the unnecessary shielding of criminals. Many of these privileges seem old-fashioned as data gathering, storage, mining, and sharing technologies foster easy access and use of personal information and nibble away at the old concepts. Perhaps someday the notion of privileged materials will be only a quaint legal footnote.

The Historic Legal Privileges

A legal privilege is a special right or an exemption from a legal duty, often held by a certain person or class with the sole ability to assert or waive it. The holder of a legal privilege may prevent disclosure of information, particularly during a trial. Legal traditions and public policy support four legal privileges[2] protecting

1. confidential communications to certain professionals (attorneys, physicians,[3] and clergy[4]);
2. communications between spouses in connection with criminal matters;
3. constitutional privileges, such as the privilege against self-incrimination;
4. privileges developed to encourage specific conduct, such as the placement for adoption of children born outside of marriage.[5]

The Attorney-Client Privilege

In addition to the historic legal privileges described above, lawyers have special ethical and fiduciary responsibilities to hold all client property, including legal files, in trust for the client.[6] In most U.S. jurisdictions, the client owns his or her legal file, even though the lawyer may hold it and may own certain work product in the file.[7] When the legal representation terminates, the attorney generally has an ethical obligation to return the file promptly to the client.[8] Archivists who accept files from lawyers and law firms must be aware that client records may not be the property of the donor-lawyer.[9] The attorney-client privilege may affect access to legal records in archives and perhaps limit the files available for donation. In addition, archivists must be able to determine which documents are privileged and whether access to them should be granted.

The long-established legal rule of attorney-client privilege[10] safeguards confidential communications made during a professional relationship in order to facilitate the provision of legal services. The rule intends to encourage full and frank communication for the best possible representation by protecting the client's confidential disclosures and the lawyer's advice, thereby preserving the client's rights. The privilege is created at the moment that an attorney-client relationship begins, generally when the attorney is engaged, regardless of whether fees are paid. Thereafter, attorneys are not permitted, and cannot be compelled, to produce communications made in confidence by clients unless the client consents.

The attorney-client privilege protects only communications between attorneys and clients or their authorized representatives, but not between family members or third parties. The privilege protects confidential communications between a corporation's counsel and its employees, and extends to bankrupt and successor corporations. Protected communications include writings, documents, and conversations by and between a client and a lawyer as part of the legal consultation, or when the attorney acts in a professional capacity for the client. To be privileged, the communication must be *confidential,* with no actual disclosure or *intent* to disclose except to those necessary to provide legal services.

The privilege is personal to the client, or by an attorney on behalf of the client. Legally, only the client may assert or waive the privilege. If several clients are involved in the same matter, all must waive the privilege to permit disclosure. Legally and ethically, an attorney may not waive the attorney-client privilege without the client's consent, and unauthorized disclosure of client information by the attorney does not eliminate the privilege, although it may lead to adverse professional consequences for the attorney.

The Extent and Limitations of the Attorney-Client Privilege

Archivists should understand that not every document or file contains legally privileged material. The attorney-client privilege protects only communications made during the attorney-client relationship. Pre-existing documents that had been transferred to an attorney for the purpose of obtaining legal advice may or may not be privileged materials, depending on the reason for their transfer. A client may not hide documents required by a court merely by turning them over to an attorney.

Materials that are not related to the specific reason that led to the creation of the attorney-client relationship may not be privileged, even if they are in legal files. Documents exchanged between an attorney and a client as friends, for general consultation, as routine communications, or for purposes other than seeking legal advice, are not privileged. The attorney-client privilege may not protect a lawyer's *business* advice to the client, or the results of administrative services provided by the lawyer. Attorneys who act as agents to negotiate contracts, prepare tax returns, advise on whether literary manuscripts are publishable, or provide general business or estate-planning services, for example, may not be creating attorney-client privileged documents. A consideration of the nature of the legal representation and the intent of the parties will help to distinguish between business and privileged legal documents.

Communications from a client who is seeking legal advice to assist in planning or committing a crime are not privileged. As of this writing, attorneys need not report a client's breaches of financial or ethical behavior, if not illegal or if the only harm is to property, not persons. Such rules may, however, be adopted by the American Bar Association in the future. If this happens, both the attorney-client privilege and the types of documents to which it pertains would be narrowed. Attorneys would be permitted to disclose information more readily, and presumably, the constraints on archival access to lawyers' papers would be limited.

Information derived from independent knowledge and observation, including police investigations, is exempt from attorney-client privilege. Only the *communication* is protected by the privilege; the underlying facts or information may be disclosed. Many of the formal documents found in legal case files are filed in court and are a matter of public record, although drafts, notes, investigative reports, research, reference material, and notes may be privileged.

Privileged materials in papers that are transferred to the archives may be identified to minimize the risk of disclosure. Substantive correspondence, memos summarizing legal research, witness statements, investigative reports, and attorney's notes might be marked as "Privileged and Confidential" or "Privileged Attorney-Client Communication." Simple procedures might be implemented in the archives to reduce the risk of mistakenly disclosing privileged materials to public scrutiny, such as separating privileged documents from other materials or, if they are commingled, limiting access to the entire file. If privileged documents accidentally are disclosed, adverse consequences may be minimized by seeking the return of any copies of the documents and prohibiting any future disclosures.

Duration of Attorney-Client Privilege

The duration of the attorney-client privilege is a matter of debate among lawyers and of particular interest to archivists. Many attorneys believe the privilege to be perpetual, permanently preventing the disclosure of confidential communications without client consent. Since the privilege is personal to the client, it survives the client's death[11] and may be exercised by the client's heirs or executor to prevent future disclosures of confidential communications. The privilege also survives the termination of the attorney-client relationship, whether by the replacement, firing, or death of the attorney, the dissolution of the law firm, or the termination of litigation.

The strictest interpretations argue that attorney-client privileged communications never can be revealed except by a client. This would deter an attorney from donating, or prevent a risk-averse archives from accepting, attorney-client privileged records if such a transfer could risk disclosure of confidential client information without the client's consent. Lawyers may, and do, elect to destroy their files. They may also return papers to clients, rather than donate them to an archives. Or, they may elect to retain but close certain privileged files, perhaps indefinitely. The Springfield, Massachusetts, law firm that represented Lizzie Borden, accused of one of America's most notorious unsolved murders, still refuses to release the records of her defense and her attorney's trial notes and diary. Acquitted in 1893 on charges of the ax murders of her parents, Borden died in 1927 without heirs. No survivor exists to waive the privilege on her behalf and open the file, and the law firm declines to do so, concerned about reaction of the lawyer disciplinary board, the Massachusetts Board of Overseers.[12] Yet it is difficult to believe that there are good legal or historical reasons to continue to keep the files closed. It seems logical that at some date, public interest in these, and other, legal records should overtake privacy, confidentiality, and legal and ethical concerns in order to permit access. This notion is not universally accepted, however, nor is there agreement on a suitable time period for closure.

Of course, many archives hold records of lawyers and law firms and must grapple with the perplexing issues of legal privileges and providing access. A donor attorney may help guide these archival decisions; however, the rules governing attorney professional conduct usually do not favor the needs of scholars and rarely assist archivists in promoting open access to legal records.[13] Attorneys contemplating donating records to archives should seek opinions of their licensing boards.[14]

Some archives have policies to protect attorney-client privileged material by closing records containing privileged information until all affected parties probably have died, perhaps for fifty or seventy-five years after the file is closed, or from some other arbitrarily chosen date. Yale University, for example, permits access to its lawyer case files fifty years after the latest date represented in the file.[15] A decision to close important legal records for a period of time may be preferable to conducting an item-level review to determine which documents are privileged, attempting to gain consent to open files from clients or heirs, or losing valuable historical material altogether. Archivists who collect attorney-client privileged records are encouraged to develop suitable access policies and to consult with legal counsel to permit the greatest possible use of records while appropriately managing privileged materials.

Attorney Work Product Privilege

The attorney work product privilege has formally existed since 1947[16] to protect against revealing attorneys' mental impressions, analyses, strategies, conclusions, opinions, legal theories, research, investigations, personal impressions, and other materials that have been prepared in contemplation of litigation. Attorney work product is owned and controlled by the lawyer, rather than the client, and the privilege is waived when protected materials are disclosed in court. This protection allows an attorney to investigate all favorable and unfavorable aspects of a legal matter without fear of forced disclosure, and it allows privacy so that the lawyer might properly prepare a case for trial. Both documents and tangible items are protected from disclosure, including materials prepared by other attorneys and by such third persons as investigators. The resulting privilege may be broader than the attorney-client privilege.

Archivists may not often encounter attorney work product in legal case files, as many attorneys remove such materials before files are stored, returned to the client, or donated. Archivists who accept active legal case files should review them for attorney work product, while corporate and organizational archivists should be cautious about disclosing privileged and confidential materials, if doing so may jeopardize litigation, strategic planning, product development, or marketing.

Conclusion

Ethically, archivists must provide equal and as much access as possible to records and information, preserve privacy and confidentiality, uphold institutional policies and further institutional objectives, obey the law, and act professionally. Attorneys must abide by their own professional ethics and rules to safeguard their clients and themselves. These sets of professional standards may conflict, and archivists must balance a host of responsibilities to donors, researchers, collections, and institutions.

12 The Buckley Stops Where? The Ambiguity and Archival Implications of the Family Educational Rights and Privacy Act

Mark A. Greene and Christine Weideman

Student records should not be written off as valueless or even as "more trouble than they are worth." Neither can archivists underestimate the difficulties of their efficient administrative use and possible archival retention.[1]

Introduction

More than twenty-five years after Congress enacted the Family Educational Rights and Privacy Act of 1974 (FERPA),[2] the implications of the law for archivists remain vague. This ambiguity owes much to a remarkable lack of precision in the act itself. But the confusion also results from the relatively passive reaction of archivists to a statute which can be, and recently has been, interpreted to restrict public access to vast segments of educational records that would otherwise be public and/or open to research.

The act was one of many to evolve from the Vietnam War and Watergate eras with the intent of protecting individual privacy and/or of providing access to information kept by the government. The legislative record demonstrates that Congress was concerned that institutional records maintained by schools concerning students contained too much misleading and inappropriate information that parents could not review and that such information was being disclosed by schools to other people making decisions about the student, such as employers and government agencies. Congress enacted FERPA to respond to these concerns. FERPA, also known as the Buckley Amendment in honor of its author, Senator James Buckley of New York, dramatically narrowed access to "educational records" kept by any school receiving federal education funds. It further ensured that students or their parents had access to, and the right to amend, their own records. To date, Congress has amended FERPA a total of six times.[3]

FERPA provides that, to receive federal educational funds, educational agencies must ensure that "education records" are accessible upon request to students or, if the students are minors, to their parents. Records can be challenged by students, or their parents, on the grounds of being misleading, inaccurate, or in violation of the students' privacy rights. Information cannot, excepting certain cases, be released to third parties without the students', or the parents', written consent.

Education records are defined by the act as "records, files, documents, and other materials" containing information directly related to a student, which "are maintained by an educational agency or institution or by a person acting for such agency or institution."[4] An education record under the act need not exist in written form: "any permanent recording such as a tape or film, a picture, or a computer file can be a record."[5] The law implies that it applies retroactively to all student records and that education records are restricted in perpetuity.

FERPA explicitly excludes four types of records. These include so-called sole possession records that are prepared by a single school employee that are neither accessible to nor actually accessed by anyone else,[6] health treatment records of students aged eighteen or older, records created and maintained for law enforcement purposes by a law enforcement unit within an educational institution,[7] and records created about former students, such as alumni directories.

While the effect of the law was sweeping, it was enacted almost as an afterthought. As Lynn M. Daggett wrote, "Congress passed Buckley as a floor amendment to other educational legislation without the benefit of public hearings, committee reports, or much floor debate."[8] The act took the academic universe by surprise. School boards, university deans, academic registrars, and law enforcement officials responded energetically to the passage of FERPA. Archivists unfortunately, in the words of Charles B. Elston, "were the last to know or react."[9] Shortly after passage of the law, Elston, then at the University of Illinois, called for archivists to work toward changes that would open records after the death of the student, permit research use of the records of living students under certain safeguards, and explicitly recognize the historical value of student records.[10]

In 1986, Marjorie Barritt, an archivist at the University of Michigan, lamented that Elston's agenda remained unfulfilled.[11] She noted that universities created less evaluative material within student files, knowing that the students would have access to them, and frequently restricted or eliminated the transfer of student records to the archives. Barritt interviewed a dozen university archivists and found no consensus regarding whether FERPA governed student records forever or whether any legal means of making FERPA records accessible for research existed.[12]

Following up on Barritt's article, Mark Greene, then the archivist at Carleton College, asked the Family Policy Compliance Office (FPCO) of the U.S. Department of Education for a formal opinion concerning the duration of the law's restrictions.[13] In a 1987 article, Greene published the office's written statement that FERPA did *not* apply once a student was deceased. The same article included the details of a protocol adopted by Carleton College that permitted limited research access to the records of living students.[14] That protocol, similar to one at the University of Wisconsin-Madison outlined by Barritt, stipulated that no name-linked data be published as part of the research. This practice appeared permissible under FERPA's exception for "developing, validating, or administering predictive tests, administering student aid programs, and improving instruction."[15]

The Situation Today

Thirty years after FERPA became law, the implications of the statute for archivists and administrators remain remarkably unclear. Not surprisingly, archivists lack consensus about the statute's scope, definition of records, and permissible uses.[16] More unusual, and more foreboding, a growing tendency exists on the part of federal and state courts to expand the reach of the law, apparently without input from the archival community. Most recently, the FERPA office itself, and even the U.S. Supreme Court, have been unable to consistently interpret or significantly clarify the true meaning of the Buckley Amendment.

The two most important unanswered questions for archivists are 1. Does FERPA apply to the records of students who attended educational institutions prior to 1974, and who are still living? 2. What exactly constitutes an "education record" under FERPA? Despite repeated attempts in writing and by phone to elicit a response to the first question from the FPCO,[17] no clear answer exists as to whether pre-1974 records are protected by FERPA. The act seems to imply retroactivity. It twice refers to the period before 1974: once to except pre-1974 letters of recommendation in student files from compulsory access by students, and a second time to reference pre-1974 state statutes that might conflict with FERPA.[18]

If, then, it is reasonable to assume that FERPA applies to all educational records of living students, what exactly is an educational record under FERPA? The definition in the act itself changed significantly within a few months of passage, as outlined in the legislative history of FERPA:

> As first enacted, FERPA provided parents with the right to inspect and review "any and all official records, files, and data directly related to their children, including all material that is incorporated into each student's cumulative record folder, and intended for school use or to be available to parties outside the school or school system, and specifically including, but not necessarily limited to, identifying data, academic work completed, level of achievement (grades, standardized achievement test scores), attendance data, scores on standardized intelligence, aptitude, and psychological tests, interest inventory results, health data, family background information, teacher or counselor ratings and observations, and verified reports of serious or recurrent behavior patterns." The December 31, 1974, amendments substituted the term **"education records"** for the "laundry list" of records subject to FERPA.
>
> **"Education records"** were defined in the December 31, 1974, amendments as "those records, files, documents, and other materials which contain information directly related to a student; and are maintained by an educational agency or institution or by a person acting for such agency or institution."[19]

The precise practical meaning of this evolving definition remains remarkably difficult to deduce. Consider the following list of material, commonly held by a typical university archives:

- Registrar's transcripts
- Teachers' grade books
- Graded student papers
- Student papers without visible grades
- Senior theses
- Records of student organizations, including minutes and correspondence
- Correspondence (or e-mail) from students to faculty, about coursework
- Correspondence (or e-mail) from students to faculty, not related to coursework (e.g., to student organizations, or to politics)
- Correspondence (or e-mail) from parents of students to faculty or administrators, not related to their students' academic performance
- Correspondence and other files of coaches and athletic directors, which contain reference to the on-field performance of student athletes

- Web sites created by students as class assignments
- Personal Web sites of students mounted on institutional servers

A recent small informal survey of ten college and university archivists who should be familiar with FERPA indicates the ambiguity of the act. The nine respondents who *were* familiar with the statute unanimously agreed about the FERPA status of only four of these sets of material. The surveyed archivists were certain that registrar's transcripts and teachers' grade books were covered by FERPA and that student and parent correspondence with faculty not related to academic performance was not covered by FERPA.[20] That certainty may be built on a poor foundation, however, if court rulings are considered.

Teachers' grade books offer a good example of the confusion surrounding the FERPA definition of an educational record. In a 2001 brief to the Supreme Court on behalf of the FPCO, the U.S. solicitor general insisted that

> The court of appeals erred in assuming . . . that a teacher's grade book is an education record under FERPA. FERPA excludes from the definition of "education records" the records of instructional personnel that are in the "sole possession of the maker thereof" and are "not accessible or revealed to any other person except a substitute."

However, the brief continues,

> Under FERPA, if a teacher discloses his or her grade book to someone other than a substitute, the grade book would then become an education record. The teacher's disclosure of the grade book would not violate FERPA, however, if it was made to another school official or teacher of the same school or school district who has been determined by the institution "to have legitimate educational interests, including the educational interests of the child for whom consent would otherwise be required."[21]

A reasonable interpretation of these statements would be that a teacher's grade book kept solely by the student's teacher is *not* normally covered by FERPA but that if the grade book is "disclosed" (transferred or donated?) to the university archives or to any other nonschool third party it might well become an educational record restricted by the act. Even if the archives was assumed to be part of the school or school district, or if the archivist was assumed to be "another school official" with "legitimate educational interests" in the grade book, FERPA would seem to apply to any disclosure of the grade book to a researcher.

Yet the situation is even more complicated by the argument in the same brief that the legislative history of FERPA clearly intended the act to apply only to a school's central or cumulative files on students, not to any and all records related to a student's education. "Significantly, the most expansive description of covered records provided parents a right to inspect 'any and all official records, files, and data directly related to their children, including all material that is incorporated into each student's cumulative record folder. . . ,'" wrote the solicitor general, adding that subsequent amendments did nothing to indicate "that Congress intended to depart from the focus of FERPA as originally enacted on 'official' records, the student's 'cumulative file,' and 'school records.'"[22]

But in deciding the case to which the solicitor general addressed these arguments, the U.S. Supreme Court explicitly refused to accept or reject either the definition of a teacher's grade book as an educational record or the related definition of such student assignments as term papers as educational records: "the instant holding is limited to the narrow point that, assuming a teacher's grade book is an education record, grades on students' papers are not covered by the act at least until the teacher has recorded them. The Court does not reach the broader question whether the Act protects grades on individual assignments once they are turned in to teachers."[23] Frustratingly, from an archival point of view, the court's decision *implied* acceptance of the solicitor general's narrow definition of educational records as those kept centrally by the institution,[24] but by not formally addressing that "broader question," it left the meaning of "educational records" very vague.

With its ruling, the Supreme Court did nothing to clarify the status of student papers, senior theses, and student Web sites that had been created as class assignments. In his brief to the court, the U.S. solicitor general argued on behalf of the FPCO that

> The fact that a particular classroom practice may disclose a grade given on a particular homework or classroom assignment does not mean that the practice violates FERPA. Many educational practices inevitably reveal aspects of a student's academic abilities and are weighed as a part of a student's final course evaluation, including, for example, the public display of science projects, the posting of a classroom chart that records the number of books read by each student throughout the school year, students' handing back graded homework and classroom assignments, and teachers' posting of homework or classroom assignments. FERPA does not invalidate such common and longstanding teaching methods.[25]

Though this argument can reasonably be read to mean that graded assignments are *not* covered by FERPA, and thus might be made accessible through a university archives to researchers, the situation is not so clear cut. The solicitor general's own argument contains a footnote that immediately muddies the water: "if a school's final evaluation of a student in an art course consisted of a portfolio of selected pieces of the student's work and that portfolio was retained in the institution's records about the student, those pieces, too, would be education records."[26] So, would a student thesis turned over by a teacher to the school library or archives in the 1950s be an educational record? And would it matter whether there was a grade on the paper?

In 1993, the FPCO had taken a stab at providing a clear answer. Jackie Esposito, an archivist at Penn State University, asked the FPCO for clarification of whether undergraduate theses constituted "education records" under FERPA. Many college and universities house such theses, sometimes dating back to the nineteenth century. In a letter to Esposito, the director of the office stated that no explicit exceptions within the act

> would permit making student theses available to the public, such as in the University library, *without first obtaining written consent from the student.* Further, the written consent must specify the records that may be disclosed; state the purpose of the disclosure; and identify the party or class of parties to whom the disclosure may be made. . . . [T]his office would consider any written statement by a student permitting publication of a thesis sufficient consent under FERPA because such statement shows that the student intended the work to become publicly available. However, any other circumstances regarding making student theses available to the public without written consent would need to be reviewed by this Office.[27]

In a subsequent "clarification" of this statement, sent in September 1993 to the ALA Washington Office Newsline (ALAWON), the office allowed that actual written consent was perhaps not strictly necessary, so long as students knew in advance of completion that a thesis would be made publicly accessible in the archives or library. "Neither the statute, the legislative history, nor the FERPA regulations require institutions to depart from established practices regarding the placement or disclosure of student theses so long as students have been advised in advance that a particular undergraduate or graduate thesis will be made publicly available as part of the curriculum requirements."[28] While this clarification makes it much simpler for schools to collect and make accessible theses prospectively, it effectively prohibits making older theses accessible. Of course, the validity of the FPCO advisory letters has recently been questioned both by the federal courts and by the solicitor general, so it remains unclear how seriously archivists should weigh this interpretation.[29]

If the FERPA status of grade books and student assignments is unclear, surely it seems incontrovertible that student correspondence with faculty members is not an educational record so long as it does not deal with the student's academic performance. But, according to a Superior Court judge in Maine, e-mail messages from students to a faculty member about the conduct of a local rabbi *are* educational records as defined by FERPA.[30] Further, a trial judge in Louisiana ruled that a decision about whether correspondence from a parent to a school about general curriculum matters, containing nothing "about her child's performance in school or other personal details about the child," constituted an educational record under FERPA seemed sufficiently uncertain that a jury should decide the case.[31] The Texas attorney general has opined that a videotape of a school board meeting, which under state law would be public, is in fact restricted by FERPA because it includes a student performance of a play.[32] An attorney for the Indiana School Boards agreed that video made by school officials of an extracurricular activity is protected by FERPA.[33] None of these instances have direct impact beyond the local jurisdictions of the respective courts. Still, the potential harm and confusion for college and university archivists is clear. Without an explicit definition of "education record" under FERPA, almost anything might be held to be covered by the act, and almost any judicial authority can make the determination.

We underscore almost anything, because, to date, there has been no indication that courts even at the local level can conceive of the material created and kept by student organizations as "education records." The Supreme Court's decision in *Owasso* is only the latest decision to clarify that students are not, in most instances, agents of the schools they attend.[34] Yet it is not absolutely clear that files or videos or other material created by students and student organizations would not *become* educational records under FERPA if owned (in FERPA's language, "maintained") by an office or official of the school—say, the university archives or university archivist. This possibility would be the FERPA equivalent to the very real situation faced by special collections repositories at some universities a decade or more ago, when the public records laws of their states were interpreted to require that any collections donated to the repository were publicly accessible regardless of restrictions negotiated with the donor. Specific amendments to state statutes were required to enable repositories in universities to maintain restricted collections.[35]

Nor are the dangers of the ambiguities within FERPA restricted to university archives. Other repositories, such as state and local historical societies and state archives, acquire materials which may be, may not be, or might once have been "education records" covered by the act. If a teacher donates his or her grade books to a historical society, have the grade books become educational records because they are no longer in the teacher's sole possession? If so, who is responsible for violating FERPA assuming that those grade books are made accessible to researchers? If the state archives acquires registrar's records—one of the few categories of materials that seems unequivocally to constitute an educational record—from a dissolved school district, are the records still protected by FERPA? To date there has been no discussion of these issues, much less any judicial rulings. And the FPCO remains silent.

What Archivists Should Do

As the past thirty years have shown, FERPA can be confusing, ambiguous, and frustrating to enforce for archivists. If archivists believe, however, that "student records" are important to preserve and make available for research, and that student privacy must be protected, then the following steps can and should be taken.

At the National Level

The Colleges and University Archives Section (C&U) of the Society of American Archivists is superbly positioned to provide leadership at the national level to address the needs of archivists and researchers concerning FERPA-covered records. The section might begin by rallying colleagues in manuscript repositories and state archives to focus attention on FERPA, since the act's ambiguities touch those institutions as well. C&U can educate lawmakers about the historical value of education records and explain the importance of clarifying FERPA so that the law both protects privacy and supports research.[36] The section can make the following recommendations to Congress:

1. Determine whether FERPA applies to student records created before 1974.
2. Define a specific duration for FERPA to apply to records, such as seventy-two years after creation, a closure period that governs United States census records, rather than leaving archivists and researchers to track the specific lifetime of every student.
3. Address the inherent ambiguity in the term "education records." The confusion over what comprises these records is causing courts, at all levels, to make such determinations. Congress could instead take the lead by delineating the kinds of materials that need

protection. Alternatively, Congress could retain the broad definition, but amend it to provide such exemptions as
- student theses placed in repositories prior to 1974;
- communications between students and school employees, and between parents and school employees, that are unrelated to academic performance, health, or disciplinary matters;
- records documenting extracurricular activities, including athletics, that are unrelated to academic performance, health, or disciplinary matters.
4. Include a provision that permits research access to FERPA-covered records if Institutional Review Board protocols are implemented so that individual privacy is protected.

Most of these recommendations have been made before by the few archivists who have written about FERPA and its implementation. They remain as valid as when first written, but no national organization has made a concerted effort to implement them.

At the Repository Level

While waiting for action at the national level, archivists who collect records covered by FERPA must assume that the definition of "education records" will remain ambiguous for the indefinite future. Each repository should write a FERPA records policy. At the very least, if a violation occurs, the repository can show courts or government officials that it made a good faith effort to prevent the problem. The policy should assume that FERPA applies to the "education records" of all living graduates/nongraduates of the institution, and it should include the following elements:

1. That the institution's definition of "education records" include the kinds of materials kept in whatever the individual institution defines as the "central student file." Recognize that the definition will probably also include records not in the central file, even though the act itself remains vague. Archivists will need to base their definition on court cases, FERPA amendments, local practices, and common sense and review it on a periodic basis. Concomitant with creating this definition, archivists should determine where "education records" are found, both in institutional offices and in archival record units and manuscript collections within the repository.
2. That FERPA coverage expires upon the death of a student. Since even the most efficient alumni office cannot track the life spans of every student, the archivist should work with other officials at the

school to define a time span that will reasonably encompass the lifetimes of all students and use that as the *practical* delimiter of FERPA's duration. For example, the Manuscripts and Archives Department in the Yale University Library uses seventy-five years from date of graduation for its closure of "education records" under FERPA. After that, the records are open for research, because the students can reasonably be presumed to be dead. Carleton College took a slightly more conservative route and chose eighty years as the practical duration of FERPA.
3. That if the institution decides to provide access to FERPA-covered records to researchers, to define the terms under which access will be granted in a policy statement that researchers must read and sign. At a minimum, the statement should provide the institution's definition of "education records" and state that researchers must agree not to publish personally identifiable information from them. The policy might also require researchers to be approved by an institutional review board, such as those used by Carleton College and the University of Wisconsin-Madison.
4. That if the institution decides not to provide access to FERPA-covered records, to develop guidelines to close any and all collections that contain "education records." The length of time that the collections must be closed will depend on the dates of the "education records" in them and the period of time that the institution has chosen to apply FERPA restrictions to the records (see point 3 above). Closed collections must include those that contain only scattered "education records," such as faculty paper collections that may contain grade books/sheets, recommendations, and student examinations and papers. The only alternative for opening the latter is to develop processing guidelines with an emphasis on item-level examination in order to remove all FERPA-covered records.

The archivist should determine whom to include in the writing of the repository's FERPA policy. Given the penalties imposed for FERPA violations, appropriate institution officials, such as the registrar or academic provost, dean, or secretary, or their representatives, and the archivist's supervisor should be included.

Archivists should assume that FERPA, in one form or another, will remain in force for the indefinite future. It affects the work of every college and university archives in the country and therefore archivists must have a voice in its definition, interpretation, and application. Since the legislation's enactment, archivists have not had that voice. Instead, individual repositories have had to define their own policies and rely on their (hopefully) good judgment to protect students' privacy while supporting research efforts. Because FERPA's impact is so far-reaching, however, and because the voice of the courts, rather than of archivists and historians, is becoming more and more determinant, it is time for archivists to speak.

APPENDIX A

November 9, 2001
Family Policy Compliance Office
U.S. Department of Education
600 Independence Avenue S.W.
Washington, D.C. 20202-4605

Dear Sir or Madam:

We write to request clarification about the application of the Federal Educational Rights and Privacy Act (FERPA), on behalf of ourselves and many colleagues who administer archives within and outside of colleges and universities. There have been instances in the past when your office was helpful in clarifying answers to these kinds of questions and we hope you can do so again. We want to disseminate the information we receive from your office through newsletters, book chapters, and/or journal articles.

I. "Education records" defined as ". . .records, files, documents, and other materials which contain information directly related to a student. . ."

1. Are papers (e.g., term papers, essay assignments) written by a student to complete course requirements, included in the definition of "education records"?
2. Are websites created by students for class assignments included in the definition of "education records"? Are personal websites of students stored on a university's webspace included in the definition of "education records"?
3. Can any "education records" be made available for research if names or personal identifying information is removed from them?
4. Are the records (e.g., meeting minutes, membership lists, activity reports) of student organizations (e.g., campus radio station, a fraternity or sorority, Hispanic students union), which might include references to individual students and their actions, included in the definition of "education records"? If so, does it matter whether the student organization is "officially recognized" by the school and/or whether it receives funds from the school?
5. FERPA was passed in 1974. Does it apply to the records of students who attended educational institutions prior to 1974 and who are still living?

Family Policy Compliance Office
November 9, 2001
Page 2

6. Collections of personal papers of faculty members often include references written by the faculty member on behalf of a former or current student. These are not formal references included in the official file of the student. Are they included in the definition of "education records"?
7. Are letters and e-mails from students to school faculty and administrators included in the definition of "education records," even if the content of the communication is unrelated to the students' classroom and/or campus activities (e.g., discussing with a professor their mutual interest in changing a local criminal ordinance; asking the university president to change the school's policy regarding investments in South Africa)?
8. Are letters and e-mails from the parents of students to school faculty and administrators included in the definition of "education records," even if the content of the communication is unrelated to their children's performance or activities at the school (e.g., complaining to the university president about changes to the school's curriculum or investment policy)?
9. Are video and audio recordings, made by a college or university of student activities—e.g., plays, performances, declamations—included in the definition of "education records"? Many university archives and libraries hold such recordings and make them accessible, but a recent interpretation by the Texas attorney general holds that a video of a school board meeting is governed by FERPA (and therefore cannot be made public) because it contained a performance of a school play.
10. Can a university/college impose restrictions on student records that are more stringent than FERPA's (i.e., can they close student records for a period of time that might exceed a student's lifetime)? If so, and someone requests access to the record of a student who has died (whose record, therefore, would be available under FERPA standards), which takes precedence, the FERPA restrictions, or the university's more stringent restrictions?
11. Finally, and most generally, is there a formal explanation of exactly what types of material are included in the term "education records"? In addition to questions about class assignments and recordings, questions have been raised about disciplinary records and other material collected or generated by schools in the course of administering student life.

Family Policy Compliance Office
November 9, 2001
Page 3

II. "Education records" defined as ". . .and maintained by an educational agency or institution or by a person acting for such agency or institution."

1. If a collection of personal papers, such as the files of a university professor, include materials which would normally be covered by FERPA, but the collection is donated to a repository unaffiliated with the educational institution at which the materials were generated (e.g., a state or local historical society), are the materials still considered to be covered by FERPA? If so, and such material is made accessible to the public as a result of such a donation, is the "violator" of FERPA the faculty member, the school that employed the faculty member, or the archival institution that receives the donation?
2. Less frequently, but on occasion, a private educational institution (academy or college) closes its doors and donates its records to a historical society. What are the obligations of such an historical society, under FERPA, for administering the "education records" of such a defunct school? Does it matter whether the material was donated to the historical society before or after passage of FERPA?

Thank you for any information you can provide. If we can help clarify any of our questions, please let us know.

Sincerely Yours,

CHRISTINE WEIDEMAN
Assistant Head Manuscripts and Archives
Yale University Library
203/432-1740 Internet: christine.weideman@yale.edu

MARK A. GREENE
Head of Research Center Programs
Henry Ford Museum & Greenfield Village
313/982-6075 Internet: MarkGr@hfmgv.org

APPENDIX B

Mark Greene (Henry Ford Museum & Greenfield Village) and Christine Weideman (Yale University Manuscripts and Archives Section) are co-authoring a chapter on the Federal Educational Rights and Privacy Act (FERPA) for an upcoming book to be published by SAA: *Privacy and Confidentiality: A Reader*, eds. Menzi L. Behrnd-Klodt and Peter J. Wosh. As part of our research for this chapter, we would like to gather information about how college and university archives currently interpret and administer FERPA. *No institution- or name-linked information will be published from this survey.* In addition to using the information from the survey in the book chapter, any information provided for question 23 will be shared (again, anonymously) with SAA Council and the leadership of the SAA C&U section. The survey itself should only take 15–20 minutes to complete. We greatly appreciate your help with this project.

1. Is your institution: __2_Public __3_Private

2. Number of students enrolled in your institution (undergraduate and graduate): *2000; 50,000; 80,000; 14,248; 12,000*

3. Approximate quantity of (check 1) ___linear feet *400; 250,000; 22,000* ___cubic feet *11,000; 16,000* in your archives (excluding manuscripts collections, if any): _____

4. Number of professional staff (FTE) working with archives (as opposed to manuscript) material: *1; 3; 8; 1; 3*

5. For how many years has your institution had an archives? *100; 36; 96; 36; 66*

6. Are you aware of the Family Educational Rights and Privacy Act (FERPA)? __4 Yes __1 No

7. Does your institution have a written policy defining what constitutes "educational records" under FERPA? __2 Yes __3 No

8. Does your institution have a written policy defining procedures under which researchers might be permitted access to educational records protected by FERPA for compiling aggregate or non-name-linked data? __3 Yes __2 No__ So far as I know no such access is permitted under FERPA.

For the following types of material, please
a) check the box if you hold such material in your archives
b) if you do hold such material, please list the approximate span dates of that material
c) whether or not you hold such material, please indicate if you believe such material is protected by the provisions of FERPA as an "educational record."

	Type of Material	Span Dates	FERPA Record
9.	_2_ Registrar's transcripts	1859–1970; 1813–2000	4 yes; 0 no
10.	_1_ Teachers' grade books	1859–1970	4 yes; 0 no
11.	_2_ Graded student papers	1880s; 1753–2000	3 yes; 1 no
12.	_2_ Student papers w/out visible grades	1880s–pres; 1758–pres	2 yes; 2 no
13.	_3_ Senior theses	1859–1990s; 1890s–pres; 1753–2000	3 yes; 1 no
14.	_5_ Records of student organizations, including minutes and corresp.	1900–1950; 1880–1998 1863–1990s; 1890s–pres; 1753–pres	1 yes; 3 no
15.	_2_ Correspondence (or e-mail) from students to faculty—about course work	1880s–1990s; up to 2000	2 yes; 2 no
16.	_2_ Correspondence (or e-mail) from students to faculty, not related to coursework (e.g., to student organizations, or to politics)	1880s–1990s; up to 2000	0 yes; 4 no
17.	_1_ Correspondence (or e-mail) from parents of students to faculty or administrators, not related to their students' academic performance.	Up to 2000	0 yes; 4 no
18.	_1_ Correspondence and other files of coaches and athletic directors,		

	which contain reference to the on-field performance of student athletes.	*1853–2000*	*2 yes; 2 no*
19.	_1_ Web sites created by students as class assignments	*1995–Present*	*3 yes; 1 no*
20.	_0_ Personal web sites of students mounted on institutional servers		*1 yes; 3 no*

21. For material you consider governed by FERPA, does your archives make them publicly accessible upon the death of the student (or a fixed time lapse to presumptively cover death) as permitted by FERPA, or does your institution restrict access longer than FERPA requires?

    2 Restricted until death of student

    ___ Restricted by institutional policy for ____ years from enrollment or graduation (circle one)

    ___ Never made public, used only by school officials

    2 Other: *varies based on mtls—thesis available for reading, copying requires permission; registrar records permanently restricted/life of student + five years*

22. What, if anything, do you most wish was clearer about FERPA?
    Procedures for handling student-related activities, i.e., correspondence, student activities
    Which documents constitute the "student file."
    Can releases be obtained from students to make materials available?
    How does FERPA relate to pre-FERPA records?

23. What, if anything, would you most like to see SAA provide guidance on, as relates to FERPA, its interpretation, and its application?
    Best practices guidelines
    How can we abide by FERPA but retain information of historical value?
    SAA workshop taught by someone who as been involved in interpreting FERPA

THANK YOU

INSTITUTIONAL PERSPECTIVES

Institutional considerations greatly affect archival programs. All archivists grapple with privacy issues, but their specific challenges vary depending upon their broader programmatic context. Governments, universities, businesses, hospitals, religious organizations, and historical societies constitute very diverse archival work environments. Archivists try to apply uniform professional principles in each of these settings, but implementation necessarily depends on the idiosyncratic work cultures, political relationships, and power structures that function within their particular organizational milieus. This section brings together articles by archivists with substantial experience in the religious, corporate, and health care sectors in an effort to examine their common problems, explore their significant structural differences, and begin to develop a more theoretical framework for considering privacy and confidentiality questions across institutional boundaries. Interestingly, records-related issues have generated heated debate and produced considerable controversy in all three sectors over the past several years.

Corporate and clergy scandals have especially highlighted the complex privacy problems facing businesses and ecclesiastical organizations. Recent recordkeeping debacles have surfaced at firms ranging from Arthur Andersen to Enron, exposing the shoddy documentation practices and remarkable inattention to records-accountability issues within many major corporate concerns.[1] In other instances, businesses and industries have suffered public relations fiascos and financial losses by actually keeping good records and permitting public access. Journalists and litigants have successfully combed through the historical records of tobacco companies, for example, to discover damning evidence concerning past company research that documented the health dangers associated with cigarette smoke. Corporate archivists and records managers occupy a particularly precarious position, seeking to satisfy regulatory demands, protect the interests of their employers, and exercise their mandate to fully document organizational life.

Religious institutions have confronted equally serious problems. When the *Boston Globe* successfully obtained the release in 2001 of previously sealed court records involving sexual abuse lawsuits against a Roman Catholic priest, the religious recordkeeping landscape shifted. Transparency, accountability, and paper trails achieved heightened significance as dioceses sought to answer charges that they had either ignored or covered up serious problems for decades. Efforts at damage control proved ineffective. Bernard Cardinal Law's claim that poor recordkeeping had prevented him from properly administering the Boston Archdiocese, for example, drew widespread derision and only increased calls for his resignation. Other dioceses began "combing their files for past complaints and jousting with authorities about what to do with their accused priests," according to *Globe* reporters. Many embittered priests fought back, claiming that their own rights to privacy had been compromised through the release of documents filled with unsubstantiated generalizations and innuendo. The long-term implications for archivists and records programs remain unclear.[2]

North American health care institutions also found themselves at the center of social debates concerning privacy and records at the turn of the twenty-first century. The immediate issues owed less to specific scandals than to federal legislation, changing information technologies, and a desire to streamline administrative costs and burdens in the medical field. The Health Insurance Portability and Accountability Act of 1996 (HIPAA) in the United States, as well as Canada's Personal Information Protection and Electronic Documents Act (PIPEDA), mandated new measures to ensure the privacy of health care information and provide patients with more control over access to their records.[3] The legislation also created some troublesome archival problems in both countries. Individual patients, or their official representatives, now needed to sign authorization forms to allow research into their medical histories. Questions surfaced concerning whether the legislation might affect the availability of nonmedical documentation within health care archives, and it remained unclear whether archivists could ever open patient records for research. Many legal departments initially adopted a very conservative stance toward allowing any access at all. Health care archivists, similar to their colleagues in the corporate and religious worlds, appeared to face an uncertain future with unpredictable long-range consequences for their operations.[4]

The contributors to this section of the reader approach these issues from a variety of perspectives, reflecting their distinct institutional experiences. They differ in their assessments of current trends, their evaluations of appropriate archival roles, and their visions for the future. Mark J. Duffy and Christine M. Taylor focus specifically on hierarchical religious organizations, exploring the concepts of organizational culture, human agency, and trust. They suggest that archivists potentially can assume influential and powerful positions within institutions, based on their professional obligation to safeguard the integrity of organizational documentation. Recordkeepers should play important roles in creating institutional meaning, spanning the boundaries between internal and external constituencies, and serving as trustworthy professionals who exemplify the virtues of reliability and authenticity. Archivists have, of course, often appeared either unable or reluctant to effectively harness the power and influence that their recordkeeping function naturally confers. Duffy and Taylor suggest the possibilities for archivists to assume a more central role within their organizations, and their argument appears especially timely in light of the scandals and uncertainties described above. Archivists may find that their core professional values have much to contribute to institutions during moments of crisis.

Paul C. Lasewicz, however, views the archival implications of social and institutional change through a very different lens. He speculates that current trends in copyright and licensing regulations will mix and blend with property law and privacy rights in ways that will erode corporate archivists' traditional roles and obligations to researchers.[5] Rights owners should fare quite well in his distopian archival future, but corporate curators will need to radically reconsider their institutional roles to remain viable. Lasewicz remains convinced that technological change has the potential to transform archival programs into significant corporate liabilities. Such factors as the increased social sensitivity over privacy violations, fears about mounting potentially sensitive information on Web sites, and a lack of clarity concerning the ownership and proper licensing of images may make archival programs a very risky business for many companies. It remains questionable whether archivists can actively influence records policies within their organizations, or whether they remain destined merely to react to broader corporate developments. Lasewicz views corporate archivists as entrepreneurial, in the sense of effectively building internal constituencies for their programs, but their inward focus makes them very vulnerable to short-term policy shifts and bottom-line considerations. They appear much less likely than religious archivists, by culture and temperament, to successfully establish their operations as repositories of reliability, authenticity, and trust.

Barbara L. Craig takes a somewhat more optimistic view of the prospects and possibilities for archivists in the medical and health care field. Echoing Duffy and Taylor, she believes that archivists can play a pivotal institutional role by balancing the interests of patients, practitioners, the broader community, and future generations. Unlike the two previous articles in this section, Craig attempts to place current debates over records privacy within a long-term historical framework. She carefully considers the origins and evolution of medical records, charts alterations in patient-practitioner relationships that have historically influenced privacy expectations, and reminds readers that change has remained a constant theme in the informational environment of health care institutions since the mid-nineteenth century. Perhaps most significantly, Craig outlines a broad social role for records professionals. She emphasizes the fact that archivists have obligations that transcend their specific institutions. They remain responsible to future generations, as well as to communities of interest that supersede the narrower interests of patients and practitioners. Historical accountability provides the ultimate justification for an archival program, and archivists can only achieve authority and influence within their own institutions by fulfilling their loftiest ethical and social roles. Craig thus moves the privacy discussion beyond the immediate challenges of HIPAA and PIPEDA, and toward a reconceptualization of medical archivists' broader responsibilities.

L. Dale Patterson concludes this section with a much more specific institutional case study, but one that reflects many of the themes exemplified in the three preceding essays. He traces the United Methodist Church's experience in drafting its open meetings and open records policy, focusing primarily on the period since the 1980s. His article highlights several factors that influenced denominational deliberations and defined institutional attitudes toward privacy and confidentiality. Historical peculiarities and cultural considerations proved determinative, as Patterson's brief survey of church history makes clear. The attitudes and interests of several key political constituencies within the Methodist fellowship also shaped the specific provisions that became part of the open records policy. Perhaps most significantly, however, Patterson's article testifies to the interpenetration of institutional sectors within American life. The United Methodist Church bore no particular legal obligation to draft an open records law or to make its deliberations more accessible. Yet, the denomination found itself operating within a post-Watergate American milieu that demanded openness, accountability, and responsibility from social institutions. The Methodists needed to respond to these demands, no less than did the federal government itself. The process by which this one religious body grappled with conflicting demands for privacy and openness thus illustrates a process shared by many other institutions. Indeed, as with all of the studies in this section, Patterson's contribution underscores the need for archivists to think broadly about the political, cultural, and social implications of their day-to-day institutional environments.

13 Trust and Professional Agency in the Archives of Religious Organizations: An Archival Perspective on Confidence Keeping

Mark J. Duffy and Christine M. Taylor

Introduction

Archivists are in a position today of rediscovering the characteristics of the trustworthy record and the expertise required to safeguard the full set of cultural activities that sit behind the creative process. Archivists are trained to apply their technical competence to the custodial task, yet they enter into already-existing relationships that form an organized setting for the documentation environment. Within this landscape, archivists apply their professional skills, but they must also learn the norms and cultural assumptions of the organization to which they belong. This essay explores the role and activity of archivists in organizational cultures, specifically those of religions institutions, where archivists exercise leadership in positions of authority, agency, and trust. The capacity for this effective role lies in their domain expertise and in the networks around which routine information exchange and decision making take place.

Organizations such as hierarchical religious institutions, as well as other nonprofit and nongovernmental organizations, are characterized by the intentional embrace of strong value and belief systems. Archivists in these environments cannot have a constricted view of their professional role, but must accommodate a professionalism that incorporates the goals and mission of the organization for which they labor. Archivists act alternately as both outsiders and insiders; they never act completely alone, but as part of the community they document. In the course of serving the information requirements of the organization, an archivist fashions a communicative space by using organizational structures to enact power and authority as fully socialized members of the institution. While professional (technical) competence is valued, the organization rewards creative and invested people, including archivists, with strategic leadership roles.[1] The ability of the archivist to recognize the situational limits and possibilities of role differentiation is at the heart of agency. Agency allows the archivist to negotiate a trusted place as both competent professional and fiduciary agent. We wonder to what extent archivists are able to communicate and structure their organizational role to achieve greater influence in the administration of privacy, confidentiality, and access to records of Catholic and mainline Protestant denominational archives, and indeed, to the recordkeeping practices of other religious and secular organizations.

The theory of agency frames the discussion of the individual archivist's responsibility for administering personal information and corporate communication, and the concept of privacy serves to illustrate how archivists can effectively generate institutional trust. Thus, archivists intentionally seek to influence the organizational environment in reference to the way records are created and valued. Each information environment creates the ethical conditions necessary for ensuring that a range of individual and group confidences is respected. In this sense, privacy is a relational concept. Personal privacy, especially the physical, constitutes an area over which individuals exercise some ultimate control and autonomy. Informational privacy is, however, the least controlled of the private realms and is a profound source of anxiety in organizational life.[2] The lack of a controlling privacy ethic in the larger social system leads one to look at organizations as the sites where individuals resolve privacy differences. Hierarchical religious institutions are the setting for this essay in order to illustrate the archivists' exercise of professional and personal judgment in the interpretation of the concept of privacy in everyday, work-centered interactions.[3]

Privacy, Confidence Keeping, and Access in a Covenantal Relationship

Privacy and confidentiality are metaphors for the complexity of modern relationships. In organizational settings, individuals will frequently consider the effects of decisions in terms of opportunities for augmenting self-management or conversely responding to forms of social control. Privacy and access are invoked alongside the "balancing" image to describe a compromise between the purely personal and the publicly accessible. Quite apart from the personal "take" that one will adopt to privacy and freedom of information, the archivist must find a way to integrate the personal and the professional into a dominant organizational interpretation and ethical framework that presuppose a vocabulary, narrative, and practice of communal privacy and confidence keeping.[4] These organizational interpretation systems are basic to what Penny Becker calls the "idioculture" of congregational and denominational life.[5] Two dominant ethical themes relating to privacy and confidentiality in the idioculture of mainline Christian religion in America are covenant and confession. Organizational church behavior depends on a tacit understanding of covenantal relationships.

Covenants are agreements ideally rooted in a reciprocal obligation to discern right conduct as part of a community-bound discourse about responsibility, moral choice, human dignity, and the sacredness of human relationships.[6] Although legal contracts may be binding, the implied covenant constitutes the moral force upon which judgments, accountabilities, and opportunism are evaluated in pastoral and professional behavior. As in any trust relationship, "the primary burden of responsibility falls on the one with the greater power."[7] Other influences such as the size of the organization, the structural placement of the position, the level of goal identification, and networks of organizational relationships merge with the covenantal ethos to place the archivists of religious organizations in potentially powerful positions of influence over management and access to institutionwide sources of information.

Confession, particularly the priest-penitent privilege, has evolved into a special instrument for protecting secrecy and confidences.[8] While it has only limited impact on recordkeeping, it has successfully infused religious organizations with the concept of the legitimate secret and the importance of nondisclosure of personal information.[9] The civil law extension of the privilege to clergy, often in the absence of historical claims by denominations, has redefined the private sphere of religion.[10] The archivist's perspective on access and privacy in the internal environment of religious organizations draws on the ethic of respect for confidences and is further qualified by the external influences of civil law and normative practice.

Privacy and access are difficult concepts for archivists of religious institutions who confront uncertainty in the prudential exercise of institutional controls for privacy, secrets, and information access. Religious organizations, especially those that have elaborate institutional structures, stake claim to an alternative experience of the fulfilling human life in the face of secular material culture. They attach great weight to the outward expression of their members' values and beliefs in the conduct of civil society. Religious organizations are unapologetic in their mission to transform individual lives and social relationships by pursuing theologically inspired conceptions of human dignity. Despite repeated observations of their decline, private religious organizations have thrived remarkably well in pluralistic twentieth-century American society. The question of privacy touches on the rights of the religious faithful, but also extends to the privileges of the institutional Church, which is obliged to protect the rights and the interests of the whole community. Archivists of religious organizations interpret this relationship when they select and manage documentation, devise procedures for the protection of confidences, and create opportunities for the membership to access information that is essential to carrying out the mission and full potential of the community.

The interplay of privacy, confidentiality, the public life, and access, as illustrated in the documentation process, presents a complex information environment for archivists. Denominational archivists who oversee programs that include the related functions of records management, electronic records, and other knowledge resources are positioned to both understand the information ecology of their organizations and to affect the way in which internal information is communicated to the advantage of the membership and leadership. It is nearly the rule that archives of denominations attempt to document the full experiential range of the faith community's history, including individual leadership, networks of ministry, loosely connected movements, affiliated and independent agencies, and related religious societies.[11] Archivists bring to this organizational mix a set of professional expectations that includes ethical judgments about the obligations to employers as well as a socialized understanding of the various and often competing institutional interests. The dual responsibilities of organizational interpretation and the fiduciary agency of the archivist in a religious organization are practiced in a variety of institutional forms of control and freedom. The perception of the archivist's role is shaped by denominational traditions, the history of the custodial relationship, the amount of centralization in recordkeeping functions and authority, and the structural relationships in place to support the agency relationship.

The Informational Environment of Religion in Society

Religious organizations have an essential ideological cohesion regarding privacy that is unlike other organizational environments of secular society, where disagreement marks the boundaries of privacy beyond the most intimate physical and mental states. An ethic of discernment, confidentiality, and respect for the dignity of the covenantal community promotes communicative interaction at a very personal level and allows reasonable discussion of such sensitive issues as the personal health and conduct of members, beginning- and end-of-life choices, rights of lay ministers, full sacramental participation of women and homosexuals, the historical exclusion of minorities, and racism. Civil litigation has stretched the meaning of privacy claims and raised organizational awareness to the risks of data collection, dereliction in document retention or disposition, and access to records of private individuals and associational bodies. Because of competing traditions of openness and data gathering, pertinent questions arise regarding the effectiveness of religious bodies to protect the confidentiality of everything from mailing lists to personnel records.

Members of religious institutions do not relinquish their expectations of privacy as participants in civil society, but rather bring them into the councils, synods, associations, and congregations. The fact that rights may not be explicitly enumerated by canon or rule is not in any sense a limitation of the claims of church members to a realm of personal privacy in the enactment of their faith.[12] The right to due process, or procedural justice, for individuals in specific situations and contexts gives meaning to privacy claims.[13] The rational/legal basis for privacy and confidentiality is a historical inheritance that dovetails with the American discovery of privacy rights. Natural rights assumptions of an inherent right of privacy strongly influence Protestant religious traditions and are supplemented by the positive rights principle of Catholic canon law that has lately encoded the rights of the Christian faithful. Together these traditions have developed into an American formulation of a protective sphere that extends to individuals in their specific community relationships.[14] The church engages these issues with a distinctly ethical language of dialogue, prayer, personal redemption, and social transformation that affects the forums of private thoughts, interpersonal behavior, and public witness.

Any approach to the issue of privacy in the religious organization must also consider the external influence of the constitutional privilege. The Establishment Clause of the First Amendment prohibits "excessive entanglements" between church and state; the Free Exercise Clause prohibits the state from impeding one's individual rights of religious freedom.[15] Recent civil jurisprudence, especially the 1997 Supreme Court decision in *City of Boerne v. Flores,* 521 U.S. 507 (1997), which found the Religious Freedom Restoration Act (RFRA) unconstitutional, has chipped away at the rights of religious institutions to have jurisdiction over their own ecclesiastical matters through use of the First Amendment protections.[16] Thus, the arguments made in court in protecting access to records become in themselves important precedents that can erode or support the separation of church and state. The judicial accommodation of church and state relations, a relentless source of environmental pressure for religious organizations, is a cultural feature of records administration insofar as that function supports the organization's interest in being both a private religion and a public church. The courts have sometimes protected disclosure of church records (*State v. Burns*, Mont. 1992; *Hadnot v. Shaw*, Okla. 1992; and *United Methodist Church v. White*, DC App. 1990), and in other cases have allowed access to previously designated confidential and ecclesiastical records (*Meyer v. Board of Managers*, Ill. App. 1 Dist. 1991; *Niemann v. Cooley*, Ohio App. 1 Dist. 1994; *Commonwealth v. Stewart*, Pa. Super. 1994; *Abrams v. Temple of the Lost Sheep*, NY, 1990; and *Hutchinson v. Luddy*, Pa. Super. 1992).[17] Arguments made to the courts against granting access have ranged from the use of the free exercise clause to the extension of the clergy-penitent privilege to recorded information. Some courts will rule that they have no jurisdiction over intrinsically ecclesiastical matters. Other courts, however, have mandated full disclosure because of the overriding consideration given to the local laws regarding rights outlined in the discovery process.[18] The courts have shown that they will enter into litigation and disputes on almost any issue, but they also have shown a history of deference in matters of religious belief and internal governance.

State laws that sometimes narrow, and at other times expand, the zone of autonomy for churches have amply supplemented federal law. Archivists must carefully read the local situation to determine the degree of public accountability or relief. Typically, however, one will find the courts willing to extend immunity from a variety of laws governing such areas as labor, tort, contractual relationships, discrimination, and confidentiality. Some have argued that, in terms of their special legal entitlement, "religious groups are best conceived as separate sovereigns, analogous more to a government than to a corporation or a club or a charity."[19] Fundamental to the archival administration of access to organizational records is an understanding of appropriate case law and legal concepts. Because of the First Amendment's separation of church and state, civil laws apply to religious institutions in oblique ways. The privilege at law enjoyed by religious organizations adds a protective mantle of informational privacy to church records, which, though not privileged *per se*, are more sheltered than records in any other private or nonprofit environment. At the same time, the courts have demonstrated a willingness to freely interpret the mission of organized religions and periodically to indulge the public interest in guarding the integrity of these constitutionally protected institutions.[20] The monitoring of this external boundary creates internal ambiguity for archivists of religious institutions who may have more discretionary input into the information system than is found in the more regulated agencies of government, education, and business. Professional administrators, archivists, and legal counsel recognize the public policy impact that case and statutory law have on religious institutions and society, and thus the spirit of the law may be followed even though the letter of the law may not apply.

Conflict can result from ambiguity over the exact nature of the church's accountability to external authorities and standards. Federal statutes such as the Freedom of Information Act and the Privacy Act of 1974 do not, for example, apply to church records, but the public's experience with other records creates the expectation that church records are available or protected to the same degree as public records, and are, therefore, subject to the same level of public scrutiny as other nonprofit organizations. This tension is played out around any number of church records, including sacramental records, clergy deployment histories, missionary personnel files, social witness programs, and individual case files. The Privacy Act of 1974 provides guidelines to religious organizations for the protection of certain types of records in instances when religious law and local norms do not.

Statutory law and common case law that does not impinge on the private pursuits of the central religious organization provide archivists of religious organizations with standards for deciding what information should be kept and used for purposes of internal and public accountability, internal audit, and risk and records management.[21] In keeping with professional practice, archivists and records managers of denominational programs adopt these external standards as benchmarks for the routine administration of common business records. Records have been identified by legal and canonical counsel and church administrators as privileged and confidential, and thus potentially adverse to the individual and the community.[22] These records vary from one denomination to the next, but five broad and somewhat overlapping functional categories capture the scope of the documentation field: *lay and clerical personnel records* (e.g., missionary assignment and maintenance, grievance and due process, compensation, and evaluation); *clergy formation, discipline, and deployment records* (e.g., psychological assessments, medical evaluations, scrutinies and tests, and complaints and inquiries); *jurisdictional and congregational records* (e.g., membership lists, tithing records, sacramental records, doctrinal and authority conflict resolution); *legal and administrative records* (e.g., internal planning and operations, fund-raising, property management, and legal and tribunal records); and *educational and social service/witness program records* (e.g., training, case files, student and other school records, member discipline and counseling reports).[23]

Federal and state statutes that privilege records from disclosure apply to several additional functions of religious organizational activity including medical records; mental health, adoption and resettlement records; mediation and due process records; and legal records. Less clear in terms of the level and authority for disclosure are the numerous records of a personal nature as well as organizational communication that is part of the public representation of church life, including the annotations and ordinary entries in parish registers, missionary files, pledge and donor records, and other case files. In the Catholic Church tradition, confidentiality is represented in a range of treatments recognized by the canonical separation of secret and ordinary archives, both of which remain under the custodial authority of the church's ecclesiastical officers.[24] Privileged records in mainline Protestant denominations are more likely to be treated by particular administrative policies, or as restricted or confidential records when in archival custody, or they may be physically relinquished to church counsel where they are further secured under the attorney-client privilege. In more fragmented governing structures, more than one organizational unit served by the denominational archives could be involved in similar data-gathering functions, producing documentation with similar content but for different organizational purposes and with varying levels of protection.

The existence of local church policies and norms is in some sense a measure of the efficacy of civil laws surrounding privacy and confidentiality. Where civil law is an inadequate guide, particularly in relation to issues of agency relationship, privacy, and internal accountability, courts will turn to the internal documents of the church for guidance in the resolution of disputes.[25] Archival policies on privacy and confidentiality should include references to the religious or canon laws of the controlling church entity in order to reproduce faithfully a public sense of a "continuation of the religious mission of the organization."[26] In Protestant denominational settings, boards and commissions of the religious society negotiate with central corporate staff and executive councils to secure authority over, and access to, private communication and confidential records. The settlement reached is likely to measure the perception of risk and the controls in place to ensure accountability in a particular jurisdictional relationship. In Protestant denominational bodies, the ethic of privacy, when it is not explicit, rests on specific assurances of due process and accountability rules, as well as on theologically based commitments to the value of confidences.[27]

The Catholic Church experience is more highly formalized in that it supports an ethic of information privacy with structural protections from which the archivist can draw considerable persuasive input. For the Catholic Church, the Code of Canon Law guides the archivist when access to confidential records is at issue.[28] Canons 483–91 deal specifically with recordkeeping functions, although other canons imply the appropriate creation and use of Catholic Church records. The economical language of Canon 220, however, captures much of the ethic of denominational archivists as they act in the spirit of advancing a beneficial social norm. The canon states that "no one is permitted to harm illegitimately the good reputation which a person possesses nor to injure the right of any person to protect his or her own privacy."[29] Official commentary on the canons places some emphasis on the use of discretionary options, including pastoral approaches and other restraints in protecting both the common good and a person's public standing in the church.[30] The right to privacy has found its greatest exercise in the due process and careful administration of confidential materials around issues of clergy misconduct. Diocesan chancellors, acting as archivists, extend this right, however, to other pastoral records maintained on clergy and laity in the secret and ordinary archives. Canons 483–91 establish the kind of custodial accountability in organizational settings that permits secrets and inspires respect for confidences: a legitimate institutional "response to what is set apart, alien, perhaps sacred, and seeming to possess a power that calls for restraint even as it generates among certain outsiders a desire to be included and to be made a participant."[31] The application of the protection in a way that balances the privacy of the institution and the accountability of those who invoke those protections on behalf of the church provides the axis for developing informational trust in a particular organizational setting.[32]

The Cultural Environment of Religious Organizations

The archivist of any organizational body must assume a cultural perspective on the selection and use of documentation, and while such a perspective is helpful in any record-producing context, it is essential to understanding the meaning of such concepts as privacy and access in organizations. The concept of organizational culture has the advantage of placing individual agents into situated, naturalized contexts of action.

The archivist inherits or develops anew an organizational role through an interpretive exchange of rituals, group dynamics, technologies and artifacts of stored memory, shared participation in office narratives, language patterns, organizational stories, and other socializing traditions.[33]

For archivists concerned with preserving institutional memory, capturing a cultural record of the organization means selecting from a range of structural, functional, and representational processes that are involved in the creation and distribution of knowledge in documentation. Using historical records, the archivist in an agency relationship looks for ways to propagate organizational communication by injecting stored knowledge into new contexts of meaning and use. In this sense, the primary value of the parish register as a record of parochial membership and personal history is superseded by its more compelling value as measured in the demographic and symbolic uses of the register in tracing the organizational history and individual lives that constitute a sacramental community. In another venue, the archivist may be asked to prepare an institutional history of offices or agencies that are under review and re-organization, an opportunity to inject not just the "facts" but a historical perspective that is organizationally sensitive, well documented, and attuned to such contemporary corporate values as group work, diversity, and individual talent. Ethnographer Harold Garfinkel's description of the organization as an interpretive system applies to the artful methods of religious organizations: "methods whereby its members are provided with accounts of the setting as countable, storyable, proverbial, comparable, picturable, representable—i.e., accountable events."[34] What to accept, what to ignore, and what to simply reframe: these are decision points for archivists of religious institutions as professional, fiduciary agents. The archivist entertains a professional assignment, but does so as a participant observer, practicing the archival craft while negotiating "accountable" responses; that is, responses that connect to the way in which such essentials as language, gesture, information, and credibility are communicated to a full range of organizational stakeholders.

Institutional religious culture is marked by a "taken for grantedness" that involves prayer, ritual greetings, gestures, celebrations, and liturgies of spoken and tacit meaning. But these cultural characteristics hang together and are routinized on a framework of institutional activity: "structures organize and cultures speak."[35] Archivists of mainline Christian denominations operate in a structural relationship constituted by the special claim of the church that it exists on three levels: the church as universal, the church as religious society, and the church as corporate entity.[36] The archivist enters into a variety of agency relationships as the church organizes itself into international bodies, national structures and councils, congregational settings, ecumenical affiliations, autonomous agencies, theological schools, and programmatic networks. Each of these entities struggles to legitimize itself as a center in the broader religious field of activity. It does so by contesting ground with other segments of the organization. These contests occur in nearly every domain, such as the appointment of staff, the establishment of new parishes, the calling of a minister, and a change in the liturgical order. In their capacity as custodians and information experts, denominational archivists develop separate agency relationships with autonomous participants representing each of these segments. The ambiguity inherent in multilayered religious organizations and the differentiated role of archivists form the structural backdrop to the mediation of privacy and access to organizational records. The level of discretion at which archivists can achieve a working balance in these complex relationships will be a measure of the level of trust that is invested in them to maintain secrecy as well as to allow legitimate access to the historical memory of the community. Archivists become curators of culture in an organizational mediation with the creators of information. The intersection of these actors introduces opportunity for the archivist to communicate informational trust to the system.[37]

The local, national, and international venues of denominational culture are differentiated by the corporate structures of congregation, diocese, synod, or conference. The diffusion of authority in denominational structures has its roots in the independent societies and boards of nineteenth-century missionary and educational missions, which were much more likely to assimilate secular forms of organizational structure and cultural behavior.[38] These structures retained the historical distinctiveness of innovation and entrepreneurial evangelism, resulting in a loosely coupled structure that at any one time spawns new networks of grassroots organizational activity.[39] These historically embedded distinctions create decentralized information-collection and distribution systems in mainline denominational agencies as well as various autonomous operations of Catholic charities, religious orders, and educational institutions. The cultural segmentation of the denominational churches sets up competing fields of interest that can signal conflicting views on legitimate information access. Archival management activities, designed at the point of records creation and intended to ensure access in the future, often reflect these disagreements. Record capture, production, and dissemination hold evidence of the ambiguous layers of the religious authority structure.

The archivist grounds the analysis of organizational culture and structure in particular worshiping communities through knowledge of the symbolic texts and the skilled routines of communicative practice. These include not only the scriptures, creeds, prayer books, and orders of service, but also the picture books, newsletters, denominational symbols, parish registers, and recently, Web sites that document the ordinary events of human spirituality. Routines of worship and rituals of discernment are vehicles by which individuals merge their personal narratives and bind themselves in relationships of informational trust.[40] Private belief systems are married to familiar rituals of re-enactment that forge a cognitive and affective link to a denomination's traditions. And while private knowledge as private religion mirrors other secular trends, the debate over the decline of institutional religion has missed the ways in which personal religion has itself become part of the institutionalizing process.[41]

Professional Agency in the Management of Access and Privacy

For the archivist, as for other information and communication professionals in religious organizations, the duty to protect confidence, privacy, and access creates a realm of professional and organizational ambiguity that can affect key decision points when administering private communications and personal data. The ethical choices that archivists of religious institutions make are contingent on the location of the archivist in the organizational hierarchy, the evaluation of complexity and risk in the situation, the commitments implied by the particular custodial arrangement, and the constituencies that define the agency relationship at a particular moment in time. The overlap of professional reputation and cultural identification with the organization creates an opening for trust as a resource in advancing the interests of the archival program in the organization. The professional archivist advocates organizational self-reflection and open access to those documentary resources that hold members, ministers, and their leadership accountable—to give free rein to the information that supports mission and covenantal trust. As they scan the information environment, archivists carry confidences and private communications across organizational boundaries and into the development of policy and practice around privacy and access.[42] Within this complex interaction, the archivist has latitude to affect the interpretation of the legal, canonical, and normative rules of procedure. Granting or restricting access to private and confidential records—for either internal units of the organization or for external parties—becomes, in effect, an ethical assessment of the human and organizational implications of decision making. The archivists' discretionary latitude to advance access and trust is an extension of the agency relationship to the broader cultural dynamics of the religious organization. Archivists who do not acquire the position and authority to exercise this latitude risk a diminished voice in organizational decision making, particularly as it affects resource allocation for effective and competitive programs.

Neither an implied or stated right to privacy, nor structures for protecting due process, are sufficient in religious organizations to explain the contextual accommodation that the professional archivist makes in managing issues of organizational privacy and access. The tendency of religious bureaucracies to be overly protective of information betrays a normative prejudice for privacy in a value-intensive culture. Confidential communication proves more useful and is tacitly accepted in organizations where power appears to be distributed more equitably.[43] Members of religious organizations rely on cultural cues and networks of communication more than formal rules both to control the flow of information and to monitor the shifting commitments in the principal-agent-member relationship. Presumably, members' trust in the informal networks of church communication is reinforced by expectations that formal structures such as archives exist for the custodial control over data.

The cultural segmentation of mainline denominations compounds the documentation activities of the archivist. Documentation activities are dispersed across vertical and horizontal lines of religious authority structures and within fragmented networks of loosely associated volunteers, clergy, and employees. Institutional programs, managed by professional agents and program staff, operate at local, national and international levels and respond to divergent logics and beliefs. "It is . . . at precisely the point where institutional logics conflict that the individual retains her greatest power—what sociologists call agency—with regard to institutions. . . . In such a situation of conflict, the individual may choose which institution's logic applies to a situation."[44] The segmented organization creates opportunities for cultural re-interpretation and strategic relationships. Issues of access and privacy are embedded in networks of organizational relationships in which agency and trust are connective cultural themes.[45]

The contractual perspective on the principal-agent relationship does not operate well within structures designed to be open to active participation, human agency, spiritual intuition, and personal experience in the search for God and community. A different concept of agency may better fit systems of intentional ambiguity and personal interpretation.[46]

Professional archivists enter into religious authority structures as deputies, anchored by the trust derived from ties to legitimate office holders and official records custodians.[47] In each case they have assumed some of the fiduciary recordkeeping functions, borrowing from the reserve of authority and trust that accompanies the office or official role.

Agency theory captures the medley of individual interest, ethical choice, and organizational relationships as effective elements of organizational conflict and change. In one sense, human agency is at the heart of all individual acts of commitment and volition, but the theory has been revived to explain the displaced goals and interests of an increasingly mobile, educated, and expectant workforce. It also reflects the cultural tension between control and innovation, and stability and change. Organizational and social theorists have taken the concept of agency along a variety of paths, several of which have insights for the management of archives, information systems, and risk in organizational settings.[48]

Organizations structure their relationships with professionals in order to bring legal, contractual, and administrative controls to bear upon outside autonomous agents. Specifically, professional archivists should reduce an institution's exposure to risk from the disclosure of personal or organizational confidences. These rules and controls operate as substitutes for trust—especially in the initial stages of professional employment before socialization and identification take effect. The costs of containing opportunistic behavior are considerable enough that trust becomes a value. One aim of the economic theory of agency, therefore, is to reduce the transactional and monitoring costs of control over professional agents.[49] In religious archives, structural buffers in the form of canonical officers and governing boards can either integrate or isolate archivists from leadership roles. The decisions over structural placement will affect the archives' involvement in the administration of confidential records as well as the full programmatic inclusion of historical archives and current records and information-management responsibilities. Agency is salient in precisely those organizational settings, especially voluntary nonprofit organizations, where formal contracts are not the norm and where trust is borrowed from the repeated interaction with informational ties and networks that carry the messages of cultural integration.[50] The archivist who deliberately becomes involved, for example, in attending missionary conferences and supporting documentation efforts on behalf of the missionary network will garner tremendous goodwill that loops back into the archivist's formal organizational relationships.

Social exchange theorists have argued for parallel ways of integrating professional agents in formally structured environments. The relationship between principal and agent is based on a universal fact of social relations: the normal course of human events is based on the reciprocal exchange of valuable internal costs (e.g., friendship, commitment, loyalty) and external rewards (e.g., participation, leadership status, monetary compensation).[51] The problem with market-oriented agency and social exchange theory is that the inequality of power and differentiation of status in organizations becomes a cloudy mixture in those organizations whose "ideational" (or theological) purpose involves engaging human agency and society in all of its fullness and diversity. In practice, ambiguity is valued precisely for the opportunities that it affords to gather knowledge and to communicate. In religious and many nonprofit organizations, these tendencies are heightened by a cultural ethic that stresses equitable power relationships, recognition of diverse viewpoints, and the blending of private and public lives.

An alternative view of human agency that better supports an interpretive and ethical role for archivists and senior information managers can be found in current sociological and organizational communication theories. Structuration theory gives prominence to the complexity of human agency in organizations as social systems.[52] Human agents actively participate in the implementation of authoritative rules in the allocation of resources, including record artifacts, stored meaning, and avenues of access and restriction. They do so, moreover, by engaging in a self-reflexive assessment of those rules and resources as situated participants in the organizational system. Sociologist Anthony Giddens's definition of expert organizational agents fits the function of the archivist of religious institutions. Archivists are "lay sociologists," equipped with specialized knowledge, which they apply to informational encounters of consequence.[53] Even the seemingly trivial acts of day-to-day routine can carry a profound cumulative effect on organizational culture and conduct. Two characteristics of daily life are especially important for professionals in maintaining a culture of trust in these power relationships: the maintenance of an essential routine or continuity that creates confidence and normal expectations; and the openness of organizational structures to individual "life chances"—opportunities when the agent can exercise personal fulfillment, special talents, and effective knowledge (e.g., exercising copyrights and permissions over intellectual property, reviewing documentation for research access, preparing historical research for operational decision making, engaging in litigation support, etc.). The duality of the archivist's role involves the continuous reproduction of meaning, particularly heightened when discretionary opportunities arise around such issues as privacy and confidentiality.

Stored and retrievable knowledge is constitutive of human agency in organizational life. Communication theorists James Taylor and Elizabeth Van Every build on structuration theory by proposing an extension of the concept of agency that entails not only the communicational interaction of individuals, but also the inherited discourse of an organization that accumulates in cultural artifacts called textual maps.[54] These maps include the familiar documents of archival work as well as vesture, architecture, song, and prayer books. The surface attributes of everyday activity in a religious organization—the rites, liturgies, personal stories, and group gatherings—are features that "play out" organizational memory. In small organizations, these connective memories are largely maintained as oral tradition. In complex organizations, the memories are institutionalized and contextualized across time in the archival maps of recordkeeping systems. Giddens observes that

> [Of] essential importance to the engendering of power is the storage of authoritative resources. . . . The storage of authoritative and allocative resources may be understood as involving the retention and control of information or knowledge whereby social relations are perpetuated across time-space. Storage presumes media of information representation, modes of information retrieval or recall and, as with all power resources, modes of its dissemination. Notches on wood, written lists, books, files, films, tapes—all these are media of information storage of widely varying capacity and detail. All depend for their retrieval upon the recall capacities of the human memory but also upon skills of interpretation that may be possessed by only a minority within any given population.[55]

At any moment in time, the archivist of a religious institution is involved in an extended organizational conversation that recalls a combination of memory objects (e.g., documents, access policies, metadata, service goals, mission statements, professional resources) and the informational themes that frame the interpersonal exchange (e.g., content knowledge, source analysis, advice and referral, instruction, values, personal kindness, and humor). Information professionals are identified by their cognitive *and* affective performance in these communication exchanges.[56] The communicational context and attitude in which information professionals frame their agency is critical to their ability to be transforming agents in an organization: For whom do they speak? For the principal? For which members of the group, the organization, or other stakeholders? For the professional interest or the surrounding community?

Fiduciary Trust in the Management of Access and Privacy

The administration of privacy is a process of understanding the cultural environment and the specific structural relationships that frame privacy, confidentiality, and access in ways that allow archivists and others to make sense of the issue in instances of conflicting interpretation. The role of the archivist is to serve as an information expert, both in terms of content and process, and as an organizational communicator. A question for the administration of privacy, confidentiality, and access is to what extent archivists are perceived as reliable risk partners. Much of organizational trust is invested in devising technical systems of retrieval, filtering, selection, and appraisal. But trust in the confidence of experts, including archivists, is a form of blind trust in the reliability of systems and in professionally credentialed people—a faith in their probity as people and in the correctness of the principles they represent.[57] In religious organizations, archivists inherit an interpretive structure that is both historically and culturally engaged in modern society's struggle to define the boundaries of the relationship between human agency (the private) and community (the public). This engagement with modernity has pressed on American religious institutions the need to accommodate "personal religion," a more active laity, and a renewed emphasis on a morality centered in the integrity of the private forum. It is as if American religion has realized Durkheim's faith in the individual conscience: "since each of us incarnates something of humanity, each individual consciousness contains something divine and thus finds itself marked with a character which renders it sacred and inviolable to others. Therein lies all individualism: and that is what makes it a necessary doctrine."[58] If the churches are themselves wrapped up with questions of authority in negotiating the limits and possibilities of human agency, archivists of religious institutions will find that they, too, will encounter instances of organizational ambiguity that will test their ability to make correct ethical choices. In a discussion of the religious features of human agency, Eric Johnson considers the scriptural and supporting themes for dissecting a professional's capacity or power to act, relationships to others, intentionality, choice, moral discernment, and accountability.[59] These themes of individual authority are matched by institutional influences and constraints: the prevailing historical narrative, the identity context, the specific environment, the language of mediation, and the perceived goods.[60] These individual and contextual pressures are captured in the process of interpreting information requests from researchers, packaging research reports for administrators, guiding other professional agents into fruitful lines of inquiry, and supporting mission advocacy staff with educational resources. When these situations of negotiation arise, the archivist also participates in a role mediation that involves personal morality, professional ethics, interpersonal trust, and institutional confidence, if not faith.

The cultural and structural segmentation of religious denominations can only exacerbate a modern trend toward specialization that plays havoc with technical and procedural approaches to professional management of privacy and access issues. Archivists share responsibility for data security and integrity not only with traditional records creators but also with a tier of secondary custodians including system administrators, legal counsel, and research consultants. Adam Seligman has given special recognition to the role of religion in his exploration of the problem of differentiated roles of agents and the effect it has had on social forms of trust.[61] Seligman echoes Bernard Barber's seminal work on trust[62] by returning to the quandary for agents who move from home, to work, to church, to a dozen social environments: expectations of trust, or alternately, confusion over responsibility, is always a characterization of a particular and ambiguous set of specific social relationships. Dilemmas of privacy and access are particularly important to archivists in their roles as trusted agents; that is, as caretakers, guardians, interpreters, mediators, and communicators of institutional memory and confidences.

For archivists in religious organizations, trust exists in a series of sometimes risk-intensive encounters of personal, professional, and organizational commitment. These interactions begin with the essential repository of trust in the individual, which is reinforced in the confidences given and received in interpersonal and organizational interaction. Individuals engaged in their ministry, vocation, or profession are believed to be "called." In the course of negotiating their role, they give shape and meaning to their associations. Trust becomes entwined with perceptions of personal dignity and intentional communication of goodwill in the process of reducing anxiety around information issues.[63] Here the archivist is not only a professional expert, but is also a reliable, trusted, indeed personable and approachable, figure. In exercising ethical discretion and procedural fairness, the archivist will ensure the perception of equitable information flow while guarding the confidences that emerge from the particular human relationships.[64]

Personal trust is extended across organizational networks and boundaries by the generalized expectation of confidentiality that comes from the repeated exchanges of information, typically exhibited in normal research and reference functions. The professional agent conducts the business at hand efficiently and prudently, enforcing policy where it applies and drawing boundaries where ambiguity or conflicting interests expose the archivist to power imbalances and risk. Professional archivists are obliged to communicate their role as information agents in order to be fully accountable and ethically responsible for the information assets of the organization. In doing so, they demonstrate both their vulnerability to risk and an essential cultural identification with the group norm of trust.[65]

Finally, the expectation is that archivists of religious institutions share in fiduciary trust; that is, a truly faith-filled covenant to protect, advance, and provide for the well-being of the community. The design of religious organizations produces a culture that supersedes secular exchange relationships and contracts by establishing tacit understandings based on unconditional trust.[66] The ethics of the private life, professional standards, and the values of the church community are folded into the mix of organizational relationships. This level of commitment can be dangerous when concealment becomes the objective of information custodians (professionals as information bureaucrats). It is also at this concentrated level of identification, however, that the well-placed archivist is most able to shape the information landscape of the organization by convincing widely dispersed leadership centers of the need for procedural fairness in standards of privacy, accountability in information gathering and sharing, retention and disposition agreements, and methods for granting access without compromising confidence. The beneficial effect of the trusted agent is in mediating an equitable approach to the way in which personal and confidential corporate records are gathered, stored, destroyed, or shared.

Archivists of religious institutions have asked whether the unique tensions and information ambiguities of religious organizations tax their ability to aspire to professional integrity, personal ethical responsibility, and organizational loyalty without compromising judgment along the way.[67] The answer may be found in the ability of human agents, situated in permissive cultural settings, to engage in the personal and professional exercise of their agential rights and responsibilities. Archivists in any value-intensive corporation exercise their ethical freedom and restructure the system each time they reinforce an unquestioned (albeit useful) routine, or question a recordkeeping practice that no longer responds to the needs of the organization. The archivist's ability to exercise reflexivity in a mediating role is an essential component of human agency: as professional, as selector, as interpreter of the record, and as participant of an organizational culture. Archivists do not relinquish their other roles when they enter into contractual relationships with organizations. Any idea that the balancing of personal, professional, and organizational interests is merely a reach for objectivity underplays the complexity of human interests and affections. Archivists bring role expectations to their organizational relationships; the fit between personal sense making and organizational demands will tell the tale of leadership, credibility, and influence. The authority to carry out one's personal, professional, and organizational roles is best captured by the Catholic concept of subsidiarity that grew out of the Second Vatican Council. As an act of delegation, "the principle of subsidiarity means that nothing should be done at a higher level that can be done as well or better than at a lower level."[68]

Subsidiarity sets up the rational and attitudinal mechanisms of relational trust: communication, integrity, fairness, reliability, consistency, goodwill, and loyalty—ethical virtues that describe individual competency. Accountability is activated by the mechanisms that institutionalize and depersonalize distrust: policies and procedures, reporting requirements, production expectations, satisfaction measures, and self-monitoring.[69] Subsidiarity does not solve but merely exposes the responsibility of the archivist to the challenge of a moral environment. What is different in religious organizations and in other value-oriented corporate environments is the prevailing sense that one is called to be both a reflexive and interpretive agent as well as a source of system responsibility and accountability for self and others.[70] Religious ethicist William Rankin borrows from a legal ethicist in asking the following:

> A philosophical question that should be answered by anyone filling a professional role is: Am I, who fill this professional role, still basically a responsible person? David Luban writes, "If the true moral agent is 'me, that poor old ultimate actuality,' whose roles are mere 'lendings,' then it appears that common morality is more truly moral than role morality and should win out in cases where the two conflict." [71]

Conclusion

Organizational culture, human agency, and trust intersect in the administration of privacy, confidentiality, and access in a religious organization. The archivist is an "access point" of professional trust where uncertainty is allayed and where personal and system trust are maintained.[72] The archivist can also be exposed to institutional situations where confidentiality can become wrapped up in a cult of secrecy that conceals wrongdoing. Here, the agency principle argues for an ethic of intentional involvement, either by introducing advice on proper recordkeeping responsibilities and accountability, or by seeking calculated distance when the archivist has no effective power or voice. In either case, the archivist acts within the organization as one of many access points. Drawing from communication theory, organizational archivists (and records managers) who spend time with a variety of employees and researchers can also be seen as acting as "boundary spanners." In this role, they use their internal and stakeholder networks to inject other perspectives into existing informational patterns, acting not as neutral professionals, but as professional members of the organization's staff who construct the organization by constructing meaning. Certainly, the structural location of the archives in the organization is a decisive variable.[73] Religious archivists in particular, because of the way they weave through an organizational culture that values ambiguity and trust, can have profound influence on organizational interpretation if they use their expertise and personal skills to attain influence and position.

The structural location is a pretext, however, for the participation of the archivist in a communication process that requires not only professional reputation and expertise, but also strategic and interpersonal communication skills and an essential identity with the organization. This combination of ethical responsibility and social mediation allows trust to flourish beyond faith in technical competence to a level where the archivist can potentially shape the information design and culture of the documented community. And while this paper focuses on religious archivists, it is our contention that these issues, which essentially define professionalism, confront archivists in business, government, and other nonprofit institutions.[74] Today's digital record environment gives archivists new reason to refocus on the diplomatics of records creation and custody, evaluating production and distribution processes ever more keenly in terms of their impact on reliability, authenticity, and integrity. Interestingly, these are the very same attributes that leaders and members of religious organizations most want to associate with the curators of these information artifacts, and why should they not? Archivists should be attentive to the source of these qualities, which is not inherent in the records alone, but in the human interpretive processes by which information is re-created as new knowledge. Archival administration in religious institutions conspicuously illustrates the possibilities for exercising an ethical approach to issues of associational and individual privacy based in a theoretical understanding of human agency in organizational settings.

14 Delta Blues: Changing Conceptions of Privacy and Property, and Their Implications for Corporate Archives

Paul C. Lasewicz

> Information only really exists in the delta.
>
> *John Perry Barlow*
>
> Lord, that I'm standin' at the crossroad, babe I believe I'm sinkin' down.
>
> *Robert Johnson, "Cross Road Blues"*

I.

Introduction

Clayton M. Christensen's influential 1997 book, *The Innovator's Dilemma*, thrust the term "disruptive technology" into the corporate vernacular. Christensen defined the term as a technology or innovation "that results in worse product performance, at least in the near-term. . . . [It] brings to the market a very different value proposition than had been available previously." For Christensen, the key moment for successful technological implementation occurs not necessarily when these technologies are created, or during the initial moment of widespread acceptance, but rather in the corporation's ability to sustain that initial momentum and turn the technology into a viable business.[1]

Christensen thought in terms of industry and society, but his concepts are relevant for corporate archives as well. Just as a river delta is subjected to the twin powers of the river and the ocean, corporate archivy is caught in the confluence of two disruptive technologies: digitization and the Internet. These technologies have already altered public policy surrounding the corporations' legal and market venues, and they promise to foster change within the traditional underpinnings of the economy in the years to come. Any alterations in the corporate environment will necessarily impact the policies and practices of a corporate archives. And, in classic Christensenian fashion, they will likely produce some pain and dissatisfaction, for they hold the potential to change the traditional value propositions of corporate archives.[2]

One of the public policy areas most affected is privacy, where digital dissemination of information potentially may change all of the rules. Increasingly, people confront the reality that such personal information as health and genetic data, Web usage patterns, purchasing behavior, and facial characteristics randomly captured by surveillance video cameras, can be collected, analyzed, and even sold without their knowledge or consent.[3] This commodification of personal data is prompting a social and legal re-evaluation of privacy concepts, which is morphing traditional perceptions of privacy to include concepts of property rights. For archivists in general, this shift in perceptions holds the potential to challenge the profession's most basic assumptions about the relationship between privacy, society, and the historical record, and possibly may threaten traditional, history-driven uses of archival records. The ambiguous nature of this anticipated broadening of privacy concepts also poses an even more vexing situation for corporate archives, for their parent organizations are subject to internal drivers and external parameters that strip away some of the safeguards traditionally accorded to such educationally oriented repositories as universities and historical societies. In addition, the impermanence of corporate life raises the stakes for an archives. A corporate archives cannot become an organizational liability, for like a river delta or a Mississippi bluesman, it is never more than one bad storm or one wrong turn from "sinkin' down."

This essay will address privacy concerns for those corporate archives that contain materials that receive considerable external use. For such archives, privacy considerations are interwoven increasingly and indelibly with property-based issues. Indeed, property-based issues themselves have been redefined in recent years and appear amorphous owing to both the unbounded nature of digital technology and the somewhat defined yet always fluctuating parameters of corporate reality. All of these issues orbit around the basic problem of how corporate archivists can balance individual and social interests with the proprietary concerns of their companies. This essay will not attempt to identify solutions to these issues, because privacy and property law remain complex, evolving, and open to widely differing interpretations. Instead, it will describe how traditional perceptions of privacy are being altered by digitization and the Internet, demonstrate how these changes are an issue for corporate archivists who disseminate their content externally, and outline some of the privacy concerns that may emerge from this practice.

II.
Shifting Sands, Changing Tonalities: Who Owns What?

> I woke up this mornin'-nnn, and all my shrimps was dead and gone.
> Robert Johnson, "Dead Shrimp Blues"

If privacy and property rights resemble shrimp, then corporate archivists perhaps may empathize with Delta bluesman Robert Johnson's lament. More than ever, they face the question of who owns the shrimp. Are they safely netted and able to be turned to an asset? Or are they out of reach, dead, and gone? The waters are too muddied to know for certain. But as dramatically disruptive as digitization and Web technologies can be to archival policies, practices, and visions, nature and business both teach that in change there is opportunity. The river delta, caught in the whipsaw of fresh-water flooding and salt-water storms, takes it in stride to create a vibrant and fertile ecosystem not only lush with life but adaptive enough to become dependent on this periodic pummeling.

Whether corporate archives can demonstrate such resiliency in the face of digital convergence remains to be seen. The profession in general has not yet taken full advantage of other disruptive technology-based experiences. For example, archivists have expended much energy over the past two decades attempting to develop an agenda for managing electronic records. Despite considerable research and discussion, they have achieved only mixed results in attempting to define, craft, and implement adequate policies and procedures for managing the media.[4] It is clear that the profession presents no completely successful digital model for corporate archivists to emulate. Brewster Kahle, the founder of the Internet Archive, presciently observes that "if the last century was built on the exploitation of oil . . . this next century is all about intellectual property and knowledge, and right now we are mishandling the most important resource [electronic content] the world has."[5]

A recent effort that illustrates these mixed results was the Society of American Archivists' endorsement of the National Humanities Alliance's

"Basic Principles for Managing Intellectual Property in a Digital Environment." Leaving aside the problems that SAA's endorsement holds for corporate archivists, the principles may be fundamentally and perhaps fatally flawed. They accept the premise that existing laws surrounding property rights will, in slightly modified forms, also govern property in the digital environment. That premise is far from certain, however, because the courts are only beginning to review the topic. For example, the Copyright Act of 1976 mentions computers only once, an absence that means that the courts will interpret old legal language in light of new technologies. John Perry Barlow, a noted Net visionary, had this absence in mind when he wrote that "we are sailing into the future on a sinking ship. This vessel, the accumulated canon of copyright and patent law, was developed to convey forms and methods of expression entirely different from the vaporous cargo it is now being asked to carry." In addition, Pamela Samuelson, dubbed by pundits "the goddess of copyright" and a crusader against those who would turn copyright into a welfare program for copyright holders, warns that "people mustn't be fooled into thinking that the way copyright works today is how it must work in the future."[6]

Certainly, rights holders would also subscribe to those notions of change, although their interpretations differ from those of Barlow and Samuelson. Software firms are developing nonpermanent licenses for their products to be renewed periodically by users, and some software companies challenge the traditional right of "first sale," which holds that the legitimate purchaser of a copyrighted work can resell the copy. Other firms are lobbying for legislative remedies, and rights holders seem to be finding sympathetic ears in the courtroom. One court has held that a private individual's republishing on the Internet of an ostensibly public government document, in this case the municipal building code for Denison, Texas, violated the copyright of the original government-contracted publisher of the thousand-page volume.[7]

As the case law develops, the question becomes who will be the winners and losers in this new information era? Will it be the information democrats, like Barlow and Samuelson? Or will it be the rights holders and content owners such as software giants and the infotainment industry? How will changing conceptions of property impact privacy laws? And what can corporate archivists, as information managers with a vested interest in stable, or at least predictable, legal environments, do now to best position the profession and its collections for the rights laws of the future?

This is an important question because the rights problems of infotainment companies today will be universal tomorrow. "Every company that has a brand will look like an entertainment company in the twenty-first century," says Michael Moon, a digital asset management consultant. "This means they'll have all the digital asset management problems of a [Walt] Disney [Co.] or a Warner Brothers." Companies already have been scouring the Internet for unsanctioned uses of their brands or names. In one instance, this practice resulted in the censoring of previously public material by the removal of a reference to a thirty-five-year-old press release from an archival Web site. Like the proverbial blues singer, corporate archivists are at a crossroads, an intersection with two divergent choices. Should they choose the path most often traveled, that of the established rights canon? Or the path less traveled, the speculations of visionaries?[8]

Traditionally, it has been possible to advance both the interests of society and to protect the creator's proprietary interests through a property canon that focused on the physical format that captured the essence of creativity. The creativity itself—the thought, the perspective, the technique, or application—fell largely outside the bounds of the legal environment. That creative essence was protected through the control of physical incarnations such as paper, books, photo, and film. Today this creative essence may never exist in a tangible physical state at all. Yet, it still finds itself treated within the legal system on increasingly inadequate physical terms. That current treatment, Barlow writes, is misguided, for information now is, more often than not, "an action which occupies time rather than a state of being which occupies physical space, as is the case with hard goods." Whereas the legal system never sought to assign property value to facts or pure thought in the predigital world, courts today find themselves grappling with exactly those property issues in cyberspace—a land without physical form, "the native home of Mind." That may be fine for blues singers, for creativity thrives on ambiguity, but archivists have difficulties arranging and describing intangibles.[9]

More tangibly, the system also finds itself dealing with the increasing commodification of information. For the first time, it is practical to acquire and analyze huge volumes of discrete, factual, and previously unrelated information, including addresses, medical records, shopping behaviors, Web site visits, and DNA patterns. In the past, such information had virtually no market value because it was too difficult to generate insight and derive financial benefit from it. Property rights, therefore, were moot. Today, however, the rapid progress in computing power, along with corresponding advances in the transparent collection and analysis of data, have created great value in previously worthless minutia. The question that emerges around any discussion of value is, of course, who owns it? Is it owned by those who collect, arrange, and analyze the minutia, or by those individuals, now reduced to highly personalized data points, who constitute the subjects?[10]

III.
Standing at the Crossroads: The Benefits and Risks of History

Well, some people tell me that the worried blues ain't bad.
Robert Johnson, "Walking Blues"

This changing nature of information holds implications for the law that will reverberate far beyond the Halls of Justice. According to Samuelson, the judicial decisions made now "will have profound consequences for the kind of information society in which we will be living in the twenty-first century." One of the places it may be felt most strongly, interestingly enough, is in corporate archives. These repositories have been relatively removed from the property right debates because of their internally focused missions, which have resulted from their pursuit of internal users as a corporate survival strategy. The archival literature abounds with discussions of internal marketing as a deterrent to elimination. Business archivists have concluded that the key to survival in their unique environments involves justifying their existence by clearly demonstrating the value that they add to the corporation. As a result, corporate archives collection policies reflect an internal focus. It follows, too, that the user base is largely internal, for the documentation's primary use relates to the business itself. Outside use of most corporate archives tends to be comparatively infrequent, and any potential legal exposures posed by external use traditionally have been managed by asserting copyright ownership, disclosing nonconfidential information, and limiting the distribution of information itself.[11]

In addition, corporate archivists are an inherently conservative crew, which is a significant factor in delaying their response to the emergent property right debate. Well aware of their vulnerability in the corporation, these keepers of the corporate memory prefer to err on the side of safety. For example, as late as 1997, a discussion on the Business Archives Discussion List found a preponderance of respondents declining to even consider disseminating corporate archives information on corporate intranets behind the safety of corporate firewalls, let alone doing so over the Internet. The prevalent belief was that sensitive information could not be adequately protected even in an entirely internal Web environment, a legitimate concern given the relative lack of sophistication of early intranet security measures and the information risks posed by disgruntled employees.[12]

Despite those legitimate and valid concerns, by 1998 corporate archival thinking had evolved to the point where some corporate archives intranet sites were emerging within Fortune 100 companies. Several corporations allowed employee access to on-line finding aids and digitized documentation. A corresponding boom also occurred in corporate history Internet sites. Texas Instruments, CIGNA, Aetna, Ford, Microsoft, and IBM constitute only a few of the companies that have created sites to convey their histories to the public.

These changing conceptions of public access to corporate archival material were triggered by a number of factors. First and foremost is the culture of corporate archives. Although risk averse when it comes to their collections, corporate archivists can be entrepreneurial. This is not as paradoxical as it seems at first blush. Corporate archivists often aggressively target records for acquisition; as part of that process they regularly build and present business cases to convince reluctant departments to transfer historically significant records to the archives.

Archivists also use that same entrepreneurial mentality to grow their internal user base. Corporate archivists are particularly attuned to organizational change and always on the lookout for a new opportunity to add value. As the initial corporate technology justification for adopting Web technology was based on its potential for creating orders-of-magnitude improvement in internal information distribution, corporate archivists early recognized an intranet's potential to seamlessly deliver content to *every* employee. Once comfortable that information security exposures were adequately addressed, some corporate archivists employed the technology to push archival information to employee desktops and to provide general historical information to every requester with computer access. It is important to note that the sharing of corporate archival information via Web technology is still very much an embryonic practice from a professional perspective. Many corporate archives have a limited Web presence at best, either by choice or owing to a lack of resources. Since 1997, however, corporate archivists' perceptions of Web risk have shifted significantly. Most business archivists no longer believe that Web technology and their holdings cannot coexist in harmony.

A second factor that worked to change corporate archival attitudes toward public dissemination of information was an increased social awareness in the 1990s of the relevance of business history. The celebration of the millennium and the aging of the baby boomer generation sparked a collective bout of societal navel-gazing and a nostalgic reassessment of the last fifty years of the twentieth century. Popular culture from bygone eras was resurrected and celebrated. Television, the dominant medium of the late twentieth century, led the way in this rediscovery. The "fill the space" imperative of cable television nurtured the nostalgia boom with such channels as Nickelodeon and ESPN Classic Sports giving new meaning to the previously pejorative term of "rerun." In fact, an entire generation coming of age today fondly remembers watching these cable reruns thereby, in effect, feeling nostalgic about nostalgia!

This celebration of things past included business-related materials, not surprising given the significance of consumerism in twentieth-century society. Always sensitive to shifts in the marketplace, corporations responded in numerous ways. Movie theaters and network television were populated with introspective portrayals of the 1960s, the 1970s, and even the 1980s. Coca-Cola opened its nostalgic "World of Coke" attraction in Atlanta. The auto industry incorporated decades-old retro styling points into vehicles like the Ford Mustang, Dodge Ram pickups, and the Chrysler PT Cruiser. It also revived old brand names like the Chrysler M Series, the Ford Thunderbird, and the Volkswagen Beetle, and it liberally utilized nostalgia in advertising campaigns. Other companies breathed new life into old advertising fixtures: Charlie the Tuna returned, accompanied by the Green Giant and the Ivory Baby. Popular music, most notably rock-and-roll classics, was rolled out to sell product, and even venerable bluesmen like B. B. King found themselves projected into the nation's living rooms.[13] Less visibly, but perhaps more significantly, corporations created new archives programs or resurrected dormant operations. AIG, Ford, The Gap, Home Depot, and IBM were a few of the companies that started or revived archival programs during the economic boom of the 1990s.

Lastly, a series of recent social and legal developments drove home the relevance of business records to society and the legitimacy of public interest in nonpublic records. The emergence of the concept of reparations to right historical wrongs, most notably concerning the Holocaust and American slavery, made clear that a compelling social interest in corporate records exists, no matter how old or how arcane. This societal interest in business history means that some corporations may find it useful to make archival information widely available in order to address these needs.[14]

In light of this rising tide of internal and external drivers, there indeed may be a corporate interest in sharing internal historical assets with the public. For example, Coca-Cola recently donated to the Library of Congress an extensive collection of film and video materials which document nearly five decades of Coke advertising; "pop" culture, so to speak. In anticipation of this trend toward providing external access to archival materials, corporate archivists are now beginning to explore the feasibility of disseminating information over the Internet. To their chagrin, they see imposing obstacles, for the sharing of information in the digital environment is a double-edged sword. On the one hand, it provides new profit opportunities for individuals and organizations, particularly in patents and data collection. On the other hand, it creates a host of additional risks pertaining to intellectual property rights.[15] Nonprofit archives are protected by carefully complying with the fair use provision of copyright law and other legacy loopholes in current property law. It remains to be seen if archives in for-profit enterprises can claim the same protections for nonprofit use of their archival materials.[16]

The ambiguity of property law in a digital environment represents perhaps the largest unknown facing corporate archivists who are considering the dissemination of digital information on the Internet. The advance of technology and the practice of digital information distribution have rapidly outpaced corresponding legal developments. The speed of technological advance and implementation even has outrun the public policy debate surrounding privacy and property concepts. As a result, the rules that exist as guides for archival policy and practice are either highly restrictive or potentially subject to change. Many are rooted largely in dated legal interpretations that addressed older physical formats and limited distribution techniques. They may prove irrelevant to the digital domain. Reliable interpretations of existing case-law applications to the digital environment are still evolving and will likely continue to do so for decades. No public policy consensus exists to guide corporate archivists.[17] The extreme fluidity of these circumstances leaves corporate archivists adrift in the information delta, subject to the whims of wind and tides, casting about for firm ground for sure anchorage.

IV.
Privacy Rights: If a Rising Tide Floats All Boats, What Does a Tidal Surge Do?

> Well, I felt lonesome, I was lonesome and I could not help but cry.
> Robert Johnson, "Love In Vain (Take 4)"

William H. Gates, Microsoft's chairman, in addressing a consumer privacy conference, stated that consumer privacy and security "are tied together in a very deep way." The debate in Congress also centers on this duality, as legislators wrestle with the need to expand federal legal protections on the Internet in a manner that will not unnecessarily stunt business growth.[18] This interrelatedness echoes the endlessly repeating cycles of the river delta, for the corporate concept of privacy of information has been an issue for decades. A United States House of Representatives subcommittee held hearings on the computer and privacy in 1967, and a U.S. Senate subcommittee examined the implications that computer data banks held for the Bill of Rights in 1971. In a *Harvard Business Review* interview in 1976, IBM chief executive officer Frank T. Cary presciently noted that "Privacy is not a passing fad," and added that "computer systems with remote access have intensified both the problem and public concern."[19]

These connections between business, technology, and privacy concerns are not new ones. Web technology, however, has exacerbated them. Increasingly invasive technology, melded with on-line commerce, poses both business opportunities and business challenges. Technology companies are both creators and victims of the phenomena. For example, even as its software has been lauded as a catalyst of the new Information Era, Microsoft has had numerous conflicts with privacy advocates over the perceived intrusiveness of its products. Yet, "the same technologies that have raised concerns about a surveillance society have historically made possible many benefits that most citizens would prefer not to surrender," writes Phil Agre, an associate professor of information studies. An example is discount shopper cards, which grant cardholders discounts that they would not otherwise receive. The same cards, however, allow stores to track individual purchasing behaviors, and therein lies the tradeoff.[20] Still, it is encouraging that in the rush for e-dollars, the issue of personal privacy has not been lost. Many corporations actively address the issue. Numerous companies have adopted and applied the principles of fair information practices outlined by the Federal Trade Commission in 2000. Companies are also adding chief privacy officers to ensure that corporate practices are in accord with standards defined and accepted by all interested parties. In a form of self-governance, organizations like eTRUST and BBBOnline have been established to accredit the information-handling practices of companies dealing with consumer data. In the storm surge that is e-business, companies recognize the importance of providing safe harbors to consumers.[21]

This corporate concern is not entirely altruistic for, as Gates accurately noted, consumer confidence in on-line purchasing is tied directly to its perceived security. "Protection of privacy is not just a moral or social issue," states Ann Cavoukian, the information and privacy commissioner of the province of Ontario. "It is also an emerging business imperative." When actor Jerry Orbach's Social Security number inadvertently was posted by an on-line electronic auction site, the ensuing negative publicity was a severe blow to the fledgling consumer e-business industry. Companies are also wary that legislative remedies to privacy abuse are a very real possibility. Congressional representatives have issued numerous calls for privacy legislation, and in February 2000, the Federal Trade Commission established the Advisory Committee on Online Access and Security. There is perhaps no more urgent incentive for corporations to deal with privacy issues than the prospect of government intervention.[22]

From an archival perspective, corporate privacy concerns fall into two categories: employee and customer/client. Employee privacy has largely been relegated to protecting personnel-related materials for x years, with x usually determined by a corporate records retention policy set by the business units and occasionally augmented and lengthened by archival policy. Employee records contain everything from hiring documentation to medical information to disciplinary material. Most corporate archives do not consider employee records to be archival and do not collect them in volume. It is likely that a few personnel files will be preserved as part of other records series, for example, in the papers of key officials of the company. Generally such materials are restricted to external access until the death of the individual. The perceived social value of such information, however, may be creating a new legal ethos. A movement exists to license personal information or even make it a property right. Law-making bodies and courts increasingly appear willing to extend information property rights to individuals and their estates. Heirs seem more inclined to protect the privacy and estates of even those ancestors who clearly constituted public figures. All of these factors could make traditional archival policies inadequate.

Part of this new legal environment is the extension of the commoditization of information rights to common folk, which is blurring the lines between property and privacy legal canons. The example of IBM's popular "Little Tramp" television commercials demonstrates how complicated this issue can be. To market its personal computers during the 1980s, IBM created a serious of popular commercials featuring a Charlie-Chaplinesque character, the "Little Tramp," after having obtained permission from the Chaplin Estate to do so. If the company wanted to revive the "Little Tramp" for a future advertising campaign, it would need to obtain the consent not only from the Chaplin Estate, but also from the actor who re-created the character in the commercials or his estate, at least until property law deems otherwise. That could be a very long time, as a recent California law accords the rights in a celebrity's image to his or her heirs for seventy years after the celebrity's death.[23]

Although it is perhaps not surprising that icons of Chaplin's stature hold such legal sway, ordinary individuals someday may receive just as much protection under the law as celebrities do now. Corporate archives must be aware of this issue, since numerous companies have featured ordinary employees in advertisements to personalize their corporate image. The employees serve as tangible representations of a corporate service or behavior. For instance, numerous insurance organizations feature the helpfulness of their agents and claims representatives in their print and television advertising. But it is possible that these employees (or their estates) may not appreciate having their names or images resurface decades later on corporate history Web pages or other vehicles of mass dissemination. Corporations that unilaterally seek to reuse an advertising asset from their archives, for example, by digitizing nostalgic advertisements featuring past employees or to revive a popular advertising persona, may risk infringing upon publicity and privacy rights. Such rights do not exist for most ordinary employees now, but since the direction of publicity and privacy rights is uncertain, many corporations may be surprised to find that they may not own all of these rights in the future. It would seem logical that a corporation could expect to list its own advertising campaigns among its wholly owned assets. As these examples demonstrate, such may not be the case. It is enough to make any corporation sing the blues. Historians, too, may be unhappy with such results, for as the Coca-Cola donation to the Library of Congress indicates, corporate advertising provides immensely valuable insights into society.

Our society, however, remains in flux. New situations continually emerge that can influence archival privacy environments by redrawing the line between private and public. For example, in 1998, the clerk of courts in Hamilton County, Ohio, began putting public court records on the Internet, including divorce cases, criminal convictions, and even speeding tickets. The site generated quite a bit of interest. It recorded 385,000 visits in August 2002, which was remarkable since the county population totaled only 850,000. The on-line publication of these records prompted a host of complaints about invasion of privacy from people whose neighbors and co-workers were learning things that had been previously unknown. In a similar instance, following the collapse of the dot-com industry in 2000, court documents pertaining to the bankruptcy proceedings of Living.com, a home furnishings company, were posted on the company's Web site. These public records also contained volumes of information about company employees: salaries, stock options, home addresses, and so forth. However, the issue of redefining public access to court records in the era of Web technology, as significant as it may be, is not the question that would face the hypothetical corporate archivist for Living.com or its successor. The question for that archivist may be: What if the archives, as part of its mission, was preserving the Web site and making it accessible, could the Web site be a legally discoverable "document"? Would there be exposures based on the preservation for internal needs of personal but public information culled from a publicly distributed medium?[24]

Another example of changing privacy environments is Canada's recent Personal Information Protection and Electronic Documents Act, which applies to every organization that collects, uses, or discloses personal information in the course of commercial activity. The act requires, except in a few narrowly defined instances, that an organization obtain an individual's consent when it collects, uses, or discloses information about that individual. While this act awaits judicial review to determine the full extent of its reach, it could potentially prohibit corporate use of the kinds of innocuous employee data that have long been considered part of any company historical collection. For example, it is highly unlikely that consent forms were preserved or even acquired in the first place for corporate photographs or films of branch office personnel, company outings, or manufacturing floors. There would be no consent forms for such historically valuable period pieces as pre-electronic salary ledgers. Even if companies acquired and preserved such forms, they still may not be construed as permission for use today or on the Internet. Since it would be prohibitive to attempt to identify and obtain permission from the individuals captured in such scenes, corporate archives could face the prospect of no longer utilizing these items. Yet, these materials are the staples of both corporate history activities and researchers in business history.

The act defines personal information as "information about an identifiable individual," including race, ethnic origin, color, age, marital status, religion, and education; as well as medical, criminal, employment, or financial history; address and telephone number, numerical identifiers such as Social Insurance number, fingerprints, blood type, tissue or biological samples, and views or personal opinions. In this light, it is clear that the act specifically targets types of information normally found in corporate archives. This law may be relevant only to multinational corporations with operations in Canada. With current U.S. legislative activity focusing on expanding privacy spheres, it is possible that similar legislation could emerge here as well. Corporate archivists south of the Canadian border, therefore, should closely follow developments surrounding the act.[25]

In the United States, the case of *Felsher v. University of Evansville* illustrates how privacy and property rights may become intertwined. In this case, Dr. William M. Felsher, a disgruntled university professor, unlawfully appropriated the names, reputations, and likenesses of his former employer, the University of Evansville, and its president, vice president, and dean who were the plaintiffs in the lower court cases. Felsher used the appropriated identities to create Web sites and e-mail addresses that seemed to belong to the plaintiffs and to send e-mail supposedly from the plaintiffs. He also published highly critical articles about the plaintiffs. The Indiana lower court found that the unlawful appropriation occurred "even though the use is not a commercial one, or even though the benefit sought to be obtained is not a pecuniary one." The university sued under the legal theory of misappropriation of privacy, which was the only theory available for corporate entities and which protects private as well as commercial interests. Of potential note to corporate archivists, the lower court's decision was based not on the *Restatement of Unfair Competi-*

tion, which governs use for purposes of trade, but on the appropriation form of privacy tort in *Restatement (Second) of Torts,* which protects private as well as commercial interests. The lower court's decision, if adopted by others, suggests that unlawful appropriation of identity includes both the privacy interests of individuals and the noncommercial use of their identities. Such a theory may prove troublesome for corporations using older images from their archives. Virtually every corporate archives has a collection of standard images and film clips, often featuring unnamed employees in the course of work or play, that are circulated whenever a nostalgic image is needed. These images, long-assumed to be safe, have been used externally in books, newspapers and magazines, company history pamphlets, broadcast news stories, and now Web sites. But if the *Felsher* logic is followed by other courts, then such traditional uses may be called into question.[26] The Indiana Supreme Court, it should be noted, ultimately overruled the lower court protection of a right of privacy for the university on the grounds that the right is personal.

It is interesting to consider the threat that an extension of the *Felsher* lower court's holding could pose to modern corporate archivy, the belief that a corporate archives adds value to a company. Traditionally, corporate archives have had to combat the notion that corporate history is trivia at worst, at best only of value to academics and proponents of business history. There are those in corporations who see an archival operation as irrelevant to the business lines and an unnecessary expense that adversely affects earnings. Proactive archivists for decades have sought to reverse these attitudes, aggressively pursuing ways to contribute to the company bottom line. The missionary fervor that has characterized this pursuit has been driven by both the desire to make meaningful contributions to the organization and the need to justify the continued existence of the corporate archivist position within the company, not necessarily in that order.

Whatever the primary reason behind the adoption of that entrepreneurial mindset may be, the fact is that corporate archivists have made great progress in demonstrating their ability to add value. Through their efforts, corporate history has been successfully incorporated into marketing and advertising campaigns, product design, strategic planning, internal cultural initiatives, and employee education curriculum. Corporate archivists also participate in many activities outside the pale of traditional archivy, serving as thought leaders and cutting-edge practitioners in knowledge management, Web technologies, electronic records management, and other corporate initiatives. They have successfully adopted the language of business in their own departments, tailoring visions, missions, and departmental policies to focus on maximizing organizational contributions and minimizing expenses.

Privacy applications such as that described above, however, hold the potential to wipe out that progress, for if a corporate archives defines itself as being a contributor to the bottom line and if it is perceived by the company as being a valued corporate resource, then any of its activities could be construed as being for the company's benefit. In this light, it is conceivable that the use of these images even for solely societal benefit, such as in a company-developed Internet exhibit focusing on the history of Louisiana's twentieth-century shrimping industry, could be interpreted as a privacy exposure. By undermining the added-value philosophical pinion of corporate archivy, this view could force corporate archivists to back pedal away from the bottom line, thereby weakening their position in financially focused organizations.

The evolution of legislative and legal canons in response to emergent technologies is not the only factor affecting privacy considerations in the practice of corporate archivy. Social mores, which can shift as often as a Delta sandbar, need to be taken into account as well. Take, for instance, the biographical forms filled out by employees explicitly for the purpose of public dissemination and filed with public relations departments. These documents were ostensibly "safe" in their day, but in fact may no longer be deemed so, for they often contain information that society now considers private. In essence, they could be shipwrecks-in-waiting.

For example, biographical sheets filled out by corporate officers in the 1920s for publicity purposes likely contained historically valuable data on family, religious preferences, and social affiliations, data that would not be captured today. Such data therefore probably would be suitable only for dissemination to qualified researchers, not over the Web. In the pre-Internet days of 1979, for example, an employee public relations biographical sheet might contain a seemingly harmless reference to membership in the Iranian-American Club. In the wake of the subsequent Iranian crisis, it is unlikely that an individual would have made such a reference. It is even more unlikely that this hypothetical employee would want to make known such an affiliation to the American or potentially global public. From a process perspective, the implication of these shifting social mores is that access to certain types of corporate archival records will need to be re-evaluated on a regular basis.

Even more problematic are the records of high-ranking corporate officials. Senior management figures rarely draw a distinction between their corporate and personal lives. They receive personal correspondence at their office address, and due to the demands placed on their time by their positions, they often conduct personal business through their office. In any files of senior executives, it is possible to find correspondence pertaining to personal bank accounts, philanthropic donations, personal acquaintances, and family matters. While these likely will not be considered historical records unless they pertain to a business figure of notable celebrity, it is possible that such personal materials may nonetheless be retained if appraisal is at the folder level only, raising potential privacy concerns for future access.

In the files of chief executive officers, one might find correspondence from irate shareholders, customer or client complaints, relatives looking for jobs, and consultants with the next big idea trolling for contracts. It can be argued that these records, by dint of having been received at a corporate office during the course of normal business activity, can and should be considered business records. It is also possible that courts will take the position that these authors would have the expectation that their correspondence was personal (from one individual to another) and therefore private.

Such an expectation of privacy may even apply to internal correspondence from employees that may be preserved in executive files. In today's era of empowered employees equipped with e-mail, executives often find themselves deluged with correspondence from employees lauding or complaining about a specific organizational development, for example, a promotion, a layoff, an alteration to benefits, a new advertising campaign, and the like. Even if this correspondence is conducted on company systems and company time, it is possible that the courts could hold that these notes were sent with the expectation that a certain element of privacy would be attached to them.[27] Given the difficulties of filtering high-volume bodies of records like e-mail, these kinds of records likely will be preserved as part of an executive's legacy. As a result, it will be a very long time after executives leave the company before their records will be entirely clear of privacy issues.

That long wake alone is capable of creating rough water for any archivist mounting information on the Web, but corporate archivists also need to be especially cognizant of the fact that they are giving up control of their information. The removal of information from the Web may return control to the archivist, although there is no guarantee that will happen. The information could have caught somebody's eye and have been downloaded for future use, or even added to someone else's Web pages. Archival initiatives, like Brewster Kahle's effort to capture and preserve the entire Internet, also may work against corporate attempts to pull back Web-mounted information. To date, Internet archives have been more successful at preserving Web pages than at indexing and providing access to them, but that is likely to change as software technology grows more sophisticated.[28] Corporate archivists could build in the same safeguards when releasing archival information on the Internet that they do when dealing one-on-one with researchers. That is, archivists could review materials for appropriateness, assess potential long-term issues that may emerge, and limit access to any items that potentially could harm the individual or his or her estate. But, as in the case of the hypothetical Iranian-American employee, even the best efforts to protect both individual and institution could be negated by entirely unanticipated factors. If what is open on the Web has to be continually reassessed for appropriateness, then the practicality of saving these materials for purely historical purposes is placed in question, for only sport fishermen have the luxury of tossing their fish back. Corporate archivists, like Gulf Coast shrimpers, cannot afford to waste their efforts.

The second area where corporate archives may face privacy issues is found in records that document consumer or customer activity. A current definition of consumer/customer privacy will vary from corporation to corporation, but it will likely include the following: privacy is the right of individuals to determine for themselves when, how, to what extent, and for what purposes their private data is used and/or communicated to others. Private data is personal information that can be used to uniquely identify an individual, and it is particularly important for a corporation to differentiate between privacy and security. Security concerns issues of access and controls, while privacy policies deal with the responsible handling of personal and identifiable information collected about individuals.[29] As companies focus on e-business as a strategic priority, it is clear that basic privacy principles and sensitivities aid in building customer relationships and promoting satisfaction in the global networked economy. Since consumer attitudes are affected by confidence in how personal information is used, consumer privacy must be a consideration in e-business implementation and products.

Emergent technologies cast familiar privacy issues in a new light. The more recent advent of massive and affordable computer power gives business the ability to collect and analyze incredible volumes of data at a very small level of granularity. That ability, known as "data mining," has led businesses to attempt to capture and collate all possible information concerning customers to better target potential buyers.[30] The dot-com companies, with their "get big fast" mantra, their lack of traditional physical assets, and their powerful high-technology orientations, quickly amassed huge volumes of customer data points. As the bloom faded off the dot-com blossom, however, failed companies found these lists to be their most valuable asset, putting them up for grabs during their last frantic hours in a desperate attempt to stave off collapse, regardless of what their privacy policies stated.[31]

The practice of micro-analyzing vast pools of seemingly unrelated data points has been seen as invasive by consumer rights advocates.[32] That perception has been fueled by blunt comments from technology industry leaders like Sun Microsystems chief executive officer Scott McNealy, who tactlessly remarked, "You have zero privacy anyway. Get over it." The discomfort that society feels with privacy issues is evident on numerous fronts. A 1999 *Wall Street Journal*–NBC survey found that Americans rated privacy as the number-one issue for the twenty-first century. Recent years have seen a spate of books trumpeting the end of privacy. A number of high-profile privacy cases, including the release of Supreme Court nominee Robert Bork's video rentals and the autopsy results of NASCAR race car driver Dale Earnhardt, have served to increase public and political discomfort with current levels of privacy protection. This discomfort is also evidenced in the uproar over the patient privacy rules written to implement the Health Insurance Portability and Accountability Act of 1996 (HIPAA), which were authorized by the outgoing Clinton administration. The adoption of these rules was delayed by more than 24,000 written comments. Public concern with privacy is likely to grow even more intense as global security practices and technologies become prevalent, and therefore intrusive, in the wake of the events of 11 September 2001.[33]

Corporate archivists must factor both public and corporate concerns into their own privacy practices, for as an extension of the corporation proper they are subject to the ebb and flow of public relations pressures. These pressures lie largely outside of the statutory and legal sanctuaries built into the traditional practices of public archival repositories. A case in point that illustrates the precariousness of this balancing act involves the research use of historic life insurance applications. One insurer has more than 10,000 life applications preserved in its corporate archives. These documents contain detailed individual and family medical history information on a large number of males from the 1850s and 1860s, and it provides an abundance of information on the physical characteristics of the wealthier members of nineteenth-century American society. Due to the age of these documents, traditional archival practices would hold them to be free of privacy concerns. But in the modern computing environment, it is not only conceivable but possible to efficiently create personal medical dossiers that can include DNA data as well as family medical histories going back as far as records exist. It is not too much of a stretch to envision information like that found in centuries-old life insurance applications winding up in a database and being used to assess the medical liabilities of descendants of those nineteenth-century policyholders. If that were to happen, public outrage likely would be swift and vocal, and it would cause significant angst for corporate public relations personnel. Adopting professionally sound privacy practices in the name of history will provide precious little protection for a corporate archives if such practices result in the corporation being swamped by a tsunami of public scrutiny or even embarrassment over the release of archival information.

V.
Conclusion: The Perfect Storm

> You better come on in my kitchen babe, it's goin' to be rainin' outdoors.
> Robert Johnson, "Come On In My Kitchen"

The Internet is changing everything, even information itself. John Perry Barlow observed that "Information only really exists in the delta," occupying time rather than a physical space.[34] Without embarking on an examination of the ontology of information, the fact remains that the exact nature of information is a crucial issue for corporate archivists, for their policies and procedures—the keel upon which they base their protection of rights holders—are predicated upon restricting access to the information that they manage. Increasingly, however, these precepts seem less relevant. In these early days of this new millennium, it seems clear that the same digital implications of the Information Revolution that are so crucial for corporate business success pose equal challenges for corporate archives. For the first time, widespread external dissemination and use of corporate historical materials may be looming just offshore.

Corporate archives collections, by dint of their traditional internal focus, are not particularly well positioned for entering the convergence of the twin currents of digitization and Internet technologies. They often contain materials of significant historical value but of uncertain rights ownership. They contain materials that can at once be an organizational risk and a business asset. They are managed by professionals with long-term perspectives who operate in a shifting, day-to-day environment. The tensions between these often conflicting and at times ambiguous positions force corporate archivists to find balance points between protecting the interests of their employers and addressing the historical interests of society. It is often difficult for corporate archivists to find a tenable fulcrum in the best of times. Therefore, they have traditionally docked their vessels in the safe harbors of corporate conservatism. But, as the perfect storm of digitization and Web technology sweeps across the information landscape, established balance points are made increasingly untenable, swamped by societal tidal surges and obliterated by shifting legal sands. Social expectations and technological developments are driving corporate archives off their traditional courses. Whether they end up safely at sea or dashed upon a river shoal remains to be seen.

No one knows what the information delta will look like in the years to come. But it is possible that corporate archives will need to alter today's existing policies and procedures in anticipation of potential changes in use patterns and to manage the exposures that come with that altered usage. If they do not, they may find themselves living the lyrics from Robert Johnson's classic "Cross Road Blues": "I tried to flag a ride, Didn't nobody seem to know me, babe, everybody pass me by."

15 Confidences in Medical and Health Care Records from an Archive Perspective

Barbara L. Craig

Contemporary Interest in Privacy and Medical Records

A search of recent literature published on the topics of health care, privacy, and medical records returned over 5,000 citations to books and articles.[1] The majority, not unexpectedly, refer to privacy and records only in the situations in which advice and care are given to clients as patients, for example, in hospitals, clinics, and doctors' offices. Nevertheless, this interest in medical records, especially regarding their confidentiality and access, extends beyond working medical professionals who deal with the practical issues of applying rules every day. It reflects heightened concern more generally about the wider uses of personal medical information for purposes imperfectly known or acknowledged in the original exchange.[2] Anxieties about the privacy of medical confidences are largely a contemporary development. Health care and medical records (HC&MRs) have always contained intimate details about people, their physical and mental conditions, and such specific treatments provided by a practitioner as remedies or palliatives. Clients trust caregivers to act always in their best interests. This trust proves mutual, based largely on the presumed confidence of information that is given and, to a certain extent, received. The patient expects the practitioner to be discrete in sharing information while the practitioner, in turn, expects to control professional disclosures. These assumptions, built over time and nurtured by experience, naturally embrace the records kept by practitioners and, to a certain extent, by institutions.[3]

Public trust in the confidentiality and security of records of care has been undermined by the phenomena of new information technologies. Detailed personal information, which in the past could only be accessed through laborious and costly manual effort, now appears readily available.[4] People remain wary of the level of security that is integrated with new systems. They seek explicit recognition of rights to control their personal information and demand a voice in determining the conditions under which such data may be used. Special concerns about the collection and use of sensitive personal information seem especially evident in health care situations where information that has been collected to serve client needs may be shared with third parties without knowledgeable compliance. Practitioners, for their part, seem to exist in more complex relationships to health care service than at any previous time. There may be many levels of interest in their records and uses for them, for example, as evidence in legal proceedings, as part of ethical accountabilities, or for scientific study and for business planning. Individual control over records or the information contained within them may be no longer either desirable or possible.[5]

All archival repositories are affected in some way by increased public concern about personal privacy, even if the effects until recently have been by implication. Most, however, will be directly embraced by statutes and regulations that govern historical records containing personally identifiable information. These laws will have a direct impact on public access to records in archival repositories. For example, in North America, legislation regarding the data collected and used by the private sector provides rules for protecting and disclosing personal information surrounding health care activities. This legislation largely extends the provisions of earlier privacy legislation that focused on information that had been collected and held by public authorities. Canada's federal Personal Information Protection and Electronic Documents Act (PIPEDA), in effect since January 2001, applies to organizations in the private sector, and since January 2002, includes those that gather health information. This legislation has prompted parallel or related legislation in many provinces. All of these statutes or proposed bills embrace health care information and records.[6]

In the United States, the Health Insurance Portability and Accountability Act of 1996 (HIPAA) and its associated regulations set new national standards protecting the privacy of personal health information. HIPAA specifies the permissible use and disclosure of personal health information about persons either alive or deceased, that is created, maintained, or received electronically by "covered entities," as defined in the act. "Covered entities" include, among others, hospitals, physicians, health plans, and health information clearing houses.[7]

Most obviously and explicitly affected by the provisions of privacy legislation are repositories with records created in the course of giving care, such as archives with large holdings from health care institutions (HCI) or repositories and archives actually located in or associated with HCIs. These institutions bear a special burden resulting from health information privacy legislation. Health care records uniquely combine intimate personal information of identifiable people with the details of professional services and actions taken on their behalf.[8] In the current environment of public concern and significant new legislation concerning privacy rights in North America and the European Union, archives have taken steps to enhance the protection of people represented in their holdings. Specifically, they now routinely make terms and conditions of acquisition and use explicit in their policies, in donor agreements, and in the research protocols completed with individual users. This essay will not review such policies—although the notes will guide you to some worthwhile examples as models—but rather hopes to raise more general points about HC&MRs and about the changing nature of confidences between health care providers and recipients over time.[9]

The shifting boundaries of individual privacy, both established by laws and sanctioned by general social agreement, have profound implications for archives that keep records for historical use. Archives often have difficulty satisfying temporal concerns about privacy while simultaneously fulfilling their broader cultural responsibility to keep records, including those that are affected by prohibitions, as sources of evidence that survive contemporary exclusions. No easy formula can be offered to circumvent excessive censorship, to resist purges, or to convince funders to assign resources to keep closed records for some unknown future time. Still, some useful ways exist to develop an archival perspective on the acquisition and administration of sensitive personal records and to establish a balance of interests that will allow the retention of sources for future historical use. This perspective begins with an understanding of the individual archives' particular, often unique, responsibility for records. It is based on the archivist's research into the history of HC&MRs, an understanding of the records' documentary forms, and a recognition of the many interests that such records embody. It requires the support of a clear institutional mandate and declaration of the repository's role. And it recognizes that time will change most things, even many that we assume to be timeless. From an archives' perspective, only the records are timeless.

What Is a Health Care or Medical Record or When Is a Record an HC&MR?

Although this question seems to be fundamental, no easy answers exist. For one thing, definitions change over time. Before the mid-nineteenth century, it is particularly difficult to define a health care or medical record in terms that are precise and exclusive, largely because healing was an art with many types of practitioners who learned as apprentices to masters.[10] The authority of these healers derived from their skilled practices, coupled with their control over learning the craft and its traditional wisdom. The efficacy of their medical treatments was anchored in a theory of balance in nature, but was based on practical knowledge built empirically. Healers relied on the power of nature to right itself and, to a certain extent, on the faith of their patients in a positive outcome of treatment.

Just as healers and the healing arts have a long history, so, too, do the types of records characteristic of their medical practices. Most records were, from our perspective, idiosyncratic, personal, and unsystematic. Diaries of herbal treatments, notes and diagrams of surgical procedures, and the personal pharmacopoeia and *vade mecums* are among the many types of records that survive today in specialist repositories.[11] Practitioners valued information that had been recorded and accumulated over time for the access that it provided to experience and for its practical support of current business. Social agreements—rather than legislation, special procedures, and court action—established and controlled the privacy of the patient and acknowledged the boundaries around the confidences exchanged in consultations.

Until the early part of the twentieth century, people who required medical or surgical treatment consulted practitioners and paid for their services. Hospitals were religious or civil charities for the infirm or the sick poor. Paying patients did not seek hospital services in any number until the second quarter of the twentieth century.[12] Hospital and clinic registers, the records of an institution's governance, and financial statements that document business activities, though recognizable to contemporary researchers, provide less medical information than is routinely collected from any person admitted to a hospital or clinic today.

The archivist who responds to requests for information about community or personal health and medical practices before the early twentieth century needs to understand distinct patterns of record making, information recognition, and privacy control that differ considerably from the situation today.[13] Moreover, the need to ensure strict privacy for either healer or healed rarely arises in archives that hold early records. Although the nature of the information remains personal regardless of the time in which it was collected and recorded, and such information would be protected today, this appears to be less necessary since information from the distant past has only a minimal impact at best on the lives of identifiable descendants. As time recedes, the records from the past assume new value for contemporaries, offering evidence about the generations that came before. Group or community interests eventually supersede strictures designed to protect a shared confidence between individuals in the distant past.

By the end of the nineteenth century, healing had taken a course in which more information about people was acquired routinely. Records assumed a larger role in care and were kept more formally by practitioners and institutions. Systems, and the standards that they fostered, emerged from the mass treatment of illness by cadres of knowledgeable professionals. Increasingly complex health care services, relying more and more on technology, measurement, and analysis, were concentrated in special institutions, rather than provided to individuals at their homes. Healing today is based on the authority of experimental science. Caregiving has been largely removed from the family and assigned to the community. The merger of healing with science, the professionalization of healers, and the institutionalizing of care have created the environments that fostered the modern health care record in the forms that we would easily recognize today. Clinical notes of care; a patient's medical history detailed in technical writing; professional assessments such as diagnoses, prognoses, and specific treatments; tracings from instruments measuring physiological processes; images of anatomy; and laboratory reports of the chemical composition of blood and body fluids are just a few examples of the types of documents that contemporary files might contain.[14]

Modern advances in the science and arts of medicine and health care continue to alter the contents of records while the application of technology, especially digital information technologies, will soon merge diagnostic testing with electronic recording.[15] Caregivers on the wards, in consultation rooms, or in surgeries will have immediate information on the current condition of their patients, their location, their clinical status, and their records through integrated medical information systems accessible through portable computers. The greatest impact on recording and records currently appears to be concentrated in clinics or hospitals. In the future, individual practitioners probably will be integrated fully with central servers and special medical Web sites supporting health professionals in their offices or at patients' homes.

Just as the answer to the question "What is a medical record?" remains relative to the time in which it is asked, it also bears a direct relation to the practitioner who makes and keeps the record. It may be somewhat surprising that today there are probably far more distinct types of health care practitioners (HCP) than at any other time in the past. The information needs of each profession shape the forms and format of the records created in their practices. Physicians, psychologists, naturopaths, pharmacists, and social workers, to list only a few examples of practitioners whose information requirements we would easily recognize as being distinct, will have their own professional definitions of the types of records appropriate to their services. Some categories of information in a record satisfy the requirements of a profession's ethical code and the customs of its practices.[16] Other types of information contain elements that are required by law in the jurisdiction in which the HCP is licensed to practice.

Requirements for records set out in laws, statutes, and regulations, and those that are strictly professional, may be either elaborated or streamlined by rules of the institution in which services are delivered, either for a salary, a fee, or gratis.[17] HCIs, for example, will have rules about preparing and keeping medical records. They often specify the time of records creation, the individual responsible for maintaining documentation, and the ways in which records should be kept for reference. Only designated individuals will have access to them. The HCI will also provide staff with guidance about the conditions under which files may be consulted by the patient or outside third parties. Since at least the mid-nineteenth century, neither professional needs for information nor the legal requirements for professional practice and recordkeeping have remained static for long. They always have changed in response to new knowledge, to reflect accumulated experience in the professions, and to recognize changes in the broader social consensus about legitimate uses. One might logically assume that change will continue to mark both the delivery of health care and the records that it creates.

Acquiring, Preserving, and Providing Access to HC&MRs

Archives generally share a responsibility for preserving records for use in the future by people and for interests as yet imperfectly seen. Nevertheless, it is incumbent on repositories to manage the acquisition, preservation, and use of their records in ways that respect the potentially competing expectations of a person today and a community tomorrow. It is not possible to prescribe a foolproof method for accomplishing this, nor to describe past successes exhaustively. One reason for our lack of knowledge about institutional experiences arises from the differences among repositories. Few archives have the same terms of reference, scope for action, level of resources, or even institutional visions. Since these features condition archives administration, generic standards remain rudimentary. It is important, therefore, that the mandated role of each archives be articulated, not only to support the archivists responsible for implementing it, but also to benefit both current and future donors and users. Without a clear role articulated in a mandate, acquisition policies may be uncertain, appraisal criteria may respond poorly to needs, and access procedures may seem difficult to ground on a foundation in principle.[18]

The acquisition of health care records, or documents with medical information, brings immediately with it the responsibility of controlling access to protect the confidences implied or articulated in the record-making environment. Archives may extend existing controls over access by using mechanisms similar to those in the originating institution. They may preserve the anonymity of people in the records before permitting use, establish research protocols to govern access, and convene research committees to authorize access to records and to determine the conditions for access. The archives will have as models for immediate reference those controls carefully embedded in procedure and documented in the creating environment, especially for records in HCIs. But acquisition also raises other issues of archival administration, especially relating to the problem of continuing preservation and its costs. The volume of medical records created by modern institutions, or even by private practitioners, in most cases exceeds the capacity of any archives to retain. Most archives, even those large institutions considered to be well endowed, must select a smaller subset from the whole. Alternative sources of concentrated information may be considered better candidates to keep for research. Medical information, after all, is not synonymous only with a personal clinical file. Personal information is expansive by nature, colonizing all types of record forms. This propensity to spread beyond the confines of one or a few types of record makes protection difficult to achieve without understanding the active information environment in which it thrived.

Sensitive and personal information is often found in hospital minute books, official reports, registers of activities and events, and financial records.[19] However, these records are more succinct than case or clinical files and, for that reason, often appear more desirable candidates for preservation. Managerial records also can be reflective and analytical in content, commenting on situations from an institutional perspective. Such contemporary assessments often are valued for their historical concentration. Reports and summary statements of activity also have the attraction of being, in some cases, statistically cleaner to use, providing a more easily discernable profile of mass activities over time. The requirements to protect privacy will still affect summary types of records, but the problem of volume is usually absent. This makes them attractive to an archives and easier to acquire, keep, and manage over the long term.

The case record, however, may provide the locus of sharpest intersection between the individual as a patient with a disease, the practitioner who provides treatment, the institution that cares for the patient, and the entity that pays for both treatment and care.[20] It may not be possible to find more concentrated informational sources that possess all of the unique evidence of individual experience. As a result, many archives will need to establish a careful plan for the acquisition of personal clinical records, employing methods of selection that have been matched to their circumstances. During archival appraisal, social and institutional values, anticipated information needs, and legal requirements contribute to a balance with the resources and capabilities of the repository. Appraising records in order to select those for continuing preservation for historical use may be a fundamental archival task, but is one for which there can be no universal criteria to apply according to technical instructions. Yet it is possible to identify the types of questions that need to be asked and the issues that must be addressed, if appraisal is to proceed methodically and on a justifiable and rational basis.

Appraisal is grounded on values. But where does the archivist seek to find these values in the records and when should appraisal be done? To answer these questions, archivists need to articulate the vantage point from which they view records and values. This is accomplished by using the mandated role of the archives as a fundamental starting point. For example, the role of the archives may be to contribute to the discovery of knowledge in medicine and the health care sciences. If so, appraisal decisions will seek to advance that role in two ways. Archivists will both establish models of evaluation and develop processes that will lead to the acquisition of records that best contribute to building medical knowledge in a systematic manner. Conversely, if the role of the institution is to maintain evidence of the development of a profession and to chart its rights, responsibilities, and practices over time, other criteria for appraisal would be developed along with a process of evaluation in which the needs and interests of the profession have a voice. And to consider a third example, if the archives has a public role, perhaps to ensure the general accountability of a public authority for the proper treatment of patients receiving care in its institutions, then the criteria for appraisal would embody guidelines for selecting records to allow this audit to be conducted.[21]

A final series of questions in any model method would address the repository's special archival responsibility. This role makes the archives an independent entity rather than a passive instrument of other interests. Every archives has this larger mission, although many archivists may not have taken the time to delineate it or to document the ideals implicit in it. An archives may see its special responsibility as being to records and accountable recordkeeping, or to the history of an institution, or to documenting the development of medical practices or a profession, or to the historical exposition of a subject, topic, or locality. It may orient itself to the needs of people alive today, or it may look to emergent human communities as time proceeds. These priorities, often embedded in assumptions, should reveal themselves in answering when the archives expects "a return" on its investment of acquiring, preserving, and describing records. Use of some kind is the ultimate justification for the existence of the repository and its practices. In other words, what are envisioned to be the use or uses for the records? Although this appears self-evident, it is nonetheless important to remember always that the uses for which the records were originally intended will rarely be those for which they are used in the future.

Recognizing Time and Different Interests that Support the Archiving of HC&MRs

Time, represented by the *longue duree* of archives, is sometimes acknowledged in society but usually obliquely, as when people consume history as a form of entertainment or pursue it for family reasons. Time and history certainly are imperfectly recognized in most institutions. Archives may cater to either clear needs or vague desires to return to the recorded past, but it is rare for society or for specific organizations to prescribe in detail either retention policies or access guidelines. This is the field of activity for the archives and archivist. Ethical issues arise because laws, regulations, rules, and customs are not universal in scope. Nor do such prescriptions continue to have the same relative voice and meaning over time. While we have seen that the nature of medical information and the definition of the constituents of an HC&MR change over time, other factors, perhaps less apparent on the surface, complicate the archival administration of HC&MRs. Some relate to the problem of identifying the parties to any HC&MR and the nature of the claim that each has to its information. The first, second, and third person are not represented equally in the HC&MR, nor are their claims to its information acknowledged equally in law, regulation, or guideline.

While it might reasonably be assumed that the principal in any record is the HCP as its author, this presumption proves to be less well founded when all other original parties to it are probed. In addition to the author, contemporary participants include both the implicit and explicit writer and the recipient. Moreover, expectations for records involve a number of participants with legitimate needs and interests. The patient, or subject of the record, has real claims, especially for the evidence that a record may provide in any lawsuit in which malpractice, negligence, or error is alleged. The information in a record becomes important in the future, if unanticipated health problems arise or should questions of genetic disorders or exposure to dangerous substances emerge. The complexity of modern health care and medical practice and the expense of supporting its infrastructure of HCIs and such fast-developing technologies as out-patient cancer screening, bring into focus third parties in the form of insurers, quality service auditors, ombudsmen, research protocols for clinical trials of newly developed drugs and therapies, medical researchers generally, and actuaries and statisticians. All of these interests have an impact on the collection and recording of personal health information, and they bring real and implied claims for access to the record, its evidence, and its information.

Today the chief frame for shaping contemporary medical records is the law.[22] Still, additional frames of view usefully contribute to our understanding of the records' continuing values. These include institutional rules, professional ethics of the HCP, especially guidelines for appropriate behavior and accountability for it in records, and social sanctions on the uses of records for unanticipated purposes that contribute to the public benefit. Social sanctions appear most elusive because these often seem endemic to a community rather than declared or articulated in some formal way. The archivist's assessment of these regimes requires research, often extensive historical research, to build an understanding of public norms and concerns at any given moment in time. Although social norms are intangible, they prove particularly useful in helping to determine collection, retention, and access policies. This can be especially helpful when considering those people who never participated as part of the original exchange, bargain, or contract implied in creating the record. Ethical acquisition and destruction of records is poorly served by embracing exclusively one perspective. Although a careful analysis of all of the contemporary contexts embracing records is fundamental, appraisal requires a sense of time that transcends current concerns by endeavoring to integrate people with their communities over time and in history.

The Ethics of Archiving: Mandates, Policy, Procedure, Documentation, and Transparency

Time has a profound impact on people, society, and records. Over time, laws have changed and will continue to do so. Over time, professional requirements have changed dramatically and in ways that no one would have or could have predicted. Time reshapes society, again in generally unpredictable ways. The views of individuals and groups concerning the information contained in records, as well as the records' uses for personal and social ends, have also undergone significant alterations.[23] But in acknowledging change and its unpredictable course, archives also need to find anchors for rational and articulate archives administration. Any record, of whatever type, always involves more than one person. The author, the intended or actual recipient, and the subject of the document or the object of the action authorized by the record all play a role. Diplomatics provides a method for analyzing documents based on these distinctions and categories. Phrased another way, there is always an inherent distinction between the OF-ness of the record and its ABOUT-ness.

All categories or classifications used for analysis recognize the third-person point of view: other parties have interests in records. One of these third parties is the community. Society has a long-term interest in ensuring the legal and, perhaps more importantly, the moral actions of its professions and institutions. This becomes especially critical for institutions that deal with individuals who, by being sick or in need, become the objects of care and the recipients of actions that affect their lives and liberties. Patients and caregivers are not equally powerful in the implied contract in care or service. A record may be the evidence of "me" either as an individual patient, or as a practitioner providing a professional service. Records, collectively, offer evidence of "us," of communities that share ties with those that came before and those who will be in the future.[24] Records serve future generations, who will need to know about the norms and practices of the groups from which they sprang. Ultimately, historical accountability is the important role of records and one that archives alone fulfill in society.

The archives, by mandating policies and procedures for appraisal, preservation, and access control, and by systematically articulating and carefully recording these policies over time, brings all of these interests into a balanced alignment. Current concerns and future needs are satisfied through donor and research agreements, and re-appraisal is greatly helped by a clear statement of criteria used in the first place, and by an articulation of the values that these policies sought to recognize.

16 The United Methodists and Their Open Records Policy

L. Dale Patterson

Introduction

Institutions often attempt to balance their privacy concerns with a commitment to records access. They generally hope that a greater openness will explain actions that seemingly affect the public good. This practice most commonly occurs within the public or governmental sector, as evidenced by open records and sunshine laws. The urge to understand organizational cultures and activities, however, transcends concerns for governmental accountability. The people who manage institutions, or who have some level of investment in their operations, expect access to the decisions and plans of their organizations. This attitude characterizes corporate shareholders and especially proves true for managers of, and financial contributors to, nonprofit organizations. In fact, the expectation of records openness and transparency probably relates directly to the size and activity of an institution. It often appears that, as organizations grow in size and develop broader constituencies, a corresponding demand for accountability and transparency occurs. This seems especially true for nonprofits, which usually have both public and private characteristics.[1]

The United Methodist Church exemplifies some of these themes and provides an especially compelling case study. The denomination reached a critical size by the mid-nineteenth century, prompting an internal discussion concerning accountability and reorganization. By 1850, the Methodists had emerged as the largest Protestant denomination in America, a status that they would retain until the 1950s. The religious historian Winthrop Hudson has described the 1800s as "the Methodist

Century" in the United States. Nathan Hatch, surveying the denomination's unique influence over the course of American religious history, recently claimed much the same for the first half of the twentieth century. Both authors eschew denominational chauvinism, and neither ignores the historical impact of other denominations and religious traditions on the American psyche. But Hudson and Hatch both note that many central themes in American religious history, such as responsibility and stewardship, popular involvement of the laity, and a plain-spoken theology easily accessible to a broad audience, were all enunciated and emphasized by the Methodists. These themes place the Methodist experience in America at the heart of the American experience itself. Broader national concerns often became mirrored within the denominational framework. Even in the 1990s, when other denominations assumed greater prominence, United Methodism remained the only Protestant denomination to maintain a local church presence in every county of the continental forty-eight states. This broad public presence and representative constituency had a substantial impact on the denomination's attitude toward archival practice, recordkeeping, and public accountability.[2]

The Methodists first developed a formal open-records policy in 1984, and the church's efforts to focus on accountability and responsibility to multiple constituencies parallels public developments within the United States. The open-records policy affected all levels of church structure, from denominational agencies to local church meetings. This policy was the latest step in the Methodists' historical experience in confronting records access issues and public information. It illustrates several themes for all institutions that seek to satisfy their constituencies' demands for accountability and transparency.

Churches: Public or Private?

Churches and religious institutions occupy a unique place within American institutional cultures and history. Religion contains both public and private characteristics. American public institutions generally encompass governmental functions. The acts of governments clearly constitute public acts, and the general population has always demanded the right to monitor governmental activities. Over the course of the past two centuries, historians generally have documented a trend toward increasing public access to the acts and actions of governmental bodies. Successful self-government appears to require access to public records, as evidenced by developments in the Jacksonian,

Progressive, and post-Watergate eras. Over time, and throughout American history, public interest and expectations have tilted toward a greater demand for public access. Generally, Americans expect their public institutions to be transparent, except within some very well-defined and carefully delineated areas.

At the other end of the privacy spectrum rests the business, or the corporation. American cultural and legal traditions generally consider it vital and reasonable that little or no information concerning corporate activities or decision-making processes need be made available to the public. In recent years, governmental regulation has required corporate concerns to make public some data, such as financial information, product contents, and health-related research. Still, corporations generally are required to disclose very little information to the public. Businesses, concerned about protecting their investments, for the most part remain exempt from revealing information about their activities.

Churches find themselves in the unique position of straddling this public-private divide. On the one hand, as defined in the U.S. Constitution, they constitute private organizations. American religious historians, in attempting to describe this fundamentally new relationship between church and state, have often characterized religious institutions as voluntary societies. Governments did not force individuals to join churches or support their activities. Yet, churches also retained a very public character. Protestant traditions generally held large open public meetings and invited everyone to attend. Even with respect to finances, churches behaved in a public fashion. Whereas corporations received money in exchange for specific goods or services, churches raised funds to maintain their institutions and to perform services and functions on behalf of their members. Expenditures might involve paying a minister's salary, publishing bibles and religious literature, creating health care institutions, financing schools, or sending missionaries throughout the nation and the world. These actions were not only done to advance the faith, but also for the public good as perceived by that faith.

Religious bodies combined funds to create supralocal agencies that carried out their missions in ways that would have been impossible for purely local churches. A religious federalism, analogous to governmental structures, developed. For the Methodists, this analogy became even more direct between the 1880s and the 1920s. During that period, the denomination reorganized its agencies and support structures so that each local church was assessed (i.e., taxed) to support more general work on the national level. Every local church, after raising the funds necessary to support its pastor and local ministries, became required to transmit a denominationally determined assessment that would support centralized efforts. Though the church remained a private entity, it behaved in very public ways.

Methodist Organization

United Methodism is organized into a three-tier interconnected structure. Its most basic and obvious presence consists of the local church. In traditional Methodist terminology, the local church may be a *charge* or a *station,* where one individual church comprises the organizational unit, or it may be a *circuit,* where two or more churches comprise a structural unit. Increasingly, the more recognizable term of *parish,* which is used to describe both charges and circuits, has become more popular. Churches within a specific geographical jurisdiction, which have been combined for ecclesiastical administrative purposes, make up a *conference.* Each conference is administered by a bishop and by a delegated body of ministers and laity, called an *annual conference.* These annual conferences appoint ministers to officiate at specific churches and to receive reports relating to the churches' activities. A third administrative jurisdiction is known as the *General Conference.* This delegated legislative body meets quadrennially to set policy, enact legislation, and establish direction for the entire denomination. The General Conference also creates *general agencies* that carry out major denominational functions. Currently, fourteen agencies conduct such tasks as publishing, overseeing mission and relief work, certifying ministers, preparing educational and worship resources for the local churches, providing higher education, addressing various social concerns, and carrying out general administrative functions. Most relevant for this discussion, all three levels create and maintain archival documentation. General agency functions, it should be noted, are mirrored at the other two administrative levels as well. No central headquarters exists for the denomination, and only the General Conference can speak for the United Methodists as a whole. A *Book of Discipline* expresses the Methodist polity.

The origins of this complex structure date to the end of the nineteenth century. Between 1872 and 1920, the shape of the current structure, as it relates to agencies, boards, and committees, came into existence. The Methodists became enamored with the corporate model of organization, as did much of the rest of the United States during the late 1800s. Calling for better organization and greater accountability, the General Conference administratively and financially absorbed the handful of independent Methodist agencies. Further, it called on annual conferences and agencies to pursue similar centralizing policies. The denomination was involved in broader social discussions concerning the best organizational method of dealing with modernization. This model of organization was viewed as a boon to efficiency and effectiveness. Many mainline Protestant denominations adopted and adapted their structures in a similar manner. Prior to this organizational shift, two or three independent Methodist agencies, accountable only to local interests, acted on behalf of the entire denomination. The General Conference hoped to forestall scandal and enhance accountability by absorbing these existing agencies and also by creating similar additional bodies. It must be noted that the board of directors of these independent organizations willingly acquiesced in the takeover by the General Conference.

To fund the work of these agencies, a tax system, known as *apportionments,* developed. Every local church was expected to send financial contributions to the general church. These donations supported the administrative and programmatic work of the church, funded missionary and other agency work, paid the salaries of bishops and board personnel, and provided basic funding for emergency relief efforts. The denomination, by mandating small contributions from its local constituencies, managed to accomplish broad national objectives. Church members understood the ways in which church structure paralleled the American political system. The Methodist analogy to American federalism became even clearer by the mid-twentieth century, when denominational leaders explicitly described the church in political terms: the General Conference constituted the legislative branch, the bishops exercised executive functions, and the Judicial Council assumed the role of a Methodist supreme court.[3]

Open-Records Legislation

As church members became more cognizant of denominational similarities to the American body politic, they expected more accountability by decision makers and by implication greater access to records and participation in the dialogue on denominational policy. Examples of such interest surface throughout Methodist history. In 1834, the official newspaper of the denomination, the *Christian Advocate,* began an editorial policy suppressing any discussion of slavery and abolition. In response to this practice, a group of dissidents started *Zion's Herald,* which was devoted to the discussion of abolition and other social issues facing the denomination. In the 1870s, when the denomination faced the issue of lay participation in leadership positions, a group wishing to expand the discussion started *The Methodist.*

In the 1880s, as mentioned above, the denomination reorganized its agencies to promote greater accountability. This process of reorganization continued until 1912. Two events in the twentieth century helped to emphasize the continued interest in transparency in the administration of general agencies. In 1951, the *Reader's Digest* published "Methodism's Pink Fringe" which broadly indicted Methodism's social concern and general agencies as Communist dupes. The article was inspired primarily from information distributed from the House Un-American Activities Committee (HUAC).[4]

The *Reader's Digest* article inspired a general call for reform and accountability of the general agencies. One example of this has just surfaced in recently opened records of the Board of Missions from the late 1940s. In the aftermath of World War II, the board sent out a general letter to the clergy, along with a small booklet on the Soviet Union. The purpose was to help the clergy understand the postwar world. The booklet, however, was perceived as being too sympathetic toward the Soviet government and served to generate criticism against the board, eventually finding its way to HUAC. The expectation of accountability is demonstrated in a series of letters between Ralph Diffendorfer, the head of the board, and those unhappy with the general mailing. In the exchange, it became clear that Diffendorfer refused to reveal whether board funds had been expended in the publication of the booklet, and he refused to assign responsibility to the individuals who selected the particular book for inclusion in the mailing. This mailing became one of the reasons for the writing of the *Reader's Digest* article.[5] Finally, in 1983, the television newsmagazine *60 Minutes* interviewed a United Methodist bishop, who also served as president of the National Council of Churches (NCC). During the interview, it became apparent that the bishop was very uninformed about the policies of the board which supported the NCC and knew little about the way in which its funds were being expended. An additional article appeared in *Reader's Digest*, which questioned how church funds were being used. In the aftermath, several agencies declared the interview to have been unfair, while others in the denomination called out for more accountability.[6]

These two events, along with the general popular cry for public accountability in the wake of the Watergate scandal, probably helped to shape the denomination's interest in records openness and accountability. By the early 1980s, the communications arm of the denomination, United Methodist Communications, as well as the council responsible for general program oversight, the General Council on Ministries, helped to set the stage for the creation in 1984 of an open-meetings/records provision in the *Book of Discipline*. As a result, all meetings of agencies in the denomination, from general denomination-wide agencies through local church gatherings, became open meetings. The Methodists first opened meetings to the news media and subsequently allowed broader public access as well. All records and reports distributed in such meetings were considered public documents. Only a limited number of exceptions for closed sessions existed. The open-records provision first appeared in 1984, and the language of the statute is worth quoting in its entirety:

> In the spirit of openness and accountability, all meetings of councils, boards, agencies, commissions, and committees of the Church, including subunit meetings and teleconferences, shall be open to news media, both church and public. Portions of a particular meeting may be closed for consideration of certain subjects, if such a session is authorized by at least a three-fourth's majority vote of duly selected members present when the vote is taken in public session and entered in the minutes. Documents distributed in open meetings shall be considered public.
>
> Subjects which may be considered in closed session are limited to considerations of sale or purchase of real property, personnel matters, [issues related to the accreditation or approval of institutions,] discussions relating to civil litigation or collective bargaining, deployment of security personnel or devices, negotiations involving confidential third-party information, and deliberations of the Judicial Council.
>
> A report of the results of a closed session is to be made immediately upon its conclusion, or as soon thereafter as is practicable.[7]

This original paragraph 821, as it was called, also related to paragraph 800, which defined the term "agency" to have a denomination-wide meaning:

> The term "agency," . . . is a term used to describe the various councils, boards, commissions, committees, divisions, or other units constituted within the various levels of church organization (General, Jurisdiction, Central, Annual, District and Charge Conferences) . . . .[8]

Thus, anyone could attend meetings at the local church, conference, or general agency level. Notably, the original text stipulates that news media may be present at the meetings. This occurred because one of the initial sponsors of the legislation included the denomination's news service.[9]

Exceptions to the open-meeting law remained limited and appeared generally logical. An entire meeting cannot be closed, but closure may occur when the deliberations focus on personnel issues or security measures. Security issues most often arise at general agency meetings, which often deal with large monetary sums or valuable historical objects. Personnel issues tend to be discussed at local church and conference levels. The conference controls the admission of individuals into the ministry and also oversees any trials that might involve those ministers. All regulations concerning ministerial conduct are promulgated within the conference, and the *Book of Discipline* stipulates detailed instructions concerning the ways in which to protect ministers' confidentiality. Similar instructions, though somewhat less detailed, exist for the laity and the local church.[10] Other aspects of the statute remain slightly less well defined. Third-party restrictions, for example, remain somewhat vague. The Judicial Council constituted the only agency, until recently, that received *carte blanche* to close its proceedings. This deliberative body differs from public judiciaries in that it does not render actual verdicts but only offers decisions in matters of church law. Its decisions involve the use of proper procedures and correct rulings. Still, the Judicial Council might well review sensitive and private material relating to ministerial conduct, and Methodist trials may be either public or private and must be conducted at the conference level. As a result, paragraph 821 allows the Judicial Council to review and discuss the trial in private, yet render its decision in public. This logically follows, since the original petition to the council that led to the trial necessarily would have been a public document.

Since 1984, paragraph 821 (now 721) has undergone only two major modifications. The first expanded its scope, and the second contracted it somewhat. In 1996, the Methodists added an explicit statement opening all meetings, which confirmed the spirit of the original legislation:

> In the spirit of openness and accountability all meetings . . . shall be open. Portions of a meeting may be closed for consideration of specific subjects if such a closed session is authorized by an affirmative public vote with at least three fourths [*sic*] of the voting members present . . . .

> Great restraint should be used in closing meetings; closed sessions should be used as seldom as possible. Subjects that may be considered in closed session are limited to real estate matters; negotiations, when general knowledge could be harmful to the negotiation process; personnel matters; issues related to the accreditation or approval of institutions; discussions relating to [pending or potential] litigation or collective bargaining; [communications with attorneys or accountants;] deployment of security personnel or devices; [and] negotiations involving confidential third-party information; *and deliberations of the Judicial Council.* [italics added][11]

In 2000, the Council of Bishops, the Judicial Council, and the General Conference apparently were empowered to define their own reasons for having a closed meeting. The new phrase has not been reviewed by the

Judicial Council, the equivalent of the Supreme Court, so the full implications of the change are not yet understood. Unfortunately little information exists on the rationale behind these changes. There has been no discussion of these issues in the United Methodist press. The changes were approved on the consent calendar at General Conference, which means there was no floor discussion of these issues. It appears that most of the changes reflect a growing concern for privacy in regard to legal matters. The General Council on Ministries and the General Council on Finance and Administration—the denomination's legal agency—suggested changes in the 1996 language. The Council of Bishops recommended the language changes for 2000, and there is no record in the council's minutes of the rationale for the change.[12]

Many records have not been affected by these directives, most notably the documentation generated by the staff of the agencies in the course of their regular work. This contrasts significantly with the situation in the public sector where public access legislation controls staff records, as well as meetings and reports. The Methodists only require that meetings of agencies, and the records created for those meetings, be made public. Nothing in paragraph 821 makes staff records open to the public. A few other denominational requirements, however, do have an impact on this broader documentary universe. The denomination mandates that agency staff and episcopal offices transfer their records to the central archives. Archives exist on denominational, conference, and local church levels, but this requirement exists only at the denominational agency level.

Archival Implications

The central archives, called the General Commission on Archives and History (GCAH), was created in 1968 at the formation of the United Methodist Church. Prior to 1968, no central denominational archives existed. Rather, an Association for Methodist Historical Societies assumed some archival functions. Since 1948, each annual conference was supposed to maintain its own history and archives, and the association served as a support and resource organization for the annual conference. The Evangelical United Brethren Church (EUB), which merged with the Methodists in 1968 to form the United Methodist Church, had a longer history of archival practice. Since 1889, the United Brethren, a predecessor body to the EUB, had an archives and historical society. Thus, the creation of GCAH owed partly to the continuation of the EUB archival tradition (the first general secretary of GCAH was the former director of the

EUB Historical Society) and somewhat to the need for denominational leadership for the annual conference archives already in existence. The General Commission is composed of twenty-four members selected from the denomination, and it provides general oversight and direction for the staff of the commission. The archives also has an explicit charge to make its records available to the public. Clearly, denominational leaders expect that a substantial portion of agency staff records will become public:

> [The General Commission on Archives and History] shall maintain archives and libraries in which shall be preserved historical records and materials of every kind relating to The United Methodist Church and shall see that such holdings are available for responsible public and scholarly use . . . . The bishops, General Conference officers, general boards, commissions, committees and agencies of The United Methodist Church shall deposit official minutes or journals, or copies of the same, in the archives quadrennially and shall transfer correspondence, records, papers, and other archival materials. . . from their offices when they no longer have operational usefulness.[13]

A crucial distinction remains in that the records covered by paragraph 821 are defined as public from the day of their creation, or at least the day of their admission into an open meeting, while staff records continue to be subject to the policies and standards of the archives.

The archives thus faces the same concerns common to many public repositories: making a series of judgment calls concerning when, and if, records might become accessible. Some decisions appear obvious. Personnel files, for example, must remain closed with restricted access and perhaps even face eventual destruction. Other records that appeared sensitive and had been closed to researchers initially often become less sensitive over time. A missionary's description of a German internment camp during World War II, for example, had been thought to pose a danger to others and had been restricted in 1942. The report poses no security issue in 2002.[14] Other records series change their fundamental characters over time and require periodic review. The Missionary Files Series offers a good example. Early files date from the 1890s and consist primarily of public reports from missionaries operating in various foreign fields. They describe general operations, and the denomination often published or summarized their contents in annual reports or publications. Over time, however, personnel issues began to creep into the files. Between the mid-1930s and 1948, the Methodists gradually stopped maintaining personnel files in a completely separate system. Mid-twentieth-century missionary files featured handwritten commentary by denominational authorities, as well as exchanges between staff and missionaries, that straddled the line between informational reports and personnel files.[15] Most of the permanently valuable records generated by agency staff, however, appear very benign. They typically are opened to researchers after some designated period of time following their creation, most often twenty-five years. Permanently valuable archival records must provide evidence of the function or functions of the agencies. Tertiary records, or records that represent any unfinished or incomplete record product such as drafts and working memos, usually are destroyed. General policy decisions are established by the commission with input from the archives staff.

Initially, the archives was very passive in its collection and management of its records. The general agencies transferred whatever they wished and managed access to those records held at the archives. The rationale for this centered around privacy issues. The policy actually created a draconian process whereby a researcher needed written permission from the archives to conduct historical research and then had to obtain written permission to view specific records from the various agencies. Some agencies closed their records for fifty years, others adopted a more liberal policy, and a few openly claimed that they would only allow friendly researchers access to records. It was entirely possible for one person to see a set of records and for another to be denied access to the same records, or for one to receive permission from an agency only to be denied access by the archives. The archives leadership in 1994 rationalized the process by approving a set of guidelines for records retention for the general agencies and put into place a uniform access policy by which patrons only deal with the archives. This has required the archives staff to conduct workshops for the general agencies on the records-retention policy and to explain the implications for certain documents that will be accessioned into the archives. The General Commission approves the retention and access policies. When necessary, denominational legal counsel reviews any suggested changes in the retention policies.

Methodists clearly have a fairly comprehensive commitment to open records and to providing general access to the archives. Born in the American milieu and affected by the same social and cultural forces that defined the nation as a whole, they developed a keen interest in organization and accountability. Part of this historical legacy involves their commitment to maintain and preserve records in an archives. The United Methodist Church attempts to walk the same difficult tightrope as many other religious and nonprofit institutions: balancing the right to privacy inherent in its status as a voluntary society with its membership's and the general public's need to know and to understand how that voluntary society operates and makes its decisions.

Appendix 1: Selected U.S. Constitutional Amendments

Amendment I, 1791

"Congress shall make no law respecting an establishment of religion, or prohibiting the free exercise thereof; or abridging the freedom of speech, or of the press; or the right of the people peaceably to assemble, and to petition the Government for a redress of grievances."

Amendment IV, 1791

"The right of the people to be secure in their persons, houses, papers, and effects, against unreasonable searches and seizures, shall not be violated, and no Warrants shall issue, but upon probable cause, supported by Oath or affirmation, and particularly describing the place to be searched, and the persons or things to be seized."

Amendment V, 1791

"No person shall be held to answer for a capital, or otherwise infamous crime, unless on a presentment or indictment of a Grand Jury, except in cases arising in the land or naval forces, or in the Militia, when in actual service in time of War or public danger; nor shall any person be subject for the same offence to be twice put in jeopardy of life or limb; nor shall be compelled in any criminal case to be a witness against himself, nor be deprived of life, liberty, or property, without due process of law; nor shall private property be taken for public use, without just compensation."

Amendment IX, 1791

"The enumeration in the Constitution, of certain rights, shall not be construed to deny or disparage others retained by the people."

Amendment XIV, Section 1, 1868

"All persons born or naturalized in the United States and subject to the jurisdiction thereof, are citizens of the United States and of the State wherein they reside. No State shall make or enforce any law which shall abridge the privileges or immunities of citizens of the United States; nor shall any State deprive any person of life, liberty, or property, without due process of law, nor deny to any person within its jurisdiction the equal protection of the laws."

Appendix 2: Selected U.S. Federal Statutes Concerning Privacy

As discussed elsewhere in this volume, United States statutory privacy law is a conglomeration of broad and narrow provisions. Federal data privacy legislation is a "fractured, episodic record targeted patchwork"[1] of separate laws that fails to protect or regulate all types of data. Enactment of statutes often reflects the events, societal needs, and political pressures extant at the time. Many of these laws have counterparts in state statutes.

Cable Communications Privacy Act of 1984, 47 U.S.C. § 551. This law protects and regulates the disclosure of the personally identifiable information of cable communications subscribers, requires cable communications operators to provide notice of information collection practices, and grants subscribers a right to consent to secondary disclosures. Regulations adopted as part of the Telecommunications Act in 1996 allow consumers to opt out of disclosures. In 2001, the USA PATRIOT Act amended this statute to provide greater government and law enforcement access to personally identifiable information relating to telephone and Internet services. The Cable Communications Privacy Act's original strict requirements still apply to records of subscribers' video programming choices. The PATRIOT Act's 2005 sunset provisions do not apply to its amendments to this statute.

Children's On-line Privacy Protection Act of 1998 (COPPA), 15 U.S.C. §§ 6501–6506, effective 21 April 2000. This law was enacted to protect children from unlawful and deceptive practices in on-line marketing, specifically, to regulate the collection and use of children's personal information. It specifies the amount and types of personal information that may be collected on-line from children under age thirteen; how such information may be stored, retained, and used; and what procedures are required for parental notification and consent. The Federal Trade Commission established related regulations. COPPA applies to operators of commercial Web sites and on-line services directed to children and to general Web sites that collect information from children. COPPA's provisions require verifiable parental consent for data collection from children, generally by independent means such as a hard copy of a consent with the parent's signature or via a separate e-mail from an adult's e-mail address. Unlike other privacy laws, COPPA provides parents with more than the typical "opt out" provisions. Parents may veto or prohibit any collection, use, transfer, or retention of children's personal data. Parents may not waive the law's requirements of notice and verifiable consent.

Communications Assistance for Law Enforcement Act (CALEA, also known as **the digital telephony law),** 47 U.S.C. §§ 1001–1021 (1994). This statute requires telecommunications common carriers to design new systems and technologies to permit law enforcement wiretapping and electronic surveillance. It was supplemented by the Telecommunications Carrier Compliance Fund, established by the Omnibus Consolidated Appropriations Act for FY 1997, which pays carriers, equipment manufacturers, and providers of support services to modify equipment and services to comply with CALEA. In 2004, the FBI began efforts to extend CALEA to include packet services that carry voice over the Internet, or Voice over Internet Protocol (VoIP).

Computer Matching and Privacy Protection Act (CMA), 5 U.S.C. § 551a(*o*) (1998). This law amends the federal Privacy Act of 1974 to regulate the practice of linking an individual's computer files through a personal identifier to "match" files in separate databases. The Privacy Act did not specifically mention this practice, and consequently, this act was passed to remedy the deficiency. Federal agencies must comply with several restrictions in order to use data obtained through a computer match.

Consumer Credit Reporting Reform Act, 15 U.S.C. §§ 1681–1681t (1997). This act closed some of the loopholes in the Fair Credit Reporting Act and narrowed the "legitimate need" purpose for which credit reports can be disseminated. It continued to allow affiliate sharing of credit reports and "pre-screening" of credit reports (i.e., unsolicited offers of credit to consumers), and it limits pre-emption of stronger state credit laws.

Crime Control Act of 1973, 42 U.S.C. § 3789g. This law stipulates that state criminal justice information systems developed with federal funds must adopt privacy and security programs to ensure the "privacy and security" of records in their criminal justice systems.

Driver's Privacy Protection Act, 18 U.S.C. § 2721 et seq. This law was passed in 1994 after the stalking and murder of actress Rebecca Schaefer by a fan who retrieved her name and address from a state motor vehicle department. It prohibits the release and use from state motor vehicle records, without the consent of the individual driver, of personal information (photograph, Social Security number, driver identification number, name, address [but not zip code], telephone number, and medical and disability information). Information about accidents and violations and driver license status is exempt from this prohibition and may be released in a "masked abstract." "Permissible uses" are mandatory disclosures regarding motor vehicle or driver safety and theft; motor vehicle emissions; motor vehicle product alterations, recalls, or advisories; performance monitoring of vehicles and auto dealers; permissive disclosures to any government agency, court, or law enforcement agency, to businesses or their agents, employees, and contractors to verify the accuracy of personal information submitted by an individual to the business and if incorrect, to obtain the correct information, but only to prevent fraud; for research and statistical purposes; to insurers; to licensed private investigative agencies and security services; and for any other use specifically authorized under state law.

Electronic Communications Privacy Act of 1986 (ECPA), 18 U.S.C. §§ 2510–2521, 2701–2711, amended February 1994, 18 U.S.C. §§ 3121–3127. This act amends the Omnibus Crime Control and Safe Streets Act of 1968 (the federal Wire Tap Statute, which permits wiretapping of voice communication), which was designed to protect wireless voice and electronic communications from government surveillance, including electronic data transmissions. The Electronic Communications Privacy Act prohibits interception of and access to stored wire, oral, or electronic communications without consent by one of the parties or under a strict business extension exemption. Like many other laws, it was amended by the USA PATRIOT Act in 2001 to add a new voluntary disclosure exception for emergency situations, so that an electronic data transmission provider may disclose data to law enforcement authorities if there is a reasonable belief that immediate threat of death or serious injury exists and justifies disclosure, which may affect colleges and universities. ECPA protections may not apply equally to private institutions. In 1998, an Illinois federal district court determined that a private company Internet network was not an Internet service provider to the public and that it fell outside of ECPA. *Andersen Consulting v. UOP and Bickel and Brewer*, 991 F. Supp. 1041 (N.D. Ill. 1998). Whether this ruling will apply outside of the Northern District of Illinois also is uncertain.

Electronic Freedom of Information Act Amendments of 1996 (EFOIA), amends 5 U.S.C. § 552 (Pub. Law 104-231) to require federal agencies to be proactive in disseminating information on-line before it is requested.

Electronic Fund Transfer Act of 1980, 15 U.S.C. §§ 1693–1693r. This law contains no specific privacy protection for electronic transfers, but establishes mandatory guidelines for the relationship between consumers and financial institutions concerning electronic fund transfers to protect the rights of individual consumers. Customers must be notified about any routine third-party disclosure of personal records made during an electronic fund transfer.

Electronic Signatures in Global and National Commerce Act (ESIGN), 15 U.S.C. § 7001 et seq., effective 1 October 2000. This law makes electronic signatures valid and binding for contracts or other records and satisfactory for notary or attestation requirements on documents. It allows the use of electronic records in lieu of many other paper documents. As important exceptions, electronic signatures may not be used on wills, in divorce or adoption papers, on official court documents and court orders, for terminations of utility service and health insurance, for mortgage foreclosures, and for product recalls involving health or safety. The law limits legal risks.

Employee Polygraph Protection Act of 1988, 29 U.S.C. §§ 2001–2009, prevents private employers from requiring employees or prospective employees to take a lie detector test or to use any such results in employment decisions.

Fair Credit Reporting Act (FCRA), 1970, 15 U.S.C. § 1681 et seq., as amended. The FCRA establishes rights and responsibilities for consumers, furnishers, and users of credit information; requires credit reporting agencies to follow reasonable procedures to protect credit information accuracy, confidentiality, and relevance; makes records available to data subjects; provides rights of data quality (procedures for accessing and correcting information) and data security; and permits disclosure only to authorized customers. The USA PATRIOT Act amendments require the credit reporting agency, upon receipt of FBI certification that an individual is being investigated to protect against terrorist attacks or "clandestine intelligence activities," to disclose the names and addresses of all financial institutions where the individual has accounts, as well as identifying information about the individual. The FBI may make further disclosures of the information to federal law enforcement agencies.

Family Educational Rights and Privacy Act of 1974 (FERPA, also known as the **Buckley Amendment**), 20 U.S.C. § 1232g, as amended several times. FERPA requires schools and colleges to grant students up to age eighteen or their parents access to student school records. It provides challenge and correction procedures, and it sharply limits disclosures of student records to third parties. Amendments in 2001 and 2002, including the USA PATRIOT Act amendments, however, permit educational institutions to disclose student records to federal law enforcement officials without student consent in certain circumstances. See Mark A. Greene and Christine Weideman, "The Buckley Stops Where? The Ambiguity and Archival Implications of the Family Education Rights and Privacy Act" elsewhere in this volume, and Menzi L. Behrnd-Klodt, "Family Educational Rights and Privacy Act: Legislative Amendments and Judicial Interpretations," appendix 3 to this volume.

Financial Services Modernization Act of 1999 (also referred to as the **Gramm-Leach-Bliley Act [GLB],** of which this act is Title V), privacy provisions codified at 15 U.S.C. § 6801–6810. This act permits mergers of banks, insurers, and stock brokerages. It provides limited privacy protections against the sale of private financial information and codifies protections against "pretexting" (obtaining personal information through false pretenses). It regulates only financial institutions engaged in banking, insurance, stocks and bonds, investments, and other financial advice and services, which must ensure the security and confidentiality of customer information and records, protects against anticipated threats or hazards to the security or integrity of such records, and protects against unauthorized access to or use of such information or records that could seriously harm or inconvenience consumers. Customers must receive notices about information-sharing policies and their right to affirmatively "opt out" of some sharing of information. The law authorizes the Federal Trade Commission and other federal agencies to develop data privacy regulations for personally identifiable financial information. It permits states to enact stricter privacy legislation for personal financial data.

Freedom of Information Act (FOIA), 5 U.S.C. § 552. In contrast to the federal Privacy Act (described below), FOIA was enacted in 1966 to provide individuals with access not only to their own files, but to provide public access to all federal agency records, with certain exemptions. FOIA does not apply to Congress, the courts, private organizations, or state or local governments, although many states have enacted their own FOIA legislation. Several FOIA provisions exempt from release certain federal agency data. The 5 U.S.C. § 552(b)(6) exemption permits withholding of personal information in "personnel and medical and similar files" where there is a "clearly unwarranted invasion" of privacy. Exemption 7(C), U.S.C. § 552(b)(7), protects personal information in "investigatory records compiled for law enforcement purposes," if the disclosure could "reasonably be expected to constitute an unwarranted invasion of privacy." If the Privacy Act and FOIA conflict in a particular instance, information that must be disclosed under FOIA is exempted from the restrictions of the Privacy Act.

A number of states have enacted their own freedom of information acts, usually patterned after the federal FOIA. State laws generally contain a privacy exemption for personal and medical records.

Health Insurance Portability and Accountability Act of 1996 (HIPAA), P.L. 104-191, 42 U.S.C. § 1320d. HIPAA's Privacy and Security Rules, 45 CFR Parts 160 and 164, have revised the future of American health data privacy. The rules are discussed in Menzi L. Behrnd-Klodt, "The Brave New World of 21st-Century Medical Records Privacy in the U.S. and Canada, Contrasted with the European Data Privacy Model," which is appendix 4 to this volume.

No Child Left Behind Act of 2001, P.L. 107-110, 20 U.S.C. § 9528. This law amended the Elementary and Secondary Education Act of 1965 (ESEA), 20 U.S.C. § 7908, in conjunction with the National Defense Authorization Act for Fiscal Year 2002 (P.L. 107-107), 10 U.S.C. § 503, 544, which provided funding for the U.S. armed forces. Together these laws require local educational agencies and school districts receiving funding under ESEA to provide military recruiters, upon request, the same access to secondary school students as schools provide to postsecondary institutions or to prospective employers. Effective 1 July 2002, local education agencies must provide military recruiters with high school students' directory information (names, addresses, and telephone listings), unless parents affirmatively opt out of the program. In addition, the No Child Left Behind Act promised parents exceptionally broad powers to require vast amounts of timely and understandable information about schools and teachers. Many parents applaud their new rights. Critics note that the law is confusing and that its potential burden on schools can be overwhelming and expensive, perhaps diverting scarce educational resources.

Omnibus Crime Control and Safe Streets Act of 1968 (also known as the **Federal Wiretap Act** or **Title III**), 18 U.S.C. §§ 2510–2520 (1970). This law was the first comprehensive federal law that regulated all forms of electronic eavesdropping devices. Title III of the law nationalized all federal, state, and private electronic surveillance. This regulation "represents an accommodation of both crime control interests and privacy concerns, which is premised on the view that electronic surveillance by the government is essential to effective enforcement of the criminal law. Title III protects the privacy of citizens by dictating the circumstances and manner in which the government may eavesdrop on conversations, rather than by severely limiting or restricting government's ability to engage in the conduct."[2]

Privacy Act of 1974, 5 U.S.C. § 552a, was enacted in 1975 after the Watergate scandal, to promote respect for citizens' privacy by establishing guidelines for federal agencies' use and disclosure of personal files. This was the first comprehensive federal statute designed to protect individual privacy rights from governmental intrusion. It includes the following "Fair Information Practices" regulating all information transactions between citizens and government agencies: no secret recordkeeping systems; information collected for one purpose should not be used for others without written consent; individuals should access and have the opportunity to correct and amend information about them; and information held by agencies should be relevant, up to date, accurate, and protected against unauthorized loss, alteration, or disclosure.[3]

The Privacy Act prohibits collection and retention of data interfering with First Amendment rights unless authorized by law, and it restricts disclosures of personal information to third parties without consent. Agencies are required to provide descriptions of their recordkeeping, collect only necessary information directly from individuals, and inform individuals of their practices. Privacy Act provisions do not apply, however, unless information is within "a system of records," a much-litigated concept that includes any group of records under agency control and housed, indexed, or otherwise kept to be retrieved by use of an individual's name or other identifier.[4] Information that is not retrievable is not considered a record within a "system of records" subject to the Privacy Act.[5]

In practice, it is difficult to amend inaccurate records, and the goal of assuring that information is collected and used for only a single purpose remains unfulfilled.

Privacy Protection Act of 1980, 42 U.S.C. § 2000aa et seq. This law was passed by Congress in response to the U.S. Supreme Court ruling in *Zurcher v. Stanford Daily,* 435 U.S. 547 (1978), which had given broad law enforcement access to a newspaper's records. It established procedures for law enforcement to gain access to newspaper files, including the requirement for a subpoena. Limited exceptions allow seizure of records by a warrant (for which a lower standard of proof is required than for a subpoena), including records of child pornography, national security materials, evidence of crimes by journalists, and records needed to prevent death or serious bodily injury. Searches of a newspaper's premises may be conducted only by those officials involved in an investigation and only upon probable cause to believe a crime is involved.

Right to Financial Privacy Act of 1978 (RFPA), 12 U.S.C. §§ 3401–3422. This law was enacted in response to the U.S. Supreme Court holding in *U.S. v. Miller* (425 U.S. 435 (1976)) that personal financial information belongs to the bank, not the bank customer, and that the customer has no reasonable expectation of privacy in records of checks he or she had written. The law provides bank customers with some privacy rights in records held by banks and financial institutions, regulates federal agencies' access to bank records, and establishes procedures for disclosures requested by the government. The law attempts to balance the privacy interests of consumers with the interests of law enforcement and creates an individual privacy interest in personal bank account information. The act does not cover state or private sector third-party inquiries to banks. The law governs a customer's individual business records, but does not protect or limit access to records of a customer's bank transactions that are kept within the bank's own business records, which may be disclosed without customer consent.

Telecommunications Act of 1996, 47 U.S.C. § 222. The Telecommunications Act requires telecommunications carriers to protect the confidentiality of, and limit access to, consumer proprietary information. The law limits access to customer information to that needed to provide services. Customers must "opt in" to agree to permit marketing based on personal information.

Telemarketing and Consumer Fraud Act, 15 U.S.C. §§ 6101–6108. This law restricts telemarketing calls and autodialers, and provides certain guidelines to protect consumers.

USA PATRIOT Act (full title: **Uniting and Strengthening America by Providing Appropriate Tools Required to Intercept and Obstruct Terrorism**

Act of 2001), Public Law 107-56; 115 Stat. 272. This law was passed by the U.S. Congress shortly after the 11 September 2001 attacks. Intended to expand federal investigative powers, it reflected the prevailing American climate of fear, secrecy, and concern. The PATRIOT Act amended most existing privacy laws to permit easier federal government and law enforcement access to personal information, and it clarified how authorities can compel disclosures of information. The law authorizes Internet service providers to permit federal law enforcement authorities to investigate computer trespass and makes it easier for law enforcement to procure student records, library circulation and use records, and a variety of individual purchasing and financial records without the consent or knowledge of the individual if it is "in the course of an ongoing investigation," which is a lower standard than needed to secure a search warrant. Portions of the law lapse on 31 December 2005, unless renewed by Congress. Strong congressional and public criticism of the law developed in 2002 and 2003. New legislation, termed PATRIOT II, was provided to Congress in January 2003 under terms of great secrecy, but was not immediately passed.

The Video Privacy Protection Act of 1988 (VPPA), 18 U.S.C. § 2710–2711. This statute was passed as a response to newspaper disclosure of the video rental records of U.S. Supreme Court nominee Judge Robert Bork during his confirmation proceedings. It protects consumer privacy by prohibiting the release of personally identifiable video rental records or the disclosure of personal rental information without written consent of the consumer. Consumers may opt out of secondary disclosures for marketing use. Video rental stores must destroy rental records no longer than one year after a customer account is terminated. The law's applicability is limited to "prerecorded video cassette tapes or similar audio visual materials," which leaves unclear whether the act applies to newer formats and media, such as DVDs, video games, and other new technologies. The intersection of VPPA with the USA PATRIOT Act also is unclear. Many states have enacted video privacy laws.

Appendix 3: The Family Educational Rights and Privacy Act: Legislative Amendments and Judicial Interpretations

Menzi L. Behrnd-Klodt

Archivists are not alone in struggling with the ambiguities of the Family Educational Rights and Privacy Act of 1974 as described elsewhere in this volume by Mark A. Greene and Christine Weideman in "The Buckley Stops Where? The Ambiguity and Archival Implications of the Family Educational Rights and Privacy Act." Yet, after nearly thirty years administrative interpretation, congressional amendments, and judicial decisions have failed to clarify basic meanings of the statute or to address its privacy-related shortcomings. All of these have provided a modicum of clarity, but much remains unclear and open to speculation.

Congressional Amendments of FERPA

Several FERPA amendments permit greater disclosure of personally identifiable student information in education records without the consent of parents or students. As a result, nonstudents' rights to access and use student records often are superior to the students' right to privacy.

Amendments in 1979 and 1994 gave state and local education officials access to student records during audits and reviews of tax-supported educational programs.[1] Those who were victims of violent crimes may see the reports of college and university disciplinary proceedings against perpetrators, regardless of the outcome of such proceedings.[2] In 1992 and 1998, Congress exempted any records that were created for law enforcement purposes at higher educational institutions from the definition of restricted "education records" that could not be released without consent under FERPA and allowed schools to disclose publicly the outcome of any student disciplinary proceeding for a crime of violence or nonforcible sex offense.[3] Postsecondary institutions may inform the parents of students under age twenty-one of any violation of a law or school rule concerning alcohol or illegal drugs. The 1998 amendment adds photographs and e-mail addresses to the definition of student "directory information"[4] that schools may release without the written consent of students or their parents. In 2000 and 2004, Congress amended FERPA to allow and then to require colleges to disclose information about registered sex offenders on their campuses.

The USA PATRIOT Act of 2001 substantially amended FERPA to permit educational institutions to disclose student records without student consent to the U.S. attorney general or his or her designee, or to other federal law enforcement officials in certain circumstances. Officials may collect, retain, disseminate, and use educational records that are considered relevant to authorized investigations or prosecutions of terrorism.[5] A written application to view records only has to certify that there are "specific and articulable facts" suggesting that the records are likely to contain information about terrorism. After the application is submitted, courts must permit access to any records requested, and educational institutions must produce the records. The U.S. Immigration and Naturalization Service (INS) has established an Internet-based monitoring system known as Student and Exchange Visitor Information System (SEVIS) to facilitate schools' transmission of student information to the INS. Schools must transmit such information to the INS for tracking and monitoring foreign and exchange students.

Recent legislation focused on the release of student "directory information" without parental consent. The No Child Left Behind Act of 2001 with the National Defense Authorization Act for Fiscal Year 2002[6] granted military recruiters the same access to high school students' personal information that is provided to postsecondary institutions and employers. Educational agencies must provide directory information including names, addresses, and telephone numbers (including unlisted numbers) to military recruiters or risk losing federal funds for all schools in their area. A notice of this disclosure requirement may be provided to parents in writing, by student handbook, or by other methods. Any parent who does not wish to have a school provide a child's information must refuse consent in writing.[7]

Judicial Interpretations of FERPA

Parents, students, and organizations all use FERPA to obtain educational records during legal actions against schools for inadequate educational services or for civil rights violations. In *Rios v. Read*, 73 F.R.D. 589 (E.D.N.Y. 1977), parents were allowed to obtain educational records to support a lawsuit alleging failure to teach English to Hispanic children. A notice, in both Spanish and English, was provided to the parents of students whose records would be disclosed. Although the disclosure was limited, the court decided that there was no need to delete students' names from the records. In *In re Kryston v. Board of Education*, 430 N.Y.S.2d 688 (N.Y.App.Div. 1980), the court permitted a parent to obtain test scores of his child's entire third-grade class, with the results scrambled and students' names deleted.

In the case of *Owasso Independent School Dist. No. I-011, v. Falvo*, 534 U.S. 426 (2002), reversed and remanded, a unanimous U.S. Supreme Court decided that the common practice of peer grading did not violate FERPA. Kristja Falvo claimed that her children had been embarrassed when students exchanged and scored papers under their teacher's direction, sometimes calling out the scores aloud in the classroom. In its ruling, the U.S. Supreme Court reviewed congressional intent behind FERPA and discussed, though it did not settle, the ambiguities surrounding the meaning of "education records and the length of time such records must be retained."[8] The court found that some formalities were required to create and maintain "education records" under FERPA, none of which were present in peer grading:

> The word "maintain" suggests FERPA records will be kept in a filing cabinet in a records room at the school or on a permanent secure database, perhaps even after the student is no longer enrolled. The student graders only handle assignments for a few moments as the teacher calls out the answers. . . . The Court of Appeals was further mistaken in concluding that each student grader is "a person acting for" an educational institution . . . The phrase "acting for" connotes agents of the school, such as teachers, administrators, and other school employees.
>
> FERPA requires "a record" of access for each pupil. This single record must be kept "with the education records." This suggests Congress contemplated that education records would be kept in one place with a single record of access. By describing a "school official" and "his assistants" as the personnel responsible for the custody of the records, FERPA implies that education records are institutional records kept by a

single central custodian, such as a registrar, not individual assignments handled by many student graders in their separate classrooms. . . . [E]ven assuming a teacher's grade book is an education record, . . . the grades on student papers would not be covered under FERPA at least until the teacher has collected them and recorded them in his or her grade book.

The court also commented with a touch of irritation, that

[Falvo's] construction of the term "education records" to cover student homework or classroom work would impose substantial burdens on teachers across the country. It would force all instructors to take time, which otherwise would be spent teaching and in preparation, to correct an assortment of daily student assignments. . . . [For example,] if a teacher in any of the thousands of covered classrooms in the Nation puts a happy face, a gold star, or a disapproving remark on a classroom assignment, federal law [would] not allow other students to see it. We doubt Congress meant to intervene in this drastic fashion with traditional state functions.

Archivists also need to understand that FERPA forbids individuals whose rights have been violated by disclosure of personal information from seeking a private legal remedy. Instead, students and parents must seek administrative satisfaction from their local educational agency. If they cannot resolve the dispute, they then may petition the U.S. secretary of education. The secretary also possesses limited options and can only take the drastic step of terminating federal funding for the educational institution as a remedy.

Some individuals have attempted to seek redress under the civil rights provisions of § 1983 of Title 42 of the U.S. Code.[9] The U.S. Supreme Court, however, in ruling on such a claim in *Gonzaga University et al. v. Doe,* 122 S.Ct. 2268 (2002),[10] refused to enforce FERPA under § 1983, and it restated FERPA's prohibition of a private right of action. Moreover, the court held that there is *no* enforceable right whatsoever under FERPA. The Supreme Court limited the law's reach and scope on the grounds that Congress never intended FERPA to accord new individual rights, but rather, enacted it as a fiscal measure. Chief Justice William Rehnquist wrote:

There is no question that FERPA's confidentiality provisions create no rights enforceable under § 1983. The provisions entirely lack the sort of individually focused right-creating language that is critical. . . . Furthermore, because FERPA's confidentiality provisions speak only in terms of institutional "policy or practice," not individual instances of disclosure, . . . they have an "aggregate" focus, they are not concerned with whether the needs of any particular person have been satisfied, and they cannot give rise to individual rights. . . . The fact that recipient institutions can avoid termination of funding so long as they "comply substantially" with the Act's requirements, . . . also supports a finding that FERPA fails to support [an individual cause of action]. . . . Finally, . . . it is implausible to presume that Congress nonetheless intended private suits to be brought before thousands of federal- and state-court judges.

Congress's intent in enacting FERPA continues to puzzle and elude administrators, jurists, and archivists. Clearly the law has been revised to meet the ebb and flow of society's needs and perceptions. In the short term, archivists can expect continued uncertainty and ambiguity about the degree and type of access and protection afforded education records and student records under FERPA.

Appendix 4: The Brave New World of 21st-Century Medical Records Privacy in the U.S. and Canada, Contrasted with the European Data Privacy Model

Menzi L. Behrnd-Klodt

The United States: Health Insurance Portability and Accountability Act of 1996 (HIPAA)

The U.S. Congress passed the Health Insurance Portability and Accountability Act of 1996 (HIPAA) to improve American health care coverage. The act, also known as the Kennedy-Kassebaum Bill, mandates the portability and continuity of individual health coverage when workers change or lose jobs. As a secondary feature, HIPAA provides the first comprehensive federal protection for the privacy of health information. Rules issued to implement HIPAA's privacy and security standards are significantly affecting the management of American health care records, including archival records. This article briefly reviews these rules.

In HIPAA, Congress addressed concerns over personal privacy and the potential misuse of genetic information. Congress also responded to the ability of contemporary technology to deliver health care more efficiently while allowing greater integration of health care providers to easily share data. These technological improvements, however, also removed "some of the barriers inherent in the antiquated, paper-based methods of gathering and storing information that served to secure information and safeguard individual privacy."[1] HIPAA's administrative simplification provisions required the U.S. Department of Health and Human Services (HHS) to establish new national standards for electronic health care transactions,[2] security, and privacy to both protect confidential health information and decrease administrative costs.[3]

HIPAA Privacy Rule

HHS initially issued HIPAA privacy regulations in 2000, but "serious unintended consequences" that "would have interfered with patients' access to quality care" immediately forced revisions. HHS's long-awaited and controversial revised privacy rule,[4] issued in August 2002, promised to "empower patients by guaranteeing them access to their medical records, giving them more control over how their protected health information is used and disclosed, and providing a clear avenue of recourse if their medical privacy is compromised."[5] The "Standards for Privacy of Individually Identifiable Health Information," or "Privacy Rule," became effective on 14 April 2003 for most health care plans and providers, and on 14 April 2004 for small health plans. The Privacy Rule applies retroactively and preempts less stringent laws and rules, though it does not preempt all state laws.

The Privacy Rule facilitates the use and sharing of health information for medical treatment and payment for health care, but *all other uses and disclosures of personal health information, including scholarly and historical research uses, require individual written authorization or strict compliance with HIPAA's "safe harbor" provisions.* The Privacy Rule regulates all uses and disclosures of "Protected Health Information" (PHI) from all medical and health records, regardless of when or by whom the records were created, or whether the subject of the PHI is alive or deceased. Except for specified permitted uses, individual consent is required for any use or disclosure of PHI that

- is individually identifiable health information;
- is transmitted or maintained electronically or in any other form or medium, including paper, speech, or memory;
- is created, maintained, or received by a "covered entity";
- relates to an individual's past, present, or future physical or mental health or condition; the provision of health care to an individual; or the past, present, or future payment for the provision of health care to an individual; and
- identifies the individual or would permit identification of the individual.

Covered Entities, Hybrid Entities, and Business Associates

Repositories, including archives, that are or are part of a "covered entity" or a "hybrid entity," or that serve as a "business associate" of a covered entity, are governed by the Privacy Rule. HIPAA directly regulates as **"covered entities"**

- **Health care providers that transmit PHI electronically,** such as hospitals, universities, nursing homes, clinics, physician practices,

pharmacies, and any person, entity, or organization that furnishes, bills, or is paid for health care[6] provided to patients
- **Health plans,** such as HMOs, PPOs, group health plans, health and medical insurers, flexible spending plans, employee assistance programs, Medicare, and Medicaid
- **Health care clearinghouses**

"Covered entities" include individuals, groups, affiliates, and organizations that are, are part of, or are located within a covered entity, are associated with a covered entity, transmit health information electronically in connection with a health care transaction, or are under common ownership or shared control.[7] Archives that are covered entities must comply with the Privacy Rule in administering current and historical medical records containing PHI.

Covered entities must appoint privacy officials and adopt written privacy procedures and policies that specify who may access PHI, how the information will be used, and when it will or will not be disclosed to others. Covered entities must audit current uses and disclosures of PHI, identify who has contact with PHI, establish administrative, technical, and physical safeguards of PHI, train employees in privacy procedures, develop sanctions for violations, create records retention and security policies, and keep records of all disclosures. Patients must have a process for making privacy-related inquiries, filing complaints, accessing and copying their records, and receiving notification of their privacy rights. The covered entity's responsibilities to protect the PHI end, however, when the data is legitimately sent outside of the covered entity, unless sent to a business associate. Any use or disclosure of PHI by a covered entity must comply with the "minimum necessary" standard, requiring that only the minimum amount of PHI necessary to accomplish the intended purposes be disclosed, unless an exception applies.[8]

A **"hybrid entity"** is a covered entity with both covered and noncovered functions, such as a university with a hospital. Hybrid entities may segregate covered and noncovered functions and erect firewalls to prevent unauthorized disclosures of PHI. An archives that is a noncovered part of a hybrid entity, and that receives PHI from the covered function, must comply with the Privacy Rule.

HIPAA also regulates **"business associates"** of covered entities that perform various services that use or disclose PHI from the covered entity. Business associates provide administrative, claims, data processing, billing, medical transcription, consulting, information technology, legal, records management, and related services for covered entities. Any archives that accepts and maintains records containing PHI from a covered entity also is the covered entity's business associate.[9] Such contractors must enter into a business associate agreement governing use of PHI.[10]

Permitted and Prohibited Uses of Personal Health Information; Authorizations

PHI *may* be used, disclosed, and shared freely among medical providers, hospitals, data processors, and insurers without patient authorization or waiver for medical treatment, payment for treatment, or health care operations. PHI *must* be disclosed, without prior written patient authorization, to the patient or at the patient's request,[11] as required by law or a court order, and, as a new provision, to HHS. Health information also *may* be disclosed without an individual's authorization for such national priority purposes as research, law enforcement, public health, organ procurement, and to report abuse, neglect, and domestic violence. Without patient authorization, PHI may be used only for research on decedents, for review preparatory to research, for certain types of specified research, or pursuant to Institutional Review Board or Privacy Board findings. Research by consultants, scholars, or the public, is NOT a valid use of records containing PHI without individual patient authorization.

Individual authorizations to use PHI must be signed by a living individual or an authorized representative[12] of a living or deceased person. Authorizations must be written in plain language, signed and dated by the authorizing individual, describe the PHI to be used or disclosed, identify the person or class of persons who may use or disclose the PHI, identify the purposes of the use or disclosure, note any possibility of redisclosure, provide an expiration date for the use or disclosure, and include a statement of the individual's right to revoke the authorization.

If use of PHI is authorized, access is permitted. PHI may not be redisclosed, however, unless permitted by the original authorization. If there is no authorization or proper waiver, PHI may not be used or disclosed except by compliance with HIPAA's "safe harbor" provisions:

- Decedents' information may be accessed solely for research on the decedents' PHI, if the death and a legitimate need to use the PHI are documented. The information may not be published or redisclosed in any identified form. These requirements apply to all medical and health care records, regardless of their age.
- PHI may be reviewed preparatory to research, if necessary, solely to prepare a research protocol. No PHI may be removed.

- A "limited data set" may be used without direct identification of the individual, relatives, employers, or household members, and if the researcher signs a data use agreement.
- "De-identified" information may be used if *all* identifiers are removed or if an expert has certified that there is a very small risk that the information could be used to identify individuals, and if all elements of dates (except the year) are removed from information about any individual under eighty-nine years of age.

An archives that is subject to the Privacy Rule must record the disclosures made to each researcher under waivers of authorization, reviews of decedents' information, or reviews preparatory to research. It must also account for disclosures upon request and provide an individual with access to his or her PHI that is held by the archives.

The HHS Office for Civil Rights enforces HIPAA's Privacy Rule through a formal complaint process and compliance reviews. It may impose civil and criminal penalties, including fines. Persons whose privacy is violated have no private right to file a lawsuit.

HIPAA's Security Rule

The HIPAA Security Rule is narrower in scope than the Privacy Rule, as it applies only to PHI in any electronic format (ePHI), but not to paper documents. HHS, however, may issue security rules for nonelectronic PHI at a later date. The Security Rule also applies to transmission of ePHI within an organization rather than by external transmission. It further establishes a set of specific standards for safeguarding ePHI. The interaction of the two HIPAA rules may require compliance with the Security Rule in order to comply with the Privacy Rule.

The Security Rule has four requirements. Covered entities must (1) ensure the integrity (i.e., assurance that ePHI has not been modified or destroyed), confidentiality, and availability of ePHI; (2) protect against reasonably anticipated threats or hazards to the security or integrity of ePHI; (3) protect against reasonably anticipated uses or disclosures of ePHI that are not permitted by the Privacy Rule; and (4) ensure that employees comply with the Security Rule. The Security Rule, in short, mandates risk assessment and risk management in order to comply with its requirements and provides some flexibility and consideration of the size of the organization and the costs involved with compliance.[13] Any health care organization that is subject to HIPAA's Privacy Rule must comply with the Security Rule effective 20 April 2005. Small health plans must comply by 20 April 2006.

In summary, HIPAA's Privacy Rule and Security Rule apply to records already held by, or to be acquired by, covered and hybrid entities and business associates, including archives. Research access to records containing PHI is permitted only with written authorization, with a waiver of informed consent, or in compliance with HIPAA's "safe harbor" or other requirements.

Canada: Personal Information Protection and Electronic Documents Act[14]

Enacted in response to "the increasing security threat in the computer age," as well as to ease concerns about uses of private information,[15] Canada's Personal Information Protection and Electronic Documents Act (PIPEDA) specifies how personal information is collected, recorded, used, or disclosed via electronic means. PIPEDA balances an individual's right to protect personal information with organizations' needs to use such information for legitimate business purposes.[16]

These federal privacy restrictions regulate not only medical or health information or records, but all forms of commercial activity. Initially, PIPEDA applied only to the federally regulated private sector (banks, telecommunications companies, airlines, railways, and trucking companies and their employee records) and to cross-border disclosures of personal data, such as sales or rentals of customer lists. As of 1 January 2002, PIPEDA applied to personal health information collected, used, or disclosed by organizations to whom the law already applied.[17] As of 1 January 2004, PIPEDA regulated the collection, use, and disclosure of personal information by any organization in the course of commercial transactions, including health information and all interprovincial and international transactions.[18]

PIPEDA requires businesses and organizations to obtain individual consent to collect, use, or disclose personal information for commercial activities, with limited exceptions for investigations or health and safety emergencies. Businesses and organizations must supply a product or service that is requested, even if the individual refuses consent, unless the data is essential for the transaction. Individuals have the right to know why an organization collects personal information, as well as who will protect personal information within the organization. They also have the right to expect that information will be accurate and complete, and that they will be able to access personal information and request corrections, as well as to register complaints.[19]

"Personal information" is defined as any information about an identifiable individual whether recorded or not, including name, age, weight, height, medical records; income, purchasing, and spending habits; race, ethnic origin, and color; blood type, DNA code, and fingerprints; marital status and religion; education; home address and telephone number. "Organizations" may be associations, partnerships, persons, and trade unions, including both "brick and mortar" and Internet e-commerce businesses.[20]

PIPEDA does not apply to Canadian federal government institutions subject to the Privacy Act; to personal information collected, used, or disclosed for personal or household reasons, for journalistic, artistic, or literary purposes;[21] or to information about employees of organizations not covered by PIPEDA.[22] The Office of the Privacy Commissioner of Canada, which acts as ombudsman between individuals and organizations, and the Federal Court oversee and provide redress for violations of PIPEDA. Obstruction of investigations or audits, destruction of personal information subject to an access request, or discipline of a whistleblower are violations punishable by fines ranging from $10,000 to $100,000.[23]

Those Canadian provinces that enact privacy legislation substantially similar to PIPEDA by 2004 are exempt from compliance with PIPEDA for intraprovince transactions. Without such separate legislation, however, federal law applies. Significant regional differences in these laws could prove troubling for archivists and records managers.

European Union: Data Protection Directive of 1995[24]

In contrast to the U.S. legislation that focuses on medical and health care records, the European Union (EU) includes such information in a broad category of regulated personal data. The differences between the European and American approaches to privacy protection are summarized as follows:

> In contrast to the diverse and targeted U.S. approach to fair information practice, most European countries have omnibus laws to regulate the use of personal information in the public and private sectors. European countries generally require the state to take an active role in protecting the fair treatment of personal information. Such laws establish comprehensive sets of rights and responsibilities that address the issues of data collection, storage, use and disclosure. Often, a single piece of legislation regulates both the public and private sectors. These laws are then supplemented by a series of laws and regulations that govern more narrow fields of processing activity. Legislative activity tends to be carried out in a complete and continuous fashion.

Within Europe, there is significant agreement on the essential principles of fair information practice. This consensus shows four elements: (a) the establishment of obligations and responsibilities for personal information; (b) the maintenance of transparent processing of personal information; (c) the creation of special protection for sensitive data; and (d) the establishment of enforcement rights and effective oversight of the treatment of personal information. These basic elements establish a comprehensive European approach to the protection of personal information. The complete set of basic principles is firmly established in existing national laws and in the Council of Europe Convention. They are also expressed in the European Union's 1995 directive on data processing and in the guidelines adopted by the Organization for Economic Co-Operation and Development.[25]

The EU's 1995 Data Protection Directive articulates some of the most sweeping developments in modern privacy law. It was designed to protect the privacy of personal information and by so doing, permit the free flow of information between European member nations. Based on the concept that privacy is a fundamental human right, the Privacy Directive creates a common standard for privacy protection for citizens of its member states and establishes governmental and judicial bodies to protect personal data and to determine the conditions under which the processing of personal data would be permitted. These regulations protect personal information and harmonize the privacy laws of the individual member states by requiring the adoption or revision of privacy laws. The directive applies to the processing of all personal data (with certain exemptions), and it provides stricter privacy rules for sensitive data that reveals "racial or ethnic origin, political opinions, religious or philosophical beliefs, [and] trade union membership" and "concerning health or sex life" (Directive 95/46/EC, Article 8(1)). The data subject must provide "explicit consent" for the use or disclosure of such sensitive data. EU member states may enact rules that would prohibit the processing of such data even if the data subject consented.

Articles 10 and 11 of Directive 95/46/EC provide that the subject receive notice of the party planning to use the subject's personal information and the purpose of the data processing. The requirement is the same whether the data is obtained from the subject or from other sources. Article 12 grants the subject the right to access information from the data processor about the source, category, recipients, and purpose of personal data that is processed. The data subject may "rectify, erase or block" the processing of such personal data, if the processing does not comply with the requirements of the 1995 directive.

An interesting feature of the 1995 directive is found in Article 15, which provides each person the right not "to be subject to a decision which produces legal effects concerning him or significantly affects him and which is based solely on automated processing of data intended to evaluate certain personal aspects relating to him such as his performance at work, credit worthiness, reliability, conduct, etc." Exemptions to these prohibitions are found in Article 9 and require member states to allow processing of personal data "carried out solely for journalistic purposes or the purpose of artistic or literary expression."

The directive further stipulates that personal data of Europeans may be transferred only to non-EU countries that provide a level of privacy protection equivalent to that of the individual's home country. All non-EU companies and organizations must comply with the Privacy Directive when using or transmitting personal information of European Union citizens.[26]

In 1997, the EU issued its Telecommunications Privacy Directive (Directive 97/66/EC), regulating telephone, digital television, mobile networks, telecommunications systems, and the Internet. The directive requires carriers and service providers to protect the privacy of users' communications and restricts access to billing data and marketing activity, thereby strengthening individual privacy rights in a "technology-neutral" sense. Legislators attempted unsuccessfully to mandate data retention and to require Internet service providers and telecommunications operators to retain logs of all telephone calls, faxes, e-mails, and Internet activity for access by law enforcement. Following the events of 11 September 2001 in the United States, however, such data retention proposals were more favorably received.

The Canadian minister of industry and minister of international trade reported in January 2002 that Canada was the first non-European nation to meet the European Union's rigorous standards for the protection and processing of personal data. The European Parliament's acceptance permitted continued commercial transfer of personal information between Canada and the EU.

The reciprocity principle in Article 25 of Directive 95/46/EC further restricts transfers of data from the EU to other countries without adequate data protection. The U.S. Department of Commerce has developed a "safe harbor" framework that was approved by the EU in 2000. Businesses and organizations voluntarily participate in the safe harbor by publicly declaring their compliance with its requirements.

Given the strict new standards of Canadian law and the EU Privacy Directive, American multinationals and other organizations that transfer personal data electronically to the EU and Canada, as well as their archives and records programs, should be aware of the legal requirements and new developments.[27]

NOTES

Introduction

1. Charles J. Sykes, *The End of Privacy* (New York: St. Martin's Press, 1999), which references a 1998 Harris poll indicating that 88 percent of Americans expressed concerns over their privacy.
2. Rodney A. Smolla, "Privacy and the First Amendment Right to Gather News," *Privacy and the Law: A Symposium. The George Washington Law Review* 67 (June/August 1999): 1098–1100.
3. For an overview of these issues, see Bruce Craig, "Executive Order 13233: We Dare Not Allow Ourselves to Be Bush-Whacked," *RBM: A Journal of Rare Books, Manuscripts, and Cultural Heritage* 3 (Fall 2002): 106–23.
4. Frank B. Evans, *Modern Archives and Manuscripts: A Select Bibliography* (Chicago: Society of American Archivists, 1975), 59–63.
5. Exceptions to the general neglect include Alan Reitman, "Freedom of Information and Privacy: The Civil Libertarian's Dilemma," *American Archivist* 38 (1975): 501–8; Virginia R. Stewart, "Problems of Confidentiality in the Administration of Personal Case Records," *American Archivist* 37 (1974): 387–98; and Charles B. Elston, "University Student Records: Research Use, Privacy Rights, and the Buckley Law," *Midwestern Archivist* 1 (1976): 16–32.
6. R. Joseph Anderson, "Public Welfare Case Records: A Study of Archival Practices," *American Archivist* (Spring 1980): 169–79, was one of the first articles to call attention to the complexities of administering these records. See also David Klaassen, "The Provenance of Social Work Case Records: Implications for Archival Appraisal and Access," *Provenance* 1 (Spring 1983): 5–30.
7. Sue E. Holbert, *Archives & Manuscripts: Reference & Access* (Chicago: Society of American Archivists, 1977).
8. Ibid., 5–6. Mark Greene, "Moderation in Everything, Access to Nothing?: Opinions About Access Restrictions on Private Papers," *Archival Issues* 18 (1993): 31–41, makes some similar points concerning the Holbert manual and the way in which access trumped privacy in most archival literature during the 1970s.
9. Gary M. Peterson and Trudy Huskamp Peterson, *Archives & Manuscripts: Law* (Chicago: Society of American Archivists, 1985), 39.
10. Mary Boccaccio, ed., *Constitutional Issues and Archives* (Mid-Atlantic Regional Archives Conference, 1988).
11. Heather MacNeil, *Without Consent: The Ethics of Disclosing Personal Information in Public Archives* (Metuchen, N.J.: Society of American Archivists and The Scarecrow Press, 1992), 5, 176.
12. Raymond H. Geselbracht, "The Origins of Restrictions on Access to Personal Papers in the Library of Congress and the National Archives," *American Archivist* 49 (Spring 1986): 142–62; Trudy Huskamp Peterson, "After 5 Years: An Assessment of the Amended U.S. Freedom of Information Act," *American Archivist* 43 (Spring 1980): 161–68; James Gregory Bradsher, "Privacy Act Expungements: A Reconsideration," *Provenance* 6

(Spring 1988): 1–25; Robert J. Hayward, "Federal Access and Privacy Legislation and the Public Archives of Canada," *Archivaria* 18 (Summer 1984): 47–57.

13. Roland M. Baumann, "The Administration of Access to Confidential Records in State Archives: Common Practices and the Need for a Common Law," *American Archivist* 49 (Fall 1986): 349–70; Alice Robbin, "State Archives and Issues of Personal Privacy: Policies and Practices," *American Archivist* 49 (Spring 1986): 163–75.

14. Marjorie Rabe Barritt, "The Appraisal of Personally Identifiable Student Records," *American Archivist* 49 (Summer 1986): 263–75; Mark A. Greene, "Developing a Research Access Policy for Student Records: A Case Study at Carleton College," *American Archivist* 50 (Fall 1987): 570–79.

15. Ruth J. Simmons, "The Public's Right to Know and the Individual's Right to be Private," *Provenance* 1 (Spring 1983): 1–4; Elena Danielson, "The Ethics of Access," *American Archivist* 52 (Winter 1989): 52–62; Sara S. Hodson, "Private Lives: Confidentiality in Manuscript Collections," *Rare Books and Manuscript Librarianship* 6 (1991): 108–18; David E. Horn, "The Development of Ethics in Archival Practice," *American Archivist* 52 (Winter 1989): 64–71; Greene, "Moderation in Everything."

16. Harold L. Miller, "Will Access Restrictions Hold Up in Court: The FBI's Attempt to Use the Braden Papers at the State Historical Society of Wisconsin," *American Archivist* 52 (Spring 1989): 180–90; Diane E. Kaplan, "The Stanley Milgram Papers: A Case Study on Appraisal and Access to Confidential Data Files," *American Archivist* 59 (Summer 1996): 288–97; Judith Schwarz, "The Archivist's Balancing Act: Helping Researchers While Protecting Individual Privacy," *Journal of American History* (June 1992): 178–89, reprinted in this volume.

17. David M. Weinberg, "The Other Side of the Human Experience: Providing Access to Social Service Case Study Files," *American Archivist* 53 (Winter 1990): 122–29; Margaret L. Hedstrom, "Computers, Privacy, and Research Access to Confidential Information," *Midwestern Archivist* 6 (1981): 5–18; Brian Bucknall, "The Archivist, the Lawyer, the Clients and Their Files," *Archivaria* 33 (Winter 1991–1992): 181–87; Doug Whyte, "The Acquisition of Lawyers' Private Papers," *Archivaria* 18 (Summer 1984): 142–53.

18. The lack of consensus can be seen in the SAA's attempts to incorporate sections concerning privacy into its Code of Ethics. See the discussion on pages 116–17 below.

19. James M. O'Toole, *Understanding Archives and Manuscripts* (Chicago: Society of American Archivists, 1990), 49.

Part 1. Legal Perspectives

1. Corporations, organizations, partnerships, and other entities do not have a right of privacy.

2. Does *U.S. News & World Report* columnist John Leo's report portend a further extension of privacy rights? "A dead giraffe's privacy was threatened by prying reporters. When the Washington Post asked to see the National Zoo's medical records of a beloved giraffe after its death, the zoo said that viewing the records 'would violate the animal's right to privacy and be an intrusion into the zookeeper-animal relationship,'" *Wisconsin State Journal,* 17 December 2002.

3. Advocates suggest that a family right of privacy is superior to an individual right of privacy in both form and function, serving to strengthen the nuclear family, protect marital privacy, and provide a new entity-based autonomy for family decision making. Feminists and others who disagree note its sometime use in obscuring

domestic violence and abuse and denying children's rights. See Martha Albertson Fineman, "What Place for Family Privacy?"; Naomi R. Cahn, "Models of Family Privacy"; and Barbara Bennett Woodhouse, "The Dark Side of Family Privacy" in *Privacy and the Law: A Symposium, The George Washington Law Review* 67 (June–August 1999): 1207–62.

4. Public status does not destroy privacy entirely, but precisely when one becomes a "public person" with fewer privacy rights is fact-specific and difficult to determine, often depending on whether a business or calling allows the public a legitimate interest in the incumbent's character, activities, or affairs, or the attainment of accomplishments, fame, or a particular mode of life.
5. The court has outlined a "penumbra of privacy" rights protected by the five cited amendments.
6. The full text of the cited amendments may be found in appendix 1.
7. Samuel D. Warren and Louis D. Brandeis, "The Right to Privacy," *Harvard Law Review* 4 (1890): 193. The authors did not invent the right of privacy, however. In 1873, writing in *Liberty, Equality, Fraternity*, Sir James Fitzjames Stephen discussed its philosophical basis; in 1880, Judge Thomas Cooley noted: "The right to one's person may be said to be a right of complete immunity: to be let alone"; and in 1881, the Michigan Supreme Court recognized a legal right to privacy that all must respect in certain circumstances. Richard C. Turkington and Anita L. Allen, *Privacy Law: Cases and Materials*, 2nd ed. (St. Paul, Minn.: West Group, 2002), 52, 23.
8. *Roberson v. Rochester Folding Box Co.*, 171 N.Y. 538, 64 N.E. 442 (1902).
9. *Pavesich v. New England Life Insurance Co.*, 122 Ga. 190, 50 S.E. 68 (1905).
10. *Meyer v. Nebraska*, 262 U.S. 390 (1923); *Pierce v. Society of Sisters*, 268 U.S. 510 (1925).
11. Quoted from *Melvin v. Reid*, 112 Cal. App. 285, 297 Pac. 91 (1931). See also William L. Prosser, "Privacy," *California Law Review* 48 (August 1960), reprinted in this volume.
12. Prosser's handbook remains an important source for law students and is currently in print as *Prosser and Keeton on The Law of Torts*, ed. W. Page Keeton (St. Paul, Minn.: West Publishing Co., 1984).
13. Turkington and Allen, *Privacy Law*, 60.
14. *Skinner v. Oklahoma*, 316 U.S. 535 (1942).
15. 367 U.S. 497, 522 (1961) (Harlan, J., dissenting).
16. *Griswold v. Connecticut*, 381 U.S. 479 (1965). John E. Nowak, Ronald D. Rotunda, and J. Nelson Young, *Constitutional Law*, 2nd ed. (St. Paul, Minn.: West Publishing Co., 1983), 738. See also *Eisenstadt v. Baird*, 405 U.S. 438 (1972).
17. *Loving v. Virginia*, 388 U.S. 1 (1967), *Boddie v. Connecticut*, 401 U.S. 371 (1971), *Zablocki v. Redhail*, 434 U.S. 374 (1978), *Roe v. Wade*, 410 U.S. 113 (1973), *Paul v. Davis*, 424 U.S. 693 (1976).
18. *Whalen v. Roe*, 429 U.S. 589 (1977).
19. *Boyd v. United States*, 116 U.S. 616 (1886).
20. *Olmstead v. United States*, 227 U.S. 438 (1928).
21. 389 U.S. 347 (1967).
22. *U.S. v. Miller*, 425 U.S. 435 (1976). In response to *Miller*, Congress passed the Right to Financial Privacy Act of 1978.
23. *Smith v. Maryland*, 442 U.S. 735 (1979).
24. *California v. Ciraolo*, 476 U.S. 207 (1986) and *California v. Greenwood*, 486 U.S. 35 (1988).
25. *International Privacy, Publicity and Personality Laws*, ed. Michael Henry (London: Butterworths, Reed Elsevier, 2001), 462–63.

Chapter 1. The Right to Privacy

1. Year Book, Lib. Ass., folio 99, pl. 60 (1348 or 1349), appears to be the first reported case where damages were recovered for a civil assault.
2. These nuisances are technically injuries to property; but the recognition of the right to have property free from interference by such nuisances involves also a recognition of the value of human sensations.
3. Year Book, Lib. Ass., folio 177, pl. 19 (1356), (2 Finl. Reeves Eng. Law, 395) seems to be the earliest reported case of an action for slander.
4. Winsmore *v.* Greenbank, Willes, 577 (1745).
5. Loss of service is the gist of the action; but it has been said that "we are not aware of any reported case brought by a parent where the value of such services was held to be the measure of damages." Cassoday, J., in Lavery *v.* Crooke, 52 Wis. 612, 623 (1881). First the fiction of constructive service was invented; Martin *v.* Payne, 9 John. 387 (1812). Then the feelings of the parent, the dishonor to himself and his family, were accepted as the most important element of damage. Bedford *v.* McKowl, 3 Esp. 119 (1800); Andrews *v.* Askey, 8 C. & P. 7 (1837); Phillips *v.* Hoyle, 4 Gray, 568 (1855); Phelin *v.* Kenderdine, 20 Pa. St. 354 (1853). The allowance of these damages would seem to be a recognition that the invasion upon the honor of the family is an injury to the parent's person, for ordinarily mere injury to parental feelings is not an element of damage, e.g., the suffering of the parent in case of physical injury to the child. Flemington *v.* Smithers, 2 C. & P. 292 (1827); Black *v.* Carrolton R.R. Co., 10 La. Ann. 33 (1855); Covington Street Ry. Co. *v.* Packer, 9 Bush, 455 (1872).
6. "The notion of Mr. Justice Yates that nothing is property which cannot be earmarked and recovered in detinue or trover, may be true in an early stage of society, when property is in its simple form, and the remedies for violation of it also simple, but is not true in a more civilized state, when the relations of life and the interests arising therefrom are complicated." Erle, J., in Jefferys *v.* Boosey, 4 H. L. C. 815, 869 (1854).
7. Copyright appears to have been first recognized as a species of private property in England in 1558. Drone on Copyright, 54, 61.
8. Gibblett *v.* Read, 9 Mod. 459 (1743), is probably the first recognition of goodwill as property.
9. Hogg *v.* Kirby, 8 Ves. 215 (1803). As late as 1742 Lord Hardwicke refused to treat a trade-mark as property for infringement upon which an injunction could be granted. Blanchard *v.* Hill, 2 Atk. 484.
10. Cooley on Torts, 2d ed., p. 29.
11. 8 Amer. Law Reg. N. S. 1 (1869); 12 Wash. Law Rep. 353 (1884); 24 Sol. J. & Rep. 4 (1879).
12. Scribner's Magazine, July, 1890. "The Rights of the Citizen: To his Reputation," by E. L. Godkin, Esq., pp. 65, 67.
13. Marion Manola *v.* Stevens & Myers, N. Y. Supreme Court, "New York Times" of June 15, 18, 21, 1890. There the complainant alleged that while she was playing in the Broadway Theatre, in a role which required her appearance in tights, she was, by means of a flash light, photographed surreptitiously and without her consent, from one of the boxes by defendant Stevens, the manager of the "Castle in the Air" company, and defendant Myers, a photographer, and prayed that the defendants might be restrained from making use of the photograph taken. A preliminary injunction issued *ex parte*, and a time was set for argument of the motion that the injunction should be made permanent, but no one then appeared in opposition.

14. Though the legal value of "feelings" is now generally recognized, distinctions have been drawn between the several classes of cases in which compensation may or may not be recovered. Thus, the fright occasioned by an assault constitutes a cause of action, but fright occasioned by negligence does not. So fright coupled with bodily injury affords a foundation for enhanced damages; but, ordinarily, fright unattended by bodily injury cannot be relied upon as an element of damages, even where a valid cause of action exists, as in trespass *quare clausum fregit*. Wyman *v.* Leavitt, 71 Me. 227; Canning *v.* Williamstown, 1 Cush. 451. The allowance of damages for injury to the parents' feelings, in case of seduction, abduction of a child (Stowe *v.* Heywood, 7 All. 118), or removal of the corpse of child from a burial-ground (Meagher *v.* Driscoll, 99 Mass. 281), are said to be exceptions to a general rule. On the other hand, injury to feelings is a recognized element of damages in actions of slander and libel, and of malicious prosecution. These distinctions between the cases, where injury to feelings does and where it does not constitute a cause of action or legal element of damages, are not logical, but doubtless serve well as practical rules. It will, it is believed, be found, upon examination of the authorities, that wherever substantial mental suffering would be the natural and probable result of the act, there compensation for injury to feelings has been allowed, and that where no mental suffering would ordinarily result, or if resulting, would naturally be but trifling, and, being unaccompanied by visible signs of injury, would afford a wide scope for imaginative ills, there damages have been disallowed. The decisions on this subject illustrate well the subjection in our law of logic to common-sense.
15. "Injuria, in the narrower sense, is every intentional and illegal violation of honour, *i.e.,* the whole personality of another." "Now an outrage is committed not only when a man shall be struck with the fist, say, or with a club, or even flogged, but also if abusive language has been used to one." Salkowski, Roman Law, p. 668 and p. 669, n. 2.
16. "It is certain every man has a right to keep his own sentiments, if he pleases. He has certainly a right to judge whether he will make them public, or commit them only to the sight of his friends." Yates, J., in Millar *v.* Taylor, 4 Burr. 2303, 2379 (1769).
17. Nicols *v.* Pitman, 26 Ch. D. 374 (1884).
18. Lee *v.* Simpson, 3 C. B. 871, 881; Daly *v.* Palmer, 6 Blatchf. 256.
19. Turner *v.* Robinson, 10 Ir. Ch. 121; s. c. ib. 510.
20. Drone on Copyright, 102.
21. "Assuming the law to be so, what is its foundation in this respect? It is not, I conceive, referable to any consideration peculiarly literary. Those with whom our common law originated had not probably among their many merits that of being patrons of letters; but they knew the duty and necessity of protecting property, and with that general object laid down rules providently expansive,—rules capable of adapting themselves to the various forms and modes of property which peace and cultivation might discover and introduce.

"The produce of mental labor, thoughts and sentiments, recorded and preserved by writing, became, as knowledge went onward and spread, and the culture of man's understanding advanced, a kind of property impossible to disregard, and the interference of modern legislation upon the subject, by the stat. 8 Anne, professing by its title to be 'For the encouragement of learning,' and using the words 'taken the liberty,' in the preamble, whether it operated in augmentation or diminution of the private rights of authors, having left them to some extent untouched, it was found that the common law, in providing for the protection of property, provided for their security, at least before general publication by the writer's consent." Knight Bruce, V. C., in Prince Albert *v.* Strange, 2 DeGex & Sm. 652, 695 (1849).

22. "The question, however, does not turn upon the form or amount of mischief or advantage, loss or gain. The author of manuscripts, whether he is famous or obscure, low or high, has a right to say of them, if innocent, that whether interesting or dull, light or heavy, saleable or unsaleable, they shall not, without his consent, be published." Knight Bruce, V. C., in Prince Albert *v.* Strange, 2 DeGex & Sm. 652, 694.
23. Duke of Queensberry *v.* Shebbeare, 2 Eden, 329 (1758); Bartlett *v.* Crittenden, 5 McLean, 32, 41 (1849).
24. Drone on Copyright, pp. 102, 104; Parton *v.* Prang, 3 Clifford, 537, 548 (1872); Jefferys *v.* Boosey, 4 H. L. C. 815, 867, 962 (1854).
25. "The question will be whether the bill has stated facts of which the court can take notice, as a case of civil property, which it is bound to protect. The injunction cannot be maintained on any principle of this sort, that if a letter has been written in the way of friendship, either the continuance or the discontinuance of the friendship affords a reason for the interference of the court." Lord Eldon in Gee *v.* Pritchard, 2 Swanst. 402, 413 (1818).

    "Upon the principle, therefore, of protecting property, it is that the common law, in cases not aided or prejudiced by statute, shelters the privacy and seclusion of thought and sentiments committed to writing, and desired by the author to remain not generally known." Knight Bruce, V. C., in Prince Albert *v.* Strange, 2 DeGex & Sm. 652, 695.

    "It being conceded that reasons of expediency and public policy can never be made the sole basis of civil jurisdiction, the question, whether upon any ground the plaintiff can be entitled to the relief which he claims, remains to be answered; and it appears to us that there is only one ground upon which his title to claim, and our jurisdiction to grant, the relief, can be placed. We must be satisfied, that the publication of private letters, without the consent of the writer, is an invasion of an exclusive right of property which remains in the writer, even when the letters have been sent to, and are still in the possession of his correspondent." Duer, J., in Woolsey *v.* Judd, 4 Duer, 379, 384 (1855).
26. "A work lawfully published, in the popular sense of the term, stands in this respect, I conceive, differently from a work which has never been in that situation. The former may be liable to be translated, abridged, analyzed, exhibited in morsels, complimented, and otherwise treated, in a manner that the latter is not.

    "Suppose, however,—instead of a translation, an abridgment, or a review,—the case of a catalogue,—suppose a man to have composed a variety of literary works ('innocent,' to use Lord Eldon's expression), which he has never printed or published, or lost the right to prohibit from being published,—suppose a knowledge of them unduly obtained by some unscrupulous person, who prints with a view to circulation a descriptive catalogue, or even a mere list of the manuscripts, without authority or consent, does the law allow this? I hope and believe not. The same principles that prevent more candid piracy must, I conceive, govern such a case also.

    "By publishing of a man that he has written to particular persons, or on particular subjects, he may be exposed, not merely to sarcasm, he may be ruined. There may be in his possession returned letters that he had written to former correspondents, with whom to have had relations, however harmlessly, may not in after life be a recommendation; or his writings may be otherwise of a kind squaring in no sort with his outward habits and worldly position. There are callings even now in which to be convicted of literature, is dangerous, though the danger is sometimes escaped.

    "Again, the manuscripts may be those of a man on account of whose name alone a mere list would be a matter of general curiosity. How many persons could be mentioned, a catalogue of whose unpublished writings would, during their lives or after-

wards, command a ready sale!" Knight Bruce, V. C., in Prince Albert *v.* Strange, 2 DeGex & Sm. 652, 693.
27. "A copy or impression of the etchings would only be a means of communicating knowledge and information of the original, and does not a list and description of the same? The means are different, but the object and effect are similar; for in both, the object and effect is to make known to the public more or less of the unpublished work and composition of the author, which he is entitled to keep wholly for his private use and pleasure, and to withhold altogether, or so far as he may please, from the knowledge of others. Cases upon abridgments, translations, extracts, and criticisms of published works have no reference whatever to the present question; they all depend upon the extent of right under the acts respecting copyright, and have no analogy to the exclusive rights in the author of unpublished compositions which depend entirely upon the common-law right of property." Lord Cottenham in Prince Albert *v.* Strange, 1 McN. & G. 23, 43 (1849). "Mr. Justice Yates, in Millar *v.* Taylor, said, that an author's case was exactly similar to that of an inventor of a new mechanical machine; that both original inventions stood upon the same footing in point of property, whether the case were mechanical or literary, whether an epic poem or an orrery; that the immorality of pirating another man's invention was as great as that of purloining his ideas. Property in mechanical works or works of art, executed by a man for his own amusement, instruction, or use, is allowed to subsist, certainly, and may, before publication by him, be invaded, not merely by copying, but by description or by catalogue, as it appears to me. A catalogue of such works may in itself be valuable. It may also as effectually show the bent and turn of the mind, the feelings and taste of the artist, especially if not professional, as a list of his papers. The portfolio or the studio may declare as much as the writing-table. A man may employ himself in private in a manner very harmless, but which, disclosed to society, may destroy the comfort of his life, or even his success in it. Every one, however, has a right, I apprehend, to say that the produce of his private hours is not more liable to publication without his consent, because the publication must be creditable or advantageous to him, than it would be in opposite circumstances."

"I think, therefore, not only that the defendant here is unlawfully invading the plaintiff's rights, but also that the invasion is of such a kind and affects such property as to entitle the plaintiff to the preventive remedy of an injunction; and if not the more, yet, certainly, not the less, because it is an intrusion,—an unbecoming and unseemly intrusion,—an intrusion not alone in breach of conventional rules, but offensive to that inbred sense of propriety natural to every man,—if intrusion, indeed, fitly describes a sordid spying into the privacy of domestic life,—into the home (a word hitherto sacred among us), the home of a family whose life and conduct form an acknowledged title, though not their only unquestionable title, to the most marked respect in this country." Knight Bruce, V. C., in Prince Albert *v.* Strange, 2 DeGex & Sm. 652, 696. 697.
28. Kiernan *v.* Manhattan Quotation Co., 50 How. Pr. 194 (1876).
29. "The defendants' counsel say, that a man acquiring a knowledge of another's property without his consent is not by any rule or principle which a court of justice can apply (however secretly he may have kept or endeavored to keep it) forbidden without his consent to communicate and publish that knowledge to the world, to inform the world what the property is, or to describe it publicly, whether orally, or in print or writing.

"I claim, however, leave to doubt whether, as to property of a private nature, which the owner, without infringing on the right of any other, may and does retain in a state of privacy, it is certain that a person who, without the owner's consent, express or implied, acquires a knowledge of it, can lawfully avail himself of the knowledge so acquired to publish without his consent a description of the property.

"It is probably true that such a publication may be in a manner or relate to property of a kind rendering a question concerning the lawfulness of the act too slight to deserve attention. I can conceive cases, however, in which an act of the sort may be so circumstanced or relate to property such, that the matter may weightily affect the owner's interest or feelings, or both. For instance, the nature and intention of an unfinished work of an artist, prematurely made known to the world, may be painful and deeply prejudicial against him; nor would it be difficult to suggest other examples. . . .

"It was suggested that, to publish a catalogue of a collector's gems, coins, antiquities, or other such curiosities, for instance, without his consent, would be to make use of his property without his consent; and it is true, certainly, that a proceeding of that kind may not only as much embitter one collector's life as it would flatter another,— may be not only an ideal calamity,—but may do the owner damage in the most vulgar sense. Such catalogues, even when not descriptive, are often sought after, and sometimes obtain very substantial prices. These, therefore, and the like instances, are not necessarily examples merely of pain inflicted in point of sentiment or imagination; they may be that, and something else beside." Knight Bruce, V. C., in Prince Albert v. Strange, 2 DeGex & Sm. 652, 689, 690.

30. Hoyt v. Mackenzie, 3 Barb. Ch. 320, 324 (1848); Wetmore v. Scovell, 3 Edw. Ch. 515 (1842). See Sir Thomas Plumer in 2 Ves. & B. 19 (1813).

31. Woolsey v. Judd, 4 Duer, 379, 404 (1855). "It has been decided, fortunately for the welfare of society, that the writer of letters, though written without any purpose of profit, or any idea of literary property, possesses such a right of property in them, that they cannot be published without his consent, unless the purposes of justice, civil or criminal, require the publication." Sir Samuel Romilly, *arg.*, in Gee v. Pritchard, 2 Swanst. 402, 418 (1818). But see High on Injunctions, 3d ed., 1012, *contra*.

32. "But a doubt has been suggested, whether mere private letters, not intended as literary compositions, are entitled to the protection of an injunction in the same manner as compositions of a literary character. This doubt has probably arisen from the habit of not discriminating between the different rights of property which belong to an unpublished manuscript, and those which belong to a published book. The latter, as I have intimated in another connection, is a right to take the profits of publication. The former is a right to control the act of publication, and to decide whether there shall be any publication at all. It has been called a right of property; an expression perhaps not quite satisfactory, but on the other hand sufficiently descriptive of a right which, however incorporeal, involves many of the essential elements of property, and is at least positive and definite. This expression can leave us in no doubt as to the meaning of the learned judges who have used it, when they have applied it to cases of unpublished manuscripts. They obviously intended to use it in no other sense, than in contradistinction to the mere interests of feeling, and to describe a substantial right of legal interest." Curtis on Copyright, pp. 93, 94.

The resemblance of the right to prevent publication of an unpublished manuscript to the well-recognized rights of personal immunity is found in the treatment of it in connection with the rights of creditors. The right to prevent such publication and the right of action for its infringement, like the cause of action for an assault, battery, defamation, or malicious prosecution, are not assets available to creditors.

"There is no law which can compel an author to publish. No one can determine this essential matter of publication but the author. His manuscripts, however valuable, cannot, without his consent, be seized by his creditors as property." McLean, J., in Bartlett v. Crittenden, 5 McLean 32, 37 (1849).

It has also been held that even where the sender's rights are not asserted, the receiver of a letter has not such property in it as passes to his executor or administrator as a salable asset. Eyre *v.* Higbee, 22 How. Pr. (N.Y.) 198 (1861).

"The very meaning of the word 'property' in its legal sense is 'that which is peculiar or proper to any person; that which belongs exclusively to one.' The first meaning of the word from which it is derived—*proprius*—is 'one's own.'" Drone on Copyright, p. 6.

It is clear that a thing must be capable of identification in order to be the subject of exclusive ownership. But when its identity can be determined so that individual ownership may be asserted, it matters not whether it be corporeal or incorporeal.

33. "Such then being, as I believe, the nature and the foundation of the common law as to manuscripts independently of Parliamentary additions and subtractions, its operation cannot of necessity be confined to literary subjects. That would be to limit the rule by the example. Wherever the produce of labor is liable to invasion in an analogous manner, there must, I suppose, be a title to analogous protection or redress." Knight Bruce, V. C., in Prince Albert *v.* Strange, 2 DeGex & Sm. 652, 696.

34. "The question, therefore, is whether a photographer who has been employed by a customer to take his or her portrait is justified in striking off copies of such photograph for his own use, and selling and disposing of them, or publicly exhibiting them by way of advertisement or otherwise, without the authority of such customer, either express or implied. I say 'express or implied,' because a photographer is frequently allowed, on his own request, to take a photograph of a person under circumstances in which a subsequent sale by him must have been in the contemplation of both parties, though not actually mentioned. To the question thus put, my answer is in the negative, that the photographer is not justified in so doing. Where a person obtains information in the course of a confidential employment, the law does not permit him to make any improper use of the information so obtained; and an injunction is granted, if necessary, to restrain such use; as, for instance, to restrain a clerk from disclosing his master's accounts, or an attorney from making known his client's affairs, learned in the course of such employment. Again, the law is clear that a breach of contract, whether express or implied, can be restrained by injunction. In my opinion the case of the photographer comes within the principles upon which both of these classes of cases depend. The object for which he is employed and paid is to supply his customer with the required number of printed photographs of a given subject. For this purpose the negative is taken by the photographer on glass; and from this negative copies can be printed in much larger numbers than are generally required by the customer. The customer who sits for the negative thus puts the power of reproducing the object in the hands of the photographer; and in my opinion the photographer who uses the negative to produce other copies for his own use, without authority, is abusing the power confidentially placed in his hands merely for the purpose of supplying the customer; and further, I hold that the bargain between the customer and the photographer includes, by implication, an agreement that the prints taken from the negative are to be appropriated to the use of the customer only." Referring to the opinions delivered in Tuck *v.* Priester, 19 Q. B. D. 639, the learned justice continued: "Then Lord Justice Lindley says: 'I will deal first with the injunction, which stands, or may stand, on a totally different footing from either the penalties or the damages. It appears to me that the relation between the plaintiffs and the defendant was such that, whether the plaintiffs had any copyright or not, the defendant has done that which renders him liable to an injunction. He was employed by the plaintiffs to make a certain number of copies of the picture, and that employment carried with it the necessary implication that the defendant was not

to make more copies for himself, or to sell the additional copies in this country in competition with his employer. Such conduct on his part is a gross breach of contract and a gross breach of faith, and, in my judgment, clearly entitles the plaintiffs to an injunction, whether they have a copyright in the picture or not.' That case is the more noticeable, as the contract was in writing; and yet it was held to be an implied condition that the defendant should not make any copies for himself. The phrase 'a gross breach of faith' used by Lord Justice Lindley in that case applies with equal force to the present, when a lady's feelings are shocked by finding that the photographer she has employed to take her likeness for her own use is publicly exhibiting and selling copies thereof." North, J., in Pollard v. Photographic Co., 40 Ch. D. 345, 349-352 (1888).

"It may be said also that the cases to which I have referred are all cases in which there was some right of property infringed, based upon the recognition by the law of protection being due for the products of a man's own skill or mental labor; whereas in the present case the person photographed has done nothing to merit such protection, which is meant to prevent legal wrongs, and not mere sentimental grievances. But a person whose photograph is taken by a photographer is not thus deserted by the law; for the Act of 25 and 26 Vict., c. 68, s. 1, provides that when the negative of any photograph is made or executed for or on behalf of another person for a good or valuable consideration, the person making or executing the same shall not retain the copyright thereof, unless it is expressly reserved to him by agreement in writing signed by the person for or on whose behalf the same is so made or executed; but the copyright shall belong to the person for or on whose behalf the same shall have been made or executed.

"The result is that in the present case the copyright in the photograph is in one of the plaintiffs. It is true, no doubt, that sect. 4 of the same act provides that no proprietor of copyright shall be entitled to the benefit of the act until registration, and no action shall be sustained in respect of anything done before registration; and it was, I presume, because the photograph of the female plaintiff has not been registered that this act was not referred to by counsel in the course of the argument. But, although the protection against the world in general conferred by the act cannot be enforced until after registration, this does not deprive the plaintiffs of their common-law right of action against the defendant for his breach of contract and breach of faith. This is quite clear from the cases of Morison v. Moat [9 Hare, 241] and Tuck v. Priester [19 Q. B. D. 629] already referred to, in which latter case the same act of Parliament was in question." Per North, J., ibid. p. 352.

This language suggests that the property right in photographs or portraits may be one created by statute, which would not exist in the absence of registration; but it is submitted that it must eventually be held here, as it has been in the similar cases, that the statute provision becomes applicable only when there is a publication, and that before the act of registering there is property in the thing upon which the statute is to operate.

35. Duke of Queensberry v. Shebbeare, 2 Eden 329; Murray v. Heath, 1 B. & Ad. 804; Tuck v. Priester, 19 Q. B. D. 629.

36. See Mr. Justice Story in Folsom v. Marsh, 2 Story, 100, 111 (1841): —

"If he [the recipient of a letter] attempt to publish such letter or letters on other occasions, not justifiable, a court of equity will prevent the publication by an injunction, as a breach of private confidence or contract, or of the rights of the author; and *a fortiori*, if he attempt to publish them for profit; for then it is not a mere breach of confidence or contract, but it is a violation of the exclusive copyright of the writer. . . . The general property, and the general rights incident to property, belong to the writer, whether the letters are literary compositions, or familiar letters, or details of facts, or letters of business. The general property in the manuscripts remains in the writer and his representatives, as well as the general copyright. *A fortiori,* third persons, standing in no privity with either party, are not entitled to publish them, to subserve their own private purposes of interest, or curiosity, or passion."

37. "The receiver of a letter is not a bailee, nor does he stand in a character analogous to that of a bailee. There is no right to possession, present or future, in the writer. The only right to be enforced against the holder is a right to prevent publication, not to require the manuscript from the holder in order to [sic] a publication of himself." Per Hon. Joel Parker, quoted in Grigsby *v.* Breckenridge, 2 Bush. 480, 489 (1867).

38. In Morison *v.* Moat, 9 Hare, 241, 255 (1851), a suit for an injunction to restrain the use of a secret medical compound, Sir George James Turner, V. C., said: "That the court has exercised jurisdiction in cases of this nature does not, I think, admit of any question. Different grounds have indeed been assigned for the exercise of that jurisdiction. In some cases it has been referred to property, in others to contract, and in others, again, it has been treated as founded upon trust or confidence,—meaning, as I conceive, that the court fastens the obligation on the conscience of the party, and enforces it against him in the same manner as it enforces against a party to whom a benefit is given, the obligation of performing a promise on the faith of which the benefit has been conferred; but upon whatever grounds the jurisdiction is founded, the authorities leave no doubt as to the exercise of it."

39. A similar growth of the law showing the development of contractual rights into rights of property is found in the law of goodwill. There are indications, as early as the Year Books, of traders endeavoring to secure to themselves by contract the advantages now designated by the term "goodwill," but it was not until 1743 that goodwill received legal recognition as property apart from the personal covenants of the traders. See Allan on Goodwill, pp. 2, 3.

40. The application of an existing principle to a new state of facts is not judicial legislation. To call it such is to assert that the existing body of law consists practically of the statutes and decided cases, and to deny that the principles (of which these cases are ordinarily said to be evidence) exist at all. It is not the application of an existing principle to new cases, but the introduction of a new principle, which is properly termed judicial legislation.

But even the fact that a certain decision would involve judicial legislation should not be taken as conclusive against the propriety of making it. This power has been constantly exercised by our judges, when applying to a new subject principles of private justice, moral fitness, and public convenience. Indeed, the elasticity of our law, its adaptability to new conditions, the capacity for growth, which has enabled it to meet the wants of an ever changing society and to apply immediate relief for every recognized wrong, have been its greatest boast.

"I cannot understand how any person who has considered the subject can suppose that society could possibly have gone on if judges had not legislated, or that there is any danger whatever in allowing them that power which they have in fact exercised, to make up for the negligence or the incapacity of the avowed legislator. That part of the law of every country which was made by judges has been far better made than that part which consists of statutes enacted by the legislature." 1 Austin's Jurisprudence, p. 224.

The cases referred to above show that the common law has for a century and a half protected privacy in certain cases, and to grant the further protection now suggested would be merely another application of an existing rule.

41. Loi Relative a la Presse. 11 Mai 1868.

"II. Toute publication dans un ecrit periodique relative a un fait de la vie privee constitue une contravention punie d'un amende de cinq cent francs.

"La poursuite ne pourra etre exercee que sur la plainte de la partie interessee."
Riviere, Codes Francais et Lois Usuelles. App. Code Pen., p. 20.

42. See Campbell *v.* Spottiswoode, 3 B. & S. 769, 776; Henwood *v.* Harrison, L. R. 7 C. P. 606; Gott *v.* Pulsifer, 122 Mass. 235.

43. "Nos moeurs n'admettent pas la pretention d'enlever aux investigations de la publicite les actes qui relevent de la vie publique, et ce dernier mot ne doit pas etre restreint a la vie officielle ou a celle du fonctionnaire. Tout homme qui appelle sur lui l'attention ou les regards du publique, soit par une mission qu'il a recue ou qu'il se donne, soit par le role qu'il s'attribue dans l'industrie, les arts, le theatre, etc., ne peut plus invoquer contre la critique ou l'expose de sa conduite d'autre protection que les lois qui repriment la diffamation et l'injure." Circ. Mins. Just., 4 Juin, 1868. Riviere Codes Francais et Lois Usuelles, App. Code Pen. 20 n (b).

44. "Celui-la seul a droit au silence absolu qui n'a pas expressement ou indirectment provoque ou authorise l'attention, l'approbation ou le blame." Circ. Mins. Just., 4 Juin, 1868. Riviere Codes Francais et Lois Usuelles, App. Code Pen. 20 n (b).

The principle thus expressed evidently is designed to exclude the wholesale investigations into the past of prominent public men with whom the American public is too familiar, and also, unhappily, too well pleased; while not entitled to the "silence *absolu*" which less prominent men may claim as their due, they may still demand that all the details of private life in its most limited sense shall not be laid bare for inspection.

45. Wason *v.* Walters, L. R. 4 Q. B. 73; Smith *v.* Higgins, 16 Gray, 251; Barrows *v.* Bell, 7 Gray, 331.

46. This limitation upon the right to prevent the publication of private letters was recognized early: —

"But, consistently with this right [of the writer of letters], the persons to whom they are addressed may have, nay, must, by implication, possess, the right to publish any letter or letters addressed to them, upon such occasions, as require, or justify, the publication or public use of them; but this right is strictly limited to such occasions. Thus, a person may justifiably use and publish, in a suit at law or in equity, such letter or letters as are necessary and proper, to establish his right to maintain the suit, or defend the same. So, if he be aspersed or misrepresented by the writer, or accused of improper conduct, in a public manner, he may publish such parts of such letter or letters, but no more, as may be necessary to vindicate his character and reputation, or free him from unjust obloquy and reproach." Story, J., in Folsom *v.* Marsh, 2 Story, 100, 110, 111 (1841).

The existence of any right in the recipient of letters to publish the same has been strenuously denied by Mr. Drone; but the reasoning upon which his denial rests does not seem satisfactory. Drone on Copyright, pp. 136-139.

47. Townshend on Slander and Libel, 4th ed., 18; Odgers on Libel and Slander, 2d ed., p. 3.

48. "But as long as gossip was oral, it spread, as regards any one individual, over a very small area, and was confined to the immediate circle of his acquaintances. It did not reach, or but rarely reached, those who knew nothing of him. It did not make his name, or his walk, or his conversation familiar to strangers. And what is more to the purpose, it spared him the pain and mortification of knowing that he was gossipped about. A man seldom heard of oral gossip about him which simply made him ridiculous, or trespassed on his lawful privacy, but made no positive attack upon his reputation. His peace and comfort were, therefore, but slightly affected by it." E. L. Godkin, "The Rights of the Citizen: To his Reputation." Scribner's Magazine, July, 1890, p. 66.

Vice-Chancellor Knight Bruce suggested in Prince Albert *v.* Strange, 2 DeGex & Sm. 652, 694, that a distinction would be made as to the right to privacy of works of art between an oral and a written description or catalogue.
49. See Drone on Copyright, pp. 121, 289, 290.
50. Comp. Drone on Copyright, p. 107.
51. Comp. High on Injunctions, 3d ed., 1015; Townshend on Libel and Slander, 4th ed., 417a-417d.
52. The following draft of a bill has been prepared by William H. Dunbar, Esq., of the Boston bar, as a suggestion for possible legislation: —

"SECTION 1. Whoever publishes in any newspaper, journal, magazine, or other periodical publication any statement concerning the private life or affairs of another, after being requested in writing by such other person not to publish such statement or any statement concerning him, shall be punished by imprisonment in the State prison not exceeding five years, or by imprisonment in the jail not exceeding two years, or by fine not exceeding one thousand dollars; provided, that no statement concerning the conduct of any person in, or the qualifications of any person for, a public office or position which such person holds, has held, or is seeking to obtain, or for which such person is at the time of such publication a candidate, or for which he or she is then suggested as a candidate, and no statement of or concerning the acts of any person in his or her business, profession, or calling, and no statement concerning any person in relation to a position, profession, business, or calling, bringing such person prominently before the public, or in relation to the qualifications for such a position, business, profession, or calling of any person prominent or seeking prominence before the public, and no statement relating to any act done by any person in a public place, nor any other statement of matter which is of public and general interest, shall be deemed a statement concerning the private life or affairs of such person within the meaning of this act.

"SECT. 2. It shall not be a defence to any criminal prosecution brought under section 1 of this act that the statement complained of is true, or that such statement was published without a malicious intention; but no person shall be liable to punishment for any statement published under such circumstances that if it were defamatory the publication thereof would be privileged."

Chapter 2. Privacy

1. "The press is overstepping in every direction the obvious bounds of propriety and of decency. Gossip is no longer the resource of the idle and of the vicious, but has become a trade, which is pursued with industry as well as effrontery. To satisfy a prurient taste the details of sexual relations are spread broadcast in the columns of the daily papers. To occupy the indolent, column upon column is filled with idle gossip, which can only be procured by intrusion upon the domestic circle. The intensity and complexity of life, attendant upon advancing civilization, have rendered necessary some retreat from the world, and man, under the refining influence of culture, has become more sensitive to publicity, so that solitude and privacy have become more essential to the individual; but modern enterprise and invention have, through invasions upon his privacy, subjected him to mental pain and distress, far greater than could be inflicted by mere bodily injury." Warren and Brandeis, *The Right to Privacy,* 4 Harv. L. Rev. 193, 196 (1890).
2. Mason, Brandeis, A Free Man's Life 70 (1946).
3. 4 Harv. L. Rev. 193 (1890).

4. Woolsey v. Judd, 4 Duer (11 N.Y. Super.) 379, 11 How. Pr. 49 (N.Y. 1855) (publication of private letters); Gee v. Pritchard, 2 Swans. 402, 36 Eng. Rep. 670 (1818) (same); Prince Albert v. Strange, 2 De G. & Sm. 652, 41 Eng. Rep. 1171, 1 Mac. & G. 25, 64 Eng. Rep. 293 (1849) (exhibition of etchings and publication of catalogue).
5. Yovatt v. Winyard, 1 Jac. & W. 394, 37 Eng. Rep. 425 (1820) (publication of recipes surreptitiously obtained by employee); Abernethy v. Hutchinson, 3 L.J. Ch. 209 (1825) (publication of lectures to class of which defendant was a member); Pollard v. Photographic Co., 40 Ch. D. 345 (1888) (publication of plaintiff's picture made by defendant).
6. Larremore, *The Law of Privacy*, 12 Colum. L. Rev. 693 (1912); Ragland, *The Right of Privacy*, 17 Ky. L.J. 101 (1929); Winfield, *Privacy*, 47 L.Q. Rev. 23 (1931); Green, *The Right of Privacy*, 27 Ill. L. Rev. 237 (1932); Kacedan, *The Right of Privacy*, 12 B.U.L. Rev. 353, 600 (1932); Dickler, *The Right of Privacy*, 70 U.S.L. Rev. 435 (1936); Harper & McNeely, *A Re-examination of the Basis for Liability for Emotional Distress*, [1938] Wis. L. Rev. 426; Nizer, *The Right of Privacy*, 39 Mich. L. Rev. 526 (1941); Feinberg, *Recent Developments in the Law of Privacy*, 48 Colum. L. Rev. 713 (1948); Ludwig, *"Peace of Mind" in 48 Pieces vs. Uniform Right of Privacy*, 32 Minn. L. Rev. 734 (1948); Yankwich, *The Right of Privacy*, 27 Notre Dame Law. 429 (1952); Daims, *What Do We Mean by "Right to Privacy,"* 4 S.D.L. Rev. 1 (1959).

    Also Notes in 8 Mich. L. Rev. 221 (1909); 12 Colum. L. Rev. 1 (1912); 43 Harv. L. Rev. 297 (1929); 7 N.C.L. Rev. 435 (1929); 26 Ill. L. Rev. 63 (1931); 81 U. Pa. L. Rev. 324 (1933); 33 Ill. L. Rev. 87 (1938); 13 So. Cal. L. Rev. 81 (1939); 15 Temp. L.Q. 148 (1941); 25 Minn. L. Rev. 619 (1941); 30 Cornell L.Q. 398 (1945); 48 Colum. L. Rev. 713 (1948); 15 U. Chi. L. Rev. 926 (1948); 6 Ark. L. Rev. 459 (1952); 38 Va. L. Rev. 117 (1952); 28 Ind. L.J. 179 (1953); 27 Miss. L.J. 256 (1956); 44 Va. L. Rev. 1303 (1958); 31 Miss. L.J. 191 (1960).

    The foreign law is discussed in Gutteridge, *The Comparative Law of the Right to Privacy*, 47 L.Q. Rev. 203 (1931); Walton, *The Comparative Law of the Right to Privacy*, 47 L.Q. Rev. 219 (1931).
7. O'Brien, *The Right of Privacy*, 2 Colum. L. Rev. 437 (1902); Lisle, *The Right of Privacy (A Contra View)*, 19 Ky L.J. 137 (1931); Notes, 2 Colum. L. Rev. 437 (1902); 64 Albany L.J. 428 (1902); 29 Law Notes 64 (1925); 43 Harv. L. Rev. 297 (1929); 26 Ill. L. Rev. 63 (1931).
8. Manola v. Stevens (N.Y. Sup. Ct. 1890), in N.Y. Times, June 15, 18, 21, 1890.
9. Mackenzie v. Soden Mineral Springs Co., 27 Abb. N. Cas. 402, 18 N.Y.S. 240 (Sup. Ct. 1891) (use of name of physician in advertising patent medicine enjoined); Marks v. Jaffa, 6 Misc. 290, 26 N.Y.S. 908 (Super. Ct. N.Y. City 1893) (entering actor in embarrassing popularity contest); Schuyler v. Curtis, 147 N.Y. 434, 42 N.E. 22 (1895) (erection of statue as memorial to deceased; relief denied only because he was dead).
10. Corliss v. E.W. Walker Co., 64 Fed. 280 (D. Mass. 1894) (portrait to be inserted in biographical sketch of plaintiff; relief denied because he was a public figure).
11. Atkinson v. John E. Doherty & Co., 121 Mich. 372, 80 N.W. 285 (1899). The man was dead, and in any case a public figure; and on either ground the same decision would probably result today. See *infra*, text at notes 205, 218–32.
12. 171 N.Y. 538, 64 N.E. 442 (1902).
13. O'Brien, *The Right of Privacy*, 2 Colum. L. Rev. 437 (1902).
14. N.Y. Sess. Laws 1903, ch. 132, 1–2. Now, as amended in 1921, N.Y. Civ. Rights Law, 50–51. Held constitutional in Rhodes v. Sperry & Hutchinson Co., 193 N.Y. 223, 85 N.E. 1097 (1908), *aff'd*, 220 U.S. 502 (1911). See generally, Hofstadter, The Development of the Right of Privacy in New York (1954).

15. 122 Ga. 190, 50 S.E. 68 (1905).
16. Restatement, Torts 867 (1939).
17. Smith v. Doss, 251 Ala. 250, 37 So.2d 118 (1948); Birmingham Broadcasting Co. v. Bell, 259 Ala. 656, 68 So.2d 314 (1953), *later appeal,* 266 Ala. 266, 96 So.2d 263 (1957).
18. Smith v. Suratt, 7 Alaska 416 (1926).
19. Reed v. Real Detective Pub. Co., 63 Ariz. 294, 162 P.2d 133 (1945).
20. Melvin v. Reid, 112 Cal. App. 285, 297 Pac. 91 (1931); Kerby v. Hal Roach Studios, 53 Cal. App. 2d 207, 127 P.2d 577 (1942); Stryker v. Republic Pictures Corp., 108 Cal. App. 2d 191, 238 P.2d 670 (1951); Gill v. Curtis Pub. Co., 38 Cal. 2d 273, 239 P.2d 630 (1952); Linehan v. Linehan, 134 Cal. App. 2d 250, 285 P.2d 326 (1955); Fairfield v. American Photocopy Equipment Co., 138 Cal. App. 2d 82, 291 P.2d 194 (1955).
21. Korn v. Rennison, 156 A.2d 476 (Conn. Super. 1959).
22. Peay v. Curtis Pub. Co., 78 F. Supp. 305 (D.D.C. 1948).
23. Cason v. Baskin, 155 Fla. 198, 20 So.2d 243 (1944), *second appeal,* 159 Fla. 31, 30 So.2d 635 (1947); and see Jacova v. Southern Radio & Television Co., 83 So.2d 34 (Fla. 1955).
24. Pavesich v. New England Life Ins. Co., 122 Ga. 190, 50 S.E. 68 (1905); Bazemore v. Savannah Hospital, 171 Ga. 257, 155 S.E. 194 (1930); McDaniel v. Atlanta Coca Cola Bottling Co., 60 Ga. App. 92, 2 S.E.2d 810 (1939); Walker v. Whittle, 83 Ga. App. 445, 64 S.E.2d 87 (1951); Gouldman-Taber Pontiac, Inc. v. Zerbst, 96 Ga. App. 48, 99 S.E.2d 475 (1957).
25. Eick v. Perk Dog Food Co., 347 Ill. App. 293, 106 N.E.2d 742 (1952); Annerino v. Dell Pub. Co., 17 Ill. App. 2d 205, 149 N.E.2d 761 (1958).
26. Continental Optical Co. v. Reed, 119 Ind. App. 643, 86 N.E.2d 306 (1949). See also Estill v. Hearst Pub. Co., 186 F.2d 1017 (7th Cir. 1951).
27. Bremmer v. Journal-Tribune Co., 247 Iowa 817, 76 N.W.2d 762 (1956).
28. Kunz v. Allen, 102 Kan. 883, 172 Pac. 532 (1918). See also Johnson v. Boeing Airplane Co., 175 Kan. 275, 262 P.2d 808 (1953).
29. Foster-Milburn Co. v. Chinn, 134 Ky. 424, 120 S.W. 364 (1909); Douglas v. Stokes, 149 Ky. 506, 149 S.W. 849 (1912); Brents v. Morgan, 221 Ky. 765, 299 S.W. 967 (1927); Rhodes v. Graham, 238 Ky. 225, 37 S.W.2d 46 (1931); Trammell v. Citizens News Co., 285 Ky. 529, 148 S.W.2d 708 (1941).
30. Itzkovitch v. Whitaker, 115 La. 479, 39 So. 499 (1905); Schwartz v. Edrington, 133 La. 235, 62 So. 660 (1913); Hamilton v. Lumbermen's Mut. Cas. Co., 82 So.2d 61 (La. App. 1955); Souder v. Pendleton Detectives, 88 So.2d 716 (La. App. 1956).
31. Pallas v. Crowley, Milner & Co., 322 Mich. 411, 33 N.W.2d 911 (1948).
32. Martin v. Dorton, 210 Miss. 668, 50 So.2d 391 (1951). See Note, 27 Miss. L.J. 256 (1956).
33. Munden v. Harris, 153 Mo. App. 652, 134 S.W. 1076 (1911); Barber v. Time, Inc., 348 Mo. 1199, 159 S.W.2d 291 (1942); State *ex rel.* Clemens v. Witthaus, 228 S.W.2d 4 (Mo. 1950); Biederman's of Springfield, Inc. v. Wright, 322 S.W.2d 892 (Mo. 1959).
34. Welsh v. Pritchard, 125 Mont. 517, 241 P.2d 816 (1952).
35. Norman v. City of Las Vegas, 64 Nev. 38, 177 P.2d 442 (1947).
36. Vanderbilt v. Mitchell, 72 N.J. Eq. 910, 67 Atl. (Ct. Err. & App. 1907); Edison v. Edison Polyform Mfg. Co., 73 N.J. Eq. 136, 67 Atl. 392 (Ch. 1907); Frey v. Dixon, 141 N.J. Eq. 481, 58 A.2d 86 (Ch. 1948); Ettore v. Philco Television Broadcasting Co., 229 F.2d 481 (3d Cir. 1956).
37. Flake v. Greensboro News Co., 212 N.C. 780, 195 S.E. 55 (1938).
38. Friedman v. Cincinnati Local Joint Exec. Board, 6 Ohio Supp. 276, 20 Ohio Op. 473 (C.P. 1941); Housh v. Peth, 165 Ohio St. 35, 133 N.E.2d 340 (1956).
39. Hinish v. Meier & Frank Co., 166 Ore. 482, 113 P.2d 438 (1941).

40. Clayman v. Bernstein, 38 Pa. D. & C. 543 (C.P.1940); Bennett v. Norban, 396 Pa. 94, 151 A.2d 476 (1959); Aquino v. Bulletin Co., 154 A.2d 422 (Pa. Super. 1959); Jenkins v. Dell Pub. Co., 251 F.2d 447 (3d Cir. 1958).
41. Holloman v. Life Ins. Co. of Va., 192 S.C. 454, 7 S.E.2d 169 (1940); Meetze v. Associated Press, 230 S.C. 330, 95 S.E.2d 606 (1956); Frith v. Associated Press, 176 F. Supp. 671 (E.D.S.C. 1959).
42. Langford v. Vanderbilt University, 199 Tenn. 389, 287 S.W.2d 32 (1956).
43. Roach v. Harper, 105 S.E.2d 564 (W. Va. 1958); Sutherland v. Kroger Co., 110 S.E.2d 716 (W. Va. 1959).
44. Miller v. National Broadcasting Co., 157 F. Supp. 240 (D. Del. 1957).
45. Graham v. Baltimore Post Co., (Baltimore Super. Ct. 1932), reported in 22 Ky. L.J. 108 (1933).
46. Mabry v. Kettering, 89 Ark. 551, 117 S.W. 746 (1909), *second appeal*, 92 Ark. 81, 122 S.W. 115 (1909).
47. Fitzsimmons v. Olinger Mortuary Ass'n, 91 Colo. 544, 17 P.2d 535 (1932); McCreery v. Miller's Grocerteria Co., 99 Colo. 499, 64 P.2d 803 (1936). In the last named case the dissent indicates that an opinion recognizing the right of privacy was written, but withdrawn.
48. Marek v. Zanol Products Co., 298 Mass. 1, 9 N.E.2d 393 (1937); Thayer v. Worcester Post Pub. Co., 284 Mass. 160, 187 N.E. 292 (1933); Themo v. New England Newspaper Pub. Co., 306 Mass. 54, 27 N.E.2d 753 (1940). In Wright v. R.K.O. Radio Pictures, 55 F. Supp. 639 (D. Mass. 1944), the court considered that the state had rejected the right of privacy; but in Kelley v. Post Pub. Co., 327 Mass. 275, 98 N.E.2d 286 (1951), the question was said to be still open. See also Hazlitt v. Fawcett Publications, 116 F. Supp. 538 (D. Conn. 1953).
49. Berg v. Minneapolis Star & Tribune Co., 79 F. Supp. 957 (D. Minn. 1948). See also Hazlitt v. Fawcett Publications, 116 F. Supp. 538 (D. Conn. 1953).
50. In Hillman v. Star Pub. Co., 64 Wash. 691, 117 Pac. 594 (1911), the right of privacy was rejected, and said to be a matter for legislation. In State *ex rel.* La Follette v. Hinkle, 131 Wash. 86, 229 Pac. 317 (1924), it was apparently recognized; but in Lewis v. Physicians & Dentists Credit Bureau, 27 Wash. 2d 267, 177 P.2d 896 (1947), the question was said to be still open in Washington. See also Hazlitt v. Fawcett Publications, 116 F. Supp. 538 (D. Conn. 1953).

    Writers have added South Dakota and Wyoming. Davis, *What Do We Mean by "Right to Privacy,"* 4 S.D.L. Rev. 1 (1959), considers that rather vague constitutional provisions in South Dakota will lead to recognition of the right; and the Note, 11 Wyo. L.J. 184 (1957), believes that the same result may follow on the basis of the Wyoming constitutional provision that truth is a defense to libel.
51. See *supra*, note 14.
52. Okla. Stat. Ann. tit. 21, 839-40 (1958). Before the statute there were numerous indications that Oklahoma would recognize the right of privacy without it. Bartholomew v. Workman, 197 Okl. 267, 169 P.2d 1012 (1946); McKinzie v. Huckaby, 112 F. Supp. 642 (W.D. Okl. 1953); Lyles v. State, 330 P.2d 734 (Okl. Cr. 1958); Paramount Pictures v. Leader Press, 24 F. Supp. (W.D. Okl. 1938), *rev'd on other grounds* in 106 F.2d 229 (10th Cir. 1939; Banks v. King Features Syndicate, 30 F. Supp. 352 (S.D.N.Y. 1939, Oklahoma law); Hazlitt v. Fawcett Publications, 116 F. Supp. 538 (D. Conn. 1953, Oklahoma law). The Note in 10 Okl. L. Rev. 353 (1957), considers that there is still some doubt as to whether the common law right may not be recognized, in addition to the statutory one. The New York statute has been held to be exclusive. Kimmerle v. New York Evening Journal Co., 262 N.Y. 99, 186 N.E. 217 (1933).
53. Utah Code Ann. 76-4-8 and 76-4-9 (1953).

54. Va. Code Ann. 8-650 (1957). See Notes, 38 Va. L. Rev. 117 (1952); 44 Va. L. Rev. 1303 (1958).
55. Henry v. Cherry & Webb, 30 R.I. 13, 73 Atl. 97 (1909).
56. Brunson v. Ranks Army Store, 161 Neb. 519, 73 N.W.2d 803 (1955). See also Schnieding v. American Farmers Mut. Ins. Co., 138 F. Supp. 167 (D. Neb. 1955).
57. Milner v. Red River Valley Pub. Co., 249 S.W.2d 227 (Tex. Civ. App. 1952); McCullagh v. Houston Chronicle Pub. Co., 211 F.2d 4 (5th Cir. 1954). See Seavey, *Can Texas Courts Protect Newly Discovered Interests,* 31 Texas L. Rev. 309 (1953).
58. Judevine v. Benzies-Montanye Fuel & Warehouse Co., 222 Wis. 512, 269 N.W. 295 (1936); State *ex rel.* Distenfeld v. Neelen, 255 Wis. 214, 38 N.W.2d 703 (1949); see Note, [1952] Wis. L. Rev. 507. The last decision, in Yoeckel v. Samonig, 272 Wis. 430, 75 N.W.2d 925 (1956), involved a particularly outrageous invasion, when the defendant intruded into a ladies' rest room, photographed the plaintiff there, and exhibited the picture to patrons in a restaurant. The court bowed to the fact that a bill providing for the right of privacy had failed to pass in the last legislature. The case is nevertheless an atrocity.
59. Cooley, Torts 29 (2d ed. 1888).
60. De May v. Roberts, 46 Mich. 160, 9 N.W. 146 (1881).
61. Young v. Western & A.R. Co., 39 Ga. App. 761, 148 S.E. 414 (1929) (search without warrant); Walker v. Whittle, 83 Ga. App. 445, 64 S.E.2d 87 (1951) (entry without legal authority to arrest husband); Welsh v. Pritchard, 125 Mont. 517, 241 P.2d 816 (1952) (landlord moving in on tenant).
62. Newcomb Hotel Co. v. Corbett, 27 Ga. App. 365, 108 S.E. 309 (1921).
63. Byfield v. Candler, 33 Ga. App. 275, 125 S.E. 905 (1924).
64. Sutherland v. Kroger Co., 110 S.E.2d 716 (W.Va. 1959).
65. Rhodes v. Graham, 238 Ky. 225, 37 S.W.2d 46 (1931).
66. McDaniel v. Atlanta Coca Cola Bottling Co., 60 Ga. App. 92, 2 S.E.2d 810 (1939); Roach v. Harper, 105 S.E.2d 564 (W. Va. 1958). The same conclusion was reached, on the basis of a criminal statute, in People v. Trieber, 28 Cal. 2d 657, 163 P.2d 492, 171 P.2d 1 (1946).
67. Moore v. New York Elevated R. Co., 130 N.Y. 523, 29 N.E. 997 (1892) (looking into windows from elevated railway; plaintiff compensated under eminent domain); Pritchett v. Board of Commissioners of Knox County, 42 Ind. App. 3, 85 N.E. 32 (1908) (relief on the basis of nuisance); Souder v. Pendleton Detectives, 88 So.2d 716 (La. App. 1956) (spying into windows).

This topic gave rise to a possible nomination for the all-time prize law review title, in the Note, *Crimination of Peeping Toms and Other Men of Vision,* 5 Ark. L. Rev. 388 (1951).
68. Bartow v. Smith, 149 Ohio St. 301, 78 N.E.2d 735 (1948).
69. *Cf.* Duty v. General Finance Co., 154 Tex. 16, 273 S.W.2d 64 (1954).
70. House v. Peth, 165 Ohio St. 35, 133 N.E.2d 340 (1956), *affirming* 99 Ohio App. 485, 135 N.E.2d 440 (1955). *Accord,* on the ground of "nuisance," Wiggins v. Moskins Credit Clothing Store, 137 F. Supp. 764 (E.D.S.C. 1956).
71. Brex v. Smith, 104 N.J. Eq. 386, 146 Atl. 34 (Ch. 1929); Zimmerman v. Wilson, 81 F.2d 847 (3d Cir. 1936).
72. Frey v. Dixon, 141 N.J. Eq. 481, 58 A.2d 86 (Ch. 1948); State *ex rel.* Clemens v. Witthaus, 228 S.W.2d 4 (Mo. 1950) (court order).
73. Bednarik v. Bednarik, 18 N.J. Misc. 633, 16 A.2d 80 (Ch. 1940). *Cf.* Hawkins v. Kuhne, 153 App. Div. 216, 137 N.Y.S. 1090 (1912), *aff'd,* 208 N.Y. 555, 101 N.E. 1104 (1913) (illegal photographing and measuring by police called an "assault").

74. Owens v. Henman, 1 W. & S. 548, 37 Am. Dec. 481 (Pa. 1841).
75. Lisowski v. Jaskiewicz, 76 Pa. D. & C. 79 (C.P. 1950); Christie v. Greenleaf, 78 Pa. D. & C. 191 (C.P. 1951).
76. Horstman v. Newman, 291 S.W.2d 567 (Ky. 1956).
77. Gotthelf v. Hillcrest Lumber Co., 280 App. Div. 668, 116 N.Y.S.2d 873 (1952).
78. Voelker v. Tyndall, 226 Ind. 43, 75 N.E.2d 548 (1947); McGovern v. Van Riper, 140 N.J. Eq. 341, 54 A.2d 469 (Ch. 1947), *affirming* 137 N.J. Eq. 548, 45 A.2d 842 (Ct. Err. & App. 1946), *which reversed* 137 N.J. Eq. 24, 43 A.2d 514 (Ch. 1945); State *ex rel.* Mavity v. Tyndall, 224 Ind. 364, 66 N.E.2d 755 (1946); Bartletta v. McFeeley, 107 N.J. Eq. 141, 152 Atl. 17 (Ch. 1930), *aff'd*, 109 N.J. Eq. 241, 156 Atl. 658 (Ct. Err. & App. 1931); Fernicola v. Keenan, 136 N.J. Eq. 9, 39 A.2d 851 (Ch. 1944); Norman v. City of Las Vegas, 64 Nev. 38, 177 P.2d 442 (1947); Mabry v. Kettering, 89 Ark. 551, 117 S.W. 746 (1909), *second appeal*, 92 Ark. 81, 122 S.W. 115 (1909); Hodgeman v. Olson, 86 Wash. 615, 150 Pac. 1122 (1915); *cf.* Sellers v. Henry, 329 S.W.2d 214 (Ky. 1959). As to the use made of police photographs, see *infra*, text at notes 143–45.

    In Anthony v. Anthony, 9 N.J. Super. 411, 74 A.2d 919 (Ch. 1950), a compulsory blood test in a paternity suit was held to be justified, and not to invade any right of privacy.

    Such cases, of course, usually turn on constitutional rights.
79. Bowles v. Misle, 64 F. Supp. 835 (D. Neb. 1946); United States v. Alabama Highway Express Co., 46 F. Supp. 450 (D. Ala. 1942); Alabama State Federation of Labor v. McAdory, 246 Ala. 1, 18 So.2d 810 (1944).
80. Chappell v. Stewart, 82 Md. 323, 33 Atl. 542 (1896). *Cf.* McKinzie v. Huckaby, 112 F. Supp. 642 (W.D. Okl. 1953), where the defendant, calling at the plaintiff's home, brought along a policeman, who remained outside in the car.

    In Schultz v. Frankfort Marine, Accident & Plate Glass Ins. Co., 151 Wis. 537, 139 N.W. 386 (1913), "rough shadowing" which was visible to onlookers, was held to be actionable as slander.
81. Gill v. Hearst Pub. Co., 40 Cal. 2d 224, 253 P.2d 441 (1953); Berg v. Minneapolis Star & Tribune Co., 79 F. Supp. 957 (D. Minn. 1948) (courtroom); Lyles v. State, 330 P.2d 734 (Okl. Cr. 1958) (television in court). *Cf.* Gautier v. Pro-Football, Inc., 304 N.Y. 354, 107 N.E.2d 485 (1952); Sports & General Press Agency v. "Our Dogs" Pub. Co., [1916] 2 K.B. 880; and cases cited *infra*, note 104. See Fitzpatrick, *Unauthorized Photographs*, 20 Geo. L.J. 134 (1932). In United States v. Gugel, 119 F. Supp. 897 (E.D. Ky. 1954), the right to take such pictures was said to be protected by the Constitution of the United States.

    The same type of reasoning, that the record does not differ from a written report, was applied to the recording of a private telephone conversation between plaintiff and defendant, in Chaplin v. National Broadcasting Co., 15 F.R.D. 134 (S.D.N.Y. 1953).

    As to publication, see *infra*, text at notes 102–08.

    In Friedman v. Cincinnati Local Joint Executive Board, 6 Ohio Supp. 276, 20 Ohio Op. 473 (C.P. 1941), a labor union which had taken pictures of customers crossing a picket line was enjoined from making use of them for purposes of retaliation.
82. Barber v. Time, Inc., 348 Mo. 1199, 159 S.W.2d 291 (1942). *Cf.* Clayman v. Bernstein, 38 Pa. D. & C. 543 (C.P. 1940) (picture of semi-conscious patient taken by physician).
83. Douglas v. Stokes, 149 Ky. 506, 149 S.W. 849 (1912) (publication of picture by photographer, breach of implied contract); Thompson v. Adelberg & Berman, 181 Ky. 487, 205 S.W. 558 (1918) (publication of debt, libel); Feeney v. Young, 191 App. Div. 501, 181 N.Y.S. 481 (1920) (exhibition of pictures of caesarian operation, breach of

trust and implied contract); Peed v. Washington Times, 55 Wash. L. Rep. 182 (D.C. 1927) (publication of stolen picture).
84. Brents v. Morgan, 221 Ky. 765, 299 S.W. 967 (1927). "Dr. W. R. Morgan owes an account here of $49.67. And if promises would pay an account this account would have been settled long ago. This account will be advertised as long as it remains unpaid."
85. 112 Cal. App. 285, 297 Pac. 91 (1931).
86. Mau v. Rio Grande Oil, Inc., 28 F. Supp. 845 (N.D. Cal. 1939).
87. Trammell v. Citizens News Co., 285 Ky. 529, 148 S.W.2d 708 (1941); Biederman's of Springfield, Inc. v. Wright, 322 S.W.2d 892 (Mo. 1959). *Cf.* Bennett v. Norban, 396 Pa. 94, 151 A.2d 476 (1959).
    In Maysville Transit Co. v. Ort, 296 Ky. 524, 177 S.W.2d 369 (1944), it was held that a corporation had no right of privacy, but that there could be recovery for disclosure of its tax returns on the basis of violation of a statute.
88. Banks v. King Features Syndicate, 30 F. Supp. 352 (S.D.N.Y. 1939) (Oklahoma law; newspaper publication of X-rays of woman's pelvic region); Griffin v. Medical Society, 11 N.Y.S.2d 109 (Sup. Ct. 1939) (publication in medical journal of pictures of plaintiff's deformed nose); Feeney v. Young, 191 App. Div. 501, 181 N.Y.S. 481 (1920) (public exhibition of films of caesarian operation). *Cf.* Clayman v. Bernstein, 38 Pa. D. & C. 543 (C.P. 1940) (doctor enjoined from using pictures of facial disfigurement taken while patient was semi-conscious).
89. Cason v. Baskin, 155 Fla. 198, 20 So.2d 243 (1945), *second appeal*, 159 Fla. 31, 30 So.2d 635 (1947).
90. Trammell v. Citizens News Co., 285 Ky. 529, 148 S.W.2d 708 (1941). *Cf.* Thompson v. Adelberg & Berman, Inc., 181 Ky. 487, 205 S.W. 558 (1918).
91. Brents v. Morgan, 221 Ky. 765, 299 S.W. 967 (1927).
92. Bennett v. Norban, 396 Pa. 94, 151 A.2d 476 (1959). *Cf.* Biederman's of Springfield, Inc. v. Wright, 322 S.W.2d 892 (Mo. 1959) (public restaurant).
93. Gouldman-Taber Pontiac, Inc. v. Zerbst, 96 Ga. App. 48, 99 S.E.2d 475 (1957), *reversed in* 213 Ga. 682, 100 S.E.2d 881 (1957), on the ground that the communication was privileged.
94. Patton v. Jacobs, 118 Ind. App. 358, 78 N.E.2d 789 (1948); Voneye v. Turner, 240 S.W.2d 588 (Ky. 1951); Lucas v. Moskins Stores, 262 S.W.2d 679 (Ky. 1953); Hawley v. Professional Credit Bureau, Inc., 345 Mich. 500, 76 N.W.2d 835 (1956); Lewis v. Physicians & Dentists Credit Bureau, 27 Wash.2d 267, 177 P.2d 896 (1947). *Cf.* Davis. v. General Finance & Thrift Corp., 80 Ga. App. 708, 57 S.E.2d 225 (1950) (telegram to plaintiff); Perry v. Moskins Stores, 249 S.W.2d 812 (Ky. 1952) (postcard to plaintiff).
95. Gregory v. Bryan-Hunt Co., 295 Ky. 345, 174 S.W.2d 510 (1943) (oral accusation of theft). On the other hand, in Kerby v. Hal Roach Studios, 53 Cal. App. 2d 207, 127 P.2d 577 (1942), the distribution of a letter to a thousand persons was held, without discussion, to make it public.
96. Berry v. Moench, 8 Utah 2d 191, 331 P.2d 814 (1958); *cf.* Simonsen v. Swenson, 104 Neb. 224, 177 N.W. 831 (1920); and see Note, 43 Minn. L. Rev. 943 (1959).
97. Warren and Brandeis, *The Right to Privacy*, 4 Harv. L. Rev. 193, 217 (1890).
98. Martin v. F.I.Y. Theatre Co., 10 Ohio Op. 338 (Ohio C.P. 1938); Gregory v. Bryan-Hunt Co., 295 Ky. 345, 174 S.W.2d 510 (1943); Pangallo v. Murphy, 243 S.W.2d 496 (Ky. 1951); Lewis v. Physicians & Dentists Credit Bureau, 27 Wash. 2d 267, 177 P.2d 896 (1947).
99. Mau v. Rio Grande Oil, Inc., 28 F. Supp. 845 (N.D. Cal. 1939) (radio); Strickler v. National Broadcasting Co., 167 F. Supp. 68 (S.D. Cal. 1958) (television); Binns v. Vitagraph Co. of America, 210 N.Y. 51, 103 N.E. 1108 (1913) (motion picture);

Donohue v. Warner Bros. Pictures, 194 F.2d 6 (10th Cir. 1952) (same); Ettore v. Philco Television Broadcasting Co., 229 F.2d 481 (3d Cir. 1956) (motion picture film on television).
100. Bennett v. Norban, 396 Pa. 94, 151 A.2d 476 (1959); Biederman's of Springfield, Inc. v. Wright, 322 S.W.2d 892 (Mo. 1959); Linehan v. Linehan, 134 Cal. App. 2d 250, 285 P.2d 326 (1955).
101. Reed v. Orleans Parish Schoolboard, 21 So.2d 895 (La. App. 1945). Compare the cases of disclosure of corporate records, *supra* note 79.
102. See *infra*, text at notes 218–63.
103. In Chaplin v. National Broadcasting Co., 15 F.R.D. 134 (S.D.N.Y. 1953), the same reasoning was applied to the broadcast of a recorded private telephone conversation between plaintiff and defendant. The case looks wrong, since one element, the sound of Chaplin's voice, was not then public, and was expected to be private to the recipient.
104. Sports & General Press Agency v. "Our Dogs" Pub. Co., [1916] 2 K.B. 880; Humiston v. Universal Film Mfg. Co., 189 App. Div. 467, 178 N.Y.S. 752 (1919); Merle v. Sociological Research Film Corp., 166 App. Div. 376, 152 N.Y.S. 829 (1915); Berg v. Minneapolis Star & Tribune Co., 79 F. Supp. 957 (D. Minn. 1948) (courtroom); Lyles v. State, 330 P.2d 734 (Okl. Cr. 1958) (television in courtroom). *Cf.* Gautier v. Pro-Football, Inc., 304 N.Y. 354, 107 N.E.2d 485 (1952) (football game); Jacova v. Southern Radio & Television Co., 83 So.2d 34 (Fla. 1955) (cigar store raid).

It may be suggested, however, that a man may still be private in a public place. Suppose that a citizen responds to a call of nature in the bushes in a public park?
105. Gill v. Hearst Pub. Co., 40 Cal. 2d 224, 253 P.2d 441 (1953).
106. Note, 44 Va. L. Rev. 1303 (1958).
107. Blumenthal v. Picture Classics, 235 App. Div. 570, 257 N.Y.S. 800 (1932), *aff'd*, 261 N.Y. 504, 185 N.E.713 (1933).
108. In Sarat Lahiri v. Daily Mirror, 162 Misc. 776, 295 N.Y.S. 382 (Sup. Ct. 1937).
109. Barber v. Time, Inc., 348 Mo. 1199, 159 S.W.2d 291 (1942) (hospital bed). *Cf.* Clayman v. Bernstein, 38 Pa. D. & C. 543 (C.P. 1940) (picture of semi-conscious patient taken by physician).
110. Peed v. Washington Times, 55 Wash. L. Rep. 182 (D.C. 1927).

In Metter v. Los Angeles Examiner, 35 Cal. App. 2d 304, 95 P.2d 491 (1939), the newspaper appears to have gotten away with a great deal. After plaintiff's wife had committed suicide, the screen of his kitchen window was forced open, and a photograph of his wife disappeared from his table. The same day the same photograph appeared in the paper. The court considered that there was no evidence that the defendant had stolen it. The actual decision can be justified, however, on the ground that the woman was dead. See *infra*, text at note 205.
111. Bazemore v. Savannah Hospital, 171 Ga. 257, 155 S.E. 194 (1930) (picture of deformed child born to plaintiff, obtained from hospital attendants). *Cf.* Douglas v. Stokes, 149 Ky. 506, 149 S.W. 849 (1912) (breach of implied contract by photographer).
112. *Cf.* Maysville Transit Co. v. Ort, 296 Ky. 524, 177 S.W.2d 369 (1944); Munzer v. Blaisdell, 183 Misc. 773, 49 N.Y.S.2d 915 (Sup. Ct. 1944), *aff'd*, 269 App. Div. 970, 58 N.Y.S.2d 360 (1945) (records of mental institution); Sellers v. Henry, 329 S.W.2d 214 (Ky. 1959) (police photograph; liability dependent upon use).
113. Meetze v. Associated Press, 230 S.C. 330, 95 S.E.2d 606 (1956).
114. Stryker v. Republic Pictures Corp., 108 Cal. App. 2d 191, 238 P.2d 670 (1951); Continental Optical Co. v. Reed, 119 Ind. App. 643, 86 N.E.2d 306 (1949).

In Thompson v. Curtis Pub. Co., 193 F.2d 953 (3d Cir. 1952), a patent obtained by the plaintiff was held to be a public matter, "as fully as a play, a book, or a song."

115. See *infra*, text at notes 285-88.
116. Bernstein v. National Broadcasting Co., 129 F. Supp. 817 (D.D.C. 1955), *aff'd*, 232 F.2d 369 (D.C. Cir. 1956) (murder trial used in broadcast); Smith v. National Broadcasting Co., 138 Cal. App. 2d 807, 292 P.2d 600 (1956) (false report to police of escape of black panther). In both cases the name of the plaintiff was not used.
117. 112 Cal. App. 285, 297 Pac. 91 (1931) (see *supra*, text at note 85). *Accord*, Mau v. Rio Grande Oil, Inc., 28 F. Supp. 845 (N.D. Cal. 1939); and see cases cited in the preceding note. The Melvin and Mau cases were explained on the basis of the use of the name in the Smith case.
118. Reed v. Real Detective Pub. Co., 63 Ariz. 294, 162 P.2d 133 (1945); Davis. v. General Finance & Thrift Corp., 80 Ga. App. 708, 57 S.E.2d 225 (1950); Gill v. Hearst Pub. Co. 40 Cal. 2d 224, 253 P.2d 441 (1953); Samuel v. Curtis Pub. Co., 122 F. Supp 327 (N.D. Cal. 1954).
119. Meetze v. Associated Press, 230 S.C. 330, 95 S.E.2d 606 (1956) (report of birth of child to girl twelve years old).
120. Garner v. Triangle Publications, 97 F. Supp. 546 (S.D.N.Y. 1951). *Cf.* Myers v. U.S. Camera Pub. Corp., 9 Misc. 2d 765, 167 N.Y.S.2d 771 (N.Y. City Ct. 1957) (nude full body photograph of model); Feeney v. Young, 191 App. Div. 501, 181 N.Y.S. 481 (1920) (exhibition of film of caesarian operation); Banks v. King Features Syndicate, 30 F. Supp. 352 (S.D.N.Y. 1939) (X-rays of woman's pelvic region).
121. Cason v. Baskin, 155 Fla. 198, 20 So.2d 243 (1944), *second appeal*, 159 Fla. 31, 30 So.2d 635 (1947). *Cf.* Stryker v. Republic Pictures Corp., 108 Cal. App. 2d 191, 238 P.2d 670 (1951).
122. 113 F.2d 806 (2d Cir. 1940), *affirming* 34 F. Supp. 19 (S.D.N.Y. 1938).
123. See *infra*, text at notes 218-63.
124. See *supra*, text at note 85.
125. Suggested by the lower court in Sidis v. F-R Pub. Corp., 34 F. Supp. 19 (S.D.N.Y. 1938).
126. See *infra*, text at note 290.
127. Lord Byron v. Johnston, 2 Mer. 29, 35 Eng. Rep. 851 (1816).
128. See *infra*, text at notes 260-63, 271-73.
129. See Wigmore, *The Right Against False Attribution of Belief or Utterance*, 4 Ky. L.J. No. 8, p. 3 (1916).
130. *Cf.* Pavesich v. New England Life Ins. Co., 122 Ga. 190, 50 S.E. 68 (1905); Manger v. Kree Institute of Electrolysis, 233 F.2d 5 (2d Cir. 1956); Foster-Milburn Co. v. Chinn, 134 Ky. 424, 120 S.W. 364 (1909); Fairfield v. American Photocopy Equipment Co., 138 Cal. App.2d 82, 291 P.2d 194 (1955).
131. Hinish v. Meier & Frank Co., 166 Ore. 482, 113 P.2d 438 (1941). *Accord*, Schwartz v. Edrington, 133 La. 235, 62 So. 660 (1913) (continued circulation of petition after plaintiff had withdrawn his signature).
132. D'Altomonte v. New York Herald Co., 154 App. Div. 453, 139 N.Y.S. 200 (1913), *modified*, however, as not within the New York statute, in 208 N.Y. 596, 102 N.E. 1101 (1913) (authorship of absurd travel story); Hogan v. A.S. Barnes & Co., 114 U.S.P.Q. 314 (Pa. C.P. 1957) (book on golf purporting to give information from plaintiff about his game).
133. State *ex rel.* La Follette v. Hinkle, 131 Wash. 86, 229 Pac. 317 (1924).
134. Hamilton v. Lumbermen's Mutual Cas. Co., 82 So.2d 61 (La. App. 1955).
135. Marks v. Jaffa, 6 Misc. 290, 26 N.Y.S. 908 (Super. Ct. N.Y. City 1893).
136. *Infra*, text at notes 258-59.
137. Peay v. Curtis Pub. Co., 78 F. Supp. 305 (D.D.C. 1948).
138. Leverton v. Curtis Pub. Co., 192 F.2d 974 (3d Cir. 1951).
139. Gill v. Curtis Pub. Co., 38 Cal. 2d 273, 239 P.2d 630 (1952).

140. Martin v. Johnson Pub. Co., 157 N.Y.S.2d 409 (Sup. Ct. 1956). *Accord,* Semler v. Ultem Publications, 170 Misc. 551, 9 N.Y.S.2d 319 (N.Y. City Ct. 1938) (pictures of model in sensational sex magazine); Russell v. Marboro Books, 18 Misc.2d 166, 183 N.Y.S.2d 8 (Sup. Ct. 1959) (picture of model used in bawdy advertisement for bed sheets).
141. Metzger v. Dell Pub. Co., 207 Misc. 182, 136 N.Y.S.2d 888 (Sup. Ct. 1955).
   More doubtful is Callas v. Whisper, Inc., 198 Misc. 829 (1950), *affirmed,* 278 App. Div. 974, 105 N.Y.S.2d 1001 (1951), where the picture of a minor, obtained by fraudulent representations, was used as background in a night club, with the innuendo that she was in a disreputable place. It was held that she had no cause of action. The facts, however, are by no means entirely clear from the summary of the pleading.
142. Thompson v. Close-Up, Inc., 277 App. Div. 848, 98 N.Y.S.2d 300 (1950).
143. Itzkovitch v. Whitaker, 115 La. 479, 39 So. 499 (1950); and see Downs v. Swann, 111 Md. 53, 73 Atl. 653 (1909); State *ex rel.* Mavity v. Tyndall, 224 Ind. 364, 66 N.E.2d 755 (1946); Norman v. City of Las Vegas, 64 Nev. 38, 177 P.2d 442 (1947). *Cf.* Vanderbilt v. Mitchell, 72 N.J. Eq. 910, 67 Atl. 97 (Ct. Err. & App. 1907) (birth certificate naming plaintiff as father of child).
144. Mabry v. Kettering, 89 Ark. 551, 117 S.W. 746 (1909), *second appeal,* 92 Ark. 81, 122 S.W. 115 (1909); State *ex rel.* Mavity v. Tyndall, 224 Ind. 364, 66 N.E.2d 755 (1946); Norman v. City of Las Vegas, 64 Nev. 38, 177 P.2d 442 (1947); Bartletta v. McFeeley, 107 N.J. Eq. 141, 152 Atl. 17 (Ch. 1930), *affirmed,* 109 N.J. Eq. 241, 156 Atl. 658 (Ct. Err. & App. 1931); McGovern v. Van Riper, 140 N.J. Eq. 341, 54 A.2d 469 (Ch. 1947); Downs v. Swann, 111 Md. 53, 73 Atl. 653 (1909).
145. Hodgeman v. Olsen, 86 Wash. 615, 150 Pac. 1122 (1915) (convict); Fernicola v. Keenan, 136 N.J. Eq. 9, 39 A.2d 851 (Ch. 1944).
146. *Cf.* Bennett v. Norban, 396 Pa. 94, 151 A.2d 476 (1959) (accusation of theft upon the street); Linehan v. Linehan, 134 Cal. App.2d 250, 285 P.2d 326 (1955) (public accusation that plaintiff was not the lawful wife of defendant's ex-husband); D'Altomonte v. New York Herald, 154 App. Div. 453, 139 N.Y.S. 200 (1913), *modified,* 208 N.Y. 596, 102 N.E. 1101 (1913) (imputing authorship of absurd travel story); Peay v. Curtis Pub. Co., 78 F. Supp. 305 (D.D.C. 1948) (imputing cheating practices to taxi driver); Martin v. Johnson Pub. Co., 157 N.Y.S.2d 409 (Sup. Ct. 1956) (use of picture with article on "man hungry" women); Russell v. Marboro Books, 18 Misc.2d 166, 183 N.Y.S.2d 8 (Sup. Ct. 1959) (picture used in bawdy advertisement).
147. See *supra,* text at notes 118–25.
148. In Strickler v. National Broadcasting Co., 167 F. Supp. 68 (S.D. Cal. 1958), it was left to the jury to decide whether fictitious details of plaintiff's conduct in an airplane crisis, as portrayed in a broadcast, would be objectionable to a reasonable man.
149. Koussevitzky v. Allen, Towne & Heath, 188 Misc. 479, 68 N.Y.S.2d 779 (Sup. Ct.), *aff'd,* 272 App. Div. 759, 69 N.Y.S.2d 432 (1947).
150. Middleton v. News Syndicate Co., 162 Misc. 516, 295 N.Y.S. 120 (Sup. Ct. 1937).
   It would appear, however, that this was carried entirely too far in Jones v. Herald Post Co., 230 Ky. 227, 18 S.W.2d 972 (1929). There was a newspaper report of the murder of plaintiff's husband in her presence, and false and sensational statements were attributed to her, that she had fought with the criminals, and would have killed them if she could.
151. Pollard v. Photographic Co., 40 Ch. D. 345 (1888).
152. Holmes v. Underwood & Underwood, 225 App. Div. 360, 233 N.Y.S. 153 (1929); Klug v. Sheriffs, 129 Wis. 468, 109 N.W. 656 (1906); Fitzsimmons v. Olinger Mortuary Ass'n, 91 Colo. 544, 17 P.2d 535 (1932); McCreery v. Miller's Grocerteria Co., 99 Colo. 499, 64 P.2d 803 (1936); Bennett v. Gusdorf, 101 Mont. 39, 53 P.2d 91 (1935).

153. *Supra,* text at note 12.
154. *Supra,* note 14.
155. It is not impossible that there might be appropriation of the plaintiff's identity, as by impersonation, without the use of either his name or likeness, and that this would be an invasion of his right of privacy. No such case appears to have arisen.
156. Mackenzie v. Soden Mineral Springs Co., 27 Abb. N. Cal. 402, 18 N.Y.S. 240 (Sup. Ct. 1891); Eliot v. Jones, 66 Misc. 95, 120 N.Y.S. 989 (Sup. Ct. 1910), *aff'd,* 140 App. Div. 911, 125 N.Y.S. 1119 (1910); Thompson v. Tillford, 152 App. Div. 928, 137 N.Y.S. 523 (1912); Brociner v. Radio Wire Television, Inc., 15 Misc.2d 843, 183 N.Y.S.2d 743 (Sup. Ct. 1959) (use in union drive for membership held advertising); Birmingham Broadcasting Co. v. Bell, 259 Ala. 656, 68 So.2d 314 (1953), *later appeal,* 266 Ala. 266, 96 So.2d 263 (1957); Kerby v. Hal Roach Studios, 53 Cal. App. 2d 207, 127 P.2d 577 (1942); Fairfield v. American Photocopy Equipment Co., 138 Cal. App.2d 82, 291 P.2d 194 (1955).

In the cases cited in the next note, the plaintiff's name accompanied the picture.
157. Fisher v. Murray M. Rosenberg, Inc., 175 Misc. 370, 23 N.Y.S.2d 677 (Sup. Ct. 1940); Russell v. Marboro Books, 18 Misc.2d 166, 183 N.Y.S.2d 8 (Sup. Ct. 1959); Flores v. Mosler Safe Co., 7 N.Y.2d 276, 164 N.E.2d 853 (1959), *affirming* 7 App. Div. 226, 182 N.Y.S.2d 126 (1959); Korn v. Rennison, 156 A.2d 476 (Conn. Super. 1959); Pavesich v. New England Life Ins. Co., 122 Ga. 190, 50 S.E. 68 (1905); Colgate-Palmolive Co. v. Tullos, 219 F.2d 617 (5th Cir. 1955) (Georgia law); Eick v. Perk Dog Food Co., 347 Ill. App. 293, 106 N.E.2d 742 (1952); Continental Optical Co. v. Reed, 119 Ind. App. 643, 86 N.E.2d 306 (1949); Kunz v. Allen, 102 Kan. 883, 172 Pac. 532 (1918); Foster-Milburn Co. v. Chinn, 134 Ky. 424, 120 S.W. 364 (1909); Pallas v. Crowley, Milner & Co., 322 Mich. 411, 33 N.W.2d 911 (1948); Munden v. Harris, 153 Mo. App. 652, 134 S.W. 1076 (1911); Flake v. Greensboro News Co., 212 N.C. 780, 195 S.E. 55 (1938).
158. Young v. Greneker Studios, 175 Misc. 1027, 26 N.Y.S.2d 357 (Sup. Ct. 1941) (manikin). In Freed v. Loew's, Inc., 175 Misc. 616, 24 N.Y.S.2d 679 (Sup. Ct. 1940), an artist used the plaintiff's figure as a base, but improved it, and it was held not to be a "portrait or picture" within the New York statute. But in Loftus v. Greenwich Lithographing Co., 192 App. Div. 251, 182 N.Y.S. 428 (1920), the artist used the plaintiff's picture in designing a poster, but made some changes, and the result was held not to fall within the statute. The difference between the two cases may have been one of the extent of the resemblance.
159. Neyland v. Home Pattern Co., 65 F.2d 363 (2d Cir. 1933) (patterns); Lane v. F.W. Woolworth Co., 171 Misc. 66, 11 N.Y.S.2d 199 (Sup. Ct. 1939), *aff'd,* 256 App. Div. 1065, 12 N.Y.S.2d 352 (1939) (lockets); McNulty v. Press Pub. Co., 136 Misc. 833, 241 N.Y.S. 29 (Sup. Ct. 1930 (cartoon containing photograph); Jansen v. Hilo Packing Co., 202 Misc. 900, 118 N.Y.S.2d 162 (Sup. Ct. 1952), *aff'd,* 282 App. Div. 935, 125 N.Y.S.2d 648 (1952) (popcorn); Miller v. Madison Square Garden Corp., 176 Misc. 714, 28 N.Y.S.2d 811 (Sup. Ct. 1941) (booklet sold at bicycle races).

Also, of course, when there is an unauthorized sale of the picture itself. Kunz v. Boselman, 131 App. Div. 288, 115 N.Y.S. 650 (1909); Wyatt v. James McCreery Co., 126 App. Div. 650, 111 N.Y.S. 86 (1908); Holmes v. Underwood & Underwood, 225 App. Div. 360, 233 N.Y.S. 153 (1929).
160. Von Thodorovich v. Franz Josef Beneficial Ass'n, 154 Fed. 911 (E.D. Pa. 1907); Edison v. Edison Polyform Mfg. Co., 73 N.J. Eq. 136, 67 Atl. 392 (Ch. 1907). *Cf.* U.S. Life Ins. Co. v. Hamilton, 238 S.W.2d 289 (Tex. Civ. App. 1951), where the use of an employee's name on company letterhead after termination of his employment was said not to invade his right of privacy (not recognized in Texas), but was held to be actionable anyway.

161. In Hogan v. A.S. Barnes Co., 114 U.S.P.Q. 314 (1957) (book); Binns v. Vitagraph Co. of America, 210 N.Y. 51, 103 N.E. 1108 (1913) (motion picture); Redmond v. Columbia Pictures Corp., 277 N.Y. 707, 14 N.E.2d 636 (1938); *affirming* 253 App. Div. 708, 1 N.Y.S.2d 643 (same); Stryker v. Republic Pictures Corp., 108 Cal. App. 2d 191, 238 P.2d 670 (1951) (same); Ettore v. Philco Television Broadcasting Co., 229 F.2d 481 (3d Cir. 1956) (motion picture exhibited on television); Almind v. Sea Beach Co., 78 Misc. 445, 139 N.Y.S. 559 (Sup. Ct. 1912), *aff'd*, 157 App. Div. 927, 142 N.Y.S. 1106 (1913) (picture of plaintiff entering or leaving street car used to teach other passengers how to do it).

In Donahue v. Warner Bros. Pictures, 194 F.2d 6 (10th Cir. 1952), it was held that a motion picture, based upon the life of a deceased celebrity but partly fictional, and using his name, came within the Utah statute. But in Donohue v. Warner Bros. Pictures Distributing Corp., 2 Utah 2d 256, 272 P.2d 177 (1954), the state court rejected this decision, and indicated that the statute was to be limited to the use of name or likeness in advertising, or the sale of "some collateral commodity." The effect of this is to nullify the federal decision.

162. *Supra*, text at note 14.
163. In Oklahoma, Utah, and Virginia. See *supra* notes 52–54.
164. See, as illustrations of possible differences: Cardy v. Maxwell, 9 Misc. 2d 329, 169 N.Y.S.2d 547 (Sup. Ct. 1957) (use of name and publicity to extort money not a commercial use within the statute); Hamilton v. Lumbermen's Mutual Cas. Co., 82 So.2d 61 (La. App. 1955) (advertising in name of plaintiff for witnesses of accident); State *ex rel.* La Follette v. Hinkle, 131 Wash. 86, 229 Pac. 317 (1924) (use of name as candidate for office by political party). See also the cases cited *infra*, notes 167 and 168.
165. Du Boulay v. Du Boulay, L.R. 2 P.C. 430 (1869); Cowley v. Cowley, [1901] A.C. 450; Brown Chemical Co. v. Meyer, 139 U.S. 540 (1891); Smith v. United States Casualty Co., 197 N.Y. 420, 90 N.E. 947 (1910); Baumann v. Baumann, 250 N.Y. 382, 165 N.E. 819 (1929); Bartholomew v. Workman, 197 Okla. 267, 169 P.2d 1012 (1946).
166. "While I know of no instance, it can safely be assumed that should *A*, by the use of *B*'s name, together with other characteristics of *B*, successfully impersonate *B*, and thereby obtain valuable recognition or benefits from a third person, a suit by *B* against *A* could be maintained." Green, *The Right of Privacy*, 27 Ill. L. Rev. 237, 243–44 (1932).

Three years after these words were published, recovery was allowed in such a case. Goodyear Tire & Rubber Co., v. Vandergriff, 52 Ga. App. 662, 184 S.E. 452 (1936), in which defendant, impersonating plaintiff's agent, obtained confidential information from dealers about tire prices.

167. Burns v. Stevens, 236 Mich. 443, 210 N.W. 482 (1926). *Contra*, Baumann v. Baumann, 250 N.Y. 382, 165 N.E. 819 (1929); *but cf.* Niver v. Niver, 200 Misc. 993, 111 N.Y.S.2d 889 (Sup. Ct. 1951).
168. Vanderbilt v. Mitchell, 72 N.J. Eq. 910, 67 Atl. 97 (Ct. Err. & App. 1907).
169. Swacker v. Wright, 154 Misc. 822, 277 N.Y.S. 296 (Sup. Ct. 1935); People v. Charles Scribner's Sons, 205 Misc. 818, 130 N.Y.S.2d 514 (N.Y. City Magis. Ct. 1954).
170. Nebb v. Bell Syndicate, 41 F. Supp. 929 (S.D.N.Y. 1941).
171. Pfaudler v. Pfaudler Co., 114 Misc. 477, 186 N.Y.S. 725 (Sup. Ct. 1920).
172. In Uproar Co. v. National Broadcasting Co., 8 F. Supp. 358 (D. Mass. 1934), *affirmed as modified*, 81 F.2d 373 (1st Cir. 1936), the comedian Ed Wynn published, in pamphlet form, humorous skits which he had performed on the radio, in which he made frequent mention of "Graham." It was held that the public would reasonably understand this to refer to Graham McNamee, a radio announcer who had been his foil.

In Kerby v. Hal Roach Studios, 53 Ca. App.2d 207, 127 P.2d 577 (1942), defendant, advertising a motion picture, made use of the name Marion Kerby, which was signed to a letter apparently suggesting an assignation. Plaintiff, an actress named Marion Kerby, was the only person of that name listed in the city directory and the telephone book. She had in fact a large number of telephone calls about the letter. It was held that it might reasonably be understood to refer to her.

In Krieger v. Popular Publications, 167 Misc. 5, 3 N.Y.S.2d 480 (Sup. Ct., 1938), a complaint alleging that the plaintiff was a professional boxer, and that the defendant had appropriated his name by publishing a story about such a boxer of the same name, which appeared more than a hundred times in twenty pages, was held sufficient to state a cause of action.

On the other hand, in Levey v. Warner Bros. Pictures, 57 F. Supp 40 (S.D.N.Y. 1944), the plaintiff, whose name was Mary, was the divorced first wife of the actor George M. Cohan. The defendant made a motion picture of his life, in which the part of the wife, named Mary, was played by an actress. The part was almost entirely fictional, and there was no mention of the divorce. It was held that this could not reasonably be understood to be a portrayal of the plaintiff.

In such cases the test appears to be that usually applied in cases of defamation, as to whether a reasonable man would understand the name to identify the plaintiff. Compare Harrison v. Smith, 20 L.T.R. (n.s.) 713 (1869); Clare v. Farrell, 70 F. Supp. 276 (D. Minn. 1947); Macfadden's Publications v. Turner, 95 S.W.2d 1027 (Tex. Civ. App. 1936); Landau v. Columbia Broadcasting System, 205 Misc. 357, 128 N.Y.S.2d 254 (Sup. Ct. 1954); Newton v. Grubb, 155 Ky. 479, 159 S.W. 994 (1913).

173. Mackenzie v. Soden Mineral Springs Co., 27 Abb. N. Cas. 402, 18 N.Y.S. 240 (Sup. Ct. 1891) (signature); Orsini v. Eastern Wine Corp., 190 Misc. 235, 73 N.Y.S.2d 426 (Sup. Ct. 1947), *aff'd,* 273 App. Div. 947, 78 N.Y.S.2d 224 (1948), *appeal denied,* 273 App. Div. 996, 79 N.Y.S.2d 870 (1948) (plaintiff's coat of arms).

174. The only cases have involved construction of the New York statute, as to the use of the plaintiff's "name." In Davis v. R.K.O. Radio Pictures, 16 F. Supp. 195 (S.D.N.Y. 1936), where a clairvoyant made use of the name "Cassandra," it was held that this was limited to genuine names. In Gardella v. Log Cabin Products Co., 89 F.2d 891 (2d Cir. 1937), a trade mark case, a dictum disagreed, and said that the statute would cover a stage name. In People v. Charles Scribner's Sons, 205 Misc. 818, 130 N.Y.S.2d 514 (N.Y. City Magis. Ct. 1954), it was said that there was no protection of an "assumed" name, and doubt as to a "stage name." In the unreported case of Van Duren v. Fawcett Publications, No. 13114, S.D. Cal. 1952, the court regarded the *Davis* case as controlling New York law, and disregarded the *Gardella* case as dictum.

Apart from statutory language, however, it is suggested that the text statement is correct. The suggestion, for example, that Samuel L. Clemens would have a cause of action when that name was used in advertising, but not for the use of "Mark Twain," fully speaks for itself.

175. Brewer v. Hearst Pub. Co., 185 F.2d 846 (7th Cir. 1950). *Cf.* Sellers v. Henry, 329 S.W.2d 214 (Ky. 1959), and Waters v. Fleetwood, 212 Ga. 161, 91 S.E.2d 344 (1956), where there were photographs of unidentifiable dead bodies.

176. Rozhon v. Triangle Publications, 230 F.2d 359 (7th Cir. 1956). In accord is the unreported case of Cole v. Goodyear Tire & Rubber Co., App. Dept. Superior Court, San Francisco, Calif., Nov. 21, 1955.

177. Branson v. Fawcett Publications, 124 F. Supp. 429 (E.D. Ill. 1954).

178. Lawrence v. Ylla, 184 Misc. 807, 55 N.Y.S.2d 343 (Sup. Ct. 1945).

179. Toscani v. Hersey, 271 App. Div. 445, 65 N.Y.S.2d 814 (1946). *Cf.* Bernstein v. National Broadcasting Co., 129 F. Supp. 817 (D.D.C. 1955), *aff'd,* 232 F.2d 369 (D.C. Cir. 1956); Miller v. National Broadcasting Co., 157 F. Supp. 240 (D. Del. 1957); Levey v. Warner Bros. Pictures, 57 F. Supp. 40 (S.D.N.Y. 1944).

180. See, for example, State *ex rel.* La Follette v. Hinkle, 131 Wash. 86, 229 Pac. 317 (1924) (use of name as candidate by political party): Hinish v. Meier & Frank Co., 166 Ore. 482, 113 P.2d 438 (1941) (name signed to telegram urging governor to veto a bill); Schwartz v. Edrington, 133 La. 235, 62 So. 660 (1913) (name signed to petition); Vanderbilt v. Mitchell, 72 N.J. Eq. 910, 67 Atl. 97 (Ct. Err. & App. 1907) (birth certificate naming plaintiff as father); Burns v. Stevens, 236 Mich. 443, 210 N.W. 482 (1926) (posing as plaintiff's common law wife).
181. Colyer v. Richard K. Fox Pub. Co., 162 App. Div. 297, 146 N.Y.S. 999 (1914).
182. See Donahue v. Warner Bros. Picture Distributing Corp., 2 Utah 2d 256, 272 Pac. 177 (1954).
183. Damron v. Doubleday, Doran & Co., 133 Misc. 302, 231 N.Y.S. 444 (Sup. Ct. 1928), *aff'd*, 226 App. Div. 796, 234 N.Y.S. 773 (1929); Shubert v. Columbia Pictures Corp., 189 Misc. 734, 72 N.Y.S2d 851 (Sup. Ct. 1947), *aff'd,* 274 App. Div. 571, 80 N.Y.S.2d 724 (1948), *appeal denied,* 274 App. Div. 880, 83 N.Y.S.2d 233 (1948).
184. Stillman v. Paramount Pictures Corp., 1 Misc. 2d 108, 147 N.Y.S.2d 504 (Sup. Ct. 1956), *aff'd,* 2 App. Div.2d 18, 153 N.Y.S. 2d 190 (1956), *appeal denied,* 2 App. Div.2d 886, 157 N.Y.S.2d 899 (1956).
185. Wallach v. Bacharach, 192 Misc. 979, 80 N.Y.S.2d 37 (Sup. Ct. 1948), *aff'd,* 274 App. Div. 919, 84 N.Y.S.2d 894 (1948).

   In accord is O'Brien v. Pabst Sales Co., 124 F.2d 167 (5th Cir. 1941), where the court refused to find a commercial use in the publication of the pictures of an all-American football team on a calendar advertising the defendant's beer, with no suggestion that the team endorsed it.
186. Dallessandro v. Henry Holt & Co., 4 App. Div. 2d 470, 166 N.Y.S.2d 805 (1957) (plaintiff's photograph while conversing with a priest who was the subject of the book).
187. Humiston v. Universal Film Mfg. Co., 189 App. Div. 467, 178 N.Y.S. 752 (1919); Merle v. Sociological Research Film Corp., 166 App. Div. 376, 152 N.Y.S. 829 (1915) (picture of plaintiff's factory showing his name).
188. Binns v. Vitagraph Co. of America, 147 App. Div. 783, 132 N.Y.S. 237 (1911), *aff'd,* 210 N.Y. 51, 103 N.E. 1108 (1913).
189. Holmes v. Underwood & Underwood, 225 App. Div. 360, 233 N.Y.S. 153 (1929); Sutton v. Hearst Corp., 277 App. Div. 155, 98 N.Y.S.2d 233 (1950), *appeal denied,* 297 App. Div. 873, 98 N.Y.S.2d 589 (1950); Garner v. Triangle Publications, 97 F. Supp. 546 (S.D.N.Y. 1951).
190. Semler v. Ultem Publications, 170 Misc. 551, 9 N.Y.S.2d 319 (N.Y. City Ct. 1938); Thompson v. Close-Up, Inc., 277 App. Div. 848, 98 N.Y.S.2d 300 (1950); Metzger v. Dell Pub. Co., 207 Misc. 182, 136 N.Y.S.2d 888 (Sup. Ct. 1955); Martin v. Johnson Pub. Co., 157 N.Y.S.2d 409 (Sup. Ct. 1956). These were all cases involving the use of plaintiff's picture to illustrate articles with which he had no connection.
191. *Supra,* text at notes 126–50.
192. See Rhodes v. Sperry & Hutchinson Co., 193 N.Y. 223, 85 N.E. 1097 (1908); Gautier v. Pro-Football, Inc., 304 N.Y. 354, 107 N.E.2d 485 (1952); Mau v. Rio Grande Oil, Inc., 28 F. Supp. 845 (N.D. Cal. 1939); Hull v. Curtis Pub. Co., 182 Pa. Super. 86, 125 A.2d 644 (1956); Metter v. Los Angeles Examiner, 35 Cal. App.2d 304, 95 P.2d 491 (1939); Ludwig, *"Peace of Mind" in 48 Pieces vs. Uniform Right of Privacy,* 32 Minn. L. Rev. 734 (1948).
193. Haelan Laboratories v. Topps Chewing Gum, Inc., 202 F.2d 866 (2d Cir. 1953), *reversing* Bowman Gum Co. v. Topps Chewing Gum, Inc., 103 F. Supp. 944 (E.D.N.Y. 1952).
194. Nimmer, *The Right of Publicity,* 19 Law & Contemp. Prob. 203 (1954); Notes, 62 Yale L.J. 1123 (1953); 41 Geo. L.J. 583 (1953).

195. The "right of publicity" was held not to exist in California in Strickler v. National Broadcasting Co., 167 F. Supp. 68 (S.D. Cal. 1958). It was rejected in Pekas Co. v. Leslie, 52 N.Y.L.J. 1864 (Sup. Ct. 1915).

It appears to have been foreshadowed when relief was granted on other grounds in Uproar Co. v. National Broadcasting Co., 8 F. Supp. 358 (D. Mass. 1934), *modified* in 81 F.2d 373 (1st Cir. 1936); Liebig's Extract of Meat Co. v. Liebig Extract Co., 180 Fed. 68 (2d Cir. 1910). See also Madison Square Garden Corp. v. Universal Pictures Co., 255 App. Div. 459, 7 N.Y.S.2d 845 (1938).

196. In Ettore v. Philco Television Broadcasting Co., 229 F.2d 481 (3d Cir. 1956).
197. Gill v. Hearst Pub. Co., 40 Cal. 2d 224, 253 P.2d 441 (1953). The complaint alleged the publication of the picture in connection with the article involved in the other case, but failed to plead that the defendant had authorized it. A demurrer was sustained, but the plaintiff was permitted to amend.
198. Gill v. Curtis Pub. Co., 38 Cal. 2d 273, 239 P.2d 630 (1952).
199. *E.g.,* the defendant breaks into the plaintiff's home, steals his photograph, and publishes it with false statements about the plaintiff in his advertising.
200. Murray v. Gast Lithographic & Engraving Co., 8 Misc. 36, 28 N.Y.S. 271 (N.Y.C.P. 1894); Rozhon v. Triangle Publications, 230 F.2d 539 (7th Cir. 1956); Waters v. Fleetwood, 212 Ga. 161, 91 S.E.2d 344 (1956); Bremmer v. Journal-Tribune Co., 247 Iowa 817, 76 N.W.2d 762 (1956); Kelly v. Johnson Pub. Co., 160 Cal. App.2d 718, 325 P.2d 659 (1958). See also the cases cited *infra,* note 202.
201. Walker v. Whittle, 83 Ga. App. 445, 64 S.E.2d 87 (1951) (intrusion into home to arrest husband). See Coverstone v. Davies, 38 Cal. 2d 315, 239 P.2d 876 (1952); Smith v. Doss, 251 Ala. 250, 37 So.2d 118 (1948); and *cf.* Bazemore v. Savannah Hospital, 171 Ga. 257, 155 S.E. 195 (1930); Douglas v. Stokes, 149 Ky. 506, 149 S.W. 849 (1912).
202. Hanna Mfg. Co. v. Hillerich & Bradsby Co., 78 F.2d 763 (5th Cir. 1939); Wyatt v. Hall's Portrait Studios, 71 Misc. 199, 128 N.Y.S. 247 (Sup. Ct. 1911); Murray v. Gast Lithographic & Engraving Co., 8 Misc. 36, 28 N.Y.S. 271 (N.Y.C.P. 1894); Rhodes v. Sperry & Hutchinson Co., 193 N.Y. 223, 85 N.E. 1097 (1908). *Cf.* Von Thodorovich v. Franz Josef Beneficial Ass'n, 154 Fed. 911 (E.D. Pa. 1907) (Austrian diplomat cannot maintain action on behalf of Emperor of Austria).
203. Reed v. Real Detective Pub. Co., 63 Ariz. 294, 162 P.2d 133 (1945).
204. Wyatt v. Hall's Portrait Studios, 71 Misc. 199, 128 N.Y.S. 247 (Sup. Ct. 1911); Lunceford v. Wilcox, 88 N.Y.S.2d 225 (N.Y. City Ct. 1949).
205. Schuyler v. Curtis, 147 N.Y. 434, 42 N.E. 22 (1895); *In re* Hart's Estate, 193 Misc. 884, 83 N.Y.S.2d 635 (Surr. Ct. 1948); Schumann v. Loew's, Inc., 199 Misc. 38, 102 N.Y.S.2d 572 (Sup. Ct. 1951), *aff'd,* 135 N.Y.S.2d 361 (Sup. Ct. 1954); Rozhon v. Triangle Publications, 230 F.2d 539 (7th Cir. 1956); Abernathy v. Thornton, 263 Ala. 496, 83 So.2d 235 (1955); Metter v. Los Angeles Examiner, 35 Cal. App.2d 304, 95 P.2d 491 (1939); Kelly v. Johnson Pub. Co., 160 Cal. App.2d 718, 325 P.2d 659 (1958); James v. Screen Gems, Inc., 174 Cal. App. 2d 650, 344 P.2d 799 (1959); Kelley v. Post Pub. Co., 327 Mass. 275, 98 N.E.2d 286 (1951); Bartholomew v. Workman, 197 Okl. 267, 169 P.2d 1012 (1946). *Cf.* Atkinson v. John E. Doherty & Co., 121 Mich. 372, 80 N.W. 285 (1899).

As in the case of living persons, however, a publication concerning one who is dead may invade the separate right of privacy of surviving relatives. See the last three cases cited *supra* and note 198.

206. *Supra,* notes 52–54. See Donahue v. Warner Bros. Pictures, 194 F.2d 6 (10th Cir. 1952); Donahue v. Warner Bros. Pictures Distributing Corp., 2 Utah 2d 256, 272 P.2d 177 (1954).

207. Jaggard v. R.H. Macy & Co., 176 Misc. 88, 26 N.Y.S.2d 829 (Sup. Ct. 1941), *aff'd*, 265 App. Div. 15, 37 N.Y.S.2d 570 (1942); Shubert v. Columbia Pictures Corp., 189 Misc. 734, 72 N.Y.S.2d 851 (Sup. Ct. 1947), *aff'd*, 274 App. Div. 571, 80 N.Y.S.2d 724 (1948), *appeal denied*, 274 App. Div. 880, 83 N.Y.S.2d 233 (1948); Maysville Transit Co. v. Ort, 296 Ky. 524, 177 S.W.2d 369 (1944); United States v. Morton, 338 U.S. 632 (1950).
208. Rosenwasser v. Ogoglia, 172 App. Div. 107, 158 N.Y.S. 56 (1916).
209. Vassar College v. Loose-Wiles Biscuit Co., 197 Fed. 982 (W.D. Mo. 1912).
210. Reed v. Real Detective Pub. Co., 63 Ariz. 294, 162 P.2d 133 (1945); Fairfield v. American Photocopy Equipment Co., 138 Cal. App.2d 82, 291 P.2d 194 (1955); Cason v. Baskin, 155 Fla. 198, 20 So.2d 243 (1945); Pavesich v. New England Life Ins. Co., 122 Ga. 190, 50 S.E. 68 (1905); Kunz v. Allen, 102 Kan. 883, 172 Pac. 532 (1918); Foster-Milburn Co. v. Chinn, 134 Ky. 424, 120 S.W. 364 (1909); Munden v. Harris, 153 Mo. App. 652, 134 S.W. 1076 (1911); Flake v. Greensboro News Co., 212 N.C. 780, 195 S.E. 55 (1938).
211. Brents v. Morgan, 221 Ky. 765, 299 S.W. 967 (1927); Rhodes v. Graham, 238 Ky. 225, 37 S.W.2d 46 (1951); Hinish v. Meier & Frank Co., 166 Ore. 482, 113 P.2d 438 (1941); Fairfield v. American Photocopy Equipment Co., 138 Cal. App.2d 82, 291 P.2d 194 (1955).
212. Pavesich v. New England Life Ins. Co., 122 Ga. 190, 50 S.E. 68 (1905); Sutherland v. Kroger Co., 110 S.E.2d 716 (W. Va. 1959). In Cason v. Baskin, 159 Fla. 31, 30 So.2d 635 (1947), where there was evidence that the plaintiff had suffered no great distress, and had gained weight, the recovery was limited to nominal damages.
213. Bunnell v. Keystone Varnish Co., 254 App. Div. 885, 5 N.Y.S.2d 415 (1938), *affirming* 167 Misc. 707, 4 N.Y.S.2d 601 (Sup. Ct. 1938).
214. Continental Optical Co. v. Reed, 119 Ind. App. 643, 86 N.E.2d 306 (1949); Manger v. Kree Institute of Electrolysis, 233 F.2d 5 (2d Cir. 1956); Hogan v. A.S. Barnes & Co., 114 U.S.P.Q. 314 (Pa. C.P. 1957). Likewise, the fact that the plaintiff has benefited in his profession by the publicity may be considered in mitigation, and may reduce his recovery to nominal damages. Harris v. H.W. Gossard Co., 194 App. Div. 688, 185 N.Y.S. 861 (1921).
215. Munden v. Harris, 153 Mo. App. 652, 134 S.W. 1076 (1911); Hinish v. Meier & Frank Co., 166 Ore. 482, 113 P.2d 438 (1941); Welsh v. Pritchard, 125 Mont. 517, 241 P.2d 816 (1952).
216. Fisher v. Murray M. Rosenberg, Inc., 175 Misc. 370, 23 N.Y.S.2d 667 (Sup. Ct. 1940); Barber v. Time, Inc., 348 Mo. 1199, 159 S.W.2d 291 (1942). But in Myers v. U.S. Camera Pub. Corp., 9 Misc.2d 765, 167 N.Y.S.2d 771 (N.Y. City Ct. 1957), punitive damages were allowed where the defendant "knew or should have known."

In Harlow v. Buno Co., 36 Pa. D.&C. 101 (C.P. 1939), the fact that the defendant had acted in good faith under a forged consent was held to defeat the action entirely. This appears to be wrong. *Cf.* Kerby v. Hal Roach Studios, 53 Cal. App. 2d 207, 127 P.2d 577 (1942), where the defendant made use of the plaintiff's name without even being aware of her existence.
217. In Themo v. New England Newspaper Pub. Co., 306 Mass. 54, 27 N.E.2d 753 (1940), it was said that these privileges are not technically defenses, and the absence of a privileged occasion must be pleaded and proved by the plaintiff. This is the only case found bearing on the question; but it may be doubted that other jurisdictions will agree.
218. Cason v. Baskin, 159 Fla. 31, 30 So.2d 635, 638 (1947).
219. The question of degree has not been discussed in the cases. In Kerby v. Hal Roach Studios, 53 Cal. App. 2d 207, 127 P.2d 577 (1942), the plaintiff was an actress, concert singer and monologist, so obscure that the defendant's studio had never heard of her. She was allowed to recover for appropriation of her name and a false light before the public,

without mention of whether she was a public figure, which obviously would have made no difference in the decision. It may be suggested that even an obscure entertainer may be a public figure to some limited extent, but that the field in which she may be given further publicity may be more narrowly limited. See *infra*, text at notes 282–84.
220. Paramount Pictures v. Leader Press, 24 F. Supp. 1004 (W.D. Okl. 1938), *reversed on other grounds* in 106 F.2d 229 (10th Cir. 1939); Chaplin v. National Broadcasting Co., 15 F.R.D. 134 (S.D.N.Y. 1953).
221. Ruth v. Educational Films, 194 App. Div. 893, 184 N.Y.S. 948 (1920); see Jansen v. Hilo Packing Co., 202 Misc. 900, 118 N.Y.S.2d 162 (Sup. Ct. 1952), *aff'd*, 282 App. Div. 935, 125 N.Y.S.2d 648 (1953). *Cf.* O'Brien v. Pabst Sales Co., 124 F.2d 167 (5th Cir. 1941) (all-American football player).
222. Jeffries v. New York Evening Journal Pub. Co., 67 Misc. 570, 125 N.Y.S. 780 (Sup. Ct. 1910); Cohen v. Marx, 94 Cal. App. 2d 704, 211 P.2d 320 (1950); Oma v. Hillman Periodicals, 281 App. Div. 240, 118 N.Y.S.2d 720 (1953).
223. Colyer v. Richard K. Fox Pub. Co., 162 App. Div. 297, 146 N.Y.S. 999 (1914) (high diver); Koussevitzky v. Allen, Towne & Heath, 188 Misc. 479, 68 N.Y.S.2d 779 (Sup. Ct. 1947), *aff'd*, 272 App. Div. 759, 69 N.Y.S.2d 432 (1947) (symphony conductor); Gavrilov v. Duell, Sloan & Pierce, 84 N.Y.S.2d 320 (Sup. Ct. 1948) (dancer); Redmond v. Columbia Pictures Corp., 277 N.Y. 707, 14 N.E.2d 636 (1938), *affirming* 253 App. Div. 708, 1 N.Y.S.2d 643 (trick shot golfer). *Cf.* Gautier v. Pro-Football, Inc., 304 N.Y. 354, 107 N.E.2d 485 (1952) (performing animal act at football game); Goelet v. Confidential, Inc., 5 App. Div. 2d 226, 171 N.Y.S.2d 223 (1958) (unspecified).
224. Martin v. Dorton, 210 Miss. 668, 50 So.2d 391 (1951) (sheriff); Hull v. Curtis Pub. Co., 182 Pa. Super. 86, 125 A.2d 644 (1956) (arrest by policeman).
225. Corliss v. E.W. Walker Co., 64 Fed. 280 (D. Mass. 1894). *Cf.* Thompson v. Curtis Pub. Co., 193 F.2d 953 (3d Cir. 1952).
226. Smith v. Suratt, 7 Alaska 416 (1926).
227. Stryker v. Republic Pictures Corp., 108 Cal. App.2d 191, 238 P.2d 670 (1951). *Accord*, Molony v. Boy Comics Publishers, 277 App. Div. 166, 98 N.Y.S.2d 119 (1950), *reversing* 188 Misc. 450, 65 N.Y.S.2d 173 (Sup. Ct. 1946) (hero in disaster).
228. See Continental Optical Co. v. Reed, 119 Ind. App. 643, 86 N.E.2d 306 (1949).
229. Sidis v. F-R. Pub. Corp., 113 F.2d 806 (2d Cir. 1940), *affirming* 34 F. Supp. 19 (S.D.N.Y. 1938).
230. Wilson v. Brown, 189 Misc. 79, 73 N.Y.S.2d 587 (Sup. Ct. 1947).
231. Cason v. Baskin, 155 Fla. 198, 20 So.2d 243 (1945), *second appeal*, 159 Fla. 31, 30 So.2d 635 (1947). A book, *Cross Creek*, which became a best seller, was written about the back woods people of Florida, and an obscure local woman was described in embarrassing personal detail. It was held that she did not became [sic] a public figure.
232. See cases cited *supra*, notes 221-231.
233. Sweenek v. Pathe News, 16 F. Supp. 746, 747 (E.D.N.Y. 1936).
234. Jones v. Herald Post Co., 230 Ky. 227, 18 S.W.2d 972 (1929); Bremmer v. Journal-Tribune Co., 247 Iowa 817, 76 N.W.2d 762 (1956); Waters v. Fleetwood, 212 Ga. 161, 91 S.E.2d 344 (1956); Jenkins v. Dell Pub. Co., 143 F. Supp. 953 (W.D. Pa. 1956), *aff'd*, 251 F.2d 447 (3d Cir. 1958); Bernstein v. National Broadcasting Co., 129 F. Supp. 817 (D.D.C. 1955), *aff'd*, 232 F.2d 369 (D.C. Cir. 1956).
235. Elmhurst v. Pearson, 153 F.2d 467 (D.C. Cir. 1946) (sedition); Miller v. National Broadcasting Co., 157 F. Supp. 240 (D. Del. 1957) (robbery); Hillman v. Star Pub. Co., 64 Wash. 691, 117 Pac. 594 (1911) (mail fraud).
236. Frith v. Associated Press, 176 F. Supp. 671 (E.D.S.C. 1959) (mob action); Coverstone v. Davies, 38 Cal. 2d 315, 239 P.2d 876 (1952) ("hot-rod" race); Hull v. Curtis Pub. Co., 182 Pa. Super. 86, 125 A.2d 644 (1956).

237. Jacova v. Southern Radio & Television Co., 83 So.2d 34 (Fla. 1955). *Cf.* Schnabel v. Meredith, 378 Pa. 609, 107 A.2d 860 (1954).
238. Metter v. Los Angeles Examiner, 35 Cal. App.2d 304, 95 P.2d 491 (1939); and see Samuel v. Curtis Pub. Co., 122 F. Supp. 327 (N.D. Cal. 1954).
239. Aquino v. Bulletin Co., 154 A.2d 422, 190 Pa. Super. 528 (1959).
240. Berg v. Minneapolis Star & Tribune Co., 79 F. Supp. 957 (D. Minn. 1948); Aquino v. Bulletin Co., 154 A.2d 422, 190 Pa. Super. 528 (1959).
241. Kelley v. Post Pub. Co., 327 Mass. 275, 98 N.E.2d 286 (1951). *Cf.* Strickler v. National Broadcasting Co., 167 F. Supp. 68 (S.D. Cal. 1958) (crisis in airplane).
242. Rozhon v. Triangle Publications, 230 F.2d 539 (7th Cir. 1956). *Cf.* Abernathy v. Thornton, 263 Ala. 496, 83 So.2d 235 (1955) (death of criminal paroled for federal offense).
243. Barber v. Time, Inc., 348 Mo. 1199, 159 S.W.2d 291 (1942).
244. Meetze v. Associated Press, 230 S.C. 330, 95 S.E.2d 606 (1956).
245. Langford v. Vanderbilt University, 199 Tenn. 389, 287 S.W.2d 32 (1956).
246. Smith v. National Broadcasting Co., 138 Cal. App.2d 807, 292 P.2d 600 (1956).
247. Smith v. Doss, 251 Ala. 250, 37 So.2d 118 (1948).
248. See, as to unspecified news, Moser v. Press Pub. Co., 59 Misc. 78, 109 N.Y.S. 963 (Sup. Ct. 1908); Themo v. New England Newspaper Pub. Co., 306 Mass. 54, 27 N.E.2d 753 (1940).
249. Ruth v. Educational Films, 194 App. Div. 893, 184 N.Y.S. 948 (1920) (baseball); Sweenek v. Pathe News, 16 F. Supp. 746 (E.D.N.Y. 1936) (group of fat women reducing with novel and comical apparatus); and see Jenkins v. Dell Pub. Co., 143 F. Supp. 953 (W.D. Pa. 1956), *aff'd,* 251 F.2d 447 (3d Cir. 1958).
250. People *ex rel.* Stern v. Robert M. McBride & Co., 159 Misc. 5, 288 N.Y.S. 501 (N.Y. City Magis. Ct. 1936) (strike-breaking); Kline v. Robert M. McBride & Co., 170 Misc. 974, 11 N.Y.S.2d 674 (Sup. Ct. 1939) (same); Samuel v. Curtis Pub. Co., 122 F. Supp. 327 (N.D. Cal. 1954) (suicide); Hogan v. A.S. Barnes Co., 114 U.S.P.Q. 314 (Pa. C.P. 1957) (golf); Oma v. Hillman Periodicals, 281 App. Div. 240, 118 N.Y.S.2d 720 (1953) (boxing); Delinger v. American News Co., 6 App. Div. 2d 1027, 178 N.Y.S.2d 231 (1958) (muscular development and virility).
251. Humiston v. Universal Film Mfg. Co., 189 App. Div. 467, 178 N.Y.S. 752 (1919). *Cf.* Gill v. Hearst Pub. Co., 40 Cal. 2d 224, 253 P.2d 441 (1953) (market place); Berg v. Minneapolis Star & Tribune Co., 79 F. Supp. 957 (D. Minn. 1948) (photograph in courtroom); Lyles v. State, 330 P.2d 734 (Okl. Cr. 1958) (television in courtroom); Middleton v. News Syndicate Co., 162 Misc. 516, 295 N.Y.S. 120 (Sup. Ct. 1937) ("inquiring photographer" on the street).
252. Jones v. Herald Post Co., 230 Ky. 227, 18 S.W.2d 972 (1929).
253. Jacova v. Southern Radio & Television Co., 83 So.2d 34 (Fla. 1955).
254. In theory the privilege as to public figures is to depict the person, while that as to news is to report the event. In practice the two often become so merged as to be inseparable. See, for example, Elmhurst v. Pearson, 153 F.2d 467 (D.D.C. 1946) (place of employment of defendant in sedition trial); Martin v. Dorton, 210 Miss. 668, 50 So.2d 391 (1951) (mass meeting complaining of conduct of sheriff); Stryker v. Republic Pictures Corp., 108 Cal. App.2d 191, 238 P.2d 670 (1951) (military career of war hero); Molony v. Boy Comics Publishers, 277 App. Div. 166, 98 N.Y.S.2d 119 (1950), *reversing* 188 Misc. 450, 65 N.Y.S.2d 173 (Sup. Ct. 1946) (conduct of hero in disaster). The outstanding example in our time has been the popular interest in Charles A. Lindbergh, after he flew the Atlantic.
255. Restatement, Torts 867, comment *c* (1939).

256. Smith v. Doss, 251 Ala. 250, 37 So.2d 118 (1948) (family of man who disappeared, was believed murdered, died, and his body was brought home); Coverstone v. Davies, 38 Cal. 2d 315, 239 P.2d 876 (1952) (father of boy arrested for "hot-rod" race); Kelly v. Post Pub. Co., 327 Mass. 275, 98 N.E.2d 286 (1951) (parents of girl killed in accident); Aquino v. Bulletin Co., 190 Pa. Super. 528, 154 A.2d 422 (1959) (parents of girl secretly married and then divorced); Jenkins v. Dell Pub. Co., 143 F. Supp. 952 (W.D. Pa. 1956), aff'd, 251 F.2d 447 (3d Cir. 1958) (family of boy kicked to death by hoodlums); Hillman v. Star Pub. Co., 64 Wash. 691, 117 Pac. 594 (1911) (son of man arrested for mail fraud). Cf. Milner v. Red River Valley Pub. Co., 249 S.W.2d 227 (Tex. Civ. App. 1952) (family of man killed in accident).
257. Such a limitation is indicated in Martin v. New Metropolitan Fiction, 139 Misc. 290, 248 N.Y.S. 359 (Sup. Ct. 1931), aff'd, 234 App. Div. 904, 254 N.Y.S. 1015 (1931), where a mother, attending her son's criminal trial, was depicted as broken-hearted in a news story. On the pleadings, the court refused to dismiss because it could not say that evidence could not be produced which would go beyond the privilege.
258. People ex rel. Stern v. Robert M. McBride & Co., 159 Misc. 5, 288 N.Y.S. 501 (N.Y. City Magis. Ct. 1936); Kline v. Robert M. McBride & Co., 170 Misc. 974, 11 N.Y.S.2d 674 (Sup. Ct. 1939).
259. Sarat Lahiri v. Daily Mirror, 162 Misc. 776, 295 N.Y.S. 382 (Sup. Ct. 1937). *Accord,* Delinger v. American News Co., 6 App. Div. 2d 1027, 178 N.Y.S.2d 231 (1958) (physical training instructor, article on relation of muscular development and virility); Dallessandro v. Henry Holt & Co., 4 App. Div. 2d 470, 166 N.Y.S.2d 805 (1957) (picture of plaintiff conversing with priest who was subject of book); Oma v. Hillman Periodicals, 281 App. Div. 240, 118 N.Y.S.2d 720 (1953) (boxer, article on boxing); Gavrilov v. Duell, Sloan & Pierce, 84 N.Y.S.2d 320 (Sup. Ct. 1948), aff'd, 276 App. Div. 826, 93 N.Y.S.2d 715 (dancer, book on dancing).
260. Peay v. Curtis Pub. Co., 78 F. Supp. 305 (D.D.C. 1948).
261. Martin v. Johnson Pub. Co., 157 N.Y.S.2d 409 (Sup. Ct. 1956). For other examples, see *supra* notes 137–42.
262. Samuel v. Curtis Pub. Co., 122 F. Supp. 327 (N.D. Cal. 1954).
263. Metzger v. Dell Pub. Co., 207 Misc. 182, 136 N.Y.S.2d 888 (Sup. Ct. 1955).
264. Discussed in Spiegel, *Public Celebrity v. Scandal Magazine—The Celebrity's Right to Privacy,* 30 So. Cal. L. Rev. 280 (1957).
265. Attributed to Greta Garbo.
266. This seems to be clear from the cases holding that the publication of stolen or surreptitiously obtained pictures is actionable, even though the plaintiff is "news." See *supra* notes 109–11.
267. Eliot v. Jones, 66 Misc. 95, 120 N.Y.S. 989 (Sup. Ct. 1910), aff'd, 140 App. Div. 911, 125 N.Y.S. 1119 (1910) (name of president of Harvard used to sell books); Lane v. F.W. Woolworth Co., 171 Misc. 66, 11 N.Y.S.2d 199 (Sup. Ct. 1939), aff'd, 256 App. Div. 1065, 12 N.Y.S.2d 352 (1939) (picture of actress sold in lockets); Birmingham Broadcasting Co. v. Bell, 259 Ala. 656, 68 So.2d 314 (1953), *later appeal,* 69 So.2d 263 (Ala. 1957) (name of sports broadcaster used to advertise program with which he had no connection); Continental Optical Co. v. Reed, 119 Ind. App. 643, 86 N.E.2d 306 (1949) (picture of soldier used to advertise optical goods); Jansen v. Hilo Packing Co., 202 Misc. 900, 118 N.Y.S.2d 162 (Sup. Ct. 1952), aff'd, 282 App. Div. 935, 125 N.Y.S.2d 648 (1953) (picture of baseball player sold with popcorn). *Cf.* Kerby v. Hal Roach Studios, 53 Cal. App. 2d 207, 127 P.2d 577 (1042) (name of actress used to advertise motion picture); State ex rel. La Follette v. Hinkle, 131 Wash. 86, 229 Pac. 317 (1924) (use of name of politician as candidate by political party).

268. Flores v. Mosler Safe Co., 7 N.Y.2d 276, 164 N.E.2d 853 (1959), *affirming* 7 App. Div. 2d 226, 182 N.Y.S.2d 126 (1959) (picture and news story of man who accidentally set a fire used to advertise safes).
269. Von Thodorovich v. Franz Josef Beneficial Ass'n, 154 Fed. 911 (E.D. Pa. 1907). *Accord,* Edison v. Edison Polyform Mfg. Co., 73 N.J. Eq. 136, 67 Atl. 392 (Ch. 1907) (Thomas Edison).
270. Goelet v. Confidential, Inc., 5 App. Div. 2d 226, 171 N.Y.S.2d 223 (1958); Bremmer v. Journal-Tribune Pub. Co., 247 Iowa 817, 76 N.W.2d 762 (1956); Jenkins v. Dell Pub. Co., 143 F. Supp. 953 (W.D. Pa. 1956), *aff'd,* 251 F.2d 447 (3d Cir. 1958); Aquino v. Bulletin Co., 190 Pa. Super. 528, 154 A.2d 422 (1959); Waters v. Fleetwood, 212 Ga. 161, 91 S.W.2d 344 (1956).

Two cases sometimes cited to the contrary, Douglas v. Stokes, 149 Ky. 506, 149 S.W. 849 (1912), and Bazemore v. Savannah Hospital, 171 Ga. 257, 155 S.E. 194 (1930), are apparently to be explained on the basis of pictures obtained by inducing breach of trust.

It may nevertheless be suggested that there must be some as yet undefined limits of common decency as to what can be published about anyone; and that a photograph of indecent exposure, for example, can never be legitimate "news."
271. Hazlitt v. Fawcett Publications, 116 F. Supp. 539 (D. Conn. 1953) (fictional account of stunt driver, tried for homicide); Sutton v. Hearst Corp., 277 App. Div. 155, 98 N.Y.S.2d 233 (1950), *appeal denied,* 277 App. Div. 873, 98 N.Y.S.2d 589 (1950) (fictional story about turret gunner); Hogan v. A.S. Barnes Co., 114 U.S.P.Q. 314 (Pa. C.P. 1957) (book purporting to give information from plaintiff about his golf game); Stryker v. Republic Pictures Corp., 108 Cal. App. 2d 191, 238 P.2d 670 (1951) (fiction in motion picture about war hero); Binns v. Vitagraph Co. of America, 147 App. Div. 783, 132 N.Y.S. 237 (1911), *aff'd,* 210 N.Y. 51, 103 N.E. 1108 (1913) (fiction in motion picture about radio operator hero); Donahue v. Warner Bros. Pictures, 194 F.2d 6 (10th Cir. 1952) (fiction in motion picture about entertainer); D'Altomonte v. New York Herald Co., 154 App. Div. 953, 139 N.Y.S. 200 (1913), *modified* as not within the New York statute in 208 N.Y. 596, 102 N.E. 1101 (1913) (authorship of absurd story attributed to well known writer). See also the last two cases cited *supra,* note 267.
272. Garner v. Triangle Publications, 97 F. Supp. 546 (S.D.N.Y. 1951) (fiction added to murder story); Reed v. Real Detective Pub. Co., 63 Ariz. 294, 162 P.2d 133 (1945) (false statements in story of crime); Annerino v. Dell Pub. Co., 11 Ill. App. 2d 205, 149 N.E.2d 761 (1958) (fiction in account of murder of plaintiff's husband); Strickler v. National Broadcasting Co., 167 F. Supp. 68 (S.D. Cal. 1958) (false details in story of plaintiff's conduct in airplane crisis); Aquino v. Bulletin Co., 190 Pa. Super. 528, 154 A.2d 422 (1959) (reporter of secret marriage and subsequent divorce drew on his imagination).
273. See the cases of pictures used to illustrate articles, *supra,* notes 137–42.
274. "In general, then, the matters of which the publication should be repressed may be described as those which concern the private life, habits, acts and relations of an individual, and have no legitimate connection with his fitness for a public office which he seeks or for which he is suggested, and have no legitimate relation to or bearing upon any act done by him in a public or quasi public capacity." Warren and Brandeis, *The Right to Privacy,* 4 Harv. L. Rev. 193, 215 (1890).
275. Jeffries v. New York Evening Journal Co., 67 Misc. 570, 124 N.Y.S. 780 (Sup. Ct. 1910); Koussevitzky v. Allen, Towne & Heath, 188 Misc. 479, 68 N.Y.S.2d 779 (1947), *aff'd,* 272 App. Div. 759, 69 N.Y.S.2d 432 (1947). *Cf.* Corliss v. E. W. Walker Co., 64 Fed. 280 (D. Mass. 1894).
276. Smith v. Suratt, 7 Alaska 416 (1926) (Dr. Cook).

277. *Cf.* Garner v. Triangle Publications, 97 F. Supp. 546 (S.D.N.Y. 1951) (relations, partly fictional, between participants in murder).
278. For example, Fla. Stat. 794.03 (1957); Wis. Stat. Ann. 942.02 (1958).
279. Pope v. Curl, 2 Atk. 341, 26 Eng. Rep. 608 (1741); Roberts v. McKee, 29 Ga. 161 (1859); Woolsey v. Judd, 4 Duer 379 (11 N.Y. Super. 1855); Denis v. Leclerc, 1 Mart. (o.s.) 297 (La. 1811); Baker v. Libbie, 210 Mass. 599, 97 N.E. 109 (1912). Usually this has been put upon the ground of a property right in the letter itself, or literary property in its contents. See Note, 44 Iowa L. Rev. 705 (1959).
280. Prince Albert v. Strange, 1 Mac. & G. 25, 64 Eng. Rep. 293 (1848), *aff'd*, 2 De. G. & Sm. 652, 41 Eng. Rep. 1171 (1849).
281. Douglas v. Disney Productions, reported in Los Angeles Daily Journal Rep., Dec. 31, 1956, p. 27, col. 3.
282. Witness the disclosure, in the election of 1884, of Grover Cleveland's parentage of an illegitimate child, many years before.
283. Stryker v. Republic Pictures Corp., 108 Cal. App. 2d 191, 238 P.2d 670 (1951); and see Continental Optical Co. v. Reed, 119 Ind. App. 643, 86 N.E.2d 306 (1949).
284. Bernstein v. National Broadcasting Co., 129 F. Supp. 817 (D.D.C. 1955), *aff'd*, 232 F.2d 369 (D.C. Cir. 1956) (murder and trial); Smith v. National Broadcasting Co., 138 Cal. App.2d 807, 282 P.2d 600 (1956) (false report to police of escape of black panther).
285. Cohen v. Marx, 94 Cal. App. 2d 704, 211 P.2d 320 (1950) (pugilist, ten years); Sidis v. F-R. Pub. Corp., 113 F.2d 806 (2d Cir. 1940), *affirming* 34 F. Supp. 19 (S.D.N.Y. 1938) (infant prodigy, seven years); Schnabel v. Meredith, 378 Pa. 609, 107 A.2d 860 (1954) (slot machines found on plaintiff's premises, six months).
286. Jenkins v. Dell Pub. Co., 143 F. Supp. 953 (W.D. Pa. 1956), *aff'd*, 251 F.2d 447 (3d Cir. 1958) (family of murdered boy, three months). *Accord,* as to pictures illustrating articles, Samuel v. Curtis Pub. Co., 122 F. Supp. 327 (N.D. Cal. 1954) (arguing with suicide, twenty-two months); and see Leverton v. Curtis Pub. Co., 192 F.2d 974 (3d Cir. 1951) (child struck by car, two years).
287. Estill v. Hearst Pub. Co., 186 F.2d 1017 (7th Cir. 1951).

The case of Smith v. Doss, 251 Ala. 250, 37 So.2d 118 (1948), where a man who had disappeared and was believed to have been murdered died in a distant state, and his body was brought back to town, is probably to be distinguished on the basis that the later event was itself "news," and so justified the revival of the story.
288. 112 Cal. App. 285, 297 Pac. 91 (1931).

The report of the case leaves the facts in some doubt. It came up on the plaintiff's pleading, which alleged that the defendant made use of the plaintiff's maiden name of Gabrielle Darley, and that "by the production and showing of the picture, friends of appellant learned for the first time of the unsavory incidents of her early life." It is difficult to see how this was accomplished, unless the picture also revealed her present identity under her married name of Melvin. At least the allegation is not to be ignored in interpreting the case.
289. Mau v. Rio Grande Oil, Inc., 28 F. Supp. 845 (N.D. Cal. 1939) (radio dramatization of robbery); and see the cases cited *supra,* note 284.

In Barber v. Time, Inc., 348 Mo. 1199, 159 S.W.2d 291 (1942), the court laid stress upon the "unnecessary" use of the name in even a current report, concerning a woman suffering from a rare disease. The decision, however, appears rather to rest upon the intrusion of taking her picture in bed in a hospital.
290. Brents v. Morgan, 221 Ky. 765, 299 S.W. 967 (1927); Melvin v. Reid, 112 Cal. App. 285, 297 Pac. 91 (1931); Mau v. Rio Grande Oil, Inc., 28 F. Supp. 845 (N.D. Cal. 1939); Barber v. Time, Inc., 348 Mo. 1199, 159 S.W.2d 291 (1942); Cason v. Baskin,

155 Fla. 198, 20 So.2d 243 (1945), *second appeal,* 159 Fla. 31, 30 So.2d 635 (1947); Themo v. New England Newspaper Pub. Co., 306 Mass. 54, 27 N.E.2d 753 (1940).
291. See *supra,* text at notes 127–50.
292. Grossman v. Frederick Bros. Acceptance Corp., 34 N.Y.S.2d 785 (Sup. Ct., App. T. 1942) (written consent a complete defense under the New York statute); Jenkins v. Dell Pub. Co., 143 F. Supp. 953 (W.D. Pa. 1956), *aff'd,* 250 F.2d 447 (3d Cir. 1958); Reitmeister v. Reitmeister, 162 F.2d 691 (2d Cir. 1947); Tanner-Brice Co. v. Sims, 174 Ga. 13, 161 S.E. 819 (1931).

In Porter v. American Tobacco Co., 140 App. Div. 871, 125 N.Y.S. 710 (1910), it was held that consent must be pleaded and proved as a defense.
293. Gill v. Hearst Pub. Co., 40 Cal. 2d 224, 253 P.2d 441 (1953); Thayer v. Worcester Post Co., 284 Mass. 160, 187 N.E. 292 (1933); Wendell v. Conduit Machine Co., 74 Misc. 201, 133 N.Y.S. 758 (Sup. Ct. 1911); Johnson v. Boeing Airplane Co., 175 Kan. 275, 262 P.2d 808 (1953).
294. In O'Brien v. Pabst Sales Co., 124 F.2d 167 (5th Cir. 1941), the fact that the plaintiff had gone to great lengths to get himself named as an all-American football player was held to prevent any recovery for publicity given to him in that capacity. *Cf.* Gautier v. Pro-Football, Inc., 304 N.Y. 354, 107 N.E.2d 485 (1952) (television broadcast of performing animal act at football game).

See also Schmieding v. American Farmers Mut. Ins. Co., 138 F. Supp. 167 (D. Neb. 1955), where the plaintiff failed to object to continued use of his rubber-stamp signature after termination of his employment.
295. Garden v. Parfumerie Rigaud, 151 Misc. 692, 271 N.Y.S. 187 (Sup. Ct. 1993); State *ex rel.* La Follette v. Hinkle, 131 Wash. 86, 229 Pac. 317 (1924).
296. Lillie v. Warner Bros. Pictures, 139 Cal. App. 724, 34 P.2d 835 (1934) (motion picture contract includes use of "shorts"); Long v. Decca Records, 76 N.Y.S.2d 133 (Sup. Ct. 1947) (contract to make records held to include use of name and picture in advertising); Fairbanks v. Winik, 119 Misc. 809, 198 N.Y.S. 299 (Sup. Ct. 1922) (motion picture actor surrenders right to use of film); Wendell v. Conduit Machine Co., 74 Misc. 201, 133 N.Y.S. 758 (Sup. Ct. 1911) (use of employee's picture in business after termination of employment); Marek v. Zanol Products Co., 298 Mass. 1, 9 N.E.2d 393 (1937) (contract consent to use of name); Sharaga v. Sinram Bros., 275 App. Div. 967, 90 N.Y.S.2d 705 (1949) (use of salesman's name after termination of employment); Johnson v. Boeing Airplane Co., 175 Kan. 275, 262 P.2d 808 (1953) (consent to picture in house organ held to include national publication).

In Bell v. Birmingham Broadcasting Co., 263 Ala. 355, 82 So.2d 345 (1955), it was held that a custom of giving consent was proper evidence bearing on the interpretation of the contract.
297. *Cf.* Manger v. Kree Institute of Electrolysis, 233 F.2d 5 (2d Cir. 1956) (letter altered to make it testimonial); Myers v. Afro-American Pub. Co., 168 Misc. 429, 5 N.Y.S.2d 223 (Sup. Ct. 1938), *aff'd,* 255 App. Div. 838, 7 N.Y.S.2d 662 (1938) (consent to use of semi-nude picture on condition that nudity be covered up).
298. Ettore v. Philco Television Broadcasting Co., 229 F.2d 481 (3d Cir. 1956) (motion picture contract held not to include use of the film on television, subsequently developed); Colgate-Palmolive Co. v. Tullos, 219 F.2d 617 (5th Cir. 1955) (use of employee's picture in advertising after termination of employment); Sinclair v. Postal Tel. & Cable Co., 72 N.Y.S.2d 841 (Sup. Ct. 1935) (picture of actor putting him in undignified light); Russell v. Marboro Books, 18 Misc.2d 166, 183 N.Y.S.2d 8 (Sup. Ct. 1959) (picture of model used in bawdy advertisement of bed sheets).
299. *Supra,* notes 14, 52-54. It has been held that the consent of an infant is ineffective under the New York statute and that of the parent must be obtained. Semler v.

Ultem Publications, 170 Misc. 551, 9 N.Y.S.2d 319 (N.Y. City Ct. 1938); Wyatt v. James McCreery Co., 126 App. Div. 650, 111 N.Y.S. 86 (1908).
300. Buschelle v. Conde Nast Publications, 173 Misc. 674, 19 N.Y.S.2d 129 (Sup. Ct. 1940); Hammond v. Crowell Pub. Co., 253 App. Div. 205, 1 N.Y.S.2d 728 (1938); Miller v. Madison Square Garden Corp., 176 Misc. 714, 28 N.Y.S.2d 811 (Sup. Ct. 1941) (reduced to nominal damages); Lane v. F.W. Woolworth Co., 171 Misc. 66, 11 N.Y.S.2d 199 (Sup. Ct. 1939), aff'd, 256 App. Div. 1065, 12 N.Y.S.2d 352 (1939); Harris v. H.W. Gossard Co., 194 App. Div. 688, 185 N.Y.S. 861 (1921).
301. Warren and Brandeis, *The Right to Privacy*, 4 Harv. L. Rev. 193, 216 (1890).
302. Application of Tiene, 19 N.J. 149, 115 A.2d 543 (1955).
303. Johnson v. Scripps Pub. Co., 18 Ohio Op. 372 (C.P. 1940).
304. Langford v. Vanderbilt University, 199 Tenn. 389, 287 S.W.2d 32 (1956). *Cf.* Lyles v. State, 330 P.2d 734 (Okl. Cr. 1958) (television in courtroom); Berg v. Minneapolis Star & Tribune Co., 79 F. Supp. 957 (D. Minn. 1948) (photograph taken in courtroom).
305. Schmukler v. Ohio-Bell Tel. Co., 116 N.E.2d 819 (Ohio C.P. 1953). *Accord*, People v. Appelbaum, 277 App. Div. 43, 97 N.Y.S.2d 807 (1950), aff'd, 301 N.Y. 738, 95 N.E.2d 410 (1950) (subscriber tapping his own telephone to protect his interests). *Cf.* Davis v. General Finance & Thrift Co., 80 Ga. App. 708, 57 S.E.2d 225 (1950) (creditor's telegram to debtor threatening suit); Gouldman-Taber Pontiac, Inc. v. Zerbst, 213 Ga. 682, 100 S.E.2d 881 (1957) (creditor's complaint to debtor's employer).
306. Holloman v. Life Ins. Co. of Va., 192 S.C. 454, 7 S.E.2d 169 (1940).
307. Ellis v. Hurst, 70 Misc. 122, 128 N.Y.S. 144 (Sup. Ct. 1910); Shostakovitch v. Twentieth-Century Fox Film Corp., 196 Misc. 67, 80 N.Y.S.2d 575 (Sup. Ct. 1948), aff'd, 275 App. Div. 692, 87 N.Y.S.2d 430 (1949).
Cf. White v. William G. White Co., 160 App. Div. 709, 145 N.Y.S. 743 (1914), where the plaintiff's sale of a corporation bearing his name was held to convey the right to continue to use it.
308. Brociner v. Radio Wire Television, Inc., 15 Misc.2d 843, 183 N.Y.S.2d 743 (Sup. Ct. 1959).
309. Prosser, *Interstate Publication,* 51 Mich. L. Rev. 959 (1953), reprinted in Prosser, Selected Topics on the Law of Torts 70–134 (1953).
310. Discussed at length in Prosser, *Insult and Outrage,* 44 Calif. L. Rev. 40 (1956).
311. Reported in a note to Rex v. Carlisle, 6 Car. & P. 636, 172 Eng. Rep. 1397 (1834).

Chapter 3. The Tort Right of Privacy

1. A "tort" refers to conduct that creates an unreasonable or unacceptable risk, or results in loss or harm, often involving fault or negligence. Torts include illegal acts and omissions that directly or indirectly cause injury to persons, property, or reputation. Through tort law, courts compensate those injured by others and deter wrongdoers by forcing them to pay the social costs of their actions. Tort law concepts change over time.
2. The *Restatements of the Law* are produced by the American Law Institute (ALI) to clarify and simplify the law, better adapt it to social needs, and promote better administration of justice. ALI "address[es] uncertainty in the law through a restatement of basic legal subjects that would tell judges and lawyers what the law was." Between 1923 and 1944, *Restatements of the Law* were prepared by legal scholars and experts who analyzed statutes, court decisions, and legal precedents and authorities to draw conclusions to guide judges and lawyers. In 1952 and 1987, the Second and Third

3. *Estate of Berthiaume v. Pratt*, 365 A.2d 792 (Me. 1976); *Clayman v. Bernstein*, 38 Pa. D. & C. 543 (1940); *Barber v. Time, Inc.*, 348 Mo. 1199, 159 S.W.2d 291 (1942).
4. *Haelan Laboratories, Inc. v. Topps Chewing Gum*, 202 F.2d 866 (2d Cir.) *cert. denied*, 346 U.S. 816 (1953). Haelan sought to prevent a competitor from using a picture of a baseball player with whom it had previously contracted.
5. In *Lugosi v. Universal Pictures*, 25 Cal.3d 813, 603 P.2d 425, 160 Cal.Rptr. 323 (1979), actor Bela Lugosi's heirs unsuccessfully sought to protect (and receive royalties from) his 1930 performance in *Dracula*. Although Lugosi could have sold or transferred his rights in his performance (i.e., his acts, poses, plays, and appearances) prior to his death, he had not, and the right to do so died with him. The California legislature subsequently enacted a law to overrule this outcome.
6. Over strenuous judicial dissent, television letter-turner Vanna White successfully stopped Samsung from advertising using a robot in a wig, gown, and jewelry standing next to a Wheel of Fortune-like game board. *White v. Samsung Electronics America, Inc.*, 971 F.2d 1395 (9th Cir. 1992).
7. In *Hirsch v. S.C. Johnson & Son*, 90 Wis.2d 379, 280 N.W.2d 129 (1979), football star Elroy "Crazylegs" Hirsch successfully prevented the use of "Crazylegs" for shaving gel.
8. Here's Johnny Portable Toilets, Inc. misappropriated the slogan of former *Tonight Show* host, Johnny Carson. *Carson v. Here's Johnny Portable Toilets, Inc.*, 698 F.2d 831 (6th Cir. 1983).
9. J. McCarthy, *The Rights of Publicity and Privacy*, Section 5.8[C], 5–69 (Release #11, 4/94). Often-cited examples include misuse of a man's name as the father of an illegitimate child (*Vanderbilt v. Mitchell*, 72 N.J.Eq. 910, 67 A. 97 (1907) and the misuse of a candidate's name in a presidential primary (*Battaglia v. Adams*, 164 S.2d 195 (Fla. 1964)). Richard C. Turkington and Anita L. Allen, *Privacy Law: Cases and Materials*, 2nd ed. (St. Paul, Minn.: West Group, 2002), 661, et seq.
10. Edward Friedan, former husband of feminist Betty Friedan, sued her and *New York Magazine* for publishing a 1949 photo of them with their son in an article about her career. His right of privacy was found to be secondary to the public's interest in news of Ms. Friedan. *Friedan v. Friedan*, 414 F. Supp. 77 (S.D.N.Y. 1976).
11. The California law overturning *Lugosi* allows personalities who died within fifty years of the statute's enactment to own a property right in certain commercial uses of their names, voices, signatures, photographs, or likenesses. Heirs and descendants may inherit these rights and own them for fifty years, but may not prohibit uses in plays, books, periodicals, films, broadcasts, political or news items, original works of art, or advertisements for them. These rights accrue even if not commercially exploited during the life of the celebrity. Cal. Civil Code Sec. 990 and 3344.
12. In Florida, a person may sue for unauthorized use of his or her name or picture for commercial advantage. Fla. Stat. Ann. sec. 540.08.
13. The Kentucky right of publicity continues for fifty years after death. Commercial uses of a person's likeness or name may be made with the written consent of the estate's administrator. Ky. Rev. Stat. Sec. 391.170.
14. N.Y. Civil Rights Law, sec. 50.
15. Oklahoma law extends the right of publicity for one hundred years after death, but protects only personalities with commercial value and celebrities who died after

1936. Survivors must register with the secretary of state. Okla. Stat. Ann. Title 12, sec. 1448-1449. See also Okla. Stat. Ann. Title 21, sec. 839.1.
16. In Tennessee, the home of Elvis Presley, an individual's property right in the use of his or her name or likeness may be transferred or assigned to another person. This right continues for ten years after death, regardless of whether such rights were commercially exploited by the individual during the individual's lifetime. Tenn. Cod. Ann. Sec. 47-25-1101-1108 (1988).
17. The right of publicity for celebrities extends beyond death in Texas. Tex. Stat. Title IV, ch. 26, sec. 26.001.
18. In Utah, the deceased's heirs or personal representatives may collect damages for wrongful use of the deceased's name, portrait, or picture for advertising or trade. Utah Sec. 76-4-8.
19. Virginia law is similar to Utah's statute, but governs Virginia residents only. Va. Code sec. 8.01–40.
20. *Martin Luther King Center v. American Heritage Prods., Inc.*, 250 Ga. 135, 296 S.E.2d 697 (1982).
21. See, e.g., *International Privacy, Publicity and Personality Laws,* ed. Michael Henry. (London: Butterworths, Reed Elsevier, 2001), 468–71.
22. In *Florida Star v. B.J.F.,* 491 U.S. 524 (1989), the *Florida Star* newspaper printed B.J.F.'s full name after she was robbed and sexually assaulted. B.J.F. sued. In a narrow ruling for the newspaper on First Amendment grounds, the U.S. Supreme Court noted: "We do not hold that truthful publication is automatically constitutionally protected, or that there is no zone of personal privacy within which the State may protect the individual from intrusion by the press, . . . We hold only that where a newspaper publishes truthful information which it has lawfully obtained, punishment may lawfully be imposed, if at all, only when narrowly tailored to a state interest of the highest order, and that no such interest is satisfactorily served by imposing liability. . . ."
23. *Restatement (Second) of Torts,* §652D, comment a.
24. In *Tellado v. Time-Life Books, Inc.,* 643 F.Supp. 904 (D.N.J.1986), a Vietnam War veteran sued the publisher for disseminating five million copies of a brochure showing him in battle twenty years earlier. The court found that the photo showed soldiers in a "clearly public setting" during wartime.
25. *Restatement (Second) of Torts,* §652D (1977).
26. *Prosser and Keeton on the Law of Torts,* ed. W. Page Keeton, (St. Paul, Minn.: West Publishing Co., 1984), Sec. 117 at p. 857.
27. In *Klein v. McGraw-Hill, Inc.,* 263 F.Supp. 919 (D.D.C. 1966), a former child inventor objected to the later use of his photograph and a description of his scientific work in a science book. The court ruled that he had become a public figure who was not entitled to the same degree of privacy as an ordinary person.
28. *Restatement (Second) of Torts,* §652D, comment h.
29. In 1964, the Supreme Court of Alabama found that it was an offensive disclosure of private facts for a newspaper to publish a photo of a woman taken as she and her children departed a carnival "fun house" when air jets blew up her dress, causing her to be embarrassed, self-conscious, upset, and tearful on occasion. *Daily Times Democrat v. Graham,* 276 Ala. 380, 162 So.2d 474 (1964). In 1976, a Pennsylvania court found that publication of a man's photo taken at a Pittsburgh Steelers football game, with his trousers' zipper open, was not an invasion of privacy. The photo was taken at a public event, with his knowledge and implied consent, and so there was no publication of private facts. Different times and places may account for these outcomes.

30. State statutes of limitations, or limitation of actions, set the period after a legal claim arises or accrues within which an action must be filed in court, or be permanently barred.
31. *International Privacy, Publicity and Personality Laws,* 471. This area of the law may be evolving.
32. As of this writing, only Nebraska, New York, North Carolina, and Oregon do not recognize this defense. See *International Privacy, Publicity and Personality Laws,* 465.
33. In *Haynes v. Alfred A. Knopf, Inc.,* 8 F.3d 1222, 1232 (7th Cir. 1993), Haynes objected to disclosure of unpleasant facts about his private life in a book about the migration of black Americans to the North from the rural South. The use was protected because his private life provided a concrete example of the black American experience.
34. Alida Brill, *Nobody's Business: Paradoxes of Privacy* (Reading, Mass.: Addison-Wesley Publishing Company, Inc., 1990), 190.

Part 2. Ethical Perspectives

1. The text of the statement, which was approved by SAA Council in December 1973, was printed in *American Archivist* 37 (January 1974): 153–54. A slightly modified version of this statement, which remained substantively similar to the committee statement, became the "ALA-SAA Joint Statement on Access to Original Research Materials in Libraries, Archives, and Manuscript Repositories."
2. The Society of American Archivists' Code of Ethics is currently (June 2004) undergoing a substantial revision.
3. Heather MacNeil, *Without Consent: The Ethics of Disclosing Personal Information in Public Archives* (Metuchen, N.J.: Society of American Archivists and Scarecrow Press, 1992). The book itself was based on MacNeil's 1987 Master of Archival Studies thesis at the University of British Columbia.

Chapter 4. Information Privacy, Liberty, and Democracy

1. Society of American Archivists, "A Code of Ethics for Archivists with Commentary." A similarly worded provision is found in the Association of Canadian Archivists' "A Code of Ethics for Archivists in Canada," available at http://archivists.ca/; and in the International Council on Archives' "Code of Ethics," available at http://www.ica.org.
2. Since 1974, most Western countries have adopted data protection legislation regulating government recordkeeping practices. The U.S. *Privacy Act* (5 U.S.C. § 552a) and the Canadian *Privacy Act* (S.C. 1980-81-82-83, c.11, Section II) are North American examples of such legislation. In Canada and Québec, such legislation has been extended to the private sector. See Canada, *Personal Information Protection and Electronic Documents Act* (S.C. 2000, c.5, Section I) and Québec, *An Act Respecting the Protection of Personal Information in the Private Sector* (L.Q., 1993, c. 17). The countries of the European Union have also negotiated a general data protection directive, which is designed to harmonize all European laws and to facilitate the flow of personal information around the single market. See European Union, *Directive 95/EC of the European Parliament and of the Council on the Protection of Individuals with Regard to the Processing of Personal Data and on the Free Movement of Such Data* (Brussels: Official Journal of the European Communities L281, 24 October 1995).
3. Margaret Cross Norton, *Norton on Archives: The Writings of Margaret Cross Norton on Archival and Records Management,* ed. Thornton Mitchell (Chicago: Society of American Archivists, 1975, 2001), 26.

4. The notion of the archivist as trusted custodian is embedded in the Society of American Archivists' very definition of an archivist, which states that: "The archivist is the trustee of the present and the past for future generations . . . a steadfast keeper of the records held in trust." See "Archivist: A Definition," *SAA Newsletter* (January 1984), 4.
5. John D. McCamus, "The Delicate Balance: Reconciling Privacy Protection with the Freedom of Information Principle," *Conference on Privacy: Initiatives for 1984* (Toronto, Ont.: Provincial Secretariat for Resources Development, 1984), 51.
6. Ruth Gavison, "Privacy and the Limits of Law," in *Philosophical Dimensions of Privacy*, ed. Ferdinand David Schoeman (Cambridge, Mass.: Cambridge University Press, 1984), 350, 347.
7. Raymond Williams, *Keywords: A Vocabulary of Culture and Society* (Great Britain: Fontana, 1976), 203.
8. Oscar H. Gandy, *The Panoptic Sort: A Political Economy of Personal Information* (Boulder, Colo.: Westview Press, 1993), 179. Gandy's point is reinforced by Barrington Moore's observation that "until near the end of the nineteenth century, the benefits of privacy and opportunities for privacy flowed almost entirely to the propertied and employing classes." Barrington Moore, Jr., *Privacy Studies in Social and Cultural History* (Armonk, N.Y.: M.E. Sharpe, 1984). For an examination of the evolution of the concept of privacy between the sixteenth and nineteenth centuries, see also Richard Hixon, *Privacy in a Public Society: Human Rights in Conflict* (New York: Oxford University Press, 1987), 3–51.
9. Williams, *Keywords*, 204.
10. Jean Marie Goulemot, "Literary Practices: Publicizing the Private," *Passions of the Renaissance*, vol. 3 of *A History of Private Life*, ed. Roger Chartier (Cambridge, Mass.: Harvard University Press, 1989), 389.
11. J. S. Mill, "On Liberty," in *Utilitarianism, On Liberty and Considerations of Representative Government*, ed. H. B. Acton (London and Melbourne: J. M. Dent and Sons, 1972), 78.
12. W. A. Parent, "Privacy, Morality, and the Law," *Philosophy and Public Affairs* 12 (1983): 276–77.
13. R. L. Nettleship, cited in J. W. Gough, *The Social Contract*, 2nd ed. (Oxford: Clarendon, 1957), 245.
14. H. Tristram Engelhardt, Jr., "Privacy and Limited Democracy: The Moral Centrality of Persons," in *The Right to Privacy*, ed. Ellen Frankel Paul, Fred D. Miller, Jr., and Jeffrey Paul (Cambridge: Cambridge University Press, 2000), 123–24.
15. Ibid., 124.
16. Michel Foucault, *Discipline and Punish: The Birth of the Prison*, trans. Ann Sheridan (New York: Vintage, 1979), 200.
17. Ibid., 201–2.
18. Michel Foucault, "The Subject and Power: Afterword," in *Michel Foucault: Beyond Structuralism and Hermeneutics*, 2nd ed., ed. Hubert L. Dreyfus and Paul Rabinow (Chicago: University of Chicago Press, 1983), 223.
19. Kevin Robins and Frank Webster, "Cybernetic Capitalism: Information, Technology, Everyday Life," in *The Political Economy of Information*, ed. V. Mosco and J. Wasco (Madison: University of Wisconsin Press, 1988), 59.
20. Jeffrey H. Reiman, "Driving to the Panopticon: A Philosophical Exploration of the Risks to Privacy Posed by the Highway Technology of the Future," *Santa Clara Computer and High Technology Law Journal* 11 (1995): 34.
21. Gandy, *The Panoptic Sort*, 180.
22. Reiman, "Driving to the Panopticon," 39.
23. Ibid., 42.
24. Gavison, "Privacy and the Limits of Law," 369–70.

25. Spiros Simitis, "Reviewing Privacy in an Information Society," *University of Pennsylvania Law Review* 135 (1986–87): 731.
26. The notion of a right "to be let alone" was first advanced in the American common law in Thomas M. Cooley, "The right to be let alone," *Torts* 29 (2nd ed. 1888). In 1890, it became the cornerstone of Warren and Brandeis's argument for the legal protection of a right to privacy. The explicit recognition of such a right was intended to protect individuals against the unjustifiable exposure of their private affairs without their consent. "Recent inventions and business methods," they asserted, "call attention to the next step which must be taken for the protection of the person, and for securing to the individual . . . the right 'to be let alone.' Instantaneous photographs and newspaper enterprise have invaded the sacred precincts of private and domestic life . . . Of the desirability—indeed of the necessity—of some such protection, there can, it is believed, be no doubt." Samuel D. Warren and Louis D. Brandeis, "The Right to Privacy [the implicit made explicit]," *Harvard Law Review* 4 (1890), reprinted in *Philosophical Dimensions of Privacy*, 76.
27. Simitis, "Reviewing Privacy," 731, 733.
28. Ibid., 733–34. The term "lifeworld" was coined by the critical theorist Jurgen Habermas, who defined it as "shared understandings about what will be treated as a fact, valid norms, and subjective experience." Cited in ibid., n. 117.
29. Paul M. Schwartz, "Privacy and Participation: Personal Information and Public Sector Regulation in the United States," *Iowa Law Review* 80 (1995): 559.
30. By "deliberative autonomy," Schwartz refers to individuals' capacity "to form and act on their notions of the good when deciding how to live their lives." This "first interest in self-determination," he maintains, is threatened by unrestricted access to personal information. By "deliberative democracy," he means "the decisional process by which individuals make choices about the merits of political institutions and social policies. [Such process] requires that citizens be permitted to apply their deliberative capacities to the consideration of the justice of basic institutions and social processes." Ibid., 560–61.
31. Quoted in Simitis, "Reviewing Privacy," 734.
32. Schafer, "Privacy: A Philosophical Overview," 19.
33. Lloyd L. Weinreb, "The Right to Privacy," in *The Right to Privacy*, 31. On the complex relationship between the public and the private spheres, see also *Public and Private: Legal, Political and Philosophical Perspectives,* ed. Maurizio Passerin d'Entrèves and Ursula Vogel (London: Routledge, 2000).
34. Ferdinand David Schoeman, *Privacy and Social Freedom* (Cambridge, Mass.: Cambridge University Press, 1992), 21.
35. Mark Kingwell, *The World We Want: Virtue, Vice, and the Good Citizen* (Toronto: Viking Penguin, 2000), 188–89.
36. Although the discussion that follows focuses on the archival management of government records containing personal information, the policies and practices it recommends may be extended by analogy to the archival management of private records. If we consider a right to be a kind of freedom that must be made available to and protected for all the citizens in a democratic society, there is no philosophical distinction between the public and private spheres in terms of an individual's right to privacy. A more specific discussion of the issues associated with administering access to records containing personal information in the private sphere may be found in Heather MacNeil, "To Close or Disclose: Evaluating Third Party Privacy Rights in Relation to Private Fonds," *AABC Newsletter* 5 (Autumn 1995): 6–14.

37. Ruth Simmons, "The Public's Right to Know and the Individual's Right to be Private," *Provenance* 1 (Spring 1983): 3.
38. The discussion that follows is drawn from Heather MacNeil, *Without Consent: The Ethics of Disclosing Personal Information in Public Archives* (Lanham, N.J.: Scarecrow Press and Society of American Archivists, 1992, 2001), 181–204.
39. The main categories of information typically protected include civil status and affiliation; health, wealth, and income; penal and criminal proceedings; professional activity; political, philosophical, and religious opinions; and basic statistical documents.
40. For a detailed analysis of each of these areas, see Gary M. Peterson and Trudy Huskamp Peterson, *Archives & Manuscripts: Law* (Chicago: Society of American Archivists, 1985), 60–71.
41. Richard Cox, "Professionalism and Archivists in the United States," *American Archivist* 49 (Summer 1986): 233.
42. See, for example, Society of American Archivists, "A Code of Ethics for Archivists with Commentary," sec. XII and XIII; Association of Canadian Archivists, "A Code of Ethics for Archivists in Canada," sec. E; International Council on Archives, "Code of Ethics," art. 8 and 9.
43. Alice Robbin, "Ethical Standards and Data Archives," in *Secondary Data: New Directions for Program Evaluation*, ed. Robert F. Boruch (San Francisco: Jossey-Bass, 1978), 15–17.
44. [United States] Privacy Protection Study Commission, *Personal Privacy in an Information Society: The Report of the Privacy Protection Study Commission* (Washington, D.C.: Government Printing Office, July 1977), 14–15.
45. The Association of Canadian Archivists' Code of Ethics specifically states that "archivists share their specialised knowledge and experience with legislators and other policy-makers to assist them in formulating policies and making decisions in matters affecting the record-keeping environment." See Association of Canadian Archivists, "A Code of Ethics for Archivists in Canada," E2.
46. Trudy Peterson, "Archival Principles and Records of the New Technology," *American Archivist* 47 (Fall 1984): 383–93.

Chapter 5. The Archivist's Balancing Act

1. Judith Schwarz, *The Radical Feminists of Heterodoxy: Greenwich Village, 1912–1940* (Norwich, Vermont: New Victoria Publishers, Inc., 1986).
2. Anna Mary Wells, *Miss Marks and Miss Woolley* (Boston: Houghton Mifflin Company, 1978), ix.
3. Jonathan Katz, "The President's Sister and the Bishop's Wife: An *Advocate* Inauguration Special," *Advocate*, 31 January 1989, pp. 34–35. The groundbreaking work of Jonathan Katz is essential reading in sexual history. See Jonathan Katz, *Gay American History: Lesbians and Gay Men in the U.S.A.* (New York: Plume, 1976); and Jonathan Katz, *Gay/Lesbian Almanac: A New Documentary* (New York: Harper and Row, 1983).
4. Dr. Grant Sanger to Jonathan Katz, 25 October 1974 (in Jonathan Katz's possession).
5. Interested readers may contact Lesbian Herstory Archives/Lesbian Herstory Educational Foundation, P.O. Box 1258, New York, NY 10116.

Chapter 6. Privacy Rights and the Rights of Political Victims

1. Joachim Gauck, *Die Stasi-Akten: Das unheimliche Erbe der DDR* (Hamburg: Rowohlt, May 1991). Written during the controversy over the opening of the files, Gauck's

firsthand account includes an impassioned plea for the rights of citizens to see their own files. At the end is a draft Stasi archives law formulated in February 1991 that eventually formed the basis of legislation passed in December 1991. Fundamental information about the structure of the Stasi and its files was promptly published by David Gill and Ulrich Schröter, *Das Ministerium für Staatssicherheit: Anatomie des Mielke-Imperium* (Berlin: Rowohlt, 1991). Later, the personnel structure was analyzed by Jens Gieseke, *Die hauptamtlichen Mitarbeiter der Staatssicherheit* (Berlin: Links, 2000). A two-part compendium of the work of the unofficial informants was edited by Helmut Müller-Enbergs, *Inoffizielle Mitarbeiter des Ministeriums für Staatsichyerheit* (Berlin: Links, 1996–1998).
2. William G. Rosenberg, "Politics in the (Russian) Archives: The 'Objectivity Question,' Trust, and the Limitations of Law," *American Archivist* 64 (Spring/Summer 2001): 78–95.
3. Wolfram Kempe, "Das vorletzte Gefecht: Besetzung und Hengerstreik in der Stasizentral im September 1990," *Horch und Gunk, Histrorisch-leterarische Zeitschrift des Bürgerkomitees 15. Januar* 9 (2000): 4.
4. The complete text of the law is available in pamphlet form from the Gauck Authority and as of 2002, on the Web in both German and English: http://www.bstu.de/home.htm. For perspectives on how the Stasi act fits into existing privacy legislation and archival law, see Dagmar Unverhau, ed., *Das Stasi-Unterlagen-Gesetz im Lichte von Datenschutz und Archivgesetzgebung. Referate der Tagung des BstU vom 26.-28. 11 1997* (Münster: LIT Verlag, 1998).
5. The Gauck-Birthler Authority Web site maintains current information on disputes over the use of the files. The effort by former chancellor Helmut Kohl to prevent the release of information about his activities acquired through Stasi surveillance has been particularly revealing. The use of the intelligence gathered on West Germans and Americans is extremely sensitive. As of 2002, details were available on the Web site: http://www.bstu.de/aktenstreit/index.htm.
6. Timothy Garton Ash, *The File: A Personal History* (New York: Random House, 1997).
7. Dagmar Unverhau, ed., *Lustration, Aktenöffnung, demokratischer Umbruch in Polen, Tschechien, der Slowakei und Ungarn* (Münster: LIT, 1999).
8. Thanks to Margit Gregory for translating the Hungarian report on the security files written by László Varga. Additional information on the Hungarian stituation was noted in converstations with both Varga and György Markó on 5 October 2000.
9. Carlo Ginzburg, *Il formaggio e i vermin: Il cosmos di un mugnaio del '500* (Torino: Einaudi, 1976).
10. Giesieke, *Die hauptamtlichen Mitarbeiter*, 538. Jens Gieseke, *Die DDR-Staatssicherheit; Schild und Schwert der Partei* (Bonn: Bundeszentrale für politische Bildung, 2000).
11. Antonio Gonzales Quintana, et al., *Archives of the Security Services of Former Repressive Regimes: Report Prepared for UNESCO on Behalf of the International Council of Archives* (Paris: UNESCO, 1997).
12. Jens Gieseke, with Doris Hubert, *The GDR State Security: Shield and Sword of the Party*, trans. Mary Carlene Forszt. Single copies in English are available free of charge from http://www.bstu.de.

Chapter 7. Ethical Issues in Constructing a Eugenics Web Site

1. James D. Watson, along with Francis Crick, won the 1962 Nobel Prize in Physiology or Medicine for discovering and describing the double helix structure of DNA.
2. There are a number of excellent histories of the eugenics movement. Among the standard literature is *In the Name of Eugenics: Genetics and the Uses of Human Heredity* by

Daniel J. Kevles (Cambridge: Harvard University Press, 1995).
3. The first sentences of the mission statement for this unique institution read: "The Dolan DNA Learning Center (DNALC) is the world's first science center devoted entirely to public genetics education and is an operating unit of Cold Spring Harbor Laboratory, an important center for molecular genetics research. The DNALC extends the Laboratory's traditional research and postgraduate education mission to the college, precollege, and public levels." The entire mission statement is on-line at http://www.dnalc.org/about/Mission.html.
4. In 2002, the Editorial Advisory Panel consisted of Garland E. Allen, Washington University, St. Louis, Missouri; Elof Carlson, SUNY, Stony Brook; Katherine N. Clapp, FRAXA Research Foundation; Patricia Colbert-Cormier, Lafayette High School; Nancy L. Fisher, Regence Blue Shield; Henry Friedlander, Brooklyn College/CUNY; Daniel J. Kevles, California Institute of Technology; Philip Kitcher, University of California; Martin L. Levitt, American Philosophical Society; Paul Lombardo, University of Virginia; Nancy Press, Oregon Health Sciences University; Philip R. Reilly, Shriver Center for Mental Retardation, Inc.; Pat Ryan, Carolina Biological Supply Company; Marsha Saxton, World Institute on Disability; Steven Selden, University of Maryland; G. Terry Sharrer, National Museum of American History; and Elizabeth Thompson, ELSI Research Program, NIH.
5. Only a small number of items were used from the Rockefeller Foundation Collection held in the Rockefeller Archives Center.
6. The Truman State University Archives is the repository of the papers of H. H. Laughlin, director of the Eugenics Records Office in Cold Spring Harbor, 1910–1940.
7. In the late 1930s and 1940s, Frederick H. Osborn (1889–1981), another leading eugenicist, led a revisionist movement away from stark racist and anti-immigration thinking. See Kevles, 170–75.
8. http://vector.cshl.org/html/eugenics/editorialpolicy.html.
9. Letter of David Micklos, DNA Learning Center, to Elizabeth Thomson, Office of Scientific Review, National Human Genome Research Institute, 18 January 2000.

Part 3. Administrative Perspectives

1. See appendix 3, in this volume, for a more complete discussion of the congressional amendments to and judicial interpretations of FERPA.

Chapter 8. In Secret Kept, In Silence Sealed

1. *The Poems of Charlotte Bronte & Patrick Bramwell Bronte* (Oxford: The Shakespeare Head Press, 1934), 56.
2. Samuel D. Warren and Louis D. Brandeis, "The Right to Privacy," reprinted in this volume.
3. William L. Prosser, "Privacy," reprinted in this volume. See also Menzi L. Behrnd-Klodt, "The Tort Right of Privacy and What It Means for Archivists . . . and for Third Parties," reprinted in this volume.
4. Society of American Archivists, "Code of Ethics for Archivists" (Chicago: Society of American Archivists, 1992).
5. See Eric Jacobs, Letter to the Editor, *Times Literary Supplement*, 15 April 1994, 17; Marianne Macdonald, "Amis Letters to Larkin Stir up Censorship Row," *The Indepen-*

dent, 17 April 1994, 5; Sale Salwak, Letter to the Editor, *Times Literary Supplement,* 22 April 1994, 17; and Eric Jacobs, Letter to the Editor, *Times Literary Supplement,* 2 June 1995, 15. Ironically, and to the chagrin of those of us at the Huntington Library, Amis held the Huntington up for praise in making his papers open, while he was criticizing the Bodleian for sealing his letters and denying copies even to him. What Amis did not reveal to the media was that his papers at the Huntington contained material that had been sealed at his request.

6. Elena S. Danielson, "The Ethics of Access," *American Archivist 52* (Winter 1989): 54.
7. For full accounts of the Freud case, see Janet Malcolm, *In the Freud Archives* (New York: Alfred A. Knopf, 1984), previously published as "Annals of Scholarship: Trouble in the Archives," *New Yorker* (5 December 1983), 59–152 and (12 December 1983), 60–119; and Jeffrey Maussaieff Masson, *The Assault on Truth: Freud's Suppression of the Seduction Theory* (New York: Farrar, Straus & Giroux, 1984).
8. *Christopher Isherwood, Diaries, Volume One: 1939–1960,* edited and introduced by Katherine Bucknell (London: Methuen, 1996).
9. Sara S. Hodson, "Private Lives: Confidentiality in Manuscripts Collections," *Rare Books & Manuscripts Librarianship* 6 (1991): 116–17.
10. Ambrose Clancy, "A Post-'Graduate' Life," *Los Angeles Times,* 14 May 2002, E4.
11. Quoted in Leon Edel, *Henry James: Volume 3, The Middle Years, 1882–1895* (Philadelphia: J. B. Lippincott Co., 1962), 219.
12. Henry James, "The Aspern Papers," in *The Great Short Novels of Henry James* (New York: Dial Press, Inc., 1944), 475.
13. See Leon Edel, *Henry James,* 5 vols. (Philadelphia: J. B. Lippincott Co., 1953–1972); Fred Kaplan, *Henry James: The Imagination of Genius, A Biography* (New York: William Morrow and Co., 1992); and Diane Middlebrook, *Anne Sexton: A Biography* (Boston: Houghton Mifflin Co., 1991).
14. "Joyce, Beckett Mss. Deliberately Destroyed," *Manuscript Society News* 9 (Fall 1988): 7. For an analysis of the relationship between the private and public ownership of important cultural artifacts, see Joseph L. Sax, *Playing Darts with a Rembrandt: Public and Private Rights in Cultural Treasures* (Ann Arbor: The University of Michigan Press, 1999).
15. Stephen J. Joyce, Letter to the Editor, *New York Times Book Review,* 31 December 1989, 2.
16. Janna Malamud Smith, "Where Does a Writer's Family Draw the Line?" *New York Times Book Review,* 5 November 1989, 44.
17. Quoted in Jerry Schwartz, "Biographers Seek to Air Subjects' Dirty Laundry," *Los Angeles Times,* 11 February 1990, E2.
18. Quoted in Andrea Chambers, "Son Ben Edits John Cheever's Latest Chronicle—the Literary Genius' Intimate, Often Scandalous Letters," *People,* 21 November 1988, 194–96.
19. See Ian Hamilton, *In Search of J. D. Salinger* (New York: Random House, 1988). For a discussion of the relationship between privacy and copyright issues in unpublished manuscripts, see Kenneth Crews, "Unpublished Manuscripts and the Right of Fair Use: Copyright Law and the Strategic Management of Information Resources," *Rare Books & Manuscripts Librarianship* 5 (1990): 61–70.

Chapter 9. Southern Family Honor Tarnished?

1. Claude G. Bowers, *Rediscovering the Old South* (Chapel Hill: University of North Carolina, 1930), [1], [14].
2. Timothy D. Pyatt, "Cooperative Collecting of Manuscripts in the 'Old South,'" *Rare Books & Manuscripts Librarianship* 14 (1999): 19–25.

3. Walter C. West, "Extending Walker Percy's Legacy, the Story of His Papers at the University of North Carolina at Chapel Hill," *St. Tammany Parish Library Walker Percy Symposium* (1992), 14–25.
4. Agreement dated 8 December 1981 in the Walker Percy control file, Southern Historical Collection, Wilson Library, UNC-CH.
5. Jay Tolson, *The Correspondence of Shelby Foote and Walker Percy* (New York: W. W. Norton & Co., 1997).
6. Ibid., *Pilgrim in the Ruins: A Life of Walker Percy* (New York: Simon & Schuster, 1992).
7. Patrick Samway, *Walker Percy: A Life* (New York: Farrar, Straus, and Giroux, 1997).
8. Bertram Wyatt-Brown, *House of Percy* (New York: Oxford University Press, 1994).
9. John Barry, *Rising Tide: The Great Mississippi Flood of 1927 and How it Changed America* (New York: Simon & Schuster, 1997), 420–21.
10. Walker Percy control file, Southern Historical Collection.
11. The Walker Percy Project at http://www.ibiblio.org/wpercy/.
12. North Carolina Writers in the Southern Historical Collection at http://www.lib.unc.edu/mss/writers/.
13. Folder 8, Shelby Foote Papers #4038, Southern Historical Collection.

Chapter 10. Balancing Privacy and Access

1. James Madison, letter to W. T. Barry, 4 August 1822, in *Letters and Other Writings of James Madison,* vol. 3, ed. Philip R. Fendall (Philadelphia: Lippincott, 1865), 276.
2. John W. Carlin, "Strategic Directions for the National Archives and Records Administration," National Archives and Records Administration, 9 September 1998 available as of 2002 at http://www.nara.gov/nara/vision/vision.html.
3. Created on 26 February 1902 by S.B. 26, *Laws of Mississippi,* chapter 52, the department followed by a year the establishment of the Alabama Department of Archives and History.
4. Madel Morgan to Raymond D. Geselbracht, Archivist, Office of the Presidential Libraries, Washington D.C., 26 November 1985, Series 1297: Division Director's Correspondence, Mississippi Department of Archives and History.
5. Dunbar Rowland, "The Concentration of State and National Archives," *American Historical Association Annual Report* (1910), 298.
6. Mississippi Department of Archives and History, *Seventh Annual Report of the Director of Archives and History of the State of Mississippi* (1 October 1907–1 October 1908), 20; *Tenth Annual Report* (1 November 1909–3 October 1910), 11.
7. *Mississippi Code Annotated* (1972), Title 25, Chapter 59, Section 17-15.
8. Ibid., 25-59-27.
9. Mississippi Attorney General's Opinion to W. R. Lewis, 7 December 1995.
10. *Mississippi Code Annotated* (1972), 25-59-29 (*Mississippi Laws,* 1996, Chapter 453, 560–64).
11. Bill Minor, *New Orleans Times-Picayune,* 22 April 1973.
12. 347 U.S. 483 (1954).
13. *General Laws of the State of Mississippi,* 1956, Chapter 365, 520–24.
14. Unsigned Sovereignty Commission speech, filing date 13 July 1958, S.C. Records id. # 7-0-1-56-2-1-1.
15. Erle Johnston, memo, 24 June 1965, S.C. Records id. # 9-31-4-3-1-1-1.
16. 42 U.S.C.A. 2000a-2000a-6.
17. 79 Stat. 437, 42 U.S.C.A. 1973.
18. Johnston, memo S.C. Records, id. # 99-34-0-14-1-1-1.

19. Johnston, memo 8 February 1965, S.C. Records, id. # 99-62-0-33-1-1-1; Johnston, memo, 11 February 1965, S.C. Records, id. # 99-62-0-196-1-1-1.
20. Johnston, memo, 23 June 1964, S.C. Records, id. # 99-36-0-21-1-1-1 to 4-1-1-1. Johnston to Hon. Doty Jackson, 10 February 1966, S.C. Records, id. # 99-62-0-94-1-1-1 to 2-1-1.
21. Johnston, letter to Federation of Constitutional Government, 4 May 1964, S.C. Records, id. # 6-70-0-165-1-1-1; Johnston, speech, Canton Lyons' Club, 13 May 1964, S.C. Records, id. # 99-62-0-16-3-1-1- to 5-1-1-1; *Laws of Mississippi*, Chapter 157, 9 April 1964, 135–36; Johnston, memo, 5 June 1964, S.C. Records, id. # 99-36-0-26-1-1-1; Johnston, memo, Senate and House Appropriations Committee, 25 May 1964, S.C. Records, id. # 99-36-0-38-1-1-1. Report, "Citizen Council Grant," S.C. Records, id. # 99-30-0-46-1-1-1 to 2-1-1.
22. Johnston, memo to Governor Johnson, 29 March 1965, S.C. Records, id. # 99-34-0-9-1-1-1 to -2-1-1.
23. *Commercial Appeal*, 28 September 1997.
24. *Journal of the House of Representatives of the state of Mississippi at a regular session thereof in the city of Jackson commencing Tuesday, January 4, 1977*, 19.
25. E. Hilliard, letter to MDAH Board, 24 January 1977, Series 1250: Minutes and Related Material, MDAH; *House Journal, Regular Session*, 1977, 19, 121, 82; *Daily News*, 28 January 1977; Erle Johnston, *Mississippi's Defiant Years, 1953–1973: An Interpretive Documentary with Personal Experiences* (Forest, Miss.: Lake Harbor Publishers, 1990), 379–80; Yasuhiro Katagiri, *The Mississippi State Sovereignty Commission—Civil Rights and State's Rights* (Jackson: University Press of Mississippi, 2001), 415–18.
26. "Department of Archives and History, Minutes of a Meeting of the Board of Trustees, January 28, 1977," Series 1250, MDAH; *Clarion-Ledger*, 29 January 1977.
27. *Tupelo Daily Journal*, 17 February 1977.
28. *Daily News*, 17 February 1977; *Clarion-Ledger*, 17 February 1977, 18 February 1977; Johnston, *Defiant Years*, 381; Katagiri, *Mississippi State Sovereignty Commission—Civil Rights and States' Rights*, note 15, 668; *Tupelo Daily Journal*, 17 February 1977.
29. *Laws of Mississippi*, 1977, Chapter 320, 447–48.
30. "Department of Archives and History, Minutes of a Meeting of the Executive Committee Board of Trustees, March 11, 1977," Series 1250, MDAH; *Laws of Mississippi*, 1977, Chapter 320, 447–48; *Clarion-Ledger*, 22 May 1977. Actually, the total number of pages would not be known for twenty-five years.
31. Four years later, the 1981 Archives and Records Management Act would give archivists the authority to "inspect closed or restricted records in order to appraise them for archival significance." Unfortunately, that law could not be applied to the Sovereignty Commission records.
32. *Clarion-Ledger*, 28 July 1989.
33. 638 F.2d 1336 (5th Cir. 1981), 31 Fed. R. Srv. 2d (Callaghan) 380.
34. Calvin Trillin, "State Secrets," *The New Yorker*, 29 May 1995, 58; *Daily News*, 30 October 1984, 29 November 1984.
35. *American Civil Liberties Union ("ACLU") v. Fordice*, 969 F. Supp. 403 (S.D. Miss. 1994).
36. *Daily News*, 31 December 1990; Civil Action J77-0047(B), *American Civil Liberties Union ("ACLU") v. Mabus*, 719 F. Supp. 1345 (S.D. Miss. 1989).
37. *Clarion-Ledger*, 28 July 1989.
38. *ACLU v. Mabus*, 719 F. Supp. 1345 (S.D. Miss. 1989).
39. Ibid.
40. *Clarion-Ledger*, 28 July 1989.
41. *ACLU v. Mabus*.
42. Series 1250: Minutes and Related Materials, 1990: Jan 19.
43. Ibid.

44. Ibid.
45. Series 1254: Executive Directors Correspondence, 1990: 27 April.
46. *American Civil Liberties Union of Mississippi, Inc. v. State of Mississippi*, 911 F. 2d 1066 (5th Cir. 1990).
47. *ACLU v. Fordice*, 969 F. Supp. 403 (S.D.Miss. 1994); *Clarion-Ledger*, 4 November 1989, 23 November 1989, 21 September 1993, 24 September 1993, 30 September 1993; *Washington Post*, 6 February 1994.
48. *ACLU v. Fordice;* Memorandum and Opinion Order, Civil Action No. J77-0047B, filed 31 May 1994.
49. *ACLU v. Fordice*.
50. *Clarion-Ledger*, 1 June 1994; Dixon Pyles to Clerk of Fifth Circuit Court of Appeals, 4 November 1994, Sovereignty Commission "Control Folder," MDAH; John R. Salter to M. Bowers, 28 December 1994, ibid.; *American Civil Liberties Union of Mississippi, Inc. v. King*, 84 F. 3d 784 (5th Cir. 1996); *Clarion-Ledger*, 14 June 1996, 16 September 1996, 19 November 1996.
51. Because the final scope of required redaction was yet to be determined, all other names were redacted.
52. Inquiry Packet rough draft and notations, Control Folder, MDAH.
53. *ACLU v. Fordice*.
54. *Clarion-Ledger*, 14 January 1998.
55. The Sovereignty Commission Records On-line are available at http://www.mdah.state.ms.us.
56. Quoted from *ACLU v. Fordice*.
57. Evers was leading an integration campaign in Jackson, Mississippi, at the time he was shot and killed outside of his home by a sniper. Byron De La Beckwith died in prison in 2001.
58. Respected grocery store owner, community leader, and activist, Vernon Dahmer offered to pay poll taxes to enable poor people to vote. Following a local radio station broadcast of his offer, Dahmer's Hattiesburg home was firebombed. He succumbed on 10 January 1966, from severe burns.
59. Wharlest Jackson was the treasurer of the Natchez branch of the NAACP. He was killed instantly on 27 February 1967 when a bomb exploded in his car.
60. *ACLU v. Fordice*.
61. Ibid.
62. Dunbar Rowland, "The Concentration of State and National Archives," *American Historical Association Annual Report* (1910), 298.
63. *Mississippi Code Annotated* (1972) Section 25-61-1.
64. *Tarlton v. United States*, 430 F.2d 1531 (5th Cir. 1970).
65. *Mississippi Code Annotated* (1972) Section 25-59-16(f).
66. Heather MacNeil, *Without Consent: The Ethics of Disclosing Personal Information in Public Archives* (Metuchen, N.J.: Society of American Archivists and Scarecrow Press, 1992), 172–73.
67. The Council of the Society of American Archivists, "Code of Ethics for Archivists" (Chicago: Society of American Archivists, 1992), 3–4.
68. MacNeil, *Without Consent*, 172–73.

Chapter 11. Archival Access to Lawyers' Papers

1. Common, or case, law developed from ancient and modern Anglo-American court decisions (except for Louisiana's law which is based on the French civil code). Portions of the common law are analyzed in such highly regarded scholarly legal works as the *Restatements of Torts* and codified in U.S. state laws.

2. Kenneth S. Broun and Walker J. Blakey, *Evidence*, 3rd ed. (St. Paul, Minn.: West Publishing Co., 2001), 194 et seq.
3. Many U.S. state laws, the federal Health Insurance Portability and Accountability Act of 1996 (HIPAA), and Canada's Personal Information Protection and Electronic Documents Act (PIPEDA) also protect the confidentiality of medical and health care records. See Barbara L. Craig, "Confidences in Medical and Health Care Records from an Archive Perspective" and Menzi L. Behrnd-Klodt, "The Brave New World of 21st-Century Medical Records Privacy in the U.S. and Canada, Contrasted with the European Data Privacy Model," appendix 4, both in this volume.

   Florida's open records law, once one of the nation's strongest, was changed to close autopsy records after the February 2001 death of the NASCAR racecar driver Dale Earnhardt at the Daytona 500. Newspapers sought access to autopsy photos and records in order to investigate race track safety. Earnhardt's widow immediately sued, fearing release of the records on the Internet and claiming an invasion of her family's right of privacy. Florida legislators swiftly passed, and the governor signed, a law that retroactively prohibited all access to autopsy photos and records, including access by police investigators and physicians (2001 Florida Statutes, Title XXIX [Public Health], Chapter 406 [Medical Examiners], Chapter 406.135 [Autopsies; confidentiality of photographs and video and audio recordings]). Florida courts upheld the new law, ignoring First Amendment concerns and the long-standing rule that privacy rights are personal to the individual and end at death. See the following articles in the *Orlando Sentinel:* Henry Curtis Pierson, "Bush Files Court Brief in Suit Over Autopsy Law," 21 December 2001; Sean Mussenden "Earnhardt Law Triggers Autopsy Debate Elsewhere," 18 February 2002; and Ludmilla Lelis, "Earnhardt Law Is Back in Court," 23 May 2002. Louisiana, Georgia, North Carolina, South Carolina, Maryland, Wisconsin, and Kentucky legislatures considered similar legislation, although it is unclear whether merely in reaction to the sudden death of a folk hero, fears of Internet disclosures, or a new protection of a "family right of privacy."

   In a slightly different vein, the U.S. Supreme Court reached a similar conclusion based on a quite different law in *National Archives and Records Administration v. Favish*, No. 02-954, slip op. at 1-17 (decided 30 March 2004). After the 1998 suicide of Deputy White House Counsel Vincent W. Foster, Jr., Allan Favish filed a FOIA request for photographs of the scene of Foster's death. The Office of Independent Counsel's denial cited FOIA exemption 7(C), which allows law enforcement records to be withheld. Favish sued to compel production. The Supreme Court upheld the denial, based on the family's right of personal privacy with respect to a close relative's death-scene images. The court felt that this outweighed the public's interest in disclosure. Concluding that Congress "intended to permit family members to assert their own privacy rights against public intrusions long deemed impermissible under the common law and cultural traditions," the court protected law enforcement activities and the "well-established cultural tradition of acknowledging a family's control over the body and the deceased's death images." The court rejected Favish's argument that exemption 7(C) was confined to an individual's right to control information about himself or herself. Finally, the court held that, when privacy interests are protected by FOIA exemption 7(C), one who requests protected records must demonstrate "an interest more specific than having the information for its own sake, and that the information is likely to advance that interest."
4. The privilege is personal to the communicant, the only person who may waive it. One who asserts the privilege may refuse to disclose and may prevent the clergy from disclosing confidential communications. Brown and Blakey, *Evidence*, 207–8. The privilege is based on an ancient rule protecting as a "sacred or moral trust" those commu-

nications required by a religion to be made; for example, a confession to a Roman Catholic priest. Many state statutes codify this privilege for all confidential communications with clergy of any denomination in the course of religious duties. This privilege has no constitutional basis. See Graham C. Lilly, *An Introduction to the Law of Evidence,* 3rd ed. (St. Paul, Minn.: West Publishing Co., 1996), 512–13, fn 2. Religious, church, and other archives may hold clergy-penitent privileged material.

5. Adoption records typically were sealed to protect privacy and anonymity, ensure equal status, promote the best interests of adopted children, and allow individuals to overcome past mistakes. See Arthur D. Sorosky, Annette Baran, and Reuben Pannor, *The Adoption Triangle* (Garden City, N.Y.: Anchor Press, Doubleday, 1978). As society's views of illegitimacy and single parenthood changed and distrust of government decisions increased, many states have opened adoption records to allow adopted children to learn their medical and family histories. As of this writing, Alaska, California, Delaware, Kansas, Ohio, Oklahoma, Oregon, Tennessee, and Washington permit adult adoptees some access to birth and adoption records, while Pennsylvania courts closed files previously available. Birth registries in some states permit willing birth parents and adult children to locate one another.

The Uniform Adoption Act, a model state law completed in 1969 and revised in 1994, suggests that adoption records be sealed for ninety-nine years after a child's birth. Alaska, Arkansas, Montana (later repealed), North Dakota, Ohio, and Vermont have passed this uniform act. Adoptee advocacy groups strongly oppose such a lengthy closure. See "Laws Giving Records Access Are Patchwork of 50 States," *San Jose Mercury News,* 6 December 1998; Associated Press, "Tennessee Justices Back Adoptees' Access to Files," *Arizona Daily Star,* 28 September 1999; Bill Graves, "Adoptees Rush to Get Copies of Birth Record," *The Oregonian,* 20 July 1999; Barbara White Stack, "Adoption Appeals Documents Concealed," *Pittsburgh Post Gazette,* 29 March 1999; Rene Sanchez, "Oregon Unseals a Painful Adoption Issue," *Washington Post,* November 1998; Kate Taylor, "Adoptees Gain Access to Their Birth Records," *The Oregonian,* November 1998; "Adoptees Speak for National Registry," 11 June 1998; Carol Christian, "A Birth Right Denied? Adoptees Seek Their Original Certificates," *Houston Chronicle,* 19 April 1999.

"Florida's Scarlet Letter Law" (2001 Florida Statues, Chapter 63.087 [Proceeding to Terminate Parental Rights Pending Adoption]) took another tack, reversing privacy safeguards for mothers and children. Any mother who places a child for adoption without identifying or locating the father must advertise in newspapers in the locality where the child was conceived, naming herself and all possible fathers, providing physical descriptions of herself and all possible fathers, and listing the likely dates and locations of conception. There are no exceptions for rape or incest victims or minors. Legislators intended to protect men who may be unaware that they are fathers, to "bring finality to the adoption process . . . and . . . make sure that adoptions don't go wrong." Adoption advocates condemn this as a draconian invasion of privacy intended to embarrass women. See Shelby Oppel, "Senate Okays Adoption Changes," *St. Petersburg Times,* 23 March 2001.

6. The requirement to return the file to the client remains if the lawyer retires or leaves the law practice, if the law firm is sold or dissolved, or if the attorney dies. New York State Bar Ethics Opinion 623 (7 November 1991). If an attorney dies, a successor attorney must locate and notify clients about the files. "Generally, the files should be returned to the client, destroyed if the client so directs, or stored as long as is necessary to protect the client's interest." Philadelphia Bar Association Opinion 88-17 (16 May 1988). In some jurisdictions, the client must agree to any transfer of closed case files to another attorney. The lawyer may be required to publish notices in local

newspapers to locate clients. The lawyer may not destroy client documents without consent and must not violate confidentiality in disposing of files. North Dakota Ethics Opinion 92-11 (16 September 1992). If client files are abandoned, a lawyer who acquires them later must treat them as client property and preserve confidences. The lawyer should attempt to notify clients and offer to forward the files to them. Philadelphia Bar Association Opinion 95-6 (1995).

The client's wishes may influence the file's disposition after the client's death. See Virginia State Bar Ethics Opinion 928 (1987). A lawyer may not provide copies of a deceased client's file to the client's children or heirs if the client had requested confidentiality. Mississippi State Bar Ethics Opinion 123 (1986). An attorney may turn over old closed files of a deceased client to a lawyer representing the client's estate only on court order or if the decedent consented prior to death. Missouri Ethics Opinion 980172 (undated). It is improper for a non-lawyer not affiliated with a firm to review its files, thus, a lawyer's heirs may not review the decedent's files. Virginia State Bar Ethics Opinion 1307 (1989).

7. Ann Massie Nelson, "File Custody Disputes Are Common When Lawyers Leave Law Firms," *Wisconsin Lawyer* 71 (September 1998); Wisconsin Ethics Opinion E-00-03 (2000); Colorado Ethics Opinion 104 (1999); Michigan Ethics Opinion RI-204 (1994); Kansas Ethics Opinion 92-05 (1992); Alaska Ethics Opinion 95-6 (1995); and South Dakota Ethics Opinion 96-7 (1996). *In re: Admonition Issued in Panel Files No. 94-24,* 553 N.W.2d 853 (Minn. S. Ct. 1995).

8. Many jurisdictions have adopted the American Bar Association's Model Rules of Professional Conduct Rule 1.16(d), Declining or Terminating Representation, "Upon termination of representation, a lawyer shall take steps to the extent reasonably practicable to protect a client's interests, such as . . . surrendering papers and property to which the client is entitled . . ." and Rule 1.17(c), Sale of Law Practice, requiring that actual written notice of the sale be given to each client, including subsection (3), "the client's right to . . . take possession of the file." If the client cannot be located, a court may authorize the transfer or disposition of client files. *Model Rules of Professional Conduct,* 2001 edition (Chicago: American Bar Association, 2000). Also see, e.g., Colorado Ethics Opinion 104 (1999) (detailing types of documents to be returned to the client or withheld by the attorney). The lawyer first must determine which materials belong to the client and which to the lawyer. The latter may be retained for the lawyer's future use, but should remain available to protect the client's rights, if needed. The client's files may be returned when the representation concludes. Attorneys should not destroy files without client consent, but may first consult with the client about the preferred disposition or merely return the files. See, e.g., District of Committee Bar Opinion 1988-1 (undated); Bar of the City of New York Ethics Opinion 1986-4 (1986); South Carolina State Bar Ethics Opinion 92-19 (1992); Wisconsin Ethics Opinion E-98-1: Disposition of Closed Client files (1998); and Bar Association of San Francisco Ethics Opinion 1990-1 (1990).

9. Ideally, lawyers arrange with the client for the disposal of closed files, document the decision in a written agreement, and develop a formal records retention plan for closed client files. Wisconsin Ethics Opinion E-98-1 (1998); Los Angeles County Ethics Opinion 473 (1993); District of Columbia Bar Ethics Opinion 283 (1998); Missouri Ethics Opinions 960224 (undated) and 000082 (2000). When clients cannot be located, many bar associations require diligent searching and notification, and if to no avail, require retention of closed case files for specific periods, e.g., a specific period after the completion of the last act that could result in assertion of a claim or malpractice action against the lawyer or periods consistent with legal requirements for maintaining records of client account funds or state abandoned property laws.

Some recommend permanent retention of intrinsically valuable items. See, e.g., Wisconsin Ethics Opinion E-98-1 (1998) (six years); 58 Alabama Law 368 (1997) (six years); Arizona Ethics Opinion (no disposal of a missing client's financial and business documents unless legally abandoned under state law); District of Columbia Bar Ethics Opinion 283, note 11 (1998) (five years); Illinois State Bar Association Opinion 94-19 (1995) (five years for legal aid agency files); Iowa Ethics Opinion 91-20 (1991) (five years after the file is closed); Los Angeles Ethics Opinion 475 (1993) (five years); Maryland Ethics Opinion (1994) (five years); Michigan Ethics Opinion R-12 (1991) (five years for files of public defenders); Missouri Ethics Opinion 000082 (2000), Nassau County (NY) Bar Association Ethics Opinion 81-10 (1981) (seven years after the case is closed); New York County Ethics Opinion 725 (1998); North Carolina Revised Proposed Rule of Professional Conduct 209 (1995) (six years); and Vermont Ethics Opinion 97-8. See also D.C. Bar Opinion 283, note 10. Following expiration of the required period, the files generally may be destroyed. In some jurisdictions, however, client property or original documents may not be destroyed under any circumstances. South Carolina Ethics Op. 95-18, ABA/BNA Man. Prof. Conduct 45:1208; D.C. Bar Op. 283, note 8; Los Angeles County Bar Association Ethics Opinion 491 (1997).

The lawyer must protect client confidentiality even during destruction, which should be by shredding, incinerating, or using a confidential commercial service. See, e.g., New York County Ethics Opinion 725 (1998).

10. Attorneys are required by ethics and professional codes of conduct to maintain client confidentiality. In addition, attorney-client privilege has been upheld by the U.S. Supreme Court in *Swidler & Berlin v. United States,* 118 S.Ct. 2081, 2084 (1998).

11. In 1998, during independent counsel Kenneth W. Starr's investigations into the Clinton administration, Starr unsuccessfully sought the notes of attorney James Hamilton of his conversations with Deputy White House Counsel Vincent W. Foster, Jr. Foster spoke to Hamilton following the firing of White House travel office employees, and shortly thereafter committed suicide. Starr sought Hamilton's notes on the grounds that upholding the attorney-client privilege would obstruct the search for truth, but the Supreme Court refused to force disclosure of the privileged conversations. *Swidler & Berlin v. United States,* 118 S.Ct. 2081. Also see Joan Biskupic, "Do Legal Secrets Outlive Clients?" *Washington Post,* 8 June 1998.

12. Jules R. Ryckebusch, "Prof. Ryckebusch: Authority on Lizzie Borden," originally printed in *Massachusetts Community College Newsletter* 9, Article 4 (November 1994), reprinted on-line at http://cite2.bristol.mass.edu/~kbjorge/LizzieBsite/JulesRyckebusch/LizzieB_Quarterly_Newsletter.

13. Few recorded ethics opinions advise attorneys who are potential archival donors. In 1996, the Standing Committee on Legal Ethics of the Virginia State Bar noted that "A lawyer whose closed case files may have historical significance may not turn them over to a university for archiving without client consent if the files contain client confidences or secrets. Even if scholars wishing access to the files are required to represent that their work will not involve any use of the former clients' names or other identifying data, the duty of confidentiality prevails." Virginia Ethics Opinion 1166 (1996).

In Oklahoma, "the files of a lawyer may not be turned over to a historical or educational institution, unless the lawyer's clients expressly consent or the files contain no information that could be classified as confidences or secrets." Oklahoma Ethics Opinion 301 (1983).

The District of Columbia Bar Committee on Legal Ethics considered a donation of papers to a university research archives specializing in U.S. domestic and foreign policy. The papers related to the lawyer's representation of private clients and his activities as a former high-level government employee. Some items already had been disclosed outside of the attorney-client relationship. The Bar provided the following responses to questions posed:

(1) May the papers be turned over to the archives without obtaining the consent of the affected clients? Answer: No. "A lawyer may not donate to a university archives papers disclosing the confidences or secrets of his or her private clients without first obtaining the informed consent of the affected clients. This is true regardless of the passage of time or changed circumstances as long as the underlying information continues to constitute a confidence or secret." The requirement applied to past and present clients while the information continued to be confidential, the client made a continuing request for nondisclosure, or disclosure was potentially detrimental or embarrassing to the client. "In the absence of [client] consent, the inquirer ethically may donate those papers only after making whatever deletions are necessary to protect his client's confidences and secrets." The requirements were absolute. Limiting the disclosures or imposing access restrictions were not permissible alternatives.

(2) Is there some reasonable period of time after which a client could not reasonably object to the disclosure of a lawyer's work product in the setting of a historic archive? Answer: No.

(3) Can distinctions be drawn between persons to whom access might be granted by the donor, e.g., to "bona fide historians" who will not directly quote any material without first checking with the donor or his representative, but denying it to those who will not abide by such an agreement or to the general public? Answer: No. Donor-imposed access restrictions on papers disclosing client confidences or secrets are not adequate unless clients agree.

(4) Can distinctions be drawn between materials that have been otherwise disclosed and those that have only been communicated to clients or the lawyer's partners and associates? Answer: It depends. Once materials have been disclosed to third parties outside of the lawyer-client relationship, they may no longer be confidential, however in some cases, courts may consider whether the client intended for the materials to be disclosed. District of Columbia Bar Association Opinion 119 (1983).

14. When the author's local bar association located old law firm client grievance files, the Wisconsin Supreme Court instructed that the files be delivered to the court for destruction rather than placed in a public archives. Archivists may disagree, but such is the safest outcome for attorneys.
15. Akiba J. Covitz, "Providing Access to Lawyers' Papers: The Perils . . . and the Rewards," *Legal Reference Services Quarterly* 20, nos. 1/2 (2001), also published separately as *Public Services Issues with Rare and Archival Law Materials,* ed. Michael Widener (New York: Haworth Press, 2001).
16. *Hickman v. Taylor,* 329 US 495 (1947).

Chapter 12. The Buckley Stops Where?

1. Marjorie Rabe Barritt, "The Appraisal of Personally Identifiable Student Records," *American Archivist* 49 (Summer 1986): 275.
2. 88 Statute 571, 20 U.S.C. Section 1232g. See Menzi L. Behrnd-Klodt, "The Family Education Rights and Privacy Act: Legislative Amendments and Judicial Interpretations," appendix 3 of this volume, for more information about FERPA. The legisla-

Notes to Pages 181–183　　**347**

tive history of FERPA is profiled in appendix 2, "Selected U.S. Federal Statutes Concerning Privacy."
3. Family Policy Compliance Office, U.S. Department of Education, "Legislative History of Major FERPA Provisions," http://www.ed.gov, provides details of the evolution of the act, including the legislative changes since it was first adopted. Congress also amended the terms of FERPA in the USA PATRIOT Act, passed in October 2001 and described more fully in appendix 3.
4. 20 U.S.C. Section 1232(a)(4)(A).
5. Lynn M. Daggett, "Bucking Up Buckley I: Making the Federal Student Records Statute Work," *Catholic University Law Review* (Spring 1997), retrieved through LEXIS-NEXIS Academic Universe, November 2001.
6. As of the August 2000 revision of FERPA regulations by the U.S. Dept. of Education, a "sole possession record" is a record that is "kept in the sole possession of the maker, [is] used only as a personal memory aid, and [is] not accessible to any other person except a temporary substitute for the maker of the record." As reported in Julie M. Slavens, "FERPA: Student Photographs and Videotapes," *NSBA Newsletter*, June 2001, http://www.nsba.org/nepn/newsletter/0601.htm, available as of 2001.
7. Law enforcement records were excluded as part of one of three significant amendments to Buckley during the 1990s. See Daggett, "Bucking Up Buckley I."
8. Daggett, "Bucking Up Buckley I."
9. Charles B. Elston, "University Student Records: Research Use, Privacy Rights and the Buckley Law," *Midwestern Archivist* 1, no. 1 (1976): 26.
10. Ibid., 27.
11. Barritt, "The Appraisal of Personally Identifiable Student Records," 265–67.
12. Ibid., 272. She notes that a minority of schools contacted for her article were relying on the opinion of in-house counsel that there was no right of privacy for the dead, and they were therefore lifting restrictions on research access to the records of deceased students.
13. On its Web site, the FPCO states that its mission is "to meet the needs of the Department's primary customers—learners of all ages—by effectively implementing two laws that seek to ensure student and parental rights in education: the Family Educational Rights and Privacy Act (FERPA) and the Protection of Pupil Rights Amendment (PPRA)."
14. Mark A. Greene, "Developing a Research Access Policy for Student Records: A Case Study at Carleton College," *American Archivist* 50 (Fall 1987): 570–79. Unfortunately, the fact that FERPA ceases to apply once a student is dead—one of the few apparent certainties in interpreting the archival implications of the act—is still not well known among college and university archivists. See Helen Willa Samuels, *Varsity Letters: Documenting Modern Colleges and Universities* (Chicago: Society of American Archivists, 1992), 36–37, which incorrectly suggests that state law on privacy rather than federal law (and FERPA itself) determines FERPA's applicability to deceased students, as well as the exchange between Ed Southern and James Simpert, 26 January 2001, on the Archives and Archivists Listserv, http://listserv.muohio.edu/archives/archives.html. Inexplicably, William J. Maher, *The Management of College and University Archives* (Metuchen, N. J.: Scarecrow Press, 1992), all but ignores FERPA.
15. Greene, "Developing a Research Policy," 572–76. The statutory exception is 20 U.S.C. 1232g(b)(1)(F).
16. The lack of consensus is illuminated in a paper by Tamar Chute and Ellen Swain, "Navigating Ambiguous Waters: Providing Access to Student Records in University Archives," 2004 (submitted for publication), received just as this article was due to be sent to the printer. Chute and Swain conducted a large survey of university archivists

and their schools' management of student records. They hope their research will be a step toward "the development of guidelines that will help standardize the ways in which archivists provide access to student records."

17. A letter, reproduced as appendix A to this article, was sent to the Family Policy Compliance Office in November 2001; despite repeated phone calls to the office by Christine Weideman and several promises by office staff to reply to the letter, nothing was received.
18. 20 U.S.C. 1232g(a)(1)(C)(ii) and 20 U.S.C. 1232g(b)(1)(E)(i).
19. "Legislative History of Major FERPA Provisions."
20. The survey and responses are reproduced in appendix B to this article. The survey was designed by the authors of this article and sent via e-mail to archivists at ten colleges and universities, including a mix of private and public, large and small, from every region of the country. Only five responses were received, including one from an archivist who admitted not being aware of FERPA and therefore was unable to answer many of the questions.
21. Amicus Curiae Brief by the U.S. Solicitor General Supporting Petitioners (No. 00-1073), in the Supreme Court of the United States, *Owasso Independent School District v. Kristja J. Falvo,* http://www.usdoj.gov/osg/briefs/2001/3mer/1ami/2000-1073.mer.ami.html (hereafter "Amicus Curiae Brief"). The case involved a parent who sought to prohibit her school district from allowing teachers to have students grade each other's papers and call the grades out loud. The complaint alleged, and a U.S. Appeals Court held, that such activities violated FERPA because the grade on a class assignment was an educational record that could not be disclosed to others, and the students in this instance were acting on behalf of the school and therefore subject to FERPA restrictions. The Supreme Court overturned the Appeals Court decision.
22. Ibid.
23. Supreme Court of the United States, No. 00-1073, *Owasso Independent School District v. Kristja J. Falvo,* February 19, 2002, at http://www.supremecourtus.gov/opinions/01pdf/00-1073.pdf.
24. For example, the decision notes that FERPA requires "a record" of access for each pupil. This single record must be kept "with the education records." This suggests Congress contemplated that education records would be kept in one place with a single record of access. By describing a "school official "and "his assistants " as the personnel responsible for the custody of the records, FERPA implies that education records are institutional records kept by a single central custodian, such as a registrar, not individual assignments handled by many student graders in their separate classrooms.

    The ramifications of this implied but not legally binding interpretation of FERPA drew a sharp response from Justice Scalia, who agreed with the majority's narrow ruling but wrote, "I cannot agree, however, with the other ground repeatedly suggested by the Court: that education records include only documents kept in some central repository at the school."
25. Amicus Curiae Brief.
26. Ibid.
27. Excerpted from posting to Archives and Archivists List by Jackie Esposito, 18 May 1993, emphasis added.
28. ALAWON 2:37 (8 September 1993), "Reinventing Government, Report Highlights, Department of Education Clarifies Access to Theses," full text available from the American Library Association, Washington, D.C.
29. In deciding *Owasso v. Falvo,* the U.S. Tenth Circuit Court of Appeals explicitly rejected the formal interpretation of FERPA provided by the office to the school dis-

trict, saying "deference does not extend to an interpretation contained in an opinion letter issued by the administering agency." (The Circuit Court's decision can be found at http://laws.findlaw.com/10th/995130.html. In his amicus brief to the Supreme Court, the U.S. solicitor general acknowledged that some of the office's prior interpretations had suggested that some instances of peer grading were a violation of FERPA and asked the court to ignore those earlier letters and accept his brief as the official position of the Department of Education.

30. Andrea L. Foster, "Judge Halts Effort by Bates to Prevent Disclosure of Student E-mail Messages," *The Chronicle of Higher Education* 47 (13 April 2001), A4, found through ProQuest. The judge ruled that e-mails from students to faculty were educational records, but that Bates College did not have standing to prevent their further dissemination once the messages were in the hands of the synagogue's board of directors.

31. American Jewish Congress, "AJ Congress Calls on Education Secretary Not to Allow Privacy Rules to Shield Ideological and Political Correspondence with School Officials," 5 March 1998, found on Lexis-Nexis Academic Universe, 21 September 2001.

32. "Video of school board meeting interpreted as 'education record'," *SPLC* (Student Press Law Center) *Report* 18 (Fall 1997), 12, at http://www.splc.org/.

33. Julie M. Slavens, "FERPA: Student Photographs and Videotapes," *NSBA* (National School Boards Association) *Newsletter,* June 2001 at http://www.nsba.org/nepn/newsletter/0601.htm . Slavens allows that videotape of public events, such as football games, may not be covered by FERPA, but suggests that schools not take any chances but make explicit announcements to parents and students whenever taping occurs so that parents can exercise the "opt out" option prescribed by FERPA for directory information.

34. For citations to several additional cases, see "FERPA Fundamentalism: How a federal law designed to protect student privacy is being misinterpreted to injure press freedom" *SPLC* (Student Press Law Center) *Report* 22 (Spring 2001): 35, at http://www.splc.org/.

35. The Midwest Archives Conference gave its 1992 Presidents' Award to two state legislators who helped draft and pass such an amendment on behalf of the special collections units at the University of Minnesota.

36. In addition to manuscript curators, college and university archivists should look to enlist the support of others with a stake in clarifying FERPA, certainly including scholars and librarians, and perhaps the media.

Part 4. Institutional Perspectives

1. Richard J. Cox and David A. Wallace, eds., *Archives and the Public Good: Accountability and Records in Modern Society* (Westport, Conn.: Quorum Books, 2002) highlights the notion of accountability, though most of the articles focus on the public sector, rather than private institutions. A thorough archival overview that focuses on record-keeping scandals within American business remains to be written.

2. The Investigative Staff of the *Boston Globe, Betrayal: The Crisis in the Catholic Church* (Boston: Little, Brown and Company, 2002), xi, xiii, 137.

3. A thorough review of this legislation is contained in Menzi L. Behrnd-Klodt, "Legislating Medical Records Privacy for the 21st-Century in the U.S. and Canada, Contrasted with the European Data Privacy Model," appendix 4 of this volume.

4. Stephen Novak, "Health Insurance Portability and Accountability Act of 1996: Its Implications for History of Medicine Collections," *The Watermark* 24, no. 3 (2003), available at the Web site of Archivists and Librarians in the History of the Health Sci-

ences at http://www.library.ucla.edu/libraries/biomed/alhhs/, offers a solid overview on medical archivists and HIPAA.
5. A counterargument may be found in Richard A. Posner, "An Economic Theory of Privacy," *Regulation* 19–26 (May–June 1978). Posner argues that privacy was not desired for its own sake, but was valued as a means to produce income or other benefit. He suggests that his economic model of privacy would not assign a property value to discrediting personal information.

Chapter 13. Trust and Professional Agency in the Archives of Religious Organizations

1. Current discussions of professional lay ministry, which is essentially a debate over the agency relationship within a clerical hierarchy, are prevalent in several religious denominations, compare United States Conference of Catholic Bishops, "Lay Ecclesial Ministry: State of the Questions," *Origins* 29, no. 31 (2000): 498–512.
2. Of particular note for informational privacy issues are articles by Weinreb, "The Right to Privacy," in *The Right to Privacy,* ed. E. Paul, F. Miller, and J. Paul (Cambridge: Cambridge University Press, 2000), 34–42; R. G. Frey, "Privacy, Control, and Talk of Rights," ibid., 45–67; and Friedman (2000, pp. 186–201); see also S. Bok, *Secrets: On the Ethics of Concealment and Revelation* (New York: Vintage Books, 1989), 73–101 and 147–48; Raymond Wacks, *Personal Information: Privacy and the Law* (Oxford: Clarendon Press, 1993).
3. Concepts of organizational culture, interpretation, and performance used in this essay are influenced by writers in cognitive, social, and managerial science who emphasize environments in which the physical and symbolic interaction of the actor takes place in an already present and historically rich narrative of interpretive agency. See especially, M. Alvesson and P. O. Berg, *Corporate Culture and Organizational Symbolism* (Berlin: Walther de Gruyter, 1992); Edwin Hutchins, *Cognition in the Wild* (Cambridge, Mass.: MIT Press, 2000); R. L. Daft and K. E. Weick, "Toward a Model of Organizations as Interpretation Systems," *Academy of Management Review* 9, no. 2 (1984); and B. Latour, "On Technical Mediation: Philosophy, Sociology, Genealogy," *Common Knowledge* 3, no. 2 (1994).
4. The concept of "social privacy" might better describe the communitarian ethic that qualifies individual freedom, duty, and virtue in organized religious life. For a discussion of this concept of privacy, see R. T. Hixson, *Privacy in Public Society: Human Rights in Conflict* (New York: Oxford University Press, 1987).
5. P. E. Becker, *Congregations in Conflict: Cultural Models of Local Religious Life* (Cambridge: Cambridge University Press, 1999), 202. Becker takes her definition of idioculture from Gary Alan Fine's *With the Boys:* "a system of knowledge, beliefs, behaviors, and customs shared by members of an interacting group to which members can refer, and that serve as the basis for further interaction. This approach stresses the localized nature of culture, implying that it . . . can be a particularistic development of any group."
6. R. M. Gula, *Ethics in Pastoral Ministry* (New York: Paulist Press, 1996), 14–25.
7. Ibid., 19.
8. W. W. Rankin, *Confidentiality and Clergy: Churches, Ethics and the Law* (Harrisburg, Penn.: Morehouse Publishing, 1990), 45.
9. Bok, *Secrets.*
10. W. Bassett, *Religious Organizations and the Law* (St. Paul, Minn.: West Group, 1999). Bassett provides a legal-historical overview of the clergy-penitent privilege; see also

Rankin, *Confidentiality and Clergy*, 21–36, who gives a thoughtful discussion of the extension of the privilege to Episcopal clergy by legislation.

11. Archives of national and regional jurisdictions for the Episcopal, Lutheran, Methodist, and Presbyterian churches document their communities beyond the sponsoring corporate bodies. Catholic diocesan jurisdictions have traditionally been more constrained in their documentation strategy, although recent trends in Chicago, Seattle, Los Angeles, and New Orleans suggest a broadening of their documentation field.

12. M. H. Shepherd, "The Rights of the Baptized," in *The Case for Freedom: Human Rights in the Church*, ed. J. Coriden (Washington, D.C.: Corpus Books, 1969); D. B. Stevick, "A Theological View of the Place of Law in the Church: An Episcopal Perspective," *The Jurist* 42 (1982), 1–13; D. J. Ward, "Privacy/Confidentiality Issues in Religious Institutes," *CLSA Proceedings* 61 (1999): 305–15.

13. Weinreb, "The Right to Privacy," 2000.

14. For a discussion of the merits of negative and positive rights theories of privacy, see Frey, "Privacy, Control," 45–67.

15. C. Whelan, "Supreme Court Doctrine and Religious Institutions," *The Catholic Lawyer* 34 (1990): 1–15; D. J. Young and S. W. Tigges, "Discovery and Use of Church Records by Civil Authorities," *The Catholic Lawyer* 30, no. 3 (1990): 198–217.

16. Bassett, *Religious Organizations*, sec. 1.8; R. R. Hammer, ed., "The Clergy-Penitent Privilege and Access to Ecclesiastical Records," *Church Law and Tax Report* 7, no. 2 (1993): 5.

17. For a review of these cases and others, see Bassett, *Religious Organizations*.

18. Ibid., secs. 7.80–82.

19. Ibid., xiv; P. Dane, "The Corporation Sole and the Encounter of Law and the Church," in *Sacred Companies*, ed. J. J. Demerath, P. D. Hall, T. Schmitt, and R. H. Williams (New York: Oxford University Press, 1998), 50.

20. Since the early 1990s, the churches have felt greater readiness on the part of the courts to become involved in what were formerly deemed ecclesiastical matters guarded by the separation clause. This trend has given archivists in religious institutions openings to collaborate closely with corporate attorneys, internal auditors, and other ecclesiastical administrators in crafting policy and liability management responses (Bassett, *Religious Organizations*, §. 1.32 and §2.44–56).

21. Ibid., §1.19 and §§5:49–51.

22. D. Ioppolo, M. Breitenbeck, E. Rinere, and R. Stake, *Confidentiality in the United States, A Legal and Canonical Study* (Washington, D.C.: Canon Law Society of America, 1988); M. A. Shaughnessy, *Ministry and the Law: What You Need to Know* (New York: Paulist Press, 1998).

23. Bassett, *Religious Organizations*, § 3:1, gives an instructive list of the many areas in which the church is active in community health, education, and welfare.

24. Insofar as any of these functions are covered by canon law, some degree of confidentiality may be constitutionally protected from disclosure except in cases of "fraud, collusion or arbitrariness," Ioppolo, et al., *Confidentiality*, 21; see also Bassett, *Religious Organizations*, § 3.10.

25. Bassett, *Religious Organizations*, §3.11.

26. Ibid., §3.8.

27. Compare Constitution and Canon for the Government of the Protestant Episcopal Church in the United States of America 2000 (New York: General Convention of the Episcopal Church, 2001), IV.5–6, 14–15; *The Book of Order: The Constitution of the Presbyterian Church USA 2000–2001* (Louisville, Ky.: 2001), G-1.0300–0305, G-2.0500 and

Section D; and *The Book of Discipline of the United Methodist Church, 2000* (New York: United Methodist Publishing House, 2000), Sec. V ¶136, ¶139.
28. Canon Law Society of America, *Code of Canon Law 1983* (Washington, D.C.: Canon Law Society of America, 1983).
29. J. P. Beal, J. A. Coriden, and T. J. Green, eds., *New Commentary on the Code of Canon Law* (New York: Paulist Press, 2000), 228.
30. Ibid., 277.
31. Bok, *Secrets*.
32. Church law is augmented by the precedent of civil litigation and case law that create an ethical and legal obligation on church leadership (including archivists) to demonstrate accountability by ensuring legitimate access to corporate documentation (Bassett, *Religious Organizations*, §§ 5:56, 5:51 §§ 3:87–88).
33. Organizational theory has looked to culture for the patterns of durability and stability in organizational structures even in the midst of sometimes bewildering tensions over goal differentiation, free agent relationships, the introduction of change, and response to external influences. The literature on organizational culture is not so much about describing institutional equilibrium, as about understanding why organizations work despite the tensions that would seem to weaken them. See Alvesson and Berg, *Corporate Culture*; N. J. Demerath, "Snatching Defeat from Victory in the Decline of Liberal Protestantism: Culture versus Structure in Institutional Analysis," in *Sacred Companies*, ed. N. J. Demerath, et al.; M. J. Hatch, "The Dynamics of Organizational Culture," *Academy of Management Review* 18 (1993): 657–93; J. Martin, *Cultures in Organizations: Three Perspectives* (New York: Oxford University Press, 1993); E. H. Schein, *Organizational Culture* (San Francisco: Jossey-Bass, 1992); L. M. Smircich, "Concepts of Culture and Organizational Analysis," *Administrative Science Quaterly* 28 (1983): 339–58; and K. E. Weick, "The Significance of Corporate Culture," in *Organizational Culture*, ed. P. J. Frost, L. F. Moore, et al. (Beverly Hills, Calif.: Sage, 1985). For the impact of organizational culture on recordkeeping and communication, see especially M. Feldman, *Order Without Design: Information Processing and Policy Making*, (Palo Alto, Calif.: Stanford University Press, 1989); and J. R. Taylor and E. J. Van Every, *The Emergent Organization* (Mahwah, N. J.: Lawrence Erlbaum Associates, 2000).
34. H. Garfinkel, "A Conception of, and Experiments with, 'Trust' as a Condition of Stable Concerted Actions," in *Motivation and Social Interaction: Cognitive Determinants*, ed. O. J. Harvey (New York: Ronald Press, 1963).
35. H. S. Stout and D. S. Cormode, "Institutions and the Story of American Religion: A Sketch of a Synthesis," in *Sacred Companies*, ed. Demerath, et al., 66.
36. Dane, "Corporation Sole," 54. Dane's analysis draws largely on the work of Carl Zollmann's 1917 classic *American Civil Church Law*. Zollmann points out the distinctive structural interaction in which Christian ecclesiastical culture is radically diffused with a secular public business structure. The implications of the structure on the archivist's documentary universe can lead to circuitous communication interactions that bring the religious archivist into advisory contact with congregational parties at one moment and multinational agencies at the next.
37. P. Bourdieu, "Genesis and Structure of the Religious Field," *Comparative Social Research* 13 (1991): 1–44, examines the secrecy of knowledge that forms a dividing line between the sacred (clergy) and the profane (lay) believers as central to the exchange of power and legitimacy in religious institutions. Access to secret (rare) knowledge (symbolic ritual, dogma, and the administration of resources) is open to competition, not least by specialists, who contribute to a structural dynamic of interpretation in which the belief system and the bureaucracy that protects it undergo constant transformation. See also D. Swartz, "Bridging the Study of Culture and Reli-

gion: Pierre Bourdieu's Political Economy of Symbolic Power," *Sociology of Religion* 57, no. 1 (1996): 71–86 for a discussion of Pierre Bourdieu's sociology of religion.
38. P. D. Hall, "Religion and the Organizational Revolution in the United States," in *Sacred Companies,* ed. Demerath, et al., 99–115.
39. M. Chavez, "Denominations as Dual Structures: An Organizational Analysis," ibid., 181.
40. T. H. Jeavons, "Identifying Characteristics of 'Religious' Organizations: An Exploratory Proposal," ibid., 79–95; R. A. Rappaport, "The Obvious Aspects of Ritual," in *Ecology, Meaning and Religion,* ed. R. A. Rappaport (Richmond, Calif.: North Atlantic Books, 1979).
41. M. P. Lawson, "The Holy Spirit as Conscience Collective," *Sociology of Religion* 60, no. 4 (1999): 341–61; M. J. Neitz, *Charisma and Community: A Study of Religious Commitment within the Charismatic Renewal* (New Brunswick, N. J.: Transaction Books, 1987); R. E. Prell, *Prayer and Community: The Havurah in American Judaism* (Detroit: Wayne State University Press, 1989); W. Swatos, "Secularization Theory: The Course of a Concept," *Sociology of Religion* 60, no. 3 (1999): 209–28.
42. Bok, *Secrets,* 119, reminds us that, "confidentiality refers to the boundaries surrounding shared secrets and to the process of guarding these boundaries."
43. J. Pfeffer, "Power and Resource Allocation in Organizations," in *New Directions in Organizational Behavior,* ed. B. M. Staw and G. R. Salancik (Chicago: St. Clair Press, 1977), 235–65.
44. Stout and Cormode, "Institutions and the Story of American Religion," 75.
45. A. B. Seligman, *The Problem of Trust* (Princeton, N. J.: Princeton University Press, 1997); M. R. Talbot, "Starting from Scripture," in *Limning the Psyche: Explorations in Christian Psychology,* ed. R. C. Roberts and M. R. Talbot (Grand Rapids, Mich.: William B. Eerdmans Publishing Co., 1997).
46. Bassett, *Religious Organizations,* §1.21.
47. In the Roman Catholic Church, the information role for recorded acts is vested in the chancellor. The chancellor is the canonical gatekeeper—the individual responsible for granting access to the courts of ancient Rome—developed into the role of recordkeeper and authenticator of official documents. The same role accrued to the office of the registrar in the Episcopal Church or the stated clerk of the Presbyterian Church.
48. Eisenhardt, "Agency Theory: An Assessment and Review," *Academy of Management Review* 14 (1989): 57–74.
49. Concepts of human agency have most recently been influenced by information economics, principally in the areas of transactional cost analysis and principal-agent relationships. The assumption behind economic agency theory is that expert human agents will act with calculated self-interest using privileged access to information resources to seek opportunistic or personal advantage at the expense of the firm or organization. P. Dasgupta, "Trust as Commodity," in *Trust: Making and Breaking Cooperative Relations,* ed. D. Gambetta (New York: Basil Blackwell, 1988); L. T. Hosmer, "Trust: The Connecting Link Between Organizational Theory and Philosophical Ethics," *Academy of Management Review* 20, no. 2 (1995); M. Jensen and W. Meckling, "Theory of the Firm: Managerial Behavior, Agency Costs, and Ownership Structure," *Journal of Financial Economics* 3 (1976): 305–60; R. Wigand, A. Picot, and R. Reichwald, *Information, Organization and Management: Expanding Markets and Corporate Boundaries* (New York: John Wiley and Sons, 1997).
50. L. Zucker, M. Darby, et al., "Collaboration Structure and Information Dilemmas in Biotechnology: Organizational Boundaries as Trust Production," in *Trust in Organizations,* vol. 3, ed. R. Kramer and T. Tyler (Thousand Oaks, Calif.: Sage Publications, 1996).

51. P. Blau, *Exchange and Power in Social Life* (New York: John Wiley and Sons, 1964), 261.
52. A. Giddens, *The Constitution of Society: Outline of the Theory of Structuration* (Berkeley: University of California Press, 1984); ibid., *The Consequences of Modernity* (Stanford, Calif.: Stanford University Press, 1990); ibid., *New Rules of Sociological Method* (Cambridge, U.K.: Polity Press, 1993).
53. Ibid., *Constitution of Society*, 26.
54. Taylor and Van Every, *Emergent Organization*.
55. Giddens, *Constitution of Society*, 261.
56. D. J. McAllister, "Affect- and Cognition-based Trust as Foundations for Interpersonal Cooperation in Organizations," *Academy of Management Review* 38 (1995), 24–95.
57. Giddens, *Consequences of Modernity*, 34.
58. Quoted in Seligman, *Problem of Trust*, 16.
59. E. L. Johnson, "Human Agency and Its Social Formation," in *Limning the Psyche*, 138–64.
60. S. L. Jones, "The Meaning of Agency and Responsibility in Light of Social Science Research," ibid., 186–205.
61. Seligman, *Problem of Trust*.
62. B. Barber, *The Logic and Limits of Trust* (New Brunswick, N. J.: Rutgers University Press, 1983).
63. N. Luhmann, "Familiarity, Confidence, Trust: Problems and Alternatives," in *Trust*, 94–107.
64. C. Moorman, "Organizational Market Information Processes: Cultural Antecedents and New Product Outcomes," *Journal of Market Research* 32, no. 3 (1995): 318–36; Seligman, *Problem of Trust*, 82.
65. Zucker, et al., "Collaboration Structure."
66. Gula, *Ethics in Pastoral Ministry;* Seligman, *Problem of Trust;* D. B. Stevick, "Canon Law," in *The Study of Anglicanism*, ed. S. Sykes, J. Booty, and J. Knight (Minneapolis: Fortress Press, 1988) 240–42.
67. J. O'Toole, "What's Different about Religious Archives?" *Midwestern Archivist* 9, no. 2 (1984): 91–101.
68. R. McBrien, *Catholicism* (San Francisco: Harper Collins, 1994), 945.
69. R. J. Lewicki and B. B. Bunker, "Developing and Maintaining Trust in Work Relationships," in *Trust in Organizations*, 114–39.
70. C. M. Hovarth, "Macro and Micro: The Emerging Field of Organizational Ethics," *Online Journal of Ethics* (1996), http://www.stthom.edu/cbes/horwath.html.; Rankin, *Confidentiality and Clergy*.
71. Rankin, *Confidentiality and Clergy*, 86. Rankin reserves an activity-theoretical area of ethical conduct where personal and professional judgment are exercised while living within a "community of faithful," i.e., a sense of individual freedom and responsibility that can only truly make sense within fiduciary relationships and social bonds. Rankin specifically examines personal and professional (ordained or lay) responsibility in a (Anglican) church context, but other organizational settings are certainly open to these interpretive moments.
72. Giddens, *Consequences of Modernity*, 84.
73. G. Duncan, T. Jabine, and V. de Wolf, eds., *Private Lives and Public Policies: Confidentiality and Accessibility of Government Statistics* (Washington, D.C.: National Academy Press, 1993).
74. Perspectives on agency and its real world impact can be found in other service professions where the obligation to stakeholders and clients is evident. One thinks of the technical role of organizational archivists in organizational relationships when read-

ing about clinical expertise in nursing where, "new possibilities of moral agency are created by clinical grasp, embodied know-how, and the ability to see likely future eventualities in clinical situations. Moral action is tied to the skills of seeing, doing, and being with others in respectful caring ways . . . skill is not the only condition for being an excellent practitioner, but it is an essential condition for acting in the moment in very complex clinical situations. . . . The development of clinical expertise inherently demands the development of ethical expertise." P. Benner, C. Tanner, and C. Chesla, *Expertise in Nursing Practice: Caring, Clincial Judgment and Ethics* (New York: Springer, 1996).

Chapter 14. Delta Blues

1. Clayton M. Christensen, *The Innovator's Dilemma* (Cambridge, Mass.: Harvard Business School Press, 1997), xv.
2. "Intellectual Property: Old Rules Don't Apply," *Wall Street Journal,* 23 August 2001, A1. For a rather grim and possibly seminal assessment of what the future of technology might hold for information and society at large, see Bill Joy, "Why the Future Doesn't Need Us," *Wired,* April 2000. For a helpful summary of Joy's apocalyptic arguments and subsequent reactions to them (both positive and negative) see, The Center for the Study of Technology and Society, Washington, D.C., "Special Focus: Bill Joy's Hi-Tech Warning."
3. The development of Web "cookies" by then-Netscape programmer Lou Montulli in 1994 greatly enabled this capability to collect information about individual Internet behaviors. For a good summary of how cookies work, how they became an Internet standard, and the potential they hold for infringement of privacy, see John Schwartz, "Giving Web a Memory Costs Its Users Privacy," *New York Times,* 4 September 2001, A1.
4. Note for example the Society of American Archivists' weakly worded position statement on the 1996 Conference on Fair Use: "The Society of American Archivists has been *monitoring with interest* the work of the Conference on Fair Use to develop guidelines for the fair use of digital images" (italics added), or Bruce Dearstyne's plaintive lament "Archivists should be among the architects of the National Information Infrastructure . . ." More often than not, archivists are on the outside looking in, powerless to do anything but comment. SAA Position Statement, "Educational Fair Use Guidelines for Digital Images," *Archival Outlook* (January 1997): 6; Bruce W. Dearstyne, "The National Information Infrastructure: Issues for Archivists," *Archival Outlook* (November 1994): 21; SAA Position Statement, "Copyright, Archival Institutions, and the Digital Environment," *Archival Outlook* (September/October 1997): 6.
5. The Internet Archive is a nonprofit organization working to preserve a record of the Internet. Michael S. James, "Fading Bits of History," at http://ABCNews.com, 9 July 2001.
6. The SAA's endorsements of principles 2, 3, and 10 clearly could conflict with the interests of those who employ corporate archivists. For example, the SAA's comment on principle 2 categorically states "Archivists therefore are opposed to efforts by copyright holders to use copyright as a means to restrict or deny access to information in primary sources made available in digital format." As of 2001, the principles themselves were available at http://www-ninch.cni.org/ISSUES/COPYRIGHT/PRINCIPLES/NHA-complete.html; the endorsement of the Society of American Archivists was available at http://www.archivists.org/governance/handbook/app_j4.htm. In addition, the 1997 SAA position statement on the digital environment states that "The archival mission is to collect, preserve, and make available to the public our nation's memory. . . . ," ignoring that such is rarely the mission of a corporate archives, Position Statement,

"Copyright," *Archival Outlook* (September–October 1997). The Supreme Court decision in *Tasini vs. The New York Times* extending an author's copyright to his contributions transferred to digital databases was one of the first decisions by the court to directly address the application of the copyright canon to new media. Betsy McCaughey, "In Digital Age, Who Owns Copy?" *Investor's Business Daily,* 25 June 2001, A20; Christopher Stern, "Freelancers Win Fight Over Reuse of Works," *Washington Post,* 26 June 2001, E1. John Perry Barlow, "Selling Wine Without Bottles: The Economy of the Mind of the Global Net," EFF "Intellectual Property Online: Patent, Trademark, Copyright" Archive, Electronic Frontier Foundation, http://www.eff.org/Intellectual_property/idea_economy.article; "Lawyer Fights for Net Freedom," *Poughkeepsie Journal,* 21 January 2001, 1D. One academic specializing in digital copyright argues that the Working Group on Intellectual Property of the Information Policy Committee of the Clinton administration's Information Infrastructure Task Force essentially reinterpreted existing copyright law in totally inappropriate fashion for use in cyberspace. She argues that the Working Group's White Paper, which formed the basis of the Digital Millennial Copyright Act of 1998, destroyed the balance between social and proprietary interests that had characterized the analog intellectual property environment. Jessica Litman, *Digital Copyright* (Amherst, N.Y.: Prometheus Books, 2001), chapters 6–9.

7. "Software Resales Entangled by Copyright Issue," *Washington Post,* 2 February 2001, E1. At the eBay auction Web site on 1 February 2001, more than 32,000 software titles were auctioned; struck by this huge market, Adobe software has on at least one instance prompted eBay to prematurely close an auction for Adobe software because the seller was not an authorized Adobe reseller. However, one technology lawyer questioned Adobe's ability to usurp the right of first sale. The transaction is equated to the resale of a CD of recorded music. In a perhaps not coincidental circumstance, given Adobe's concern with defending its property, the company also instigated the July 2001 arrest of Dmitry Sklyarov, a Russian citizen who was the first person to be charged under the 1998 Digital Millennium Copyright Act's provision against developing technical solutions designed to circumvent proprietary encryption technologies. The arrest prompted a chilling of research and discussion of the effectiveness of technology-based property protections, because the law is so broad that the mere discussion of flawed protections may be construed as an attempt to circumvent them. "We Own That Law," *Forbes,* 30 April 2001, 60; Steven Levy, "Busted By the Copyright Cops," *Newsweek,* 20 August 2001, 54. If the past is precedent, a combination of both secure systems and legislative clout may be the most effective solution. Secure systems technology was applied to the property protection of VCR videotapes in the mid-1980s, but manufacturers quickly sidestepped those technical barriers and not until Congress intervened in 1998 to outlaw circumventing technology did the secure system approach work universally. In 2001, the motion picture industry threw its weight behind the proposed Security Standards and Certification Act to protect its creative works by forcing original-equipment manufacturers to build governmentally sanctioned secure access technologies into their digital appliances. Junko Yoshida and George Leopold, "Copy Protection Bill Divides Industry, Hollywood," *EE Times,* 28 September 2001, available in 2001 at http://www.eetimes.com/story/OEG20019928S0110. John Borland, "CD Copy Compromise in the Works," CNET News.com, 28 September 2001, http://news.cnet.com/news/0-1005-201-7320279-0.html.

8. An example of intellectual property and Web issues as challenged in the courts is whether computer code should be protected by the First Amendment as free speech. The first lawsuit to address this issue revolved around the Internet publication of a computer program to break the security lock on a digital videodisc in violation of the

Digital Millennium Copyright Act's prohibition against distributing any device that essentially breaks the encryption schemes of copyrighted materials. Amy Harmon, "Judges Seek Answers on Computer Code as Free Speech," *e New York Times*, 11 May 2001, C4. Moon is quoted in Sara Robinson, "Putting it Together," *Interactive Week*, ZDNet, 10 July 2001.

9. Barlow, "Selling Wine."
10. Samuelson discusses the commodification of personal data in her writings. Privacy advocates also are concerned about the commercial value that could conceivably be collected by bio-electromechanical monitoring devices such as Digital Angel, a remote health monitoring system. Similarly, the advancement of biometric technologies such as facial recognition software poses the potential to encroach on both personal liberties and individual property right. Toby Lester, "The Reinvention of Privacy," *Atlantic Monthly*, March 2001; Ross Kerber, "Face Off," *Boston Globe*, 20 August 2001, C1.
11. Anne Van Camp, "Access Policies for Corporate Archives," in *Corporate Archives and History: Making the Past Work,* ed. Arnita A. Jones and Philip L. Cantelon (Malabar, Fla.: Krieger Publishing Company, 1993), 77–80.
12. "Lawyer . . .," *Poughkeepsie Journal,* 21 January 2001. This is not to say it doesn't affect noncorporate archives. For example one major concern is the applicability of fair use doctrine to digital information. Also, will repositories facing Internet user expectations of instant access, grappling with lengthening copyright lifetimes, and confronting increasing resource drains have the patience and commitment to preserve digital information without the prospect of being able to benefit from it for decades? For examples of the variety of uses a corporate archives can be put to, see Paul C. Lasewicz, "Strangers in a Strange Land: Archival Opportunities in a Multinational Corporation," *Archival Issues* 19, no. 2 (1994): 131–42; ibid, "Riding Out the Apocalypse: The Obsolescence of Traditional Archivy in the Face of Modern Corporate Dynamics," *Archival Issues* 22, no. 1 (1997): 61–76; Marcy Goldstein, "The Evolving Role of In-House Business Archives: From Tradition to Flexibility," *The Records of American Business,* ed. James M. O'Toole (Chicago: Society of American Archivists, 1997), 41–56.
13. Stuart Elliot, "Ads From the Past With Modern Touches," *New York Times*, 9 September 2002.
14. Numerous European and American companies have been asked to produce documents pertaining to their German operations between 1933 and 1945. In addition, activists have made highly publicized demands on several American insurers to explain the involvement of their corporate antecedents in the slave economy. Of course the flip side of the reparations movement is that it may drastically alter the interpretation of what corporations currently consider to be "safe" historical records.
15. William Maher's 1998 Society of American Archivists Presidential Address expressed the frustrations of those charged with managing content not their own. But Maher's condemnation of corporate activities in expanding content control is not entirely on target, for individuals benefit from copyright expansions as well. A differing point of view is that individual pursuit of individual property rights is not an unmitigated blessing, for it "facilitates private censorship of popular culture." It may also dilute the available materials for future historical scholarship. See William Maher, "Lost in a Disneyfied World: Archivists and Society in Late-Twentieth-Century America," *American Archivist* 61 (Fall 1998): 259–65; Felicity Barringer and Ralph Blumenthal, "Big Media v. Freelancers: The Justices at the Digital Divide," *New York Times*, 19 March 2001; Michael Madow, "Private Ownership of Public Image: Popular Culture

and Publicity Rights," The Berkman Center for Internet & Society at Harvard Law School, 1993.

16. There's a glimmer of hope for corporate information managers at least, as the majority opinion in *American Geophysical Union v. Texaco* did not find that photocopying of articles by a for-profit institution was necessarily a commercial activity. *The Digital Dilemma, Intellectual Property in the Information Age* (National Research Council), chapter 4, page 7.

17. Referencing publicity rights, one lawyer perhaps unknowingly summed up the situation for the majority of the current case law pertaining to the digital domain when he wrote, "it is exceedingly difficult to reconcile them either with each other or with any single, coherent rationale." Mark D. Robins, "Publicity Rights in the Digital Media, Part II," *The Computer & Internet Lawyer* 17 (December 2000): 31.

18. "Conference Seeks to Balance Web Security and Privacy," *New York Times,* 8 December 2000, C4; Jonathan Krim and Robert O'Harrow, Jr., "Democrats Focus on Internet Privacy," *Washington Post,* 12 July 2001, E2.

19. William J. Curan, Eugene M. Laska, Honora Kaplan, and Rheta Bank, "Protection of Privacy and Confidentiality," *Science* 182 (November 1973): 797. Cary noted IBM's leadership on policies protecting employee privacy, tracing the roots to CEO Thomas J. Watson, Jr.'s direct involvement in an employee privacy issue in the mid-1960s. "IBM's Guidelines to Employee Privacy: An Interview with Frank T. Cary," *Harvard Business Review* 54 (September–October 1976): 82–90.

20. See http://www.junkbusters.com/new.html MSFT for a listing of Microsoft's perceived transgressions. Agre's quote is from Lester, "Reinvention of Privacy." See also John Schwartz, "Opting In: A Privacy Paradox," *Washington Post,* 3 September 2000, H1. For a discussion of RealNetworks' balancing act between personalization and privacy—two fundamental yet contradictory Internet concepts—see Pam Blackstone, "Developing Content, Reaching Customers," Publish, http://www.publish.com/features/0011/feature7.html, available as of 2001.

21. The Federal Trade Commission testimony is found at http://www.ftc.gov/os/2000/05/testimonyprivacy.htm (available as of 2001). IBM appointed its first chief privacy officer in November 2000.

22. Cavoukian quoted in Lester, "Reinvention of Privacy." The same might be true of the American Civil Liberties Union concerning government invasion of privacy via technologies like Carnivore, the FBI's Web-monitoring technology. "ACLU Seeks Details on FBI's New Plan to Monitor the Web," *Wall Street Journal,* 17 July 2000, B7. In an interesting twist, another incentive for keeping the government out is the burgeoning privacy "industry," a $300-million business in 1999 of technology vendors, consultants, accountants, public relations experts, and lawyers estimated to reach $1.8 billion by 2003. Edmund Sanders, "Privacy Is Becoming Everyone's Business," *Los Angeles Times,* 22 May 2001 NA, C1. "'Law & Order' Star Sues eBay," at CNN.com. Similarly, thousands of reporters using an on-line story source locator service had their names, contact information, and story ideas accidentally spilled onto the Internet. Stephanie Mills and Timothy Hanrahan, "List of Reporters' Story Ideas Hits the Web," *Wall Street Journal,* 13 June 2001, B8.

23. Rick Lyman, "Movie Stars Fear Inroads by Upstart Digital Actors," *New York Times,* 8 July 2001, 1.

24. "Employee Data Posted on Living.com Yanked After Complaints," at CNET News.com, 20 October 2000, http://www.news.com; "As Online Firms Go Bust, Privacy Goes to the Top Bidder," *USA Today,* 19 July 2000, 12A.

25. Gordon Rabchuk made the connections between this act and corporate archives and shared his perspectives on its potential implications. A primer on the act can be found at Industry Canada, http://e-com.ic.gc.ca/english/privacy/632d30.html 12/11/2000.

26. *The Computer and Internet Lawyer* 17 (November 2000): 5.

27. One example of the blurring of the public and the private in executive records is the seemingly straightforward practice of corporate philanthropy. See Stephanie Strom, "In Charity, Where Does a C.E.O. End and a Company Start?" *New York Times,* 22 September 2002. Courts have found to date that employers have every right to monitor employee on-line behaviors, perhaps largely because courts have held employers legally and severely accountable for racial discrimination, sexual harassment, and other forms of inappropriate workplace behavior by employees. But the privacy concerns of individuals engaged in appropriate business behavior have not yet been trumped by employer interests. Patti Waldmeir, "US Employees Find No Right to Privacy in Cyberspace," *Financial Times,* 31 August 2001, 12.
28. Kahle is not the Internet's only archivist. For other Web site archives, see Paul Andrews, "Failed Web Sites Live On, Gone But Not Forgotten," *New York Times,* 24 May 2001, G8; Ted Bridis, "U.S. Archive of Hacker Attacks to Close Because It Is Too Busy," *Wall Street Journal,* 24 May 2001, B10. Google's purchase of Deja.com gave the Internet search engine an instant archive of over 650 million Usenet newsgroup messages, dating from 1995. This "archive of human conversation" poses privacy issues for those Usenet participants who had initially assumed their postings would disappear within a matter of weeks, and who are now finding them posted at groups.google.com. Those concerns appear to be legitimate, based on a University of California at Berkeley project to develop data-mining technology to analyze the Usenet postings for sociological, linguistic, and business market information. Susan Stellin, "New Economy," *New York Times,* 7 May 2001, C4; Claire Tristam, "Mining for Meaning," *Technology Review* (July–August 2001): 31.
29. The distinction between the two was clearly demonstrated by a 2001 security breach at Microsoft, where customer data was unintentionally left unprotected on the Internet, open to anybody who was nosy enough to try variations on commonly used Microsoft IP addresses. One such individual hit the proverbial jackpot when one address he typed in opened up a Web-mounted database containing thousands of records on Microsoft customers. Dan Richman, "Security Hole Leaks Microsoft Records," *Seattle-Post Intelligencer,* 12 October 2001, A1.
30. For an excellent case study of data mining and its uses in the retail industry, see Mary Wagner, "Mountains of Data," *Internet Retailer* (May 2001).
31. Joeller Tessler, "FTE Tries to Block Toysmart's Data Sale," In-Depth News, Silicon Valley.com, 10 July 2000, http://SiliconValley.com. Another asset with property implications that the dot-coms tried to market was the custom software that they developed to conduct their business. Greg Sandoval, "Finding Gold In Dot-bombs Idle Software," CNET News.com, 20 August 2001, http://news.cnet.com/news/0-1007-200-6931563.html.
32. One privacy advocate stated that "Most companies don't take privacy seriously. The general view is: Collect as much data as you can, as quietly as possible. It's dirt-cheap to store, and you never know when it'll come in handy." Dana Hawkins, "Gospel of Privacy Guru: Be Wary; Assume the Worst," *U.S. News & World Report,* 25 June 2001, 71. See also Lester, "Reinvention of Privacy."
33. As might be expected, industry groups warned against the HIPAA rules, arguing that they could cost $18 billion over ten years to implement. *USA Today,* 10 April 2001, 8a. Scott McNealy, CEO of Sun Microsystems, argues that absolute privacy in areas such as medical records is not always desirable and may perhaps even be dangerous, "The Case Against Absolute Privacy," *Washington Post,* 29 May 2001, A15. In 2001, at least fifty privacy bills were presented to Congress for consideration. John Schwartz, "Government Is Wary of Tackling Online Privacy," *New York Times,* 6 September 2001, C1. The U.S. Department of Health and Human Services was forced to hold up imple-

menting the rules to be able to adequately review them. These rules required doctors and hospitals to obtain written consent from patients before using health information, even for routine purposes. They also guarded against unauthorized use of health records by companies hiring employees.
34. Barlow, "Selling Wine."

Chapter 15. Confidences in Medical and Health Care Records from an Archive Perspective

1. These citations were located in Medline databases using the search terms "privacy," "medical records," "confidentiality," "law," and "health records" and combinations using the Boolean operators "and" and "or." From this large number of citations, and an equally large number from a search of the Web of Science databases, 460 titles up to the year 2001 were identified as being relevant to the broad topic of health care records, privacy, and confidentiality. These were arranged into twelve categories: records and documentation; health information databases; medical informatics; electronic patient record, information systems, and networked environments; security; access, privacy, confidentiality, and ethics; structure, modeling, and mark-up of records and knowledge; use of records in medical research; governance, standards, and the law; theory and philosophy. The notes provide reference to selected titles from these groups.

   A small subset of this literature comprising forty-one titles deals with topics of relevance to the archives administration of health care records including use of records in historiography and general archives issues. The archives literature, especially the journals *American Archivist, Archivaria, Archives and Manuscripts*, and the Society of Archivists *Journal*, contains the most professionally relevant discussions of health care records in archives, particularly their appraisal, acquisition, and servicing. Two annotated bibliographies on the archival administration of medical and health care records are especially useful compendia: Carl Spadoni, "Medical Archives: An Annotated Bibliography," *Archivaria* 28 (Summer 1989): 75–119 (to 1985); and Barbara L. Craig and Geoffrey Reaume, "Medical Archives: An Update of the Spadoni Bibliography, 1986–1995," *Archivaria* 41 (Summer 1996): 121–57.

   The historical uses of health care and medical records and the needs of historians for particular health care records are found largely in the literature of the history of medicine, especially the journals *Bulletin of the History of Medicine* (U.S), *Canadian Bulletin of the History of Medicine*, and *Social History of Medicine* (U.K.).

   The World Wide Web has the potential to broaden communications among repositories. However, there are no agreed standards for the content of Web sites nor for their maintenance. The following three institutions are useful examples of archives with significant medical holdings that are well represented electronically; the Calgary Regional Health Authority (integrated archives, records management, and administration of access/privacy legislation, available at http://www.crha-health.ab.ca/infoprivacy/ExAIMintro.html/), the Alan Mason Chesney Medical Archives at the Johns Hopkins University (medical and health care archives and manuscript collections, available at http://www.medicalarchives.jhmi.edu/awelcome.htm), and the Contemporary Medical Archives Centre at the Wellcome Institute for the History and Understanding of Medicine (integrated archives, library, historical collections, and interpretive center, available at http://www.wellcome.ac.uk/).

   The two indispensable texts for archives and archivists with responsibilities for medical and health care records, and the best place to begin understanding issues in this area of archives administration, are Nancy McCall and Lisa A. Mix, eds., *Designing Archives Programs to Advance Knowledge in the Health Fields* (Baltimore: Johns Hopkins University Press, 1995) and Joan D. Krizack, ed., *Documentation Planning for the U.S. Health Care System* (Baltimore: Johns Hopkins University Press, 1994).

I am grateful to Ann Simonds and Sarah Bradley for help in the literature search.

2. Some examples are R. Baker, C. Shiels, et al., "What Proportion of Patients Refuse Consent to Data Collection from Their Records for Research Purposes?" *British Journal of General Practice* 50 (August 2000): 655–56; Kenneth D. Manda, Peter Szolovits, et al., "Public Standards and Patients' Control: How to Keep Electronic Medical Records Accessible but Private; Commentary: Open Approaches to Electronic Patient Records; Commentary: A Patient's Viewpoint," *British Medical Journal* 322 (2001): 283–87; J. F. Merz, B. J. Spina, and P. Sankar, "Patient Consent for Release of Sensitive Information from Their Medical Records: An Exploratory Study," *Behaviourial Sciences & the Law* 17, no. 4 (1999): 445–54; P. S. Applebaum, "Threats to the Confidentiality of Medical Records—No Place to Hide," *Journal of the American Medical Association* 283 (9 February 2000): 795–97; and Mark A. Rothstein, ed., *Genetic Secrets: Protecting Privacy and Confidentiality in the Genetic Era* (New Haven: Yale University Press, 1997).

3. Confidentiality between patient and physician dates at least to the Hippocratic Oath. The confidentiality of information in records of institutions where physicians deliver services was circumscribed by a number of practical factors in admitting and discharging patients and in providing services for them by a group or team. Records of hospitals, particularly those providing acute care, were also valued for their presumed richness as sources for statistical analysis and for medical research. The needs of management and of research provided justification for others to have access to confidences.

A brief historical review of hospital records generally, including those of managers and clinicians, is provided by Barbara L. Craig in "Hospital Records and Record-keeping, c. 1850–c. 1950: Part 1, The Development of Records in Hospitals," *Archivaria* 29 (Winter 1989): 57–87; "Part II, The Development of Record-keeping in Hospitals," *Archivaria* 30 (Summer 1990): 21–38; and "Role of Records and Record-keeping in the Development of the Modern Hospital in London, England and Ontario, Canada, c. 1890–c. 1940," *Bulletin of the History of Medicine* 65 (Fall 1990): 376–97. Also see Joel D. Howell, *Technology in the Hospital: Transforming Patient Care in the Early Twentieth Century* (Baltimore: Johns Hopkins University Press, 1995).

From the extensive literature on the topics of managing clinical records for the approved uses of the hospital and its researchers, see Edna K. Huffman *Medical Record Management*, which was published in six editions up to 1972. Most illuminating from a historical and archival perspective is the 1941 edition, which has an extensive bibliography of works on the uses of clinical records for analysis, teaching, and research extending back to the turn of the century.

4. Edna K. Huffman's textbook of clinical records management provides good examples of the effort required to coordinate and collate information manually from volumes of clinical records. In the 1940s, many hospitals introduced mechanical devices, such as the Hollerith or Powers-Samas machines, for punching cards and counting them, to assist in the collection of mass data from volumes of clinical files. See Craig, "Hospital Records and Record-Keeping Part I and Part II."

5. Third-party interest in the information contained in HC&MRs grew in tandem with the state's larger role in medicine and health care. Public payment for treatments, for example, for venereal disease or for tuberculosis, was accompanied by stipulations that required institutions and practitioners to divulge information about the patient, his or her contacts, and the disease. State intervention in medicine and its growing role in public health are explored in an extensive historical literature.

Some useful titles concerning contemporary multiple interests in records are D. Y. Dodek and A. Dodek, "From Hippocrates to Facsimile—Protecting Patient Confidentiality Is More Difficult and More Important than Before," *Canadian Medical Association Journal* 156 (15 March 1997): 847–52; A. Samuels, "Access to Health Records," *Medicine, Science and the Law* 36 (October 1996): 317–19; Judith W. DeCew "Alternatives for Protecting Privacy while Respecting Patient Care and Public Health Needs," *Ethics and Information Technology* 1/4 , no. 4 (1999): 249–55; and T. R. Knapp, J. Walter, and C. P. Renaudin, "Property Rights and Privacy Principles," *Journal of Health Information Management* 14 (Winter 2000): 83–93.

6. A succinct review of the archival implications of the draft act in the Province of Ontario, and by its references, of the archival implications of PIPEDA, is provided by the discussion paper/informational brief of the Archives Association of Ontario, "Archives and the Proposed Ontario Privacy of Personal Information Act," located at http://aao.fis.utoronto.ca/aa.

7. A good place to begin a review of HIPAA and its associated rules is the United States Department of Health and Human Services Web site at http://www.hhs.gov. A summary of modifications to the rules, issued in early August 2002, gives a succinct overview. Modifications to the standards for privacy of individually identifiable health information are located at http://www.hhs.gov/news/press/2002pres/20020809.html.

8. Archival concerns about the privacy of HC&MRs are revealed most starkly when acquisitions are contemplated. Few archives have either the resources or expertise to preserve documentary collections in the history of medicine and health care. See Irene Kiersey, "Some Problems Placing Medical Records in Public Archives," *Archives and Manuscripts* 17 (1989); David Pearson "Medical History for Tomorrow—Preserving the Record of Today," *Health Information and Libraries Journal* 18 (September 2001): 139–43; and E. Higgs and J. Melling, "Chasing the Ambulance. The Emerging Crisis in the Preservation of Modern Health Records," *Social History of Medicine* 10, no. 1 (1997): 127–36. A measured and sympathetic assessment of the problems of acquiring HC&MRs is J. Melling, "A Healthy Future for Medical Records?" *Health Information and Libraries Journal* 18 (September 2001): 162–64. His assessments, while specific to Britain, would resonate in other jurisdictions.

9. See Menzi L. Behrnd-Klodt, "The Brave New World of 21st-Century Medical Records Privacy in the U.S. and Canada, Contrasted with the European Data Privacy Model," appendix 4 in this volume, for a fuller discussion of HIPAA, PIPEDA, and the changing legal environment that governs medical records.

10. J. H. Warner, *The Therapeutic Perspective: Medical Practice, Knowledge and Identity in America, 1820–1885,* 2nd ed. (Princeton, N. J.: Princeton University Press, 1997) is an invaluable monograph on the changes in medical education and practices.

11. See Roy Porter, *Health for Sale: Quackery in England, 1650–1850* (Manchester, England: Manchester University Press, 1989). Three repositories with significant holdings from early and unorthodox health care practitioners are the National Library of Medicine, in Bethesda, Maryland; the Wellcome Library for the History and Understanding of Medicine Library in London, with its Western Manuscripts Division and Contemporary Medical Archives Centre; and the British Library in London.

12. There is a substantial literature on the history of hospitals. From among many excellent titles, the following provide a good beginning: Brian Abel-Smith, *The Hospitals 1800–1948: A Study in Social Administration in England and Wales* (London: Heinemann, 1964) and Joel D. Howell, *Technology in the Hospital: Transforming Patient Care in the Early Twentieth Century* (Baltimore: Johns Hopkins University Press, 1995). Two articles that address the impact of modern management on records are S. J. Reiser, "Creating Form Out of Mass. The Development of the Medical Record," in *Transfor-*

mation and Tradition in the Sciences, ed. F. Mendelsshon (Cambridge: Cambridge University Press, 1983) and S. Sturdy and R. Cooter, "Science, Scientific Management and the Transformation of Medicine in Britain, c. 1870–1950," *History of Science* 36/114 Pt. 4 (December 1998): 421—66. In addition, histories of individual hospitals are valuable sources for information about individual institutions. A search of your local library or on-line through a university OPAC will bring up any titles relevant to the institution in which you have special interests.

13. See Porter, *Health for Sale.* Also see Barbara L. Craig, "The Role of Records and of Record-keeping in the Development of the Modern Hospital in London, England, and Ontario, Canada, c. 1890–c. 1940," *Bulletin for the History of Medicine* 65 (1991). For a perspective on the published care report, see Laine H. McCarthy and Kathryn E. H. Reilly, "How to Write a Case Report," *Family Medicine* 32 (March 2000): 190–95.

14. The literature of the health care profession is a fruitful place to begin investigation of records from the point of view of ethics, services, and history. Four useful contributions for archivists are Robert Hall, "Confidentiality as an Organizational Issue," *Journal of Clinical Ethics* 10 (Fall 1999): 230–36; Higgs and Melling, "Chasing the Ambulance"; S. J. Reiser, "The Clinical Record in Medicine Part I: Learning for the Case," *Annals of Internal Medicine* 114 (15 May 1990): 902–7 and "Part II: Reforming Content and Purpose," *Annals of Internal Medicine* 114 (June 1991): 980–85.

15. From the extensive literature on the electronic patient record, information systems, networked environments, security, and access, see P. W. Moorman and J. Van der Lei, "An Inventory of Publications on Electronic Patient Records," *Methods of Information in Medicine* 38 (December 1999): 294–97; "Physicians Go Online for Medical Records," *Data Strategies & Benchmarks* 4 (December 2000): 183–85; M. Madjaric, V. Nesek-Madjaric, H. Leitner, et al., "Paperless Hospital: Reality, Dream or Nightmare?" *Studies in Health Technology and Informatics* 77 (2000): 1028–32; M. J. Barrett, "The Evolving Computerized Medical Record," *Health Care Informatics* 17 (May 2000): 85–88; 90, 92–93; and Part II 17 (September 2000): 83–84, 86, 88; "Abstract of MEDINET 2000: The 5th World Congress on the Internet in Medicine: Brussels, 23–26 November 2000," *Technology & Health Care* 8, nos. 3–4 (2000): 165–250; V. L. Patel, A. W. Kushniruk, S. Yang, et al., "Impact of a Computer-based Patient Record System on Data Collection, Knowledge Organization, and Reasoning," *Journal of the American Medical Informatics Association* 7 (November–December 2000): 569–85; J. A. Holland "Worlds Collide: Health Information Meets the Internet," *Journal of Ahima* 71 (November–December 2000); 50–53; D. W. Chadwick, P. J. Crook, A. J. Young, et al., "Using the Internet to Access Confidential Patient Records: A Case Study," *British Medical Journal* 321 (9 September 2000): 612–14; and P. M. Yellowhees and P. M. Brooks, "Health Online: The Future Isn't What It Used to Be," *Medical Journal of Australia* 171 (15 November 1999): 522–25.

16. In addition to the codes of ethics and guidelines for standard recordkeeping practices of the health care professions, Edna K. Huffman's *Medical Record Management,* especially the 1941 and 1972 editions, provides a historical review of professional responsibilities for recordkeeping.

17. The framework for recordkeeping typically is provided by the statutes or laws and associated regulations of the jurisdiction governing in-patient services, typically in a hospital or term care facility. Most institutions have their own rules and procedures for their own records systems, whether these are manual or automated.

Recently, data protection legislation of generic application to data collected outside specified institutions either is being considered or has passed. Such laws stipulate which data may be acquired, how it must be kept, who may use it, and under what circumstances it may be shared. Health data protection laws may neglect the historical dimension. Archivists should be cognizant of draft laws and should consult with legislators before laws or regulations are in place. Among the issues for archives with records for historical uses: ensuring a succinct definition of personal information; reducing the impact of retrospective application on records already accessible for historical research; creating exemptions for historical uses, research, and archives purposes; permitting reasonable periods of closure not to exceed about one hundred years; provisions for research agreements; exemption of personal records acquired from persons or private sources; notification to historical repositories of proposed records destruction; recognizing the social role of archives; and acknowledging the importance of historical research.

18. Archivists' professional codes of ethics all recommend that institutions articulate their mission and policies so that records are accessioned with all requirements fully understood and in place. The joint document developed by the Society of Archivists and the Records Management Society "Draft Code of Practice for Archivists under Section 51(4) of the Data Protection Act 1998, version #2, 20 April 2002" is an example of professional response to changes in legislation, accessed 15 November 2002 at the Web site of the Society of Archivists, http://www.archives.org.uk/.

    A useful example of research agreements for access to records with personal information is the "Special Undertaking" for use of records at Kings College London available at the college archives Web site, http://www.kcl.ac.uk. Also see the "Policy on Access and Use" of the Alan Mason Chesney Archives at the Johns Hopkins University at http://www.medicalarchives.jhmi.edu/awelcome.htm.

19. The medical, audit, and morbidity committees of hospitals, their admission and discharge registers, and in earlier times, even published hospital reports contain confidential information that is protected today. Some of these types of records are obvious places to find personal information. However, others do not immediately come to mind. For example, the government of the Province of Ontario, Canada, published information about asylum patients in the last century. Today, this information is carefully protected.

20. This phrase is gratefully borrowed from Terry Cook whose discussions of macro-appraisal introduced the method of appraisal used by the National Archives of Canada. Cook developed the conceptual ground for viewing accountable record-keeping around "points of intersection" between a powerful institution, in this case the state in the form of the Government of Canada, and a client or citizen. See Terry Cook's "Mind Over Matter: Towards a New Theory of Archival Appraisal," in *The Archival Imagination: Essays in Honour of Hugh A. Taylor,* ed. Barbara L. Craig (Ottawa: Association of Canadian Archivists, 1992).

21. For a valuable example of an appraisal matrix and criteria for a health care archives, see McCall and Mix, *Designing Archives Programs.* Also see H. Maxwell-Steward, J. Sheppard, and G. Yeo, *Hospital Patient Care Records: A Guide to Their Retention and Disposal* (London: Health Archives Group, 1996) and H. Maxwell-Stewart and A. Tough, "Cutting the Gordian Knot: Or How to Preserve Non-current Clinical Records without Being Buried in Paper," *Archivaria* 41 (1996): 61–77.

22. Each jurisdiction has a number of laws that apply to the handling of information generated by professional services. These statutes and regulations should be the first stop for archivists responsible for administering an archives of medical or related records. A good place to start your search is, for the United States, the Department of Health and Human Services at http://www.hhs.gov/foia/; for the United Kingdom, http://www.dataprotection.gov.uk; for Australia, http://www.privacy.gov.au; and for Canada, http://www.privcom.gc.ca.

More general context about the legal nature of the health or medical records is provided by a number of very useful works on the topic of the law and medicine. From this very large and diverse group, the following titles are recommended as useful general reading for the archivist regardless of his or her specific jurisdiction: W. H. Roach, *Medical Records and the Law* (Aspen, Colo.: Aspen Health Law and Compliance Center, 1998); K. Gormley, "100 Years of Privacy," *Wisconsin Law Review* 5 (1992): 1335–41; B. McIsaac, R. Shields, and K. Klein, *The Law of Privacy in Canada* (Toronto: Carswell, 2000); "US Sets National Standards for Patient Privacy," *British Medical Journal* 322 (2001): 8; and R. A. Epstein, "Deconstructing Privacy and Putting It Back Together Again," *Social Philosophy & Policy* 17 (Summer 2000): 1–24.
23. R. Huebert, "The Early Social History of a Word," *Sewanee Review* 105 (Winter 1997): 21–38.
24. Sue McKemish, "Evidence of Me," *Archives and Manuscripts* 24 (May 1996): 28–45.

Chapter 16. The United Methodists and Their Open Records Policy

1. The story of size and accountability first surfaces in William McGuire King, "Denominational Modernization and Religious Identity: The Case of the Methodist Episcopal Church," *Methodist History* 20 (January 1982): 75–89. For the public sector, several studies focus on the growth of accountability: see Samuel Hays, *The Response to Industrialism, 1885–1916* (Chicago: University of Chicago, 1957); and Robert Wiebe, *The Search for Order* (New York: Hill and Wang, 1967).
2. Efforts to count denominational membership often prove tricky. The claim here is based on the combined membership of the three nineteenth-century Methodist bodies that eventually merged in 1939 to form the Methodist Church. While the combined membership of all Baptist denominations in the late nineteenth century proved larger than that of the Methodists, no individual Baptist denomination claimed more members, and they never merged together in the twentieth century. Only in the mid-1960s did the Southern Baptist Convention become the largest Protestant denomination in the United States.

    Winthrop Hudson, "Methodist Age in America," *Methodist History* 12 (April 1974): 3–15; Nathan Hatch, "The Puzzle of American Methodism," *Church History* 63 (June 1994): 175–89; Penny Long Marler and C. Kirk Hadaway, "Methodists on the Margins: 'Self-Authoring' Religious Identity," in *Connectionalism: Ecclesiology, Mission and Identity*, ed. Russell E. Richey, Dennis M. Campbell, and William B. Lawrence (Nashville: Abingdon, 1997), 295.
3. King, "Denominational Modernization"; Russell E. Richey, "Introduction," in *Connectionalism: Ecclesiology, Mission, and Identity*, 15–16.
4. Stanley High, "Methodism's Pink Fringe," *Reader's Digest*, February 1950, 134–38.
5. "Behind Soviet Power," Diffendorfer Special Series in Records of the General Board of Global Ministries, United Methodist Church Archives, Madison, N.J.
6. "The Gospel According to Whom?" *60 Minutes*, 23 January 1983; Rael Jean Isaac, "Do You Know Where Your Church Offerings Go?" *Reader's Digest*, January 1973, 120–24; New Releases, Records of United Methodist Communications; Subject Files, Records of the General Board of Global Ministries, United Methodist Church Archives, Madison, N.J.
7. *The Book of Discipline of the United Methodist Church*, 1984 edition, paragraph 820. Bracketed phrase added in 1988.
8. Ibid., paragraph 800.

9. Petition AD-1024-0800 (0370), 1984 Petition Series, Records of the General Conference, United Methodist Church Archives, Madison, N.J.
10. *The Book of Discipline of the United Methodist Church,* 2000 edition, paragraphs 2701–2719.
11. *The Book of Discipline of the United Methodist Church,* 1996 edition, paragraph 721. Bracketed material was added in 2000. Also, the material in italics concerning the Judicial Council was removed and the following added: "While it is expected that the General Conference, the Judicial Council and the Council of Bishops will live by the spirit of this paragraph, each of these constitutional bodies is governed by its own rules of procedure."
12. 1996 General Conference Records, Petition 21594-GJ-821-D; 2000 General Conference Records, Petition 31168-GJ-721-D.
13. *The Book of Discipline of the United Methodist Church,* 2000 edition, paragraphs 1703.1 and 1711.3b.
14. Diffendorfer Records, Records of the World Division of the General Board of Global Ministries, United Methodist Church Archives, Madison, N.J.
15. It is worth noting that the same series now seems to be converting back to one of public reports. As missionary activity for the United Methodists has changed to one of support work with native churches, the need for reports which can be shared with others has apparently risen. So, in a few years, the Missionary File Series may once again be an open series.

Appendix 2. Selected U.S. Federal Statues Concerning Privacy

1. Richard C. Turkington and Anita L. Allen, *Privacy Law: Cases and Materials,* 2nd ed. (St. Paul, Minn.: West Group, 2002), 463.
2. Ibid., 295–96.
3. Marc Rotenberg, *The Privacy Law Sourcebook 2001* (Washington, D.C.: Electronic Privacy Information Center, 2001) 39 et seq.
4. 5 U.S.C. § 552a(a)(5).
5. Turkington and Allen, *Privacy Law,* 467.

Appendix 3. The Family Educational Rights and Privacy Act

1. Improving America's Schools Act, 1994, P.L. 103–382.
2. Campus Security Act, 1990 amendment to FERPA.
3. Higher Education Amendments of 1998. § 1232g(b)(6)(A) of the law applies to postsecondary institutions.
4. "Directory information" currently also includes a student's name, address, birthplace, date of birth, telephone number, participation in sports, attendance records, and degrees and awards received. FERPA, § 1232g(a)(5)(A)–(B).
5. See 18 U.S.C. § 1232g(j).
6. The No Child Left Behind Act of 2001 (P.L. 107-110), 20 U.S.C. § 9528, amended the Elementary and Secondary Act of 1965 (ESEA), 20 U.S.C. § 7908 and made sweeping changes to the federal government's role in K–12 education. The National Defense Authorization Act for Fiscal Year 2002 (P.L. 107-107), 10 U.S.C. § 544, funds the U.S. armed forces. See also appendix 2 to this volume.
7. Not all are pleased with the No Child Left Behind Act's possible limitations of student privacy rights. For an opposing view, see "No Child Left Unrecruited?" by University of Washington law professor Anita Ramasastry, available as of January 2003, at

http://writ.news.findlaw.com/ramasastry/20021204.html. Prof. Ramasastry explores the reversal in privacy law standards from "opt in" to an "opt out," requiring greater vigilance by parents to protect students' rights once sharing of personal information is compulsory unless consent is denied in writing. She notes that "opt out" rules benefit commercial entities and perhaps, military recruiters, as obtaining each individual's consent is burdensome and that, while sending a blanket notice to parents is easy, it may be ineffective.

8. The Court of Appeals had found that student assignments, as soon as they were graded, became education records under FERPA. The U.S. Supreme Court disagreed.
9. 42 U.S.C. § 1983, allows a private civil rights action to be brought against any person who under color of law deprives one of "any rights, privileges or immunities secured by the Constitution and laws." This section derives from the Civil Rights Act of 1871 and the Thirteenth and Fourteenth Amendments to the U.S. Constitution. It has often been used to bring lawsuits against state and local government officials who violate individuals' civil rights.
10. In *Gonzaga,* a teacher certification specialist at Gonzaga University, a private educational institution, overheard a student relate his personal sexual misconduct. The specialist launched an investigation and notified the state agency responsible for teacher certification, which declined to certify the student as a teacher. The student sued the university and the specialist under FERPA, alleging an unlawful release of his education records without parental written consent.

Appendix 4. The Brave New World of 21st-Century Medical Records Privacy in the U.S. and Canada, Contrasted with the European Data Privacy Model

1. Arthur S. Di Dio, *The Hype About HIPAA: Standards for Privacy of Individually Identifiable Health Information* (Washington: D.C.: National Legal Center for the Public Interest, 2002), 3–4.
2. HIPAA requires use of nationally standardized formats, content, and code sets (e.g., medical diagnostic or procedural codes) for certain electronic transactions between covered entities and business associates. As of this writing, HIPAA does not yet require the exclusive use of electronic transactions, although such is likely in the future.
3. HIPAA's administrative rules also affect records managers, as they set a six-year retention for documents that must be created under the Privacy Rule (e.g., disposition of complaints, written privacy policies and procedures, and privacy notices), running from the date of the document's creation or its last effective date. 45 C.F.R. § 164.530(j).
4. See 65 Fed. Reg. 82,462 (2000) and 45 C.F.R. § 164. Initial controversy concerned the length and complexity of the rules (over 350 pages in the *Federal Register*), implementation costs, and whether they may stifle medical technology research and innovation and require physicians to "facilitate violations of the Fourth Amendment prohibition against unreasonable searches and seizures." Di Dio, *Hype About HIPAA,* 2, also quoting from *The Association of American Physicians & Surgeons, Inc., et al. v. United States Department of Health and Human Services,* Complaint for Declaratory Relief ¶ 2. By some interpretations, the Privacy Rule is illegal. HHS estimated implementation costs to be $17.6 billion over ten years. The American Hospital Association calculated implementation costs of three provisions of the law to be $22 billion over five years. Yet, privacy advocates charged that the rules fail to protect privacy, since pharmaceutical companies, hospitals, and for-profit businesses may use personal

medical records for marketing, and the federal government now has greater access to personal medical records. See Di Dio, *Hype About HIPAA*, 2.

5. "HHS News," U.S. Department of Health and Human Services, press release, 9 August 2002.
6. "Health care" means preventive, diagnostic, therapeutic, rehabilitative, maintenance, or palliative care, and counseling and related assessment services.
7. "Covered entities" do not include the Social Security Administration, non–health insurance functions (e.g., workers' compensation, automobile, general liability, disability, and accident insurance without medical coverage), and employers or health plan sponsors who merely provide third-party health plans to employees (unless such employers or sponsors receive PHI by administering health plans).
8. 45 C.F.R. § 164.502(b).
9. Di Dio, *Hype About HIPAA*, 38.
10. Business associate agreements specify how PHI may or may not be used or disclosed; require safeguards, audits, reports of unauthorized uses or disclosures; require return or destruction of PHI at the end of the contract, if feasible; and require agents and contractors who access PHI downstream to agree to similar terms. See 45 C.F.R. § 164.504(e)(ii).
11. Under HIPAA, a patient has a right to all of his or her medical records, except psychotherapy notes; information compiled for civil, criminal, or administrative action; and certain exempt data within a prescribed time frame and with a right to amend PHI.
12. State laws for similar types of authorizations likely will determine who is an authorized representative.
13. See 45 C.F.R. 164.308 and 164.306.
14. The law's full title is "An Act to Support and Promote Electronic Commerce by Protecting Personal Information That Is Collected, Used or Disclosed in Certain Circumstances, by Providing For the Use of Electronic Means to Communicate or Record Information or Transactions and by Amending the Canada Evidence Act, the Statutory Instruments Act and the Statute Revision Act." The law became effective 1 January 2001. See Statutes of Canada, 2000, Chapter 5 (Bill C-6). Also see the Web site of the Privacy Commissioner of Canada, http://www.privcom.gc.ca.
15. John Shoesmith, "Privacy Matters," Canadian Healthcare Manager (undated), 4 pp, http://www.chmonline.ca.
16. Privacy Commissioner of Canada, "Backgrounder," at http://www.privcom.gc.ca.
17. Ibid. See also *eCMAJ NewsDesk* (Canadian Medical Association Journal), "Provinces Need to Get Their Privacy Legislation in Order," by Ann Silversides, 17 August 2001, at http://www.cma.ca/CMAJ/cmaj_today/2001/08_20.htm, reporting on comments by attorney Rick Shields, McCarthy Tétrault, Ottawa, Ontario, Canada, at a conference, "Managing Privacy of Health Information," August 2001, sponsored by the Canadian Institute in Toronto. See also *Canada NewsWire*, "European Commission Recognizes Canadian Legislated Privacy Protection," press release, 14 January 2002, an Office of the Minister of Industry and Office of the Minister of International Trade announcement, available at http://www.newswire.ca/releases/January2002/14/c2203/html (active as of December 2002).
18. Privacy Commissioner of Canada, "Backgrounder," at http://www.privcom.gc.ca.
19. Privacy Commissioner of Canada, "A Guide for Canadians," "What Is the Personal Information Protection and Electronic Documents Act?" at http://www.privcom.gc.ca.
20. Ibid., and Privacy Commissioner of Canada, "Backgrounder," at http://www.privcom.gc.ca.

21. This exception to PIPEDA may permit historical and journalistic uses of personal information. The development of business practices, and possibly, the courts, may determine whether such is the case.
22. Privacy Commissioner of Canada, "Backgrounder," at http://www.privcom.gc.ca.
23. Ibid.
24. Directive 95/46/EC of the European Parliament and of the Council of 24 October 1995 on the protection of individuals with regard to the processing of personal data and on the free movement of such data. *Official Journal L 281, 23/11/1995 P. 0031-0050.*
25. Paul M. Schwartz and Joel R. Reidenberg, *Data Privacy Law*, Ch. 2, § 2.2 (1996), quoted in Richard C. Turkington and Anita L. Allen, *Privacy Law: Cases and Materials*, 2nd ed. (St. Paul, Minn.: West Group, 2002), 437.
26. *Canada NewsWire*, "European Commission Recognizes Canadian Legislated Privacy Protection," press release, 14 January 2002, http://www.newswire.ca.
27. For more information about the implications for data processing between the U.S. and Europe, see Peter P. Swire and Robert E. Litan, *None of Your Business* (Washington, D.C.: Brookings Institution Press, 1998).

EDITORS AND CONTRIBUTORS

Menzi L. Behrnd-Klodt is both an archivist and an attorney, holding advanced degrees in history, library and information science, and law, all from the University of Wisconsin. Currently she is corporate counsel for American Girl, Inc., a children's book publisher and toy company that is part of Mattel, Inc., where she focuses on intellectual properties, licensing, and business agreements, and she oversees the corporate archives and records programs. Previously she managed research and library services and established the corporate archives at American Girl. She also established the corporate archives at CUNA Mutual Insurance Group, Madison, Wisconsin; was archivist at Circus World Museum, Baraboo, Wisconsin, and the Wisconsin Historical Society, and consulting archivist at Bishop Museum, Honolulu, Hawaii. Menzi consults to many other historical societies, museums, cultural organizations, and businesses on legal, archives, and records issues. Her legal practice encompassed business and insurance law. She frequently speaks at professional meetings on legal issues for archives and teaches basic archival workshops and is a past chair of SAA's Privacy and Confidentiality Roundtable.

Peter J. Wosh is the director of the Program in Archival Management and Historical Editing at New York University, a position he has held since 1994. Prior to that, he served as director of Archives and Library Services at the American Bible Society and University Archivist at Seton Hall University, where he was also responsible for administering the Archives of the Archdiocese of Newark. Wosh holds a Ph.D. (1988) and an M.A. (1979) in American History from New York University, as well as a B.A. with Highest Distinction in History from Rutgers University (1976). He is a fellow of the Society of American Archivists and has written and spoken widely on archival and history topics. Previous books include *Covenant House: Journey of a Faith-Based Charity* (Philadelphia: University of Pennsylvania Press, 2005); *Spreading the Word: The Bible Business in Nineteenth-Century America* (Ithaca: Cornell University Press, 1994); with Joseph Mahoney, *The Diocesan Journal of Michael Augustine Corrigan, Bishop of Newark, New Jersey, 1872–1880* (Newark: New Jersey Historical Society, 1987); and *Guide to Northern New Jersey Catholic Parish and Institu-*

tional Records (South Orange: New Jersey Catholic Historical Records Commission, 1984).

Sandra Boyd received her B.A. and M.A. degrees in English from Mississippi College and her M.L.S. from the University of Southern Mississippi. She heads the Mississippi Department of Archives and History Paper Archives section and was responsible for the day-do-day implementation of the court order in the Mississippi Sovereignty Commission case.

Louis Dembitz Brandeis (1856–1941) and **Samuel Dennis Warren II** (1852–1910) first met at Harvard Law School, where they became fast friends and graduated in 1877. Warren, who hailed from a distinguished and socially prominent New England family, invited his former classmate to form the law firm of Warren & Brandeis in Boston in 1879. Brandeis continued on to a very distinguished legal career. He became known as the "people's attorney" through his commitments to public service and pro bono work, and he served on the U.S. Supreme Court from 1916 through 1939. Warren ceased practicing law in the late 1880s, electing instead to manage his family's lucrative paper mill business and devote his spare time to social and philanthropic endeavors.

Barbara L. Craig is an associate professor of Archives in the Faculty of Information Studies at the University of Toronto. She has earned a B.A. (honours) and M.A. from McMaster University and a Ph.D. in Archive Studies from the University of London, England, and has published widely on archives theory, archives history, and the history of medicine. Professor Craig has held a number of executive positions in national professional organizations and served as the *American Archivist* reviews editor and the editor of *Archivaria*.

Elena S. Danielson is director of Library and Archive of the Hoover Institution, Stanford University, where she formerly was the curator of its West European Collection, archivist, and associate archivist. She received her Ph.D., A.M., and A.B. in German and Slavic Studies from Stanford University and her M.L.S. from University of California, Berkeley. She also was assistant professor of Modern Languages at Santa Clara University. Among many other honors, Dr. Danielson received the Laurel Award of the Polish Prime Minister, a Fulbright Fellowship, and Phi Beta Kappa. She writes and speaks on international archival topics, the Hoover Institution and Hoover legacy, and ethical and legal issues for archivists.

Mark J. Duffy is canonical archivist and director of The Archives of the Episcopal Church USA. He is formerly associate archivist of Harvard University Archives and chief archivist of the City of Boston. He is enrolled in the doctoral program of the University of Texas at Austin. He currently serves on the ICA Steering Committee of the Section on Archives of Churches and Religious Denominations (SKR).

Mark A. Greene currently directs the American Heritage Center at the University of Wyoming, is a fellow of the Society of American Archivists, and writes widely on historical and archival matters. Formerly he was the archivist of Carleton College. He received a B.A. in history and political science from Ripon College, Ripon, Wisconsin, and an M.A. in history from the University of Michigan.

Sara S. Hodson is the curator of literary manuscripts at the Huntington Library, where she administers all of its British and American literary manuscripts. A past chair of the Society of American Archivists' Privacy and Confidentiality Roundtable, she received a B.A. and M.A. in English from Whittier College and an M.L.S. from UCLA. She has written and spoken extensively on privacy and confidentiality issues and other archival and literary topics, and she received the Lifetime Achievement Award from the Society of California Archivists, and is a fellow of the Society of American Archivists. She co-edited a volume of scholarly essays entitled *Jack London: One Hundred Years a Writer*, published by The Huntington Press.

H. T. Holmes, director of the Mississippi Department of Archives and History Archives and Library Division, was associated with the Mississippi Sovereignty Commission court case from its beginning in 1977, and since 1988 has been responsible for the administration of the court-ordered program. He received a B.A. from Millsaps College and an M.L.S. from the University of Southern Mississippi.

Paul C. Lasewicz has been the corporate archivist at International Business Machines, Armonk, New York, since 1998. Previously he was the corporate archivist for Aetna Life and Casualty, Hartford, Connecticut. He received an M.A. in history from University of Connecticut. An active member in local, regional, and national archival organizations, Lasewicz is a frequent presenter on topics of archival and historical interest.

Martin L. Levitt is the acting director of the American Philosophical Society Library and Temple University Professor of History. He holds the M.A., M.S.L.S., and Ph.D. degrees and is both a former Fulbright Scholar and an Andrew W. Mellon Fellow. Levitt has published several articles concerning the history of twentieth-century science and technology.

Heather MacNeil is an assistant professor in the School of Library, Archival and Information Studies at the University of British Columbia. She holds an M.A. in English Literature from Simon Fraser University and a Master of Archival Studies and Ph.D. (interdisciplinary studies) from the University of British Columbia. She is the author of *Without Consent: The Ethics of Disclosing Personal Information in Public Archives* (1992; reprinted 2001) and *Trusting Records: Legal, Historical and Diplomatic Perspectives* (2000).

L. Dale Patterson received a B.S. from the University of Denver, an M.C.S. from Regent College, British Columbia, and a Ph.D. from Drew University, New Jersey. He has served as archivist/records administrator for the General Commission on Archives and History of the United Methodist Church since 1994. He also is a Certified Archivist, chaired the Archivists of Religious Collections Section of the Society of American Archivists, and teaches courses concerning archives and history at Drew University.

William Lloyd Prosser (1898–1972) received an A.B. from Harvard College in 1918 and an LL.B. from the University of Minnesota in 1928. He taught at the University of Minnesota Law School until entering the active practice of law in 1943. Prosser resumed his teaching career in 1948 at Harvard, and the next year he became dean of the faculty at Boalt Hall, the law school at the University of California, Berkeley. His seminal legal work, *Handbook of the Law of Torts* (currently in its fifth edition as *Prosser and Keeton on The Law of Torts*, 1984) and other writings greatly influenced the development of late twentieth-century American law. Excerpts from his work appear in many American legal opinions and state privacy statutes. Following his resignation from Boalt Hall in 1961, Dean Prosser taught at Hastings College of Law in San Francisco until his death in 1972.

Timothy D. Pyatt, Duke University archivist, was educated at Duke University and North Carolina Central University. He formerly was director, Southern Historical Collection and curator of Manuscripts at University of North Carolina at Chapel Hill, where he taught in the School of Information and Library Science; curator of Marylandia & Rare Books and Special Collections librarian/university archivist at the University of Maryland; and Rare Books/Special Collections librarian at the University of Oregon. Pyatt has written and spoken extensively on manuscripts collection development, access, and digital archives, and he was the 2003 chair of the SAA's Privacy and Confidentiality Roundtable.

Sarah Rowe-Sims received a B.A. (Hons.) in History and American Studies from the University of Wales Swansea and her M.L.I.S. from the University of Southern Mississippi. She was one of three archivists who implemented the court-ordered redactions of the Mississippi Sovereignty Commission records prior to public access. She now serves as an electronic records archivist with the Mississippi Department of Archives and History.

Judith Schwarz approaches privacy from the point of view of both an archivist and a historian. As a charter member of the pioneer group of academics who virtually invented the field of gay and lesbian history in the 1970s, she well understands the value of opening seemingly sensitive materials to responsible scholarly inquiry. She was a founder of the Lesbian Herstory Archives and is a professional archivist who has worked in a variety of repositories. Her article originally appeared in a professional historians' journal.

Christine M. Taylor is the chancellor of the Roman Catholic Archdiocese of Seattle. In that capacity, she is responsible for the archives and records management programs of the archdiocese. She is currently matriculating in the graduate program in canon law at Catholic University in Washington, D.C. She is a member of the ICA Steering Committee of the Section on Archives of Churches and Religious Denominations (SKR).

Christine Weideman received her M.A. from the University of Michigan. She began her archival career at the Bentley Historical Library at the University of Michigan, where she managed collection development projects and arranged and described university records. Since 1993, she has been assistant head of Manuscripts and Archives in the Yale University Library.

INDEX

Abernathy v. Hutchinson, 23
Abrams v. Temple of the Lost Sheep, 210
Academic research trends, changing, 65
Access
    archival, to lawyers' papers, 175–80
    archival management of, to records, 78–79
    balancing privacy and, 159–74, 206–7
    in covenantal relationship, 206–8
    defined, 2
    donor rights to privacy versus, 157
    to electronic records, 160–61
    establishing guidelines for, 78–80
    fiduciary trust in management of, 221–24
    open, to information, 1, 61
    to police files, 93–111
    professional agency in management of, 216–20
    restrictions on, for records, 78–79
    selective, 134–35
Administrative perspectives, 6, 127–98
Administrative records, 212
Advertising, privacy rights and, 33, 41–42
Advisory Committee on Online Access and Security, establishment of, by Federal Trade Commission (FTC), 235
Aetna, Internet sites of, 232
Agency principle, 224–25
Agency theory, 206, 218
Agre, Phil, 235
AIG, archival programs of, 233
Alexander II, assassination of, 107
Algonquin Books, 150
Allen, Garland, 119
Alumni directories, 182
American Civil Liberties Union/ Mississippi (ACLU/M), 163–65
American eugenics movement, establishment of, 114–15
American Eugenics Society, papers of, 119

American Library Association's Task Force on Gay Liberation, 87
American Philosophical Society (APS), 115, 117, 119
Amis, Kingsley, 133
    papers of, 146–47
Andersen Consulting v. UOP and Bickel and Brewer, 274
Appraisal as grounded on values, 253
Appropriation
    of identity, 239
    of likeness, 54–55
    methods of invasion of, 132
    of name, 54–55
    right to privacy and, 41–43, 44, 52
Archival policy, development of,
    to protect privacy, 85
Archives and Records Management Act (1981), 160
Archives & Manuscripts: Law (Peterson and Peterson), 4
Archives & Manuscripts: Reference & Access (Holbert), 4
Archives of repression, 93
Archivists
    balancing responsibilities, 63–64, 82–92, 159–74, 206–7
    concerns with institutional memory, 214
    corporate, 201–2
    duality role of, 5, 174, 219
    government, 67–68, 77, 159–60
    health care, 200–201
    input into records-related legislation, 127–28
    religious, 208
    research into history of medical records, 248
Aristotle, 69
Arthur Andersen, 199
Artistic property, law of, 26–27
Ash, Timothy Garton, 100
Ashcroft, John, 1

377

Aspern, Jeffrey, 140
"The Aspern Papers" (James), 139–40
Association for Methodist Historical Societies, archival functions of, 265
Attorney-client privilege, 4, 129, 176–77
  duration of, 178–79
  extent and limitations of, 177–78
Attorney work product privilege, 179–80
Authors' papers
  collection of, during lifetime, 146
  high market value of, 147–48
  privacy in, 131–48

Bachardy, Don, 135
Balfour, Patrick, papers of, 137–38
Bancroft Library at University of California, 147–48
Barber, Bernard, 222
Barbour, William H., Jr., 164, 165, 166, 167–68, 169, 171
Barlow, John Perry, 229, 230, 244
Barritt, Marjorie, 183
Barry, John, 154
Bayard, Mabel, 10
BBBOnline, 235
Becker, Penny, 207
Beckett, Samuel, 141
Behrnd-Klodt, Menzi L., 10, 129–30
Bentham, Jeremy, 71, 72, 75
Berlin Wall, fall of, 93
Bertram Rota Ltd., 137
Bierce, Ambrose, 144
Bill of Rights, 10, 53. *See also specific amendments*
Birthler, Marianne, 99
Blum, Harold, 135
Bodleian Library at Oxford University, 133
Boerne, City of, v. Flores, 209
Bohley, Bärbel, 95
Borden, Lizzie, 179
Bork, Robert, 243, 279
Bowers, Sam, 171
Box Ten Affair, 87–88
Boyd, Sandra, 129
Brandeis, Louis D., 2–3, 7, 10, 13, 31–32, 33, 37
  creation of independent basis of liability and, 51
  false light in public eye and, 39–41
  intrusion and, 34
  invasion of privacy and, 50
  public disclosure of private facts and, 36–39, 48
  "The Right to Privacy" by, 15–30, 132
Brill, Alida, 60
Brown v. Board of Education, 161
Buckley, James, 182
Buckley Amendment, 275. *See also* Family Educational Rights and Privacy Act (1974) (FERPA)
Bucknell, Katherine, 135
Bundesarchiv, 94, 96
Burns, Ken, 152
Bush, George W., 1
Business history, relevance of, 232–33
Byatt, A. S., 140
Byron, Lord, 39–40

Cable Communications Privacy Act (1984), 271
Carlin, John, 159–60, 174
Cary, Frank T., 234–35
Case records, 253
Cavoukian, Ann, 235
Celebrities, privacy in papers of, 131–48
Censorship, 8, 46, 52, 127
Chaney, James, 171
Cheever, Ben, 142
Cheever, John, papers of, 142–43
Cheever, Susan, 142
Cheka, 107, 108
Children's On-line Privacy Protection Act (1998) (COPPA), 271–72
Christensen, Clayton M., 226–27
Christian Advocate, 261
Churches. *See also* Denominations
  local policies and norms of, 212–13
  position in American institutional culture, 258
  as public or private institution, 258–60
  research use of sacramental registers, 3
CIGNA, Internet sites of, 232
Citizens' Council, 162
Civil libertarians, 70
Civil Rights Act (1964), 162
Civil rights movement, importance of Mississippi Sovereignty Commission in, 171
The Civil War: A Narrative (Foote), 153
Civil War manuscripts, 150
Clemens, Samuel, 144
Clergy
  extension of priest-penitent privilege to, 207

formation, discipline, and
deployment records of, 211
personnel records of, 211
scandals involving, 199–200
Cleveland, Rose Elizabeth, 87
Cleveland-Whipple affair, 87–88
Clinical notes of care, 250
Closure, development of archives policy
to provide, 85
Coca-Cola, donation of archives to
Library of Congress, 233, 237
Code of ethics
of International Council of Archives, 81
of Society of American Archivists (SAA),
61–62, 65, 67, 133, 137, 146, 174
Cold Spring Harbor Laboratory
Archives, 119
Collective memory, issue of individual
privacy versus, 91–92
Collectors, motives of, 83
Colleges and University Archives
Section (C&U) of Society of
American Archivists, 189–90
Commission on Archives and History,
United Methodist Church, at Drew
University, Madison, New Jersey,
records in, 84
Commodification
of information, 230
of personal data, 227
Common law, 18–19, 175, 211
Commonwealth v. Stewart, 210
Communications Assistance for Law
Enforcement Act (CALEA)
(1994), 272
Community standards, 57
privacy rights and, 56
Computer age, 7
Computer databases, information held
in, 70
Computerized records, 7
Computer Matching and Privacy
Protection Act (CMA) (1998), 272
Confession, 207
Confessor-priest privilege, 4
Confidences
archival perspective on, 205–25
breach of, 32
in covenantal relationship, 206–8
in medical records, 246–56
Confidentiality, 78
defined, 2
issues of, and eugenics, 117

problems of, in handling research
requests, 84
Congregational records, 211–12
Consent, 50, 78–79
to disclosure, 58
Consumer Credit Reporting Reform Act
(1997), 272–73
Contractual perspective on principal-
agent relationship, 217–18
Control Commission for the Dissolution
of the Ministry of Security (Federal
Republic of Germany), 94–95
Cook, Blanche Wiesen, 88
Cooley, Judge, 16, 34
Coordinating Committee for
Fundamental American
Freedoms, 162
Copyright, 128
current trends, 201
laws on, 19
ownership of, 231
privacy and, 138–39, 144–46
Copyright Act (1976), 229
Corporate archives
added-value philosophy of, 240
benefits and risks of history, 231–34
biographical sheets in, 240
changing conceptions of privacy and
property for, 226–45
correspondence in, 240–41
culture of, 232
data mining and, 242
documentation of consumer or
customer activity in, 242–43
ownership issues at, 228–30
potential for internal information
distribution, 232
privacy rights in, 227–28, 234–44
public and corporate concerns over,
243–44
public dissemination of information
and, 232
resiliency in, 228
safeguards in, 241–42
targeting of records for
acquisition, 232
traditional internal focus of, 244–45
value of, to company, 239
view of, as entrepreneurial, 201–2
Corporate scandals, 199–200
Correspondence files
of literary manuscript collection, 143
privacy and, 137–38

Counter-Reformation, 106
Covenantal relationship
  access in, 206–8
  confidence keeping in, 206–8
  privacy in, 206–8
Covenants, 207
Cox, Richard, 79
Craig, Barbara L., 202
Crime Control Act (1973), 272
Cross-referencing, procedures for, 79
Cultural environment of religious organizations, 213–16
Czechoslovakia, lustration law in, 101–2

Daggett, Lynn M., 182
Dahmer, Vernon, 171
Danielson, Elena, 64
Darley, Gabrielle, 36
Darwin, Charles, papers of, 119
Data banks, 7
  proliferation of, 3
Data mining, 242
Data Protection Directive (1995), in European Union (EU), 291–93
Data-protection laws, 67, 75–76, 78
  strengths and weaknesses of current, 76
Datenschutz, 99
Daughters of Bilitis (DOB), 91
Davenport, Charles Benedict, 114–15
  papers of, 119
Death, 55
  privacy rights and, 79, 132
Defamation, 17–18, 32
  false light claims and, 57–58
  legal distinctions between, and invasion of privacy, 58
De La Beckwich, Byron, 171
Deliberative autonomy, 76
Deliberative democracy, 76
De Mille, Agnes, 85, 86
De Mille, Anna George, 85–86
Democracy
  data-protection laws and, 75–76
  ownership of public records in, 67
  privacy rights and, 74, 77
Denominational archivists, 208
Denominations. *See also* Churches
  cultural segmentation of mainline, 215, 217
  ethic of privacy in, 212–13
  privileged records in, 212
Descendability, right to privacy and, 55
Diaries, restriction on, 135
Dickens, Charles, 144

Diffendorfer, Ralph, 262
Difficulties with Girls (Amis), 147
Digital dissemination of information, 227
Digital telephony law, 272
Digitization, 227
Disclosure
  ethics of, 174
  of private facts, 55–57
Discount shopper cards, 235
Disruptive technology, 227
  defined, 226
  privacy and, 227–28
Doctor-patient relationship, 4
  right to privacy privilege inherent in, 121
Dolan DNA Learning Center, 112, 117
  Editorial Advisory Panel of, 119–25
Donation, 82
Donors, 82
  privacy rights of, 156
  rights to privacy versus access, 157
Driver's Privacy Protection Act (1994), 272
Duberman, Martin, 88
Duffy, Mark J., 201, 202
Durkheim, 221
Dzerzynskii, Feliks, 108

Earnhardt, Dale, 243
East German State Security Service (*Ministerium für Staatssicherheit* called MfS or Stasi)
  opening of records of, 93–94
  records relating to, 64
Eavesdropping, intrusion and, 35
Edel, Deborah, 88, 91–92
Edel, Leon, 141
Education records, 212
  coverage of, under Family Educational Rights and Privacy Act, 181–98
  defined, 184–85
Eissler, Kurt, 135
Electronic Communications Privacy Act (1986) (ECPA), 272–73
Electronic Freedom of Information Act Amendments (1996) (EFOIA), 274
Electronic Fund Transfer Act (1980), 274
Electronic records, 7
  access to, 160–61
  developing agenda for managing, 228
Electronic Signatures in Global and National Commerce Act (ESIGN) (2000), 274

Electronic surveillance, 54
Elementary and Secondary Education
    Act (1965), 276
Elston, Charles B., 182–83
Emerson, Ralph Waldo, 144
Employee Polygraph Protection Act
    (1988), 274
Employee privacy, 235–36
Employee records, 236
Engelhardt, Tristram, Jr., 71
Enron, 199
Equi, Marie, letters written by, 88
ESPN Classic Sports, 232
Esposito, Jackie, 187
Ethical, Legal, and Social Issues
    (ELSI) Program of the National
    Human Genome Research
    Institute, 112, 116
Ethical perspectives, 6, 61–125
Ethical review boards, establishment of,
    by archives, 64–65
Ethical standards, purposes served by, 80
Ethics
    access to records of repressive
        regimes, 64
    of archiving health care and medical
        records, 256
    in constructing Eugenics Web site,
        112–25
    of disclosure, 174
    of privacy in protestant
        denominational bodies, 212–13
ETRUST, 235
Eugenics, 114
    coining of term, 112
    scientific plausibility of, 114
Eugenics Archive, home page of, 113
Eugenics movement
    creation of Web site documenting
        history of, 64–65
    establishment of American, 114–15
Eugenics Records Office (ERO), 115, 119
    public relations arm of, 115
European Data Privacy Model, 276
European Union (EU)
    Data Protection Directive (1995) in,
        291–93
    Telecommunications Privacy
        Directive in, 293
Evangelical United Brethren Church
    (EUB), 265
Evans, Frank B., 3
Evers, Medgar, 171

Fair Credit Reporting Act (FCRA),
    274–75
Fair information practices, 80
    principles of, 235
Fair use, 145, 152
False light
    methods of invasion of, 132
    in public eye, 39–41, 44
    publicity placing person in, 57–58
    tort of, 59
Family Educational Rights and Privacy
    Act (1974) (FERPA), 3, 5, 7, 130,
    275, 280
    ambiguity and archival implications
        of, 181–98
    congressional amendments of, 280–82
    judicial interpretations of, 282–84
Family Policy Compliance Office, 130
Federal Trade Commission (FTC),
    Advisory Committee on Online
    Access and Security establishment
    of, 235
Federal Wiretap Act (1968), 277
Felsher, William M., 238
Felsher v. University of Evansville, 238
Fiduciary trust in management of access
    and privacy, 221–24
Fields, James and Annie, 143–44
Fifth Amendment, 10, 13–14, 269
Financial Services Modernization Act
    (1999), 275
First Amendment, 10, 11–13, 269, 277
    defense of newsworthiness, 59
    Establishment Clause of, 209
    private facts and, 57
    separation of church and state, 210–11
Fitter Family Contest, 115, 122
Flynn, Elizabeth Gurley, 85, 86
Follow Me Down (Foote), 152, 153
Foote, Shelby, 151–52
    correspondence between Percy
        and, 153
    letters by, 155–56
    papers of, 128, 150–51, 153–56
Ford Motor Company
    archival programs of, 233
    Internet sites of, 232
Foucault, Michel, 71–72
Fourteenth Amendment, 10, 11–13, 270
Fourth Amendment, 10, 13–14, 269
Frederick Osborn Papers, 119
Freedom of Information Act (FOIA)
    (1966), 1, 3, 7, 109, 211, 276

Freedom of information laws, drafting of, by states and municipalities, 3
Freedom of press, 46
  constitutional guarantee of, 45
Freedom Summer (1964), 162
Freud, Anna, 135
Freud, Sigmund, papers of, 135
Freud Archives, 135

Gale, Zona, 85
Galton, Francis, 112
Gandy, Oscar, 69, 73
The Gap, archival programs of, 233
Garfinkel, Harold, 214
Gates, William H., 234, 235
Gauck, Joachim, 95–96, 96, 97–98, 99, 104, 109, 111
Gauck Authority, 100–101, 104, 105, 110
Gavison, Ruth, 68, 74
Gay American History (Katz), 87, 88
General Commission on Archives and History (GCAH) (1968), creation of, 265
Giddens, Anthony, 219, 220
Gilman, Charlotte Perkins, 85
Ginzburg, Carlo, 106
Gittings, Barbara, 87, 88, 91
Glaspell, Susan, 85
Globalization of archival issues relating to files of repression, 108–10
Gonzaga University et al. v. Doe, 283
Goodman, Andrew, 171
Gordon, Caroline, 152
Gossip, 17
Government archivists
  access guarantor role of, 68, 77
  public service role of, 67–68, 77
  role of, 159–60
Grade books, Family Educational Rights and Privacy Act (1974) (FERPA) status of, 188
The Graduate (Webb), 139
The Gramercy Winner (Percy), 152
Gramm-Leach-Bliley Act (GLB) (1999), 275
Greece, police files in, 109–10
Greene, Mark A., 130, 183
Grégoire de Roulhac Hamilton, Joseph, aggressive collecting techniques of, 149–50

Habeas data, 100
  link between concepts of lustration and, 110

Hadnot v. Shaw, 210
Hamilton, Ian, unauthorized biography by, 145
Handbook of the Law of Torts (Prosser), 12
Harlan, Justice, 12
Harriman, Mrs. E. H., 115
Harvard Law Review (Warren and Brandeis), 10–11, 15–30
Hatch, Nathan, 258
Havel, Vaclav, 101–2
Hawthorne, Nathaniel, 144
Health care records. *See* Medical records
Health Insurance Portability and Accountability Act (HIPAA) (1996), 7, 200, 202, 243, 247–48, 276, 285–91
  business associates regulation, 287–88
  covered entities, 247–48, 286–87
  health care clearinghouses under, 287
  health plans under, 287
  hybrid entity under, 287
  Personal Health Information, permitted and prohibited uses of, 288–89
  Privacy Rule, 286, 289, 290
  safe harbor provisions, 288–89
  Security Rule, 289–90
Hentz, Caroline, writings of, 150
Heterodoxy Club (Greenwich Village, NYC), 83, 85
Hilliard, Elbert, 163
Hirsch, Ralf, 95
Hodson, Sara S., 128
Hoffman, Dustin, 139
Holbert, Sue E., 4
Holmes, H. T., 129
Holmes, Oliver Wendell, 144
Home Before Dark (Cheever), 142
Home Depot, archival programs of, 233
Horton, George Moses, works by, 150
House of Percy (Wyatt-Brown), 153–55
Howard, Elizabeth Jane, 147
Howe, Marie Jenney, 85
Hudson, Winthrop, 257–58
Hull, Helen, papers of, 86
Human Genome Project (HGP), 115–16
Human rights movement, support from, in opening of police files, 93
Human sexuality, 63
Hungary, access to police files in, 103
Huntington Library, 134, 136
  Amis, Kingsley, papers at, 146–47

Fields, James and Annie, papers at, 143–44
Howard, Elizabeth, papers at, 147
Isherwood, Christopher, papers at, 135, 148
Kinross, Patrick Balfour, papers at, 137
London, Jack, papers at, 145–46
Mantel, Hilary, papers at, 147
Hurst, Fanny, 85
Hutchinson v. Luddy, 210

IBM, 236
  archival programs of, 233
  Internet sites of, 232
Identity, unlawful appropriation of, 239
Idioculture, 207
Immigration and Naturalization Service, U.S. (INS), Student and Exchange Visitor Information System (SEVIS), 281
Immortality, right to privacy and, 55
Immunity to lawsuit, 58
Implied contract, breach of, 32
Individual, identification of, 56
Individuality, impoverishment of, 73–74
Individual privacy
  balancing protection of, with research rights, 82–92
  issues of, versus collective memory, 91–92
  need to protect, 1
  rights of, 9
  shifting boundaries of, 248
Informants
  ability of victims to learn identity of, 99–100
Information
  changing nature of, 231
  commodification of, 230
Information privacy
  debates over, 76–77
  defenses of right to, 68
Information seclusion model, limits of, 76
Information technologies, public trust and, 247
Informational environment, of religion in society, 208–13
Informational seclusion model of privacy, 75–76
The Innovator's Dilemma (Christensen), 226–27

Institute for National Memory (Poland), 103
Institutionalized altruism, 79
Institutional memory, archivists concerned with preserving, 214
Institutional perspectives, 6, 199–267
Intelligence records, opening, 64
International Council of Archives (ICA)
  Code of Ethics of, 81
  report to UNESCO, 108–10
Internet, 227
Internet Archive, 228
Internet service providers, failure of, to guarantee confidentiality, 1
Intrusion, 44, 51
  upon seclusion or solitude, 53–54
Invasion of privacy, risks and defenses, 58–60
Iraqi security service files, 108
Isherwood, Christopher, 147–48
  papers of, 135

Jackson, Wharlest, 171
Jacobs, Eric, 133
James, Henry, 139–40, 141, 156
Johnson, Eric, 221
Johnson, Grace Nail, 86
Johnson, Robert, 228, 245
Jordan Country (Foote), 152
Joyce, James, 141, 156
Joyce, Lucia, 141
Joyce, Nora, 141
Joyce, Stephen, 141, 142
Judicial proceedings, use of archives as evidence in, 110
Jurisdictional and congregational records, 211–12

Kahle, Brewster, 228, 241
Kaplan, Fred, 141
Katz, Jonathan, 87–88, 88
Katz v. United States, 13
Kempe, Wolfram, 97
Kennedy-Kassebaum Bill, 285
King, B. B., 233
King, Edwin, 170
King, Martin Luther, Jr., common-law right of publicity, 55
Kingwell, Mark, 77
Kohl, Helmut, 94
Kryston, In re, v. Board of Education, 282
La Follette Family Papers (Library of Congress), 86
Lancelot (Percy), 151

Lanterns on the Levee (Percy), 151
Lapse of time, right to privacy and, 49
Larkin, Philip, 147
Lasewicz, Paul C., 201–2
The Last Gentleman (Percy), 151
Laughlin, Harry H., 115
Law, Bernard Cardinal, 200
Law enforcement purposes, records created and maintained for, 182
Lawrence, Ken, 164
Lawyers, archival access to papers of, 175–80
Lear, Edward, 144
Lee, Vernon, 140
Legal perspectives, 6, 9–60
Legal privilege
 attorney-client, 4, 176–77
  duration of, 178–79
  extent and limitations of, 177–78
 attorney work product, 179–80
 defined, 175
 doctor-patient, 121
 historic, 129
 holder of, 175–80
 priest-penitent, 4, 207
Legal records, 212
Legislative issues, 5
Lesbian Herstory Archives (LHA), 63, 83–84
 Lesbian Herstory Educational Foundation, 83–84, 89–91
Lesbian materials
 institutions' handling of, 84–89
 suppression of, 84–89
The Letters of John Cheever (Cheever), 142
Levitt, Martin, 64–65
Libel, 17, 26–27, 39, 50, 52
Life insurance applications, research use of, 243
Likeness, appropriation of, 54–55
Literary manuscript collection and correspondence, 143
Literary or artistic property, right to, 20
Literary property, law of, 26–27
Lobdell, Mary Pratt, 152
Lombardo, Paul, 119
London, Jack, 145–46
 papers of, 145–46
Longfellow, Henry Wadsworth, 144
Lost in the Cosmos (Percy), 151
Love in a Dry Season (Foote), 152, 153
Love in the Ruins (Percy), 151
Luban, David, 224

Lustration, 101
 link between concepts of *habeas data* and, 110
 passage of law on, in Czechoslovakia, 101–2

MacNeil, Heather, 5, 62, 64, 174
Maddox, Brenda, 141
Madison, James, 159
Majority rule, 74
Malamud, Bernard, 142
Mantel, Hilary, 147
Markó, György, 103
Marks, Jeannette, 87
Masked abstract, 272
Masson, Jeffrey, 135
Mazowiecki, Tadeusz, 102–3
McNealy, Scott, 243
Medical records, 246–56
 acquiring, preserving, and providing access to, 251–54
 defined, 249–51
 ethics of archiving, 256
 Family Educational Rights and Privacy Act exclusion of medical records, 182
 North American health care institutions, privacy concerns, 200–201
 origins and evolution of, 202
 recognizing time and different interests that support archiving of, 254–55
Melvin v. Reid, 36, 38, 39, 49
Mendel, Gregor, 114
The Message in the Bottle (Percy), 151
The Methodist, 261
Micklos, David, 117
Microsoft, 235
 Internet sites of, 232
Mid-Atlantic Regional Archives Conference (MARAC) (1988), 4–5
Middlebrook, Diane, 141
Mill, John Stuart, 69–70
Minnesota Historical Society (MHS), Box Ten Affair and, 87–88
Misappropriation of name or likenesss, 54–55
Missionary Files Series, 266
Mississippi Department of Archives and History (MDAH), 129
 access to records and, 165–70

efforts to prevent destruction of records, 163
establishment of privacy officer position, 172–73
history and legal mandate of, 160–61, 171–72
imaging and indexing of records, 168
rejection of optical character recognition (OCR) technology, 167
Mississippi Public Records Act (1983), 172
amendments to, 160–61
Mississippi State Sovereignty Commission, 129
advisory role of, 161
availability of all records in electronic format, 169
importance of records of, in civil rights movement, 171
investigative functions of, 161–62
opening records of, 159–74
public relations role of, 161
racism and, 161–62
records collected by, 161–62
Miss Marks and Miss Woolley (Wells), 87
Modern Archives and Manuscripts: A Select Biography (Evans), 3
Moon, Michael, 229–30
Moral autonomy, association of privacy with individual, 69
Moral interest in privacy, 68
"Mores" test, 39, 41, 49, 52
Mount Holyoke College Library, papers of Marks and Woolley at, 87
The Moviegoer (Percy), 151, 152
Municipalities, drafting of freedom of information laws by, 3

Name, appropriation of, 54–55
National Archives (U.S.), 159
National Defense Authorization Act for Fiscal Year (2002), 281
Natural rights, emergence of, 69–70
Negligent conduct, liability for, 59
Nestle, Joan, 88, 91, 92
New Cardiff (Webb), 139
News, 46
Newsworthiness, First Amendment defense of, 59
Nickelodeon, 232
Niemann v. Cooley, 210
Ninth Amendment, 10, 270

No Child Left Behind Act (2001), 276–77, 281
Nora: The Real Life of Molly Bloom (Maddox), 141
North Carolina Writers Web site, 155
Norton, Margaret Cross, 67
Nuisance, law of, 16

Okhrana, 107
Omnibus Consolidated Appropriations Act for FY 1997, 271
Omnibus Crime Control and Safe Street Act (1968), 273, 277
Open access to information, 61
Open-records legislation, 7, 261–65
Open records policy of United Methodist Church, 202–3, 257–67
Oral history interviews, 136
Orbach, Jerry, 235
Organizational culture, 213–14
O'Toole, James, 8
Owasso Independent School Dist. 1-011 v. Falvo, 130, 188, 282
Ownership issues, at corporate archives, 228–30
Oyster Boy Review, 157

Panopticon, 71, 75
Panopticon gaze, 72
Paparazzi, rise of, 1
Patient medical histories, research use of, 3
Patient-physician privilege, 4, 121
Patterson, L. Dale, 202–3
Pavesich v. New England Life Insurance Co., 33
Pedigree analysis, 112
Peer grading, 130
Percy, Camille, 151
Percy, Leroy, 151
Percy, Mary "Bunt" Townsend, 152
Percy, Walker, 151
acquisition of papers of, 150–53
correspondence between Foote and, 153
papers of, 128
use and privacy issues with papers of, 153–56
Percy, William Alexander, 151
Periodic re-review of restricted records, procedures for, 79
Permanent visibility, 75
Personal data, commodification of, 227

Personal Health Information, permitted and prohibited uses of, 288–89
Personal identity, impoverishment of, 73–74
Personal information
    collection and analysis of, 75
    concerns about collection and use of sensitive, 247
Personal Information Protection and Electronic Documents Act (PIPEDA) (Canada), 200, 202, 237–38, 247, 290–91
Personal physical and psychological space, exclusiveness of, 2
Personal privacy, societal debate concerning protection of, 80–81
Personal rights, 5
Personal trust, 222–23
Peterson, Gary M., 4
Peterson, Trudy Huskamp, 4, 81
Photocopying restriction on archival material, 152–53
Plaintiff, privacy rights of, 35
Plantation records, 150
Poe v. Ullman, 12
Poland, access to police files in, 102–3
Police files, collapse of repressive regimes and demand to open, 93–111
Political victims, privacy rights and rights of, 93–111
Pollard v. Photographic Co., 24
Possession (Byatt), 140
Post-Communist countries, opening of police files in, 101–4
Pound, Ezra, 141
Presidential records, 3
Presidential Records Act, efforts to overturn access provision of, 1
Priest-penitent privilege, 207
Prince Albert v. Strange, 20–21, 23
Principal-agent relationship, contractual perspective on, 217–18
Prior publication, principle of, 172
Privacy, 132
    access versus donor rights to, 157
    administrative challenges of, 127–98
    association of, with moral autonomy, 69
    balancing access and, 159–74, 206–7
    balancing protection of individual, with research rights, 82–92
    changing conceptions of, for corporate archives, 226–45
    as continually changing concept, 7–8
    copyright and, 138–39, 144–46
    in covenantal relationship, 206–8
    defined, 68–69
    disruptive technology and, 227–28
    efforts to define, 2
    eugenics and, 117
    fiduciary trust in management of, 221–24
    as intertwined with property rights, 238–39
    invasion of, 9
    medical records and, 246–56
    microphones, intrusion and, 35
    modern concept of, 132
    moral interest in, 68
    in papers of authors, 131–48
    in papers of celebrities, 131–48
    in Percy and Foote papers, 149–58
    privilege and, 69
    professional agency in management of, 216–20
    protection of, 2
    public responses generated by, 1
    of third parties, 132–33
Privacy Act (1974), 3, 7, 99, 106, 109, 211, 272, 277
Privacy-as-participation model, 75–76, 76
Privacy officer, establishment of, as position, 172–73
Privacy Protection Act (1980), 277
Privacy rights, 2–3, 9, 15–30. *See also* Tort right of privacy
    appropriation and, 41–43
    common features of, 43–45
    community standards and, 56
    constitutional origins of, 10
    in corporate archives, 234–44
    death and, 132
    debate on existence of, 33–34
    defenses to claim of invasion of, 50–51
    descendability/immortality and, 55
    of donor, 156
    existence of, in state courts, 33
    false light in public eye, 39–41
    Fifth Amendment and, 13–14
    First Amendment and, 11–13
    Fourteenth Amendment and, 11–13

Fourth Amendment and, 13–14
   intrusion upon, 34–36
   lapse of time and, 49
   limitations on, 47–49
     for employees, in workplace, 14
   private letters and, 133
   public disclosure of private facts, 36–39
   public figures and public interest, 45–47
   recovery on basis of, 32
   rights of political victims and, 93–111
   Supreme Court recognition of, 12–13
   third-party considerations and, 56–57
   tort of, 53–60
   unconscionability and, 56
   Warren and Brandeis on, 10
Private facts, 51–52
   disclosure of, 55–57, 59
   or information, 56
   public disclosure of, 36–39
Private letters
   privacy rights and, 133
   publication of, and consent, 48
Private life, publicity given to, 55–57
Private sector
   intersection of public sector and, 7
   mutual dependence of public sector and, 77
Privileges, 69. *See also* Legal privilege
   legal, 129
   effect of legal, 175–80
   privacy and, 69
   against self-incrimination, 176
Professional agency
   in management of access and privacy, 216–20
   in religious organization archives, 205–25
Property, 15
   changing conceptions of, for corporate archive, 226–45
Property rights, 9
   invasion of, 32
   privacy as intertwined with, 238–39
Prosser, William L., 12, 132
   Restatement (Second) of Torts, Privacy and, 53
Protected communications, attorney-client privilege and, 176–77
Proust, Marcel, 156

Public court records, availability of, on the Internet, 237
Public figures
   defined, 45
   privacy of, 48, 57, 139
   public interest and, 45–47
Publicity given to private life, or disclosure of private facts, 55–57
Publicity placing person in false light, 57–58
Public sector
   intersection of private sector and, 7
   mutual dependence of private sector and, 77
Public service, role of government archivists in, 67–68
Public welfare records, research use of, 3
Punitive damages, 45
Pyatt, Timothy D., 128–29

Racism, Mississippi State Sovereignty Commission and, 161–62
The Radical Feminists of Heterodoxy, 85
Rankin, William, 224
Reasonable degree, concept of, 68–69
Reasonable expectation of privacy standard applicable to persons, 13
Reasonable man defense, 38
Reasonable person, offensiveness to, 56–57
Recordkeeping debacles, 199
Records
   administrative, 212
   archival management of access to, 78–79
   case, 253
   computerized, 7
   congregational, 211–12
   destruction of, in maintaining favorable image, 82–83
   education, 181–98, 212
   electronic, 7, 160–61, 228
   employee, 236
   historical, 82–92
   of House Un-American Activities Committee, 163
   intelligence, 64
   jurisdictional and congregational, 211–12
   lay personnel, 211
   legal, 212
   medical, 246–56

plantation, 150
presidential, 3
proper archival management of, 78
public court, 237
public welfare, 3
sole possession, 182
Records-accountability issues, 199
Records maintained on individuals, 106
Records professionals, social role for, 202
Records-related issues, debate over, 199
Records-related legislation, archivist's input into, 127–28
Rehnquist, William, 283–84
Reiman, Jeffrey, 72–73
Religion, informational environment of, in society, 208–13
Religious Freedom Restoration Act (RFRA), 209–10
Religious organizations
  ambiguity inherent in multilayered, 215
  concerns over records of, 84
  cultural environment of, 213–16
  position in American institutional culture, 258
  sexual abuse lawsuits and, 200
  trust and professional agency in archives of, 205–25
Reparations, 233
Repression, globalization of archival issues relating to files of, 108–10
Repressive regimes
  collapse of, and demand to open police files, 93–111
  ethical approach to records of, 64
Reputation, damage to, false light claims and, 57–58
Research
  balancing protection of individual privacy with rights of, 82–92
  changing trends in academic, 65
  into church sacramental registers, 3
  into historic life insurance applications, 243
  into history of medical records, 248
  interest in full access to historical record, 82–92
  into patient medical histories, 3
  problems of confidentiality, in handling requests, 84
  into public welfare records, 3
  into social work case files, 3
Restatement of Unfair Competition, 238–39

Restatement (Second) of Torts, 12, 33, 53, 238–39
Right of publicity, 43, 54
Right to Financial Privacy Act (1978) (RFPA), 277
Right to liberty, 15
Right to life, 15
"The Right to Privacy" (Prosser), 10
Right to vote, 74
Rios v. Read, 282
Rising Tide (Barry), 154
Robbin, Alice, 80
Roberson v. Rochester Folding Box Co., 32–33, 41
Robins, Kevin, 72
Rockefeller Archives Center, 119
Rogues' gallery, inclusion of plaintiff in, 40
Romania, access to police files in, 104
Roman Catholic Church
  Code of Canon Law in, 213
  confidentiality in tradition of, 212
  positive rights principle of Canon Law, 209
  primary value of parish register, 214
  sexual abuse lawsuits and, 200
  subsidiarity and, 224
Roman Inquisition, 106
Rosenberg, William G., 96
Rousseau, 69
Rowe-Sims, Sarah, 129
Rowland, Dunbar, 160
Rubin, Louis, 150, 153
Russia
  access to police files in, 102, 107–8
  KGB in, 108
Russian Federation, national archives of, 102
Russian rehabilitation rules, 109
Russian Revolution (1917), 107–8

Salinger, J. D., unauthorized biography of, 145
Salter, John, 164, 170
Samuelson, Pamela, 229, 231
Samway, Patrick, 153
Sanger, Margaret, love letters written to, 88
Schaefer, Rebecca, 272
Schnur, Wolfgang, 95
Schwartz, Paul, 76
Schwarz, Judith, 63
Schwerner, Michael, 171

Seclusion, intrusion upon, 53–54
The Second Coming (Percy), 151, 152
Second Vatican Council, 224
Seldon, Steven, 119
Selective access, 134–35
Self-incrimination
 privilege against, 176
 protection against, 13
Self-ownership, 73
Seligman, Adam, 222
Sensations, legal value of, 15–16
September, September (Foote), 152, 156
Sexton, Anne, 141
Sexual abuse lawsuits, court records involving, 200
Sexuality, study of history of, 83
Sexual relations, right to privacy and, 38–39
Shiloh (Foote), 152, 153
Shrader, Richard, 154
Sidis, William James, 39
Sidis v. F-R Publishing Corporation, 39
Simitis, Spiros, 74–75, 75
Simmons, Ruth, 78
Simpson, Evangeline Marrs, 87–88
Slander, 17, 26–27, 39, 50, 52
Slowakia, access to police files in, 102
Smith, Janna Malamud, 142
Smith, Sophia, collection at Smith College, 88
Smith College, 88
 Sophia Smith Collection at, 88
Smolla, Rodney A., 1
Social contract theorists, 70–71
Social Darwinism, 114
Social exchange theorists, 218–19
Social service/witness program records, 212
Social work case files, research use of, 3
Society of American Archivists (SAA)
 Code of Ethics, 61–62, 67, 137, 146
 Colleges and University Archives Section (C&U) of, 189–90
 Committee on Reference, Access, and Photoduplication, 61
 Council, 133
 endorsement of National Humanities Alliance's "Basic Principles for Managing Intellectual Property in a Digital Environment," 228–29
 establishment of Privacy and Confidentiality Roundtable by, 5

Sole possession records, exclusion of, under Family Educational Rights and Privacy Act (1974) (FERPA), 182
Solitude, intrusion upon, 53–54
Southern Economics Journal, 157
Southern Historical Collection at University of North Carolina, 128–29, 149–58
Southern Historical Journal, 157
Southern Writers: A Biographical Dictionary (Rubin), 150
Spanish Inquisition, 106–7
Spender, Stephen, papers of, 147–48
Spies, adverse information compiled by, 106
Spouses, communications between, 176
Stasi Records Act (1991), 96–101, 105, 106
States
 drafting of freedom of information laws by, 3
 role in regulating marriage, 12
State v. Burns, 210
Station for Experimental Evolution (Cold Spring Harbor), 115
Statute of limitations, expiration of, 58
Statutory law, 211
Sterilization, 114
Stowe, Harriet Beecher, 144
Structuration theory, 219, 220
Student assignments, Family Educational Rights and Privacy Act (1974) (FERPA) status of, 188
Subsidiarity, Catholic concept of, 224
Sun Microsystems, 243
Sunset provisions, 271
Sunshine laws, 105
Surveillance, threat to individual autonomy, 73
Swales, Peter, 135

Tabloid culture, 1
Tabloid journalism, growth of, 139
Tamiment Library (New York University), 86
Tarlton v. United States, 172
Tate, Allen, 152
Taylor, Christine M., 201, 202
Taylor, James, 220
Teachers' grade books, exclusion of, from educational records, 185–86
Technological developments, 65

Technological implementation, successful, 226
Telecommunications Act (1996), 278
Telecommunications Carrier Compliance Fund, 272
Telemarketing and Consumer Fraud Act, 277
Texas Instruments, Internet sites of, 232
Textual maps, 220
The Thanatos Syndrome (Percy), 151
Third parties
 aggressive efforts to protect rights of, 8
 confidentiality and, 148
 disclosure of personal information to, 71
 privacy rights and, 56–57, 63–64, 132–33, 146
Thoreau, Henry David, 144
Ticknor and Fields (firm), 144
Tolson, Jay, 153–55, 155
Tort right of privacy, 53–60
 appropriation of name or likeness, 54–55
 intrusion upon seclusion or solitude, 53–54
 publicity given to private life or disclosure of private facts, 55–57
 publicity placing person in false light, 57–58
Tournament (Foote), 152, 153
Townsend, Mary, 151
Trait books, 115
Transitional justice, 93
 perpetrators in, 104–6
 victims in, 104–6
Transparency, 75
Triviality, 17
Truman, David, 87
Truman, Harry S., 89
Truman State University Archives, 119
Trust
 fiduciary, in management of access and privacy, 221–24
 personal, 222–23
 in religious organization archives, 205–25
Trust relationship, 67–68
Truth Commission, 104
 extrajudicial, 110
Tuck v. Priester, 23

Unconscionability, privacy right and, 56
UNESCO, International Council of Archives (ICA) report to, 108–10
United Brethren, 265
United Methodist Church, 265
 classified records of, 84
 Commission on Archives and History, 84
 General Board of Global Ministries (GBOGM), 83–84
 open records policy of, 202–3, 257–67
 structure of, 260–61
United Methodist Church v. White, 210
United Methodist Communications, 262
U.S. v. Miller, 277
United States House Un-American Activities Committee, handling of records of, 163
Unofficial informers, 104–5
USA PATRIOT Act (2001), 7, 14, 271, 273, 274–75, 278–79, 281
 passage of, 2
Use agreement, 120–21
Use and privacy issues, with Foote and Percy Papers, 153–56

Van Every, Elizabeth, 220
Victims
 opening of Stasi archives to, 96–101
 in transitional justice, 104–6
Video Privacy Protection Act (1988) (VPPA), 279
Voting Rights Act (1965), 162

Walker Percy and Shelby Foote Papers, issues of privacy in, 149–58
Walker Percy Project, 155
Waller, William, 162
War on terrorism, 14
Warren, Samuel D., 2–3, 7, 10–11, 31–32, 33, 37
 creation of independent basis of liability and, 51
 disclosure of private facts and, 48
 false light in public eye and, 39–41
 intrusion and, 34
 invasion of privacy and, 50
 media coverage of social life of, 31
 public disclosure of private facts and, 36–39
 "The Right to Privacy" by, 132
 wedding of daughter of, 52
Watson, James D., 112
Webb, Charles, 139
Webster, Frank, 72
Weideman, Christine, 130

Weinreb, Lloyd, 77
West German archival policy, need for consistent, 94
Westley, Helen, 85
Whipple, Henry, 88
Whipple-Scandrett Papers, 88
Whittier, John Greenleaf, 144
Williams, Raymond, 69
Winter, William, 163
Wiretapping, 54
  intrusion and, 35
Wire Tap Statute, 273
Without Consent: The Ethics of Disclosing Personal Information in Public Archives (MacNeil), 5, 62–63

Women's papers, lack of indexes to, 86
Woolley, Mary Emma, papers of, 87
Wyatt-Brown, Bertram, 153–55
Wyatt v. Wilson, 21

Yeats, William Butler, 141
Yellow journalism, 31
Yeltsin, Boris, efforts to outlaw the Russian Communist party, 102
Yovatt v. Winyard, 25

Zion's Herald, 261
Zurcher v. Stanford Daily, 277